Sounding the Center

VI G-6

Chicago Studies in Ethnomusicology

A Series Edited by Philip V. Bohlman and Bruno Nettl

Sounding
the
Center

History and Aesthetics
in Thai Buddhist Performance

Deborah Wong

The University of Chicago Press
Chicago and London

Deborah Wong is associate professor of music at the University of California, Riverside.

The University of Chicago Press, Chicago 60637
The University of Chicago Press, Ltd., London
© 2001 by The University of Chicago
All rights reserved. Published 2001
Printed in the United States of America

09 08 07 06 05 04 03 02 01 00   1 2 3 4 5
ISBN: 0-226-90585-3 (cloth)
ISBN: 0-226-90586-1 (paper)

Library of Congress Cataloging-in-Publication Data

Wong, Deborah Anne.
  Sounding the center : history and aesthetics in Thai Buddhist performance /
Deborah Wong.
    p.   cm.
  Includes bibliographical references and index.
    ISBN 0-226-90585-3 (cloth : alk. paper)—ISBN 0-226-90586-1 (pbk. : alk. paper)
    1. Rites and ceremonies—Thailand—Bangkok.   2. Ritual—Thailand—Bangkok.
3. Ethnomusicology—Thailand—Bangkok.   4. Folklore—Thailand—Bangkok—
Performance.   5. Oral tradition—Thailand—Bangkok.   6. Dance—Religious
aspects—Thailand—Bangkok.   7. Music—Religious aspects—Thailand—Bangkok.
8. Bangkok (Thailand)—Social life and customs.   9. Bangkok (Thailand)—Religious
life and customs.   I. Title.
GN635.T4 W66 2000
306.4'84'09593—dc21   00-033775

To my parents
(who encouraged me to see the world)

and to René

Contents

....

List of Figures

Attending a Ritual, Thinking about Ritual

A Ritual at Home

Around nine o'clock on Thursday morning, September 28, 1989, I took the ferry across the Chao Phraya River to Thonburi, got off at the pier in front of an old Buddhist temple, and went through the temple grounds to a small lane. A weathered house near the mouth of the lane was my destination. One of the few traditional Thai houses left in Bangkok, it was gray with age, sagging on its stilts. Its door was uncharacteristically open. I went up the wood steps, took off my shoes, and went in.

This was the home of a musical family. For at least four generations, the Phaatayakoosol family had lived and rehearsed in this house, built probably near the beginning of the twentieth century. Several of these generations were busily passing out cold drinks to arrivals like myself; others were dashing around carrying pillows, candles, and small tables. *Khunying*, or "Lady," Phaithuun Kittiwan, seventy-eight years old and the grande dame of the family, was everywhere, greeting guests and ordering around her children and grandchildren (see fig. P.1). Music had been performed all night long: the musicians, someone told me, went home at dawn to sleep for an hour or two before returning for the ceremony, and yet more music was to come during the afternoon and evening after the ritual's celebration.

The ritual began a little after 10:00 A.M., led by an impressively obese older man who walked with a cane. I asked several people his name, but no one knew—they only said, with great respect, that he was "from the palace" and was an old friend of *Khunying* Phaithuun's. He was dressed in a dark blue suit and didn't change into white for the ceremony. The audience included many members of the extended Phaatayakoosol family, a number of young military bandsmen, a handful of elementary schoolgirls, and some older men who had been disciples of the family's; some forty or fifty people were present, seated on the wooden floor, facing the permanent altar.

Figure P.1   Khunying Phaithuun Phaatayakoosol at a *wai khruu* ritual at Chulalongkorn University in 1988. Photograph by Deborah Wong.

This altar was located in a slightly raised alcove that completely filled one end of the room—a veritable museum of musical instruments, dance masks for worship, and photographs of eminent musicians connected with the family. The area was dominated by funeral ensemble instruments whose frames were beautifully inlaid with mother-of-pearl and inscribed with the family crest. Small glass cabinets holding masks of various deities were set high on the walls near the ceiling, their doors now hanging open so that candles could be lit inside. Large framed portraits of the deceased Thua Phaatayakoosol, his wives Plang and Caroen, his father Thap Phaatayakoosol, his son Theewaprasit, his patron Prince Boriphat, and a number of other famous musicians were placed at intervals around the walls, and today each was decorated with flowers and candles. Food offerings were laid out below: lots of fruit, several pigs' heads, ducks and chickens, whole fish, several bottles of liquor. The total effect was cluttered but extremely impressive, almost like an ancestor shrine.

The officiant sat on the platform facing the altar, with his back to the audience. His book of ritual texts lay on a pillow in front of him, and

Khunying Phaithuun sat behind him. Incense was passed out to the audience and then collected and placed in a big urn filled with sand; a long candle rack in the shape of a magical serpent stood nearby. The ritual began unobtrusively, in silence, with the officiant lighting the candles in front of him and family members lighting three sets of candles on smaller altars. Two final sets of candles were lit beneath the photographs of Thua and his son Theewaprasit.

The officiant first requested the power and forgiveness of the many teachers and then opened his book of ritual texts. While some officiants recite the texts from memory, this man actually read them, periodically turning the pages and even unfolding special inserted pages that had been glued in. His texts were in clear sections that he announced. The first was for "the teachers," the second for the Buddha, and the third for the teachers again; each of these sections was preceded by standard Buddhist prayers recited three times in unison.

After this, he said, "We will now say the words for the *wai khruu*," and began with the formulaic phrase, "Today is a good day." With everyone following phrase by phrase, he read a text that went approximately as follows:

> I would like to *wai* Isuan, Narai, the many deities, my father and mother, my teachers, and everyone who taught me. I would like to ask all of you to watch over me and to grant me happiness. I would like to prostrate myself before you and to *wai* you. I would like to salute the three Great Deities: Wisanuukaam; Pancasingkhaun, who plays the harp; and Parakhonthap, who passed on what he knew. I would like to fold my hands together and salute you, and I entreat you to help me and to look after me. I would like to invite the eight hermits to help me and bless me. I would like to entreat all of the many deities to protect me from danger.

After presenting the food offerings to the now-present deities, the officiant uttered propitiary verses to himself, almost silently, as three or four male family members ritually cut and sliced the offerings. One final text was read about the offerings, and then the officiant simply said, "This concludes the ritual." He prostrated himself over his book, touching his forehead to its pages three times, and then closed it as family members began to bustle about. Banana leaf plates, piled high with food offerings, were taken outside. The entire ritual had taken a mere forty minutes.

During the next half hour, a table was set up where the audience had been sitting and lunch was served. *Khunying* Phaithuun remained seated on the edge of the platform as many people came up to say hello and to express respect by *wai*-ing, that is, by putting their hands palm-to-palm and raising them to their foreheads. She answered questions in a no-nonsense manner and was almost gruff, but this was clearly just her way—she was treated affectionately by all. As she talked to people, her nephew Uthai placed a brass bowl of water and a whisk beside her. Not long after, a group of about fifteen young Navy band members in uniform came and knelt at her feet, and their leader, a middle-aged man, asked for her blessing. She briefly held the whisk to her forehead in a *wai*, turning toward the photograph of her father as she muttered a propitiatory phrase to herself, and then scattered sacralized water over them all. They prostrated themselves and were about to move away on their knees when she engaged them in talk, the young men looking shy and rather overcome with awe, but they eventually smiled and answered her questions. She repeatedly urged them to eat lunch before letting them go.

At this point, about ten close family members approached her, and the tableau of their faces, many strongly resembling the long-dead *Caangwaang* Thua, was striking. They all knelt at her feet, *wai*-ing but smiling, and her nephew handed her a small bowl of powder paste so she could anoint their foreheads. She blessed each of them, including an infant in arms, smiling and talking as she wrote a sign of power and protection on each person's brow. When others saw this going on, they came up as well, and in the end she anointed at least forty people. An older man in his sixties came up to her *wai*-ing. Almost brusquely, she said, "No, no—I won't, go away," waving her hands at him in shooing gestures, but he persisted, smiling more and more broadly. I sensed that he was an old acquaintance of status equal to or higher than hers—possibly even an officiant himself—and that she was acknowledging his authority by demurring, though she anointed him in the end. Some of her family returned to be blessed with the water, and she playfully banged a nephew on the head with the whisk while scattering water over him as he laughed.

Eventually she went off to eat lunch, and the crowd thinned out as people left. A brief but furious cloudburst drove everyone else inside. During the afternoon and evening, there would be live music, so everyone settled in to wait for the rain to stop and the musicians to arrive.

Ritual about Performance

This study is an extended look at the idea of power behind classical music and dance in Bangkok, the capital and sacred center of Thailand. I have talked with Thai musicians since 1986. Actually, "talking" has meant getting to know musicians in all the ways that one can—by taking lessons, running errands for them, interviewing them, becoming friends with them, and so forth. Whether rehearsing, hanging out, teaching in university contexts, playing in rituals, or trying to help me understand their thought and be-liefs, these musicians have been agreed upon the continuing importance of ritual in the post-court life of Thai court music. The connections between kings, teachers, knowledge, and performance form a network of power ex-change and renewal that continues to impel the classical court arts. Chang-ing patronage and new institutional structures exist in dynamic relationship with older epistemologies of ritual and performance.

The Thai ritual honoring teachers of music and dance, called the *wai khruu* ritual, transfers the spiritual power of the first, primordial teacher to present-day performers. The relationship between Thai ritual and perfor-mance is intimate and fundamental, and the reflexivity of ritual performance *about* performance is my focus in this study. This Thai ritual is an event that opens up through the process of performance. Therefore, my scholarly strategy is to look closely at particular ritual moments, thereby catching a glimpse of Thai musicians as they construct new bureaucracies using old ritual technologies.

The Thai belief that knowledge is power is reflected in the limited num-ber of male master musicians who have access to esoteric knowledge about the sacred repertoire. Thai musicians and dancers who perform the reper-toire for this ritual must be initiated by a master teacher before they can actualize the sacred with their bodies and produce the sound and move-ment that manifest the divine in the human realm. The national con-servatory, a government institution that replaced the old court system of musicians and dancers in 1934, employs many of the master teachers who perform the initiation ceremony. I see the ritual authority of these master teachers as the basis for other kinds of authority—authorities born of a postcolonial Southeast Asia—for they are not just ritual experts but also leaders of contemporary state institutions for music and dance.

Metaperformance and Metaritual:
The *Wai Khruu* as a Theory of Performance

This study inevitably becomes part of the larger body of work on Buddhist practice in Southeast Asia, but as an ethnomusicologist and ethnogra-pher, I am more invested in matters of practice than in longtime debates within religious studies attempting to reconcile "animism," Hinduism, and Buddhism. I believe that the *wai khruu* speaks to those debates, but, more importantly, it offers a chance to observe and reconsider the place of the-ory and practice in performance studies.

Thais, whether laypersons or monks, regard the relationships between

animism, Hinduism, and Buddhism as both problematic and nonproblem-
atic. The *wai khruu* contains explicit elements of each, as do many Thai ritual practices. One might say that such practices reflect an additive approach
to ritual as well as a window on the history of ritual belief in Thailand that
stretches over several millennia: animism was an indigenous belief system,
Hinduism was introduced to mainland Southeast Asia by Indian traders, and
Buddhism arrived much later.

This chronology of religious systems in what is now Thailand does little
to explain why Thais and many Southeast Asians maintain older practices
while adding on new ones. Some scholars have argued that this is due to the
tolerant ideologies of Hinduism and Buddhism, though it is also clear that
more than a few Thai Buddhist monks take a dim view of "Brahmanism,"
encouraging a more doctrinal approach to Buddhism. In her study of
the highland Shan in Thailand, Nicola Tannenbaum (1995) concludes that
"power-protection" is a "logic" that underlies and makes coherent Shan
belief in both Buddhism and animism. She suggests that scholars would do
better to accept multiple meanings of "Buddhist," and that this would do
away with constructions such as "corrupt" Buddhism or "Buddhism as a
thin veneer over other practices" (205). Looking at the question another
way, she suggests that Buddhism may be part of deeper patterns of belief,
and that models positing multiple religious systems at work in Southeast
Asia may miss ways that they are part of broader, more encompassing belief.

Rather than attempt to explain why Thai religious practice is multifaceted—and thus take less inclusive, less tolerant doctrines as normative—I
would argue that the *wai khruu* is one example out of many demonstrating
not only how Thais have a more-is-more ritual aesthetic, but that ritual
practice is constantly contemporized, even when it is felt to maintain ancient
values. As part of a widespread phenomenon in mainland (and to some extent insular) Southeast Asia, the Thai *wai khruu* takes matters a step further:
its reflexivity suggests that theory and practice converge in this particular
form, offering a theory of ritual.

Most Thai performers love to sit around and talk about the particularities of the *wai khruu* ritual. I spent many long enjoyable hours chatting with
performers about the different kinds of fruit offerings used in southern
Thailand, about how opium was formerly laid out as an offering along with
cigarettes and betel nut, about how one officiant absolutely refused to begin a ceremony until his tin offering bowl was replaced with one of silver,
and so on. Such conversations revolved around details of ritual practice and
were of infinite interest to performers and officiants—and in the end to me
as well. Furthermore, performers moved with utter matter-of-factness from

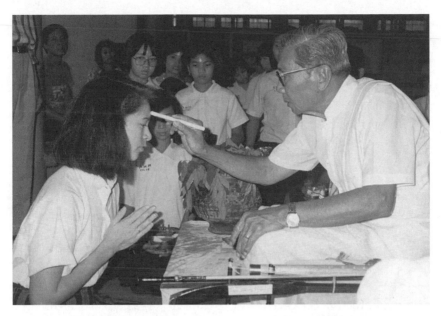

Figure P.2   Being "covered" by *Khruu* Chüa Dontriirot at my first *wai khruu* ritual in 1987 at the Department of Music Education, Srinakharinwirot University–Prasanmit. Photograph by a student friend.

talking about the precise kind of banana that should be presented as an offering to accounts of golden-faced deities talking to them in their dreams. Talking about the sacred required no reframing, no step back; it was, rather, a daily reality for the performers I came to know. I have tried to write about the *wai khruu* in a way that would please and satisfy them, trying to include much of the detail that interests them so intensely by invoking the names and histories of important teachers, by trying to describe the weight and mystery of the ritual texts without violating that mystery, and finally, by trying to recreate in words a few actual ritual events with all their bustle and solemnity and (again) matter-of-factness intact. I participated in any number of *wai khruu* rituals and thus carry the power and responsibility of many teachers' blessings (see fig. P.2).

But I must take a step back that Thai performers would never take and try to frame these ritual gestures in a way that highlights how performers and ritual experts talk to themselves about themselves through performance and ritual. I am reminded of two very different comments I received as I did my research in Bangkok. In one case, an American friend and scholar was visibly surprised when I told him that the *wai khruu* was my research topic. "But," he said, "what do you spend all your time *doing?*" He could not see how such an apparently narrow topic might involve extended examination. On the other hand, as I will reiterate at the beginning of Chapter 1, an eminent musician called me to task, asking how I would know what was correct and what wasn't when I wrote about the *wai khruu*. The implication was clear: he didn't think I would, or *could*, know, and in fact felt that it was presumptuous of me to even try.

In many ways, he was quite right. Taking the step back and arriving at the point where I wanted to put the *wai khruu* in a larger context has been a journey in itself. By making authoritative statements about what the *wai khruu* is and how it means what it does, I am intruding into areas that are not my place, but are instead the right of officiants. By taking this stance, I know that the experience of immersing myself in the ritual and in the lives of its performers is really over. As Edward Bruner writes (1986, 5), "We can have an experience, but we cannot have a behavior; we describe the behavior of others but we characterize our own experience." In addressing the experience of Thai performers and its expression in ritual, I had my own experience of their belief system; as I attempt to "re-experience, re-live, re-create, re-tell, re-construct, and re-fashion" (ibid., 11) what I saw and heard, I feel them reading over my shoulder (though I doubt many of them will ever go through these pages) and can sense their surprise and sometimes discomfort. *How* they talked about the *wai khruu* was yet another way of performing its possible meaning, of expressing their own experience of it. Some of the issues I address in this book (e.g., the interface of ritual and institutional authority) would strike them at best as misguided, at worst as inappropriate.

So I must now problematize my entire study and call into question the notion of description, especially in matters of belief and its coherence. As the anthropologist Dorinne Kondo (1990) has written, a specific eye/I was the lens through which these pages came into focus, though I have tried to bring in other eyes throughout. Kondo addresses "the richness and complexity of experience," saying, "to examine that complexity and richness in its specificity leads toward a strategy that expands notions of what can count as theory, where experience and evocation can *become theory*, where the binary between 'empirical' and 'theoretical' is displaced and loses its force" (8).

Clearly, all Thai performers do not have the same experience of the *wai khruu* ritual. The eight-year-old elementary school student whose hands are grasped and put through the motions of *Saathukaan* by a solemn stranger does not have the same experience as one of the music majors at Srinakharinwirot University who is "covered" for the fourth level of the ritual repertoire, or yet again the experience of a Department of Fine Arts performer playing in his fifth *wai khruu* ritual of the month. But there are also commonalities of experience between these three performers, commonalities that emerge *through* performance: the child absorbs them as her hands are led through the sacred piece, and the seasoned *piiphaat* musician reaffirms them every time he plays through the ritual and goes up to be "covered" by the officiant at the ritual's conclusion.

These commonalities include certain assumptions about performance, ritual, and their relationship. There are two sides to this relationship: first, ritual is always *performed*, and second, performance itself is ritual in Thailand.

That ritual is performance is axiomatic for anthropologists and scholars in performance studies. By definition, ritual is a multimedia event, involving sounds, sights, smells, and movement; ritual combines the spoken word with music and dance and then intensifies them with smoke and flame and the redundant, even excessive use of all these things together. Redundancy, strict patterning, and parallelism are nearly always essential: certain words/songs/dances are appropriate while others are not, certain words/songs/dances refer to each other across their respective media, and some may well "say the same thing" more than once (Tambiah 1985, 137–46).

Victor Turner, the moving force behind the idea that ritual is performance, would have been delighted by the *wai khruu*. His view of ritual (to quote Geertz quoting him) was "the whole human vital repertoire of thinking, willing, desiring, and feeling [as] said, painted, danced, dramatized, [and] put into circulation" (Geertz 1986, 375). Turner's broadened view of ritual as social, religious, or aesthetic performance puts a greeting between friends (at least on the face of it) on the same continuum with the Catholic Mass. Pondering Turner's contribution to the study of ritual, Richard Schechner half-seriously complains, "Even to say it in one word, *ritual*, is asking for trouble. Ritual has been so variously defined—as concept, praxis, process, ideology, yearning, religious experience, function— that it means very little because it can mean too much" (1986b, 10). The *wai khruu* is, of course, all these things and more, but the important point is that ritual is acted out by people who move and speak creatively while following established guidelines. Ritual does not sit still on paper, and it represents at least as many frames of experience as there are participants, and probably more. The pleasure of studying the *wai khruu* lies in seeing an ostensibly single ritual moment that is acted out over and over again and driven by performers' desire to integrate different media as creatively as possible. After all, who could be better at staging a ritual event than performers?

If the relationship between ritual and performance is intimate, then Thai classical performers have known this for a long time. For them, the *wai khruu* is not merely a matter of performing ritual, but is, rather, part of an aesthetic in which all performance is ritual (at some level) and in which the felicitous combination of certain movements and sounds brings the human and sacred realms closer together, opening up the possibility of encountering spiritual potency in a nearly unadulterated state. Not for nothing is the *wai khruu* so closely associated with the preperformance invocation called the "opening of the stage" (*boek roong*): performance opens up a channel between alternate realities. A performance is also entertainment, but not in the sense of "mere" entertainment. In its vital role as an offering—as entertainment for spirits and deities—a Thai performance takes on a dimension of meaning that does not disappear when a human audience is also watching it with pleasure and enjoyment. Rather, the difference between "performance" and "the performative" becomes problematic.

It is the way that the *wai khruu* doubles back on itself in what Tambiah calls a "recursive loop" (1985, 139) that grants it its force and, indeed, its reason for being. The *wai khruu* is a performance *about* performance and a ritual *about* ritual. This double step back acts as an intensifier, making the event "good to think": the form of the process exemplifies the process itself. Just as we send each other messages during conversation (smiling, yawning) in a kind of discourse Gregory Bateson called "metacommunication" (1972, 210–11), signaling how we feel the conversation is going, the *wai khruu* is simultaneously metaperformance and metaritual.

Anthropologist Kenneth George has considered the role of headhunting rituals in the upland communities of Sulawesi, Indonesia, where a late-twentieth-century political context no longer permits the taking of heads (1996). Commemorative ritual, as he calls it, is central to identity maintenance, and he frames a central moment in ritual performance when choruses "sing about singing" in a way that reconstitutes community. The reflexive moment when villagers join voices in a ritual chorus and sing about ritual practice is commemorative, in other words, it "reveals another aspect, that of imitating its prior incarnations. In a sense, it is the purpose of commemorative tradition to produce a kind of simulacrum" (187), a copy with no original. George suggests that headhunting ritual is a "crucial political act" as it entails an "effort to retain ideological control of the past" (192). Reproducing the community through metaperformance (as I would call it) is thus key to maintaining particular histories. The *wai khruu* is similarly commemorative and reflexive in its purpose of controlling the past for real political purposes. It too gestures back, but it gestures to an original that doesn't recede but rather steps forward—no simulacrum but inarguably foundational and authentic, over and over again.

The *wai khruu* recreates the basic structure of performance: its form draws self-conscious attention to the performance sequence. First, an area in which the ritual performance can take place is established; in temples or homes where no stage is available, the area is carefully defined both physically, with an altar and rugs or mats, and musically, with the piece *Saathukaan*, which defines the space with sound. The entrance of the "actors" into this space is repetitively played out a number of times, first with the entrance of the officiant (who has been there all along, but must "enter" along a path of white cloth), and then with the successive entrances of one deity after another. At the center of this drama is the *performance* of the transmission of performance knowledge: all the nonverbal aspects of performance are passed on by nonverbal means (grasping the student's hands, holding masks over the student's head, etc.). Finally, the process of evaluation is also performed: students are transformed from outsiders into successful insiders through initiation. All these basic elements of performance "craft" are carefully acted out.

Perhaps most importantly, the transformational aspect of performance is enacted over and over again in the *wai khruu:* teachers are revealed as spirits and deities, children are transformed into dancers and musicians, and each master teacher shows his other face as the sage from the beginning of time. Richard Schechner has pondered this dimension of performance in which, at some point, performers and even spectators are transformed by the activity of performing. His experience of watching the deer dance of the Arizona Yaqui could be mine watching a *wai khruu* officiant dance into the ritual, wearing the mask of the Old Father:

> I wondered if the figure I saw was a man and a deer simultaneously; or, to say it in a way a performer might understand, whether putting on the deer mask made the man "not a man" and "not a deer" but somewhere in between. The top of his head (man/deer's), with its horns and deer mask, is a deer; the bottom of his head below the white cloth, with its man's eyes, nose, and mouth, is a man. The white cloth the dancer keeps adjusting is the physicalization of the impossibility of a complete transformation into the deer. At the moments when the dancer is "not himself" and yet "not not himself," his own identity, and that of the deer, is locatable only in the liminal areas of "characterization," "representation," "imitation," "transportation," and "transformation." All of these words say that performers can't really say who they are. Unique among animals, humans carry and express multiple and ambivalent identities simultaneously. (1985, 4)

In the *wai khruu*, the distance between the participants and the "characters" they become is highlighted. The bottom line, however, is that none of this is make-believe, no mere gestures before a mirror but in fact a

doubling-back on the process of performance precisely because of its transformative nature.

And this is where the *wai khruu* crosses over from metaperformance (an
extended meditation on the nature of performance) to metaritual. When it
is successful, performance creates an intensity of experience: a threshold
is crossed into a shared, collective experience that is difficult to describe
but familiar, I think, to most human beings. Turner called it "flow," and
Schechner (1985, 11) comes close to articulating it, saying, "Performances
gather their energies almost as if time and rhythm were concrete, physical,
pliable things. . . . These elements are woven into a complicated yet apparently inevitable (experienced as simple) pattern." This intensity of performance is the axis on which the *wai khruu* turns, because the experience
it sets up necessarily involves the sacred realm: in Thailand, a ritual about
performance is also, by definition, a ritual about ritual.

Judith Butler reminds us: "The normative force of performativity—its
power to establish what qualifies as 'being'—works not only through reiteration, but through exclusion as well" (1993, 188). The *wai khruu* "works"
because it reiteratively creates insiders and outsiders, in other words, it
maintains the terms of exclusion. The extent to which all performance is
performative, and ritual performance especially so, is one of the main contributions of performance studies as a field. In her essay on performance as
a key concept in folklore studies, Deborah A. Kapchan provides a useful en-
capsulation of metaperformance: "Performances, as such, are characterized
by a higher than usual degree of reflexivity, whether calling attention to the
rules of their own enactment (metapragmatics) or talking about the performance event (metadiscourse). It has been the task of performance studies to
understand what constitutes the differences between habitual practices and
heightened performances, and how and why these differences function in
society" (1995, 479). Considering the divine embodiment of Afro-Brazilian
candomblé, Barbara Browning (1995, 72–73) arrives at a reflexive configuration of dance, the divine, and belief. She writes that the deities *(orixás):*

> can *only* come down in their choreographies, their own writing. As what
> you read now is *my* writing, it can't contain divinity. But each time we
> attempt to serve a principle—of self-reflexive lyricism or feminism, for
> example—we are being written by the *orixás*, and in this sense we embody
> them. It is not an imitation of the *orixás* but an offering to them.
>
> The only meaningful human writing, as I have come to see it, is done
> in the service of belief.

Following her lead, I am thus able to locate my attempts to describe the *wai
khruu* and its aesthetic principles. Kapchan (1995, 500) notes that "perfor-

mative ethnography incorporates indigenous theory while indexing history as embodied in social practice." If I can begin to communicate the ritual choreographies that shape Thai performers' beliefs, then I also enact a kind of praise and respect that is fitting and appropriate.

Thai classical musicians and dancers construct their knowledge of performance through performance and construct their *experience* of this knowledge through performance. The constellation of performance and its attendant transfer of power from one realm to another has fundamental implications for its relation to kings and other institutions of authority. Music and dance are not imitative but constructive; dance-drama is not a pale reflection of reality but its template. In this environment, Thai performers' respect for knowledge and for the holders of knowledge is both a binding emotion and a driving aesthetic.

Of course, no one ever said that to me, nor would they have if I had asked. This is my own eye/I, my own experience of seeing many performers act out their beliefs over many years' time. I decided to write myself into this book but not to make myself its protagonist, as this would be entirely inappropriate for my subject matter. The reader will encounter the ritual through my experiences, but I do not believe the *wai khruu* is the place for deeply reflexive writing. At what point can contemporary critical theory violate the belief system on which it is brought to bear? The ethnographic and authorial voice has been thoroughly problematized since the 1980s; I acknowledge the imprimatur of that work on my own even as I decide that this book is about my experiences but not about me.[1] I take on several roles in this book—ethnomusicologist, participant, student, friend, reader and interpreter of texts—and of course these ways of being were interlocking and interpenetrating while I made my way through Bangkok. Indeed, they still are and will always be so.

As I wrote and rewrote the following pages, I reexperienced a number of exemplary moments that encapsulated what I have tried to articulate: the first time I saw *Khruu* Nim, deeply absorbed in his sacred texts in front of the towering altar that nearly filled the small building he called home; *Mom* Caruun quietly removing the Old Father's mask at the end of a long ritual; a moment when a mask maker I knew turned to me at Wat Phra Phireen and said, "You can't *not* believe." In the pages that follow, I describe and analyze the particularities of the ceremony—in other words, the way it is enacted and the people who perform it—in detail. I especially emphasize how Thai musicians and dancers construct the ritual through words, writing, and, of course, performance: conversation, writings about the ritual, and enactments of the ritual itself are all active sites for the construction of performers' beliefs. Finally, I address the performing arts of the

Thai courts in terms of secrecy, sound, and the sacred, and I suggest that esoteric knowledge has helped Thai classical music endure in the face of changing patronage even while the ontological nature of that knowledge is actively challenged by the late-twentieth-century urban environment that supports it.

Acknowledgments

It all started during my first week at the University of Pennsylvania when I was an undergraduate in 1977. Playing the flute was at the center of my concerns but I thought I wanted to be an archaeologist. Thus, I took a work-study job in the Ban Chiang archaeological lab at the University Museum and was immediately thrown into long pleasant hours pushing around potsherds and putting them together like five-thousand-year-old jigsaw puzzles. At that point, I wasn't even sure where Thailand was, but I soon found out, especially from Professor Chester (Chet) Gorman, director of the Ban Chiang Project, and from Joyce White, then a doctoral student and now the project director. You might say that my first experience of Thailand was tactile, material: I would go home with a dusting of Thai soil on my hands, thinking about the ancient potters' fingerprints I had found on some of the shards. I thank Chet for suggesting that maybe I should consider changing majors: one day, after yet another round of my questions (Did men or women make the pots? Why did they bury pots with their dead?), he said, "You know, you're asking about the kinds of things that anthropologists look at. Check out some of those courses." Planting my interest in cultural anthropology and in Thai culture was Chet's work.

My ethnomusicological fieldwork in Thailand was made possible in 1986–1987 by a Fulbright IIE Fellowship; in 1988–1989 by the Social Science Research Council and the American Council of Learned Societies, the Asian Cultural Council, a Foreign Language and Area Studies Fellowship (Title VI), and the University of Michigan Alumni Council; in 1994 by the Research Foundation of the University of Pennsylvania; and in 1998 with support from the American Philosophical Society. Back in the United States, my dissertation write-up was generously supported by the Association of American University Women (1990–1991), the Rackham School of xxvii

Graduate Studies at the University of Michigan, and the Social Science Research Council (1989–1990). All this support is deeply appreciated.

I want to thank the National Research Council of Thailand for granting me permission to conduct research, and Doris Wibunsin and the Thailand-U.S. Educational Foundation staff for being cheerful and supportive. At the Siam Society in Bangkok, the library staff photocopied more of their Thai performance materials for me than they probably realize; Virginia and James Di Crocco (then Honorary Treasurer and Editor, respectively, of the *Journal of the Siam Society*) welcomed me into both the Society and their home; and Dacre Raikes (Honorary Vice President) was a good friend, always ready to show me the whimsical side of things.

At the Witthayalai Phau Chaang (College of Arts and Crafts), Professor Manas na Chiang Mai and Professor Varravinai Hiranmas spent several afternoons sharing their thoughts on the school's famous book of *wai khruu* texts for the artisans' ritual, and on the dangerous and exacting craft of making dance masks. At the Withayalai Khruu Baan Somdet, I thank Professor Sangat Phukhaothaung for many long, pleasant afternoons and enlightening conversations. At the Fine Arts Department's College of Dramatic Arts, a number of professors and performers were very helpful. Professor Montri Tramote and his son Silapi Tramote answered many questions. Professor Manat Khaoplüüm spent much time explaining the *naa phaat* repertoire to me and supplied me with valuable written sources. Professor Udom Angsuthaun and Professor Thongchai Phothayarom granted me important and illuminating interviews about the *wai khruu* ceremony for *khoon* and *lakhon* dance-drama. Leading dancer Ranee Chaisongkram pulled me right into the thick of things. At Mahidol University, Dr. Phunphit Amatayakul and Dr. Sugree Charoensook were consistently helpful. At Chulalongkorn University, Dr. Norut Sutcit (Chair of the Music Division, Faculty of Education) made sure I witnessed their remarkable *wai khruu* ritual (presided over by the Crown Princess), and Professor Orawan Chongsilpabanleng and Dr. Surapone Virulrak were both hospitable and fun to talk with. Dr. Paritta Chalermpow Koanantakul was a scholarly soulmate. Pranee and Sujit Wongthes routinely suggested new ways of thinking about what I was witnessing—my long Friday nights spent listening to Sujit hold forth and sing songs were memorable indeed. A number of master teachers and officiants granted me interviews, particularly *Momrachawong* Caruunsawat Suksawat, *Khruu* Sakol Kaewpenkhat, and *Khunying* Phaithuun Kittiwan. At the Luang Pradit Phairau Foundation, Malini Sagarik, Chanok Sagarik, and their mother, *Khun* Mahathepkasatsamu (Banleeng Sagarik) received me with great warmth and impressed me with their enthusiasm and commitment to classical Thai music.

I owe a special debt to the following:

Khruu Nim Pho-iam (d. 1994), who lived at Wat Phra Phireen in Bangkok, gave me a glimpse of the worlds in which a *wai khruu* celebrant can live.

Camphau Srisawang arranged for a number of my most interesting interviews with teachers and musicians to whom I would not otherwise have had access.

The professors and students in the Music Education Department at Srinakharinwirot University–Prasanmit welcomed me into their midst. My thanks go out to Professor Kanchana Intarasunanont for being a friend and for including me in her classes at the Siam Society; to Professor Prateep Lountratana-ari for showing me Thailand and for adding to my information on the *Luang* Pradit Phairau lineage; to Professor Chalermpon Ngamsutti for *sau duang* lessons; to Professor Rangsi Kasemsuk for friendship; and to Professor Manop Wisutthipaet for giving me a hard time and being a good friend.

I owe a special debt of gratitude to Professor Nikorn Chanthasorn at Srinakharinwirot University–Prasanmit. Professor Nikorn's words, thoughts, and opinions appear frequently on these pages. I spent more time with him than anyone else and hope that his spirit and ideas will engage my readers as much as they engaged me.

In the United States, Dr. Prasert Luangkesan and Mr. Sitsak Chanyawat welcomed me into their *wai khruu* ceremony at Wat Dhammaram in Chicago, Illinois. Ellsworth Peterson, Sue Darlington, and Mary Grow shared the adventure in Thailand, and their support and advice was a great help in putting it all together back home. A special thanks goes to Sarah Grew for photographing the *wai khruu* ritual at Srinakharinwirot University–Prasanmit in 1989 while I videotaped; a number of her fine photographs are featured here with her permission. Fred Lau and Inne Choi were the perfect companions during a period of follow-up research in 1994. Terry Miller has been a generous and supportive colleague, and Pamela Myers-Moro's work has consistently inspired me—her *Thai Music and Musicians in Contemporary Bangkok* (1993) is a model of its kind.

My doctoral committee members saw me through my graduate work from start to finish. Through their teachings and writings, Judith and Pete Becker shaped me in all the right ways; their influence looms large in these pages. Rich Crawford provided a demanding, exciting, and often humorous vision of the scholarly life. Tom Hudak was there from my first attempts to learn Thai to the final versions of the dissertation.

Revisiting doctoral research and making a dissertation into a book is no simple thing. Time goes on; current issues in the discipline change; *you* change. Still, revisiting those vivid months of fieldwork through revision was a rewarding experience made all the more pleasant by support and suggestions from friends and colleagues. A Faculty Fellowship from the University of Pennsylvania during the fall semester of 1995 gave me the time and mental space to begin revising the manuscript. The Center for Southeast Asian Studies at the University of Wisconsin–Madison provided a College Faculty Access grant (1997) that allowed me to update my bibliography. Thongchai Wininakul made thoughtful suggestions, and Patcharin Bickner carefully read through some of the more esoteric Thai texts central to this work. Maya Lysloff-Giles and Kimo Giles housed me during that intense stint in the University of Wisconsin library and greeted me every night with wonderful dinners and hospitality of the most generous sort. A grant from the American Philosophical Society allowed one more trip to Bangkok in 1998, where I brought the manuscript up to date. All photos not my own are reproduced here with permission, and the process of revisiting musicians and their families to get that permission was thoroughly enjoyable. At the University of California–Riverside, a subvention from the Academic Senate helped allay publication costs. Over the years, Andy Sutton has come through over and over again; this time, he provided detailed comments that got me back into the music. Philip Bohlman made crucial suggestions — twice — and helped me think through the transformation from dissertation to book. A reader's report by Frank Reynolds pointed the way into really revising my final chapter. Two anonymous readers' reports were invaluable.

As for René T. A. Lysloff, I hardly know where to start. Thanks for all those terrific discussions comparing your experiences of performance in Java to mine in Thailand; thanks for twice following me to Bangkok and helping with the camera work; thanks for doing the laundry; and thanks for being both my *faen* and my very closest colleague.

As I write this, I am reminded once again that some of the Thai teachers and performers who shared their world with me have passed on and been absorbed into the ritual memories that they helped to sustain. Montri Tramote (d. 1995), Nim Pho-iam (d. 1994), *Momrachawong* Caruunsawat Suksawat (d. 1997), and Manat Khaoplüüm (d. 1998) are all gone. I *wai* each of them and *thawaai* this book to their memory.

Conventions and Orthography

The Thai language does not romanize gracefully. I have largely used the system suggested by the Royal Institute, but with certain modifications.

I have attempted to differentiate between long and short vowels because this is helpful to Thai readers. For example, rather than use the more standard *piphat*, I romanize it as *piiphaat*, and so forth.

Proper names often fall outside this system: if a person has a preferred romanized version of their name, or if their name is spelled in a certain way in published English-language sources, I have deferred to these forms. Citations and bibliographic references to Thai writers are alphabetized by *first* name, following Thai practice.

Titles, for example, *Phra, Luang*, and so forth, are italicized throughout. Again, I have deferred to certain standard romanized forms of some titles (e.g., *Momrachawong*) rather than adhere to the Royal Institute system.

When citing Thai sources, I have noted both their Thai (Buddhist-era) and Western (Anno Domini) year of publication. Thailand observes the Buddhist-era calendar, which began in 543 B.C. with the birth of the Gautama Buddha. Therefore, I cite sources by both the Thai- and Western-calendar year of publication, separated by a slash (/), for example, Dhanit (2530/1987).

My modified version of the Royal Institute system is shown in the following Thai orthography table. Although central Thai has five tones, these are not indicated.

Conventions and Orthography

Thai Orthography: Consonants

Thai letter	Romanization	
	Initial position	*Final position*
ก	k	k
ขคฆ	kh	k
ง	ng	ng
จ	c	t
ฉชฌ	ch	t
ญ	y	n
ด(ฎ)ฑ	d	t
ตฏ	t	t
ถฐฑทฒ	th	t
นณ	n	n
บ	b	p
ป	p	p
ผถ	ph	p
ฝฟ	f	p
ม	m	m
ย	y	i
ร	r	n
ลฬ	l	n
ว	w	w
ซ ทร ศ ษ	s	t
หฮ	h	—
อ	—	—
-รร	—	-an
-รร-	—	-a-
-ร	—	-aun
ฤ	rü	—

Thai Orthography: Vowels

Thai letter	Romanization
กะ กั	ka
กา	kaa
กำ	kam
กิ	ki
กี	kii
กึ	kü
กื	küü
กุ	ku
กู	kuu
เกะ เก็	ke
เก	kee
แกะ	kae
แก	kae
โกะ	ko
โก	koo
เกาะ	kau
กอ	kau
เกอะ	koe
เกอ เกิ	koe
เกียะ	kia
เกีย	kia
เกือะ	küa
เกือ	küa
กัวะ	kua
กัว กว-	kua
ใก ไก	kai
ไกย กัย	kai

Thai Orthography: Vowels (*continued*)

Thai letter	*Romanization*
กาย	kaai
เกา	kao
กาว	kaao
กุย	kui
กอย	kooi
โกย	kooi
เกย	koei
เกือย	küai
กวย	kuai
กิว	kiu
เก็ว	keo
แกว	kaeo
เกียว	kieo

One

Men Who Become the Deity:
The Thai Body in Performance,
the Thai Body as History

Introduction

I first saw the Thai ritual honoring teachers of music and dance in 1986, at the music education department of Srinakharinwirot University in Bangkok. Although at that time I was doing research about the cassette industry, I was also taking classical Thai music lessons at the university. Early in February, after I had been taking lessons for less than three months, one of the professors casually mentioned that I should make a point of coming to the department that Sunday for a special ceremony. When I asked what kind, he said, "A ceremony to offer thanks to teachers."

Imagining that the affair would be yet another university function (even after my brief time there, I was getting used to the frequent assemblies and special holidays), I tried to avoid committing myself by saying I would try to come. The next day, however, my private teacher, Professor Nikorn, told me I *had* to come. For one thing, he said, I had to be in the ceremony. For another, I had to play afterward because there would be special performances. Finally, he wanted me to tape record the pieces performed in the ceremony because he was going to be one of the musicians. Somewhat alarmed, I said I'd be happy to tape the event, but that it would be better if I didn't play since I had just started studying and I knew I still sounded, 1

Figure 1.1   Wai khruu ritual musicians performing at Srinakharinwirot
University, Department of Music Education, in Bangkok, February 1987. My
teacher, Nikorn Chanthasorn, is fourth from the left in a dark shirt, playing
the great gong circle. I sit in the rear recording the performance.
Photograph by Manop Wisuttipaet.

frankly, bad. That didn't matter, my teacher said; what was important was
simply that I play.

In the days that followed, we went over and over this. I vigorously
resisted (as I saw it) being put on public display, but my teacher was increasingly adamant that I perform. Not only that, but the piece I had to
play was a long overture that was clearly beyond my abilities at that time.
In the end, my teacher told me to come to the department at 8:30 A.M. on
Sunday morning and not on any account to be late because he wanted a
complete tape recording of the event. I realized that, rather than having
lost control of the situation, I had never been in control of it to begin with.
Several days later, my performance in the ritual was as bad as I had known
it would be, but the ritual itself was a revelation. I realized I was witnessing
something of fundamental importance and beauty, and I felt compelled to
understand it. (See fig. 1.1.)

I have related this rather long anecdote about my first *wai khruu* ceremony not to portray the anthropologist as hero or to suggest that opacity
and mystery were eventually replaced by discovery, because neither was
the case. The *wai khruu* ritual (*wai,* "to salute," *khruu,* "teacher") is about the
power and ability of Thai classical music and dance-drama to connect with

the sacred world, and it is, as Thai musicians say, a profound matter that cannot be explicated in any simple way. It is indeed so fundamental that even I, a foreign student and rank beginner, had to participate in its celebration. Toward the end of an extended period of fieldwork in 1989, a well-known and respected ritual musician put me on the spot in front of a group of musicians, asking how I would know what was right and what was wrong when I was writing up my research.[1] I have replayed that moment in my mind many times since then. His point was well taken, and I want to make my approach clear.

This book lays out many of the particularities of the *wai khruu* ceremony: the way it is enacted, the ritual foods and objects that make it efficacious, the people who perform it. Ultimately I am most interested in how Thai musicians and dancers construct and describe the ceremony in words, in writing, and, of course, in performance. These three avenues—conversation, writings about the ritual, and enactments of the ritual itself—actively construct a belief system addressing the physical connection between performance and the sacred world. It is not coincidence that this most central Thai ritual involves performance or, in fact, that all Thai ritual *is* performance. Thai performers act out their relation to the nonhuman realm of gods and spirits to affirm their right to and respect for the sometimes dangerous power of their arts. Finally, performers and teachers are quite articulate about these matters, so it is all the more important that I emphasize the structures and discourse that *they* use to frame the *wai khruu* ceremony. In the end, however, the heart of the *wai khruu* is secret and silent, and I respect the silence I encountered in more than one teacher.

In the largest sense, this book addresses the relationship between ritual and performance and the role of performed sound in Thai ritual. Ritual has been of long-standing interest to anthropologists, but I must stress that I am not drawn to what Bruce Kapferer has called "the grail-like anthropological concern with discovering a unifying definition of ritual" (1986, 191). Rather, I am interested in how Thai ritual is performance and, even more particularly, what happens in Thai rituals *about* performance. This double step back—the reflexivity of ritual performance about performance—is at the center of my study. Once its reflexivity became clear to me, I was pleased to find that Thai performers themselves were not surprised I had chosen the *wai khruu* for study—that the ritual addressed fundamental qualities of performers and performance was also clear to them.

I do not feel that the *wai khruu* ritual is a summing-up or an all-encompassing statement about the nature of central Thai court performance traditions. Rather than treating ritual as a series of symbolic statements through which a society talks to itself, I will look at the *wai khruu* ritual as what Kapferer (ibid.) calls "a complex compositional form . . . revealed through the process of performance." The *wai khruu* ritual articulates matters of economic and institutional authority as well as deliberately esoteric, epistemological, and symbolic concerns.

Ritual as Performance

The intimate connection between expressive culture and ritual is foregrounded in performance studies, an approach that explores the idea (to use Kapferer once more) that much ritual is performance and vice versa. This approach was first developed by Victor Turner (1974, 1982, 1986) and pursued further by Richard Schechner (1977, 1985, 1986a), Stanley Tambiah (1985), and Bruce Kapferer (1983, 1986). The methodological effects of the dramatic metaphor, where the social world is seen as a stage with actors, has been even more far-reaching, as seen in Erving Goffman's work (in which discourse and experience are discussed as social "scripts" that are then departed from or manipulated) and in Clifford Geertz's description of nineteenth-century Bali as a "theater state" (1980), in which pomp and spectacle are treated not as mere artifice, rhetoric, and illusion, but as active constructions of kingship and statehood. By drawing on anthropology, performance studies, and cultural studies, I show how a particular Thai ritual is a constitutive site for certain kinds of social authority and that Thai performers are well aware of this.

Definitions of ritual that emphasize its formal, patterned behavior abound, but Roy Rappaport (1979, 176) noted that "performance as well as formality is necessary to ritual." Tambiah focuses on the media that constitute performance, in what he calls a "working definition of ritual":

> Ritual is a culturally constructed system of symbolic communication. It is constituted of patterned and ordered sequences of words and acts, often expressed in multiple media, whose content and arrangement are characterized in varying degree by formality (conventionality), stereotypy (rigidity), condensation (fusion), and redundancy (repetition). Ritual action in its constitutive features is performative in three senses: in the Austinian sense of performative, wherein saying something is also doing something as a conventional act; in the quite different sense of a staged performance that uses multiple media by which the participants experience the event intensively; and in the sense of indexical values—I derive this concept from Peirce—being attached to and inferred by actors during the performance. (1985, 128)

The key contribution of performance theory to the study of ritual is the emphasis on how ritual is created from various kinds of media, including music, dance, and the spoken word, and how each of these media structures ritual performance in specific ways. Also, the "meaning(s)" of the ritual do not stand apart from these media, just as the kings of Geertz's theater state (1980) did not stand apart from the ritual spectacle that created them. Music, dance, the sounded word, the silent word, and ephemeral substances like incense smoke and candle flame structure the *wai khruu* ceremony, and they punctuate and, indeed, make the ritual effective in ways that collapse the real and the symbolic.

Is the *wai khruu* an example of metaperformance or metaritual? The ceremony is certainly a performance about performance, but if ritual itself is performance, then the *wai khruu* also addresses the very nature of Thai ritual. It also foregrounds the features of performance most salient for Thais, highlighting and celebrating how music and dance not only cross the human and sacred realms but are truly *performative*. By this I mean that the Austinian sense of performative, "wherein saying something is also doing something," is old news to Thai musicians and dancers. Musical works and dances do not simply reflect or act out these realities, but actually make them happen. Playing certain pieces or dancing certain dances manifests divine beings and powers in the human world. When performers enact these special combinations of bodily movement and instrumental sound, the boundaries of the human and sacred realms blur. The paradox is that performance makes this happen but wouldn't be possible without it: when these boundaries shift, the persons at its axis encounter a kind of power that enables them to reenact the process again and again.

Nor is this process timeless and eternal, and in saying this I contradict Thai performers. The practice of the *wai khruu* ritual has certain enduring elements, but the purposes it serves in specific communities of Thai performers have changed along with its social context. In this sense, musicians have responded to their changing circumstances, and the ritual's results have new implications in the Bangkok of the late twentieth century. As Kenneth George has asserted, "thinking about ritual language and tradition as idealized and invariant structures seems less useful than examining the ways communities make and authorize 'ritual texts' for *ongoing* projects of interpretive and pragmatic work" (1996, 201). The pragmatic effects of making late-twentieth-century authority through the *wai khruu* ritual surfaced again and again in my research, though performers themselves acknowledged the differences between then and now with assertions that the more things change, the more they stay the same in the *wai khruu*. Still, as I address in the final chapter, the *wai khruu* of the late twentieth century by no means stands apart from the nation-state that helps support it; the conflicted relationship between the monarchy and state bureaucracy is embedded in its practitioners' prestige. I address these apparent contradictions and refusals by looking closely at the aesthetics and poetics of time and authority.

I realize now that my interest in the *wai khruu* was motivated by my long-time interest in issues of pedagogy. By "pedagogy," I mean not only teaching but also more broadly the field of relational power and control created by the transmission of knowledge. More recently, I have addressed the roles that ethnomusicologists hold in American and Thai educational systems (Wong 1999, n.d.) and the ways that critical pedagogy offers new ways of thinking about each. As an Asian American educator committed to the exploration of feminist and multicultural pedagogies, I must say that Thai performers' traditional pedagogical models lie at the opposite end of the spectrum from mine. I continue to find the logic of their system beautiful and convincing, however, and I simply accepted it on its own terms during the extended periods when I immersed myself in it as a participant. In fact, I continue to consider myself a participant in it, as the ties it creates don't dissipate over time and space. The forms of absolute authority that the system is predicated upon simply form an alternative to the pedagogical strategies I explore in the world of the American academy, but the questions posed by critical pedagogy—How are certain kinds of knowledge established and maintained as authoritative? and What's at stake politically in any given pedagogical model?—have proven useful in my thinking about the *wai khruu* even as they have been challenged by it and vice versa.

The people who wield ritual authority in Bangkok are (mostly) men, are regarded by other musicians as important teachers, draw on several kinds of spiritual force when conducting a ritual, and undergo a particular transformation during ritual events that is key to the spiritual and social constitution of other performers. These men are the heart and soul of this book. They are performers who create other performers. They are performers who allow the first great teacher to speak through them. They do what they do by doubling up particular kinds of performative acts in particular ritual contexts, and thereby quite literally keep Thai music and dance alive. They perform transmission in ways that are epistemologically irrevocable: they do it, so it is.

In the following chapters, I address the construction of ritual performance and the performative in some detail, but as an ethnomusicologist I am particularly concerned with Thai epistemologies of performed sound, whether music or texts read aloud. I suspect that dance enacts a bodily extension of this idea, representing a "sounding" of the body in space. But first I need to establish that knowledge, power, and performance are intensely interrelated in the Thai imagination.

Embodying the Hermit

The first teacher of music and dance directly empowers living teachers. This teacher, referred to as the "Old Father" by performers, lived in the distant past and was an ascetic, a hermit—a man so totally dedicated to knowledge and learning that he lived apart from others in the forest, the better to devote himself to his craft. He was present at one of the moments when Shiva, creator and destroyer of the universe, danced the cosmos into oblivion and then created it anew. For reasons utterly unexplained, the Old Father lived through this ultimate, cyclic destruction and wrote down all of Shiva's music and dance. This repertoire is the basis for Thai ritual music and dance, and it comes to us from the Old Father.

The Thai word for teacher, *khruu*, comes from the Sanskrit word *guru*, and implies a person with mystical knowledge. For as long as performers can remember, the great teachers of music and dance have been not just master performers but also carriers of esoteric knowledge about the sacred power of performance. This knowledge is given to them by other great teachers: master teachers identify pupils whose technical skill, personality, and intellect mark them as appropriate for contact with the sacred. The right to lead the *wai khruu* ceremony has been passed down from certain teachers to certain pupils for as long as anyone knows. Paying respect to teachers in ritual is a combination of ancestor worship (in the sense that deceased teachers are ancestors) and direct contact with the Hindu deities of performance. Human teachers who act as officiants in the *wai khruu* ceremony are in a real sense only one step away from the divine teachers worshipped in the ceremony; many are elderly, all are acclaimed, and there is no doubt that they are seen as transitional figures between the human and sacred realms.

I felt this especially strongly when watching Montri Tramote act as officiant. Montri (1900–1995) was unanimously regarded as the great teacher of this generation. He was personally empowered by H. M. King Bhumibol Adulyadej in the mid-1980s, and this, in combination with his experience and knowledge, gave him an aura of greatness that the Thais call *baaramii*.[2] When I knew him in the last years of his life, Montri was in good health but had the fragility and distance of the very old. I once saw him perform the ceremony in a way that accentuated his transitional qualities: he had a slight

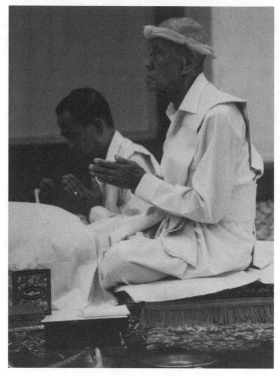

Figure 1.2   Montri Tramote leading a *wai khruu* ritual in 1987,
assisted by his son Silapi Tramote. Slide by Deborah Wong.

cold, and though he went ahead and acted as officiant, he had his son Silapi
(whom he himself had made an officiant) sit beside him at the altar and lead
the prayers. Montri silently moved his lips as his son "spoke" the prayers
through a microphone; although clearly leading the ceremony, he was also
removed from it, and I had the strong sense that he was on a slightly different plane (see fig. 1.2).

In fact, such teachers, from the moment they begin the ritual, are not
normal human beings. At its outset, a teacher is transformed into a "Brahmin" *(phraam)*, and by its end he has become the Old Father. Although I
have been referring to the *wai khruu* as a single ritual, it is actually two con-
secutive rites. The *wai khruu* proper must be done first, because it assembles
all the deities and teachers in the ritual area; this ritual is followed without
pause by the *phithii khraup*, an empowering ritual that combines blessing and
initiation. The *wai khruu* transforms the officiant into the Hermit, and the
Hermit then transforms ordinary people into performers.

The movement from man to Brahmin to Hermit is, of course, highly
symbolic, but it is also dramatic. At the heart of its drama is the fact that

performance in this context isn't "just" performance in the secular Western sense of pretense, posturing, and make-believe. It is performative: the ritual creates a context in which playing a piece of music, dancing a dance, or wearing a mask makes things real. Most importantly, music, dance, and masking open up a channel between this realm and another, a channel embodied in the officiant.

Though it is not made explicit, the parallel between the Hermit's control of sacred texts and Thai master musicians' access to esoteric knowledge is certainly the operating metaphor. The deep cultural connection between Brahminical knowledge and ritual efficacy is enacted by Thais in any number of ways. One way is the everyday Thai practice of making offerings at altars to Hindu deities while asking for help or assistance. Though the majority of Thais self-identify as Theravada Buddhists, most also participate in ritual practices that might be called Hindu and animist, but this poses no theological challenge to most laypersons. Brahminism (*saasanaa phraam*) in Thailand is associated with deep esoteric religious knowledge. I was told over and over again that officiants in the *wai khruu* ritual dress in white and utter magical prayers "like a Brahmin." There are real Brahmins of South Asian descent in Thailand who oversee royal ritual, but I know no officiants even remotely related to them.[3] Officiants are usually devout Buddhists who eat meat and dress normally; Thailand has no caste system.

Brahmanism, the ancient past, and spiritual power are thus imaginatively and affectively linked. Their confluence is actualized in ritual by men who are connected to the past in a physical, material manner. At this point, the English language fails me, as it allows only choices between past and present: the simultaneity of times and persons is the crux of the *wai khruu*, and is best described through the lens of recent Western scholarship on the body.

The Body of the Teacher

The officiant's transformation into a Brahmin begins in the days before the ritual with the careful observation of the Five or even the Eight Precepts.[4] Most officiants observe the Precepts for twenty-four hours before the ceremony, but I was told that three to five days was the norm in the past. Sleeping alone and avoiding sexual contact is also common, even among married officiants—the goal is to be pure (*baurisut*) for a certain amount of time before the ceremony. Many officiants also attend the Evening Prayers (*Suat mon yen*) held the night before the ceremony; this standard chant by Buddhist monks is the actual beginning of the ritual, a first step in creating a sacred frame for the event. The next morning, the officiant dresses completely in white *(nung khao hom khao)* for the ceremony, usually changing out of his street clothes after he arrives at the site. Most wear a white *phaanung* (a sarong-like length of cloth wound around the lower body and pulled up between the legs to form a pair of loose trousers), a white cloth wound around the waist like a cummerbund, a white long-sleeved dress shirt, and a white sash draped over the left shoulder and tucked into the waistband. Some officiants also wear a white headband, usually putting it on after they are seated in place, ready to begin the ritual.

When led by an officiant who is a dancer, the ritual opens with the explicit transformation of the human officiant into a Brahmin. His assistants unroll a length of white cloth (approximately 10 feet long x 3 feet wide) on the floor behind the officiant's seat, perpendicular to the altar and the offerings. Standing at the far end of the cloth (but not on it), the officiant calls out, *"Phraam khao!"* to the *piiphaat* ensemble (an ensemble of xylophones, gong circles, drums, and a quadruple-reed aerophone), which immediately begins to play this piece, literally "The Brahmin enters." The officiant then steps onto the cloth and performs the sacred dance of the same name, slowly proceeding forward. One particular officiant[5] always carried a conch shell filled with holy water[6] in one hand during this dance, turning and scattering the water over the onlookers as a blessing at the conclusion of the dance.

Thongchai Phothayarom, a long-time leading dancer at the National Theater and (at the time of this writing) head of its Performing Arts Division, has for some years led the annual *wai khruu* at the College of Performing Arts associated with the government Department of Fine Arts. He explained to me that *Phraam Khao* changes the officiant into a Brahmin and makes it possible for him to "replace" *(choei)* the Hermit later in the ceremony. The white cloth on the floor is a kind of bridge that paves the way for the Brahmin with purity:

> It's believed that the cloth paves the route *(phaa puu thaang doen)* traveled by the person who does the ceremony. It's completely pure. It's like with monks, you know: you sit on the floor below them, because they should sit higher than you, right? It's the same idea: the Brahmin should walk a path not used by others, paved with a white cloth that's completely pure. It must be white, the color of purity, just as the officiant should dress all in white.

The Brahmin-officiant becomes the Hermit at the end of the *wai khruu* ceremony, a transformation that can be the focus of attention or, sometimes, a moment lost in the flurry of activity preceding the initiation ritual. The officiant lifts his mask of the Old Father[7] and utters certain auspicious verses *(khaathaa)* over it; he then lights a white candle, holds it inside the mask, blows it out, and puts the mask on. Some officiants make this one of the most highly charged moments of the ritual. Udom Angsuthaun, one of Thongchai's colleagues at the College of Performing Arts and also an officiant, sits with his back to the watching students as he recites the efficacious verses and dons the mask; when he stands and faces the audience, brandishing the Hermit's staff, there is a hush like an indrawn breath from all the students, who *wai* or even prostrate themselves *(kraap)*. Watching him, a student sitting next to me turned and whispered, "The Old Father is here!" *(Phau Kae maa laew!)* with some awe. The ritual is less orderly at other locations, and the officiant often completes this transformation attended only by his assistants, while everyone else rushes around removing the food offerings and rounding up students for the imminent initiation ritual.

What exactly happens in this crucial transformation is a matter of great mystery and importance even to officiants themselves. Few are hesitant to talk about it because it is an honor that they are proud to have been granted. All agree that, from the moment they put the mask on to the moment that they formally remove it, they *are* the Old Father. But the conjunction of themselves and the Hermit is less easily explained. Thongchai was especially concerned that it not be seen as spirit possession. He emphatically explained that being possessed *(khao song)* and *inviting* a spirit to come into you are two different things. Inviting a spirit implies control and choice of a higher, more powerful sort than that of the spirit mediums found throughout Thailand. *Choen* or *anchoen* means "to invite" and is primarily used to describe the summoning of deities from the Hindu-Brahman pantheon.[8] Thongchai had a lot to say about this:

> It's not like the teacher just enters you—no! You invite him to come and bestow himself on you, invite him to come into you and make you a deity, invite him to come and imprint himself upon you as a deity—invite him to come and be an officiant through you. At that time, you *are* the deity. But if you're going to invite him down into you, you have to use special knowledge *(withayaakaun)*, which involves receiving magical verses *(khaathaa)* and the right to use them. You don't just walk out and he suddenly comes into you. Being in the ceremony means that you sit and invite him to enter you. You *invite* him to come into you. There are those who believe that you *are* him.

Curious about the nature of this "entering," I asked Thongchai whether, at that moment, he was actually the Old Father or rather a symbol *(sanyalak)* of him. His answer was a marvelous example of the collapsing of categories so central to ritual performance: he simply said, "Yes— you're a symbol of the Old Father, and you are the Old Father." In other conversations, he said that he acted as a *phuu thaen* for the Old Father, an expression that can mean "representative" or "replacement" or someone who acts on behalf of someone else. For Thongchai, the slippage between being and representing wasn't an issue but was, rather, an expectation.

To undergo this entering, this simultaneity, is not easy, however. Thongchai said that wearing the mask (i.e., being occupied by the Old Father) is a strong experience. After searching for words, he said that he feels "all choked up" with strong emotion for that stretch of time, but by the same token is not aware of himself—his voice may change, or he may weep, and he isn't really mindful of it. "The strength and power of the Teacher passes through you, and you don't know it," he said.

The transformation certainly involves the supernatural power called *aphinihaan*, defined by one dictionary as "the power of greatness" (*amnaat haeng baaramii*, in Manit 2528/1985, 1074). As Thongchai said, "When you go out, *aphinihaan* comes into you and makes you into the Teacher." But he also said that he "belonged" (*pen khaung ong thaan*) to the deity during those moments; at other times in the same conversation he said he "became" the deity in the ceremony and that the soul (*winyaan*) of the deity was brought into the mask and then into him when he wore it. He consistently used the word *ong*, a general noun or classifier for supernatural beings and sacred objects, to refer both to the Old Father and the being that he himself becomes in the course of the ritual.[9]

Spirit possession and divine embodiment remain uneasily theorized in anthropology and religious studies. Joanne Punzo Waghorne admits that "When the embodiment of god in the divine image or the holy person is mentioned, authors often adopt the stoic guidelines of a teacher forced to explain sex in class—keep it short, keep to the facts, and provide some solid assurances that it is not so mysterious after all" (1985, 1). The two dominant paradigms for explaining such "shockingly direct experience of god" (ibid.) treat possession as symbolic either of an individual's psychological state or of a particular society's problems. Emic epistemologies of embodiment have received much less attention. Waghorne traces the South Asian Hindu emphasis on the senses and "matter-based religion" as a problem referenced by concepts like "idolatry" (3–6). She puts the old question of possession in a new way, useful for this study as well: "How does the process of god embodiment operate and how do the Hindus themselves discuss the subtle relationship between the 'ordinary' concrete world of experience and the concretization of god" (6)? Similarly, I focus on the centrality of a material divine presence for Thai musicians by looking at what they do with it and listening to what they say about it.

Stephen Inglis (1985) has considered the "affinity" between those who are possessed by a deity and those who create the deity's image; he examines the Velar, a hereditary group of potters in Tamilnadu who make clay images of deities for local temples and who are also possession specialists known as *camiyati*, "god dancers." The right to act as a *camiyati* is passed between male relatives, for example, from father to son, grandson, or nephew. "The *camiyati* and the clay image are essentially identical," Inglis says (98): both are impermanent, and both become temporary vessels of the divine, designed to be reactivated periodically over a lifetime of service. Inglis theorizes that the very process of creativity connects the Velar to the deities:

> In Tamilnadu the creative act is always one of pain, vulnerability, and danger, and any creation exposes those involved to the deterioration that preceded it and that will inevitably follow. The Velar often speak of being involved in both birth and death in their work. This conception lies at the root of the social stigma which afflicts all craftspeople in south India and especially potters, for whom the creative cycle is collapsed into a relatively short temporal sequence. The new clay pot, purest of all ritual objects, quickly becomes the used pot, the archetypal symbol of impurity. When the deity departs from either the human *(camiyati)* or earthen (image) vessel, this vessel is drained and at least symbolically destroyed so that the renewed vessel can be re-created. . . . The specialized skills of a community like the Velar derive not only from their ability to create, but also from their ability to survive the dual nature of the creative process. (99)

The parallels between Velar belief and Thai musicians' worldview are extensive, partly because of a shared Hindu epistemology of divine embodiment. Making/enacting is seen by both groups as infused with vulnerability, divinity, and power, all of which are located in male bodies that are socially linked to one another. The materiality of the divine is realized through creative activity.

Paul Stoller explores bodily epistemologies of power among the Songhay of Mali and Niger, linking decades of work on the anthropology of the senses to the bodies of Songhay sorcerers and bards, as well as to the body of the scholar-ethnographer. In *Sensuous Scholarship* (1997), he draws on George Lipsitz's work to propose that Songhay spirit possession "is a sensory arena of counter-memory" (63), that is, a site of subaltern, counterhegemonic, or subversive discourses "more likely to be stored in tales, objects and bodies than in texts" (60). Stoller focuses on the Hauka, a group of European spirits who appeared among the Songhay after 1925 during the colonial era, suggesting that their continued importance in the 1980s and 90s is a "second contact" in which the Songhay address post/colonial memories and anxiety. Such spirit possession, Stoller says, points in several directions: "How can we explain the power of spirit possession to evoke the past, manipulate the present, and provoke the future? How can we explain the power of spirit possession to shape both local and state politics? My tentative answer is that spirit possession is an arena of sensuous mimetic production and reproduction, which makes it a stage for the production and reproduction of power" (65). Thai performers' mimesis does not construct otherness (à la Taussig 1993) as much as it constantly reconstructs (reproduces) original power, drawing it again and again into the moment, reflecting Thai attitudes toward a present that can never measure up to the past in sheer power, authority, and knowledge. When the Old Father walks through a university auditorium full of worshipful music majors, does he become a stage for the production and reproduction of late-twentieth-century power—or does the university become a staging ground for an elemental presence? Is the Old Father modernized or is the university traditionalized? In the context of the Thai university and public school systems, I am not convinced that the Old Father is simply a subaltern countermemory resisting the tide of modernity even as I discard the traditional/modern binary. Stoller notes that "the Hauka are seen as powerful political beings: they get things done quickly, efficiently," they solve problems in the here-and-now with European swiftness. One might say that the Old Father identifies new music and dance department chairs and even National Artists as much as he creates new performers; he has real-world effects.

Struggling to describe what happens in Afro-Brazilian *candomblé*, Barbara Browning (1995) looks at the dancing body and its relationship to the *orixás*, the Yoruba deities. "Divinity cannot be represented mimetically but only contiguously or metonymically," she writes. "The manifestation of the *orixás* is pure presence" (44). She argues that studying *candomblé* is equivalent to studying divine liturgy; in short, she treats the dancing body in *candomblé* as "writing through motion" in which "the dancer in a state of an *orixá*'s incorporation is not a writer of that dance but rather becomes the text, written by the *orixá*" (50). Though not equivalent to Thai beliefs about the embodied presence of the Old Father, Browning's scheme relating deity, performing human body, and choreography/writing can help us to see beyond mimesis and impersonation to that moment in performance when the Old Father makes his embodied presence known.

Anthropologists focused on the performance of healing practices in cross-cultural context have begun to look more closely at the poetics of the body and the senses. Robert R. Desjarlais notes how "the visceral reaches of the eyes, the ears, the skin and the tongue" are central to the efficacy of healing among the Yolmo Sherpa, a Tibetan-Burman group (1996, 159). Similarly, Thomas J. Csordas notes that "the body is the existential ground for efficacy in general" (1996, 107), in other words, bodily experience is the meeting point for the symbolic and the discursive. In short, bodily experience doesn't take place in the head, and a belief system centered on embodiment is surely about something more than mimesis.

The epistemology of the Thai performing body opens up questions that reach far beyond issues of Buddhism and its boundaries. Experience, belief, and authority join viscerally and irrevocably in the person of the empowered teacher. For the Thai officiants of music and dance, the Hermit is a meeting point of different kinds of power that can be experienced or disseminated only through the body, and this has deep implications for performers' beliefs. The materiality of spiritual presence helps to explain why Thai performers' discursive systems are centered so profoundly in particular bodies, and this in turn implicates performers' understandings of time and history. The ritual technologies that create performers are wielded by men who are not only exemplary teachers in the here-and-now but who are also routinely collapsed with the first teacher of all time. They not only bring the past into the present but literally *become* the past in ritual contexts. They are elisions of then and now, and their presence suggests that Thai theories of embodiment are literally and aesthetically powerful indeed, implicating the poetics of time and history.

....

Two

Performing the *Wai Khruu* Ritual

Thai performers love to talk about the details of the *wai khruu* ritual—they are always ready to have a conversation about the particularities of the ritual food offerings, for instance, or to talk about how *their* teacher used to do it. *How* the ritual is performed and where are topics that are interesting and indeed enjoyable; *why* the ritual is done is less easily (or perhaps comfortably) discussed. Most performers' experience of the ritual is from doing, participating: this experiential base of understanding was readily and enthusiastically shared with me. Performers were invariably pleased when I told them about my research and were eager to tell me where I should go to learn more and who I should talk to. The ritual is such an elaborate performance in and of itself that it is essential to consider the details of its enactment, not least because those details are so important to the performers.

No two *wai khruu* rituals are ever performed in exactly the same way, even by the same teacher. Each teacher establishes his own way of leading the ritual but follows the same general tripartite structure of first inviting the deities of performance to congregate in the ritual area, presenting them with elaborate food offerings, and finally empowering and initiating certain participants. Variation abounds within this basic structure. Different teachers ask for different musical pieces from the *piiphaat* ensemble; the particular deities summoned may vary, as do the food offerings; and more mundane factors such as the sheer number of participants and the amount of time available for the ritual (i.e., what time it starts, since the first two parts of the ceremony must end by eleven o'clock[1]) shape the course of the event.

Whether the ceremony is for musicians alone or for dancers as well constitutes another basic difference in ritual practice: the *wai khruu* ritual for dance-drama includes musicians, but the ceremony for music is more specialized. The *wai khruu* ritual for dance-drama is more theatrical in a performative sense because the Old Father enters the officiating teacher between the second and third sections of the ceremony. This embodiment does not occur in the music ritual: a mask of the Old Father dominates the altar, but the officiating teacher never dons it, nor does he use it for initiation, so the ritual as a whole is much more sedate.

Below I describe two of the many *wai khruu* rituals that I attended. I chose these particular performances with an eye for contrast—of place, participants, and performative drama. One event—the largest annual *wai khruu* ceremony held in Bangkok—was held at a Buddhist temple, and the other at the music education department of a major university. Both contrast with the *wai khruu* described in the Preface. One was for both music and dance-drama, while the other emphasized music. One involved working-class professional performers, the other students and professors. They could not have been more different, yet both followed the same ritual template.

The Annual *Wai Khruu* at Wat Phra Phireen

The biggest and most spectacular *wai khruu* ceremony in Bangkok is the annual ritual at Wat Phra Phireen, sponsored by the Association for Assistance to Friends and Performers. This event draws well over a thousand participants, mostly noninstitutional performers such as *likee* and *lakhon chaatrii* actors,[2] but the attendance is so huge it is difficult to generalize about who comes. Occurring as it did near the end of my extended fieldwork, I was especially struck by the intersection of different performers' circles: people I had known from entirely separate venues came together at Wat Phra Phireen. During the nights before and after the ritual, as well as at the ceremony itself, I ran into a mask maker from the College of Arts and Crafts, several musicians from the troupe at the Bangkok Bank, a few musicians from the Department of Fine Arts (though not many), some music majors from Prasanmit and Chulalongkorn University, some *likee* actors who performed near the old city wall, a private dance teacher, and so on. The cross-section of social status and performance genres was quite striking and stands out for both its size and inclusiveness.

Figure 2.1 Sign at the gate to the Wat Phra Phireen temple grounds announcing *likee* performances in conjunction with the annual *wai khruu* ritual in 1989. Slide by Deborah Wong.

Wat Phra Phireen is a quiet, slightly rundown temple in old Bangkok on the edge of Chinatown, just off Woracak Road and not too far from Caroenkrung Road; it is at the end of a long lane of mechanics' shops, off the main streets. The temple was an informal gathering place for performers when its abbot was *Phra Khun Cao* Phrathep Khunathan, a great supporter of the performing arts. This monk was venerated for his compassion in sponsoring the cremations of destitute performers who didn't have relatives or the means for a proper funeral. As one publication put it, Wat Phra Phireen was variously known as the "*likee* and *piiphaat* temple" and "the cemetery for performers" (Prong 2516/1973, 1). When the abbot died in 1969, various performers came together and formed the Performers' Association (as it is called for short), using members' donations and dues to continue sponsoring needy performers' funerals.

In 1989, the Association's *wai khruu* ceremony was held on Thursday, September 21st, but the ritual itself was the culmination of a week of special events. The annual temple fair always coincides with the week of the ritual, so the grounds were full of food vendors, a Ferris wheel, shooting galleries, and so forth. A big painted sign at the gate to the temple grounds read as follows (see fig. 2.1):

The Schedule for the Wai Khruu Festival of
the Association for Assistance to Friends and Performers:

Sunday the 17th of September:
16:00: The beginning of the festival.
19:00: Performances by five *likee* troupes.

Monday the 18th of September:
19:00: Performances by five *likee* troupes.

Tuesday the 19th of September:
19:00: Performances by five *likee* troupes.

Wednesday the 20th of September:
16:00: Monks will chant Buddhist prayers.
19:00: Performances by five *likee* troupes.

Thursday the 21st of September:
7:00: Food offerings will be made to all the temple monks.
9:00: The *wai khruu* ceremony begins.
19:00: Thai music performances.

The night performances preceding the *wai khruu* are famous for the talent of the performers as well as for the unrestrained atmosphere. Beginning around 9 or 10 P.M. (despite the stated starting time of 7 P.M.), the *likee* performances often go on until dawn. Two different professors at Prasanmit said they avoided these nighttime events. One told me that fights are common and that someone actually got killed in 1988. The other said he wouldn't go for fear that he might "sin" (which in his case probably meant get drunk)—the festivities were simply irresistible.

I went to the temple late on Wednesday afternoon, the day before the ritual, and found the place bustling with activity and filled with a celebratory feeling like Christmas in the United States, with many cheerful people dashing around preparing things. The feeling of community was strong— I had been told that any *wai khruu* ritual was supposed to promote brotherhood between musicians but that the ceremony at Wat Phra Phireen was especially open, and this proved to be true. The altar was already set up, and it was an impressive sight indeed, crammed with masks of the Old Father in every size imaginable. The altar was in the middle of the temple's main *saalaa*, or large open-air pavilion, where funerals were usually held. A long platform about two feet above the floor had been set up, with the altar at one end. Hundreds of chairs were lined up in rows, still facing the side stage where the nightly *likee* performances were held.

I watched nine temple monks chant for about an hour, until 5:00. *Khruu* Nim, one of the Association's most remarkable members (I discuss him at more length in Chapter 5), sat close to the monks during the chanted

Figure 2.2   Khruu Nim Pho-iam sitting in front of the altar at Wat Phra
Phireen's annual *wai khruu* ritual in 1989. Slide by Deborah Wong.

prayers, his eyes closed and his hands in a *wai*. When the prayers ended, the
present abbot sacralized a basin of water and anointed *Khruu* Nim's forehead. *Khruu* Nim had lived at Wat Phra Phireen since 1949, when he retired from performing female roles in *likee*. From that time on, he lived a
disciplined life, observing the Eight Precepts, dressing only in white and
performing a daily *wai khruu* ceremony for himself. Until his death in
1994, he lived in a small building (beside the main *saalaa*) that was almost
entirely filled by a huge *wai khruu* altar. Quite elderly in 1989, he was a quiet
but authoritative man and a driving force behind the big annual ceremony.
(See fig. 2.2.)

Many of the Association's officers (mostly middle-aged male performers) were there, and I was introduced to *Khruu* Thaungbai Rüangnon,
an ebullient older man who told me he had helped organize the ritual
for over eighteen years. He himself was a *wai khruu* officiant (though he
wouldn't be leading the ritual the next morning), and his father had been
one, too: he showed me an amulet he kept in his back pocket of his father
wearing the mask of the Old Father. A normal *wai khruu* ritual, he said,

Figure 2.3   Food offerings at Wat Phra Phireen in 1989.
Slide by Deborah Wong.

costs 20,000–30,000 *baht* (then U.S.$800–$1,200), but the one at Wat Phra
Phireen comes to over 100,000 *baht* (U.S.$4,000). He proudly said that the
Association's ceremony was certainly the biggest in the city. A young woman
who had been listening to us said, "The 'highest' *wai khruu* is at the Depart-
ment of Fine Arts in August, attended by the Crown Princess, but the one at
Wat Phra Phireen is the biggest one for common people."

When I arrived the next morning at about 8:00 A.M., the pavilion
and temple grounds were already full of people. Association officers wearing ribboned badges bustled around looking serious and frazzled. The rows
of seats had been turned around to face the altar, and were already almost
full of people.

It took almost an hour for some ten officers to set out the elaborate food
offerings. The officers were closely supervised by *Khruu* Nim, the acknowledged authority on *wai khruu* food offerings: entire sets of special foods were
arranged for a number of different groups of deities (unlike most such rituals, where only three sets are prepared; see fig. 2.3). Indeed, the array of
food offerings was staggering. At any *wai khruu* ritual, the arrangements of

food offerings are central to the visual splendor of the altar—multitudes
of fruit (bananas, tangerines, and more), at least two pigs' heads (one raw
and one cooked), chickens, ducks, and crabs (the crabs sometimes escape
their bindings and begin to sidle away), curries, noodles, and so forth are
always prepared and laid out as beautifully as possible on platters and in
bowls. Today, though, the usual plenitude was expanded to match the size
and importance of the occasion. At least eighty offerings were laid out on
several levels of the altar as well as on the bottom platform at its base. *Khruu*
Nim kept a close eye on their groupings, meticulously directing the officers
to arrange and rearrange what went where. Demonic deities eat only raw
foods, for instance, so these offerings were all placed on the left side of the
altar for their pleasure and consumption. Everyone deferred to *Khruu* Nim's
knowledge of particular deities' preferences: he sat and pointed to where
each offering should be placed while the officers crawled back and forth on
their knees, shifting plates of food into ever better configurations.

The celebrant, or officiant, *Momrachawong*[3] Caruunsawat Suksawat
(1918–1997), was already there and dressed in ritual white; he sat back from
the commotion of the preparations and simply watched. *Mom* Caruun, as he
was called, is best known for his skill as a mask maker, but he was admired
as a dancer in his younger days and received the right to lead the *wai khruu*
ceremony for dance from three different teachers, including *Khruu* Nim. A
popular and respected *wai khruu* officiant, he performed one or two ceremonies almost every week between June and September.

A long table was set up near the pavilion entrance, manned by Association officials. I went over and found that they were selling commemorative
booklets from past ceremonies, as well as small amulets of the Old Father.
Since these amulets are famous in performers' circles, I bought one for forty
baht. The female officer told me to treat it well—to keep it somewhere up
high when I wasn't wearing it—and the Old Father would look after me.

By 9:00, the pavilion was filled to overflowing, and the air was full of
the noise of people talking and continuous announcements over the P.A.
system. *Mom* Caruun's two assistants—his son and a disciple studying mask
making—set up the area where he would sit facing the altar. His seat was
a low table below the platform, draped with a tigerskin with the head glar-
ing out at the people behind him. All of his equipment was on the platform
itself: trays bearing his big basin for sacralized water, a small statue of Shiva
as Lord of the Dance, his oblong book of ritual texts, heaps of incense sticks,
a conch shell, and so on.

A number of people, many dressed in white, had seated themselves on
the mats directly behind *Mom* Caruun's seat. Most were spirit mediums,
made obvious later in the ceremony by their behavior.[4] I recognized one

woman as Rachani Phimthon, a dancer then in her late thirties who was trained at the College of Dramatic Arts; I had seen her remarkable performance some ten months earlier at another *wai khruu* ritual, where she was entered by the Old Father (described in Chapter 7).[5]

The *piiphaat* musicians, known as the Duriyapranit Ensemble and closely associated with the famous Duriyapranit family of musicians, took their places around 9:30. That day they were wearing matching blue polo shirts with a logo for a restaurant, presumably one of their sponsors. They immediately began playing the Morning Overture *(Hoomroong Chao)*, a ritual suite of five pieces that took ten minutes to perform as the final touches were put on the food offerings. *Mom* Caruun took his seat as the overture ended. He spent a moment praying over his necklace of prayer beads, then hung them around his neck and put on a white headband. The crowd noise continued unabated as *Mom* Caruun and *Khruu* Nim reenacted the transmission of knowledge and ritual rights between them: sitting above *Mom* Caruun on the platform, *Khruu* Nim took the book of ritual texts in both hands and held it out to *Mom* Caruun, who accepted it; they held it together for a moment as *Khruu* Nim silently uttered a magical verse and then let the book go. *Mom* Caruun *wai*-ed deeply, which *Khruu* Nim answered with another *wai*. *Mom* Caruun then put the book on a raised tray, opened it, and proceeded to sacralize the basin of water. *Khruu* Nim remained sitting on the platform near *Mom* Caruun for the rest of the ceremony, mostly praying with his eyes closed.

At about 9:50 *Mom* Caruun filled the conch shell with sacralized water and stood up as his assistants unrolled a long length of white cloth on the platform behind his seat. Stepping onto it, he called out, *"Phraahm Khao!"* to the *piiphaat* ensemble, which started playing the piece as *Mom* Caruun danced in as the Brahmin, holding the conch shell high. His dance movements were not as fluid as those of a young dancer but nevertheless had an impressive majesty and gravity. While the *piiphaat* played the concluding free-meter *rua*, he quickly turned in a circle and scattered water from the shell in a wide arc, everyone *wai*-ing as the water touched them. Rachani, close behind him, was up on her knees in a dancer's stylized *wai*.

The Association president ceremoniously lit the candles on the altar, and *Mom* Caruun rapidly began reading the ritual texts and calling for various pieces. For the first half hour, he simply read the texts aloud without having the audience repeat each phrase after him; everyone held their hands to their chests in a *wai* and listened respectfully. Incense was passed out and then collected. *Mom* Caruun was clearly abbreviating the ritual, sometimes turning several pages at a time: the ritual had started a bit late and had to be finished by 11:00, so he was cutting corners.

By the time *Mom* Caruun read the text welcoming the many *rüsii* (hermits), three women behind him were in trance, dancing on their knees and sinuously moving their arms; Rachani was now on her feet dancing in place whenever the *piiphaat* played. The trance dancing stopped whenever *Mom* Caruun recited ritual texts but resumed with ever-increasing intensity whenever the *piiphaat* ensemble played. At 10:30, *Mom* Caruun read the text inviting Parakhonthap, the deity of *piiphaat*, and it was clear that Rachani was now the Old Father: she sat in place tapping out the drum rhythms of *Tra Parakhonthap*, her face contorted into an old man's smiling but toothless visage.

Mom Caruun now instructed the audience to repeat the texts after him, phrase by phrase. The dangerous and important text inviting *Phra* Phiraap followed that for Parakhonthap. (I will discuss *Phra* Phiraap's significance in subsequent chapters, but at this point let it suffice to say that inviting him into the ritual releases his dangerous power—his presence is difficult to control and is especially risky for the officiant.) Despite all the ambient noise in the pavilion, a palpable tension settled over the gathering as this text began. As *Mom* Caruun led the second repetition of the text, his hands, clasped in a *wai*, began to tremble and then to shake rhythmically, and he controlled his voice with obvious effort. A man sitting near him began to shake in a similar manner, his eyes closed. By the third and final repetition of the text, *Mom* Caruun's voice was strangled and his hands were being violently pulled up and down, pounding against his thighs each time they came down; his assistant first held his chair to keep it from moving, and then grasped *Mom* Caruun's shoulder in concern. Just when it seemed he couldn't take anymore, the text came to an end and he was released: he sat stunned for a second and then came to himself, shaking his head. His disciple quickly handed him a cup of water, and he drank a little. He then called out for the next piece, "*Phra Phiraap Tem Ong!*" ("*Phra* Phiraap, the whole deity," discussed in Chapter 4) and sat back, but the words were no sooner out of his mouth than a bellow came from a woman somewhere in the audience as she was entered by a spirit. Everyone turned to see who it was as the music began.

The piece lasted for twenty minutes and prompted a wave of possessions among different audience members, both men and women. The women already in trance continued to behave as they had before, but even more vigorously. Rachani got to her feet and danced over to the *piiphaat* ensemble, but was shooed away by a female Association officer who directed her back to her place, firmly but without touching her. A man standing beside me suddenly let out a roar of demonic laughter, and I turned to find him half-

crouched, his arms flung wide and his fists clenched, his face in the gri-
mace of a demon. Everyone near him stood back, leaving him alone in a
little circle but watching him with a mixture of repugnance and fascination.
Three men were kneeling by the president's seat, trying to resist being possessed; one even had his hands (in a *wai*) and forehead pressed against the
president's knee.

Several more women were possessed, standing in place and gracefully
moving their arms in dance motions. Off to the side of the platform, a man
suddenly sprang to his feet, his eyes open wide, showing the whites. A moment later, he danced up behind *Mom* Caruun in a demon's stance, but *Mom*
Caruun didn't even look: he was quietly preparing the mixture of powder
and water he would soon need to anoint people. Everyone in the man's
path backed away, and several male Association officers (including *Khruu*
Thaungbai) gestured them back even further, concerned for their safety.
The man danced and gesticulated for a few more minutes and then abruptly
fell to the ground, lying on his back. Two officers immediately hurried over
to him and lightly slapped his cheeks, trying to bring him out of it, but he
responded only by convulsing slightly. After a while they left him alone, and
Mom Caruun turned to scatter sacralized water over him with his whisk, but
to no visible effect. An onlooker stood up and took a snapshot of the oblivi-
ous man with a pocket camera.

The *piiphaat* ensemble played on, and more and more people were being possessed as officers quietly prepared big banana leaves for the next part
of the ritual. An albino woman began to dance in place. The various women
in trance moved in sinuous dance gestures, usually in place, whereas men
were possessed by demons or had their *wai*-ing hands pulled violently up
and down, as *Mom* Caruun's had been, by unseen forces. An officer checked
on the unconscious demon, and when *Mom* Caruun once again sprinkled
him with water, he went into fierce convulsions. At that moment, *Phra
Phiraap Tem Ong* ended. The *piiphaat* ensemble went straight into the coda
of *Pathom* and *La*, and the man began to come to himself. A moment later,
he pulled himself to his knees, looking stunned but human, and he prostrated
himself, touching his forehead to the floor. He sat on his heels for a moment
more, breathing hard, his face covered with perspiration, and then went off
into the crowd, everyone cautiously watching him.

The music ended, and *Mom* Caruun took command of the situation,
immediately beginning to read a ritual text without asking the audience to
repeat it after him. He quickly called for *Long Song* and the Association president came over to pour water over *Mom* Caruun's small Shiva image; other
officers took their turns after him, and Association officials invited an elderly

man in white to anoint the image with the powder paste. An assistant took the image back to *Mom* Caruun, who poured water over it from the conch shell and then anointed it himself. He moved the image to another tray and poured the water collected from its washings back into the main bowl.

Going on, he read the ritual text presenting the food offerings to the deities and had the audience repeat them after him. It was nearly 11:00. He called for *Nang Kin* and *Sen Lao* ("Sitting to Eat" and "Offering Liquor") together, and a group of Association officers descended on the offerings as the music began, cutting and slicing the food. A few people were still sitting in trance, but in the flurry of activity surrounding the offerings, most people visibly relaxed and talked amongst themselves. The noise level rose again, augmented by an official making announcements over the P.A. system: a series of dance offerings were about to start, and the first was by two famous *likee* actors who were announced by name. Two officials cleared a space on the mats where the spirit mediums had been sitting, gesturing for everyone to move back. Dressed in costumes elaborate even by the gaudy standards of *likee*, two middle-aged men emerged from the crowd and began to dance the *Ram Thawaai Müü* ("The Offering of the Hands Dance") to taped music and the great interest of the audience. *Mom* Caruun sat in place as they danced, sometimes watching over his shoulder as he directed his two assistants to rearrange his area for the initiation ritual. His assistants moved all of his equipment up onto the platform, cleared his many little tables, and set them up in a semicircle.

The dance ended after about ten minutes to applause from the onlookers. The two men knelt and *wai*-ed, smiling, as two officials formally placed flower garlands around their necks, and they then went off into the crowd. A second group of dancers, six young women, performed a long dance, holding flowers and bending gracefully to the distorted sound of taped music blaring from the P.A. system. They too were given garlands by Association officials, and then the final dance offering began: a man and woman from the Department of Fine Arts, wearing long brass fingernails, did a *lakhon chaatrii* dance called *Ram Sat Chaatrii* that honors teachers and often precedes performances. Several of the *piiphaat* musicians accompanied this dance with live music, including the small double-reed instrument called *pii chawaa*, a pair of small drums called *klaung chaatrii* played with sticks, a pair of woodblocks, and the *ching*, played very quickly.

When this dance ended at about 11:35, *Mom* Caruun was helped up onto the platform and seated himself once again on his tigerskin. He led the audience in a recitation of a final, brief ritual text and then called for the *piiphaat* ensemble to play a piece as his assistants went up to the altar and took down the things he needed for the initiation ritual: the Old Father's staff, Rama's bow, two gold masks of the Old Father, a gold mask of Phra Phiraap, the green-faced mask of Wisanuukaam (Vishnu), a *soet* (a particular dance headdress), and the flat facial mask worn by jokers, with a thick tuft of hair glued on top. One by one, these objects were carefully removed from the crowded altar and arranged in a semicircle around *Mom* Caruun's seat on stands; one by one, he briefly donned them and whispered magical verses into their interiors, activating their spirits. His son unrolled the length of white cloth on the platform, creating a path to the altar. *Mom* Caruun put on one of the masks of the Old Father, uttered another silent magical verse, took the staff, and got to his feet. The audience watched reverently, their hands in *wai*-s, once again quiet. *Mom* Caruun slowly danced down the white cloth to the altar, holding the staff high, taking the dignified but majestic steps of the Old Father. When he reached the end of the cloth, he walked off it and put the staff back on the altar. People immediately began surging toward the platform. The officials had meanwhile set up a railing in front of *Mom* Caruun's seat, to control the movement of the crowd. Still wearing the mask, *Mom* Caruun reseated himself and began the initiation ritual. The dancers who had performed the dance offering pressed forward first. Efficiently aided by his assistants, *Mom* Caruun sprinkled each person with sacralized water and "covered" their heads with three objects —the Old Father, *Phra* Phiraap, and the *soet* headdress—in quick succession. That is, one of *Mom* Caruun's assistants would hand him the mask of the Old Father, and *Mom* Caruun would then hold it over the head of the kneeling performer, lightly touching the crown of the performer's head while silently uttering blessings. He repeated these actions with the mask of *Phra* Phiraap and with the dance headdress, one after the other, and handed each mask back to his assistants when done. Each "covering" imbued the performer with a different kind of blessing and spiritual power, though all three kinds are necessary. The combination of physical contact with the sacred objects and *Mom* Caruun's whispered prayers effected the transfer. Dipping his finger in the powder mixture, *Mom* Caruun then drew a magical symbol on each person's forehead and uttered a propitiary formula. He ended by blowing one short, sharp breath over each person's head.

 Mom Caruun "covered" hundreds of people in the next hour or so. He also covered many small masks of the Old Father that performers had brought from home, performing the ritual blessing on the mask just as he did on a person's head. As his assistants handed him the three masks over and over again, *Mom* Caruun was an impressive sight: the gold mask of the

Old Father, high on his head, gave him an imposing height even seated, and the gravity with which he executed the ritual actions inspired a special respect from onlookers.

As the initiation ritual went on, the crowd began to disperse. The general mood was festive, and food seemed to be on everyone's mind. People moved toward the food vendors' stalls in the temple grounds, while Association officers and especially eminent members ate lunch at communal tables in a room behind the pavilion, served in family style.

Exhausted by the crowd, I went home and returned to Wat Phra Phireen later that night to hear the *piiphaat* competition, arriving after 9:00 P.M. After strolling through the temple grounds and enjoying the fair, I joined some students from Prasanmit and spent several hours listening to one virtuoso group after another, each faster and more brilliant than the last. Hundreds of people were sitting and listening, chatting, and snacking on the night vendors' wares. I ran into a number of acquaintances. A musician from the Department of Fine Arts told me about a *wai khruu* ceremony to be held the following week and told me not to miss it. Rachani, whom I knew only slightly, greeted me like a long-lost friend and we talked about the morning's ritual: she said the Old Father was "everyone's teacher," full of compassion and kindness, and certainly not to be feared. Later still I crossed paths with Varravinai Hiranmas, a mask maker from the College of Arts and Crafts, who told me that most of the people who were "entered" during the ritual were not performers but rather mediums *(khon khao song)* or practitioners of magic *(saiyasaat)*, and that *Phra* Phiraap never enters women (though years later, I heard of women whom he did enter). Furthermore, he said, those who are easily entered are probably a bit weak-spirited *(cit aun)*, not strong. Was the possession behavior for real? I asked him. He smiled and shrugged: "When it comes to the *wai khruu*," he said, "you can't *not* believe." (See fig. 2.4.)

When I went home after midnight, the Ferris wheel was still turning and the umpteenth *piiphaat* ensemble was racing through another piece. My friends from Prasanmit stayed on—the playing wouldn't *really* get good, they said, until the wee hours.

A *Wai Khruu* Ceremony at Srinakharinwirot University–Prasanmit

I studied classical Thai music at the Prasanmit campus of Srinakharinwirot University for two years (1986–1987 and 1988–1989). Their *wai khruu* ceremony in 1987 was the first that I witnessed and in which I participated. In a very real sense, that event inspired this entire study. I came to know the

Figure 2.4 Varravinai Hiranmas and his teacher, *Momrachawong* Caruunsawat Suksawat, looking at Wat Phra Phireen's *wai khruu* altar together in 1989. Slide by Deborah Wong.

students and professors in the Department of Music Education well, both as musicians and as people. I have no illusions about having been privy to everything that went on at the department, but my research there was certainly enriched by glimpses of how personal and professional concerns affected its running and organization. Although I documented and participated in some twenty-eight *wai khruu* rituals during my research, I saw only the 1989 ceremony at Prasanmit from start to finish—a tall order, since the preparations for any *wai khruu* ceremony take days, and the ritual rarely has a clear ending point. At Prasanmit, I also had an in-depth understanding of the participants' relationships, and this, of course, is what the *wai khruu* is really all about: the links, both pedagogical and personal, between teachers and students.

Srinakharinwirot University is one of the largest university systems in Thailand, with (then) a total of eight campuses;[6] Prasanmit, where I studied, is the main campus, situated on a large tract of land between Phetburi and Sukhumwit Roads in the center of Bangkok. The Department of Music Education *(Phaak Wichaa Duriyangsaat)* was founded only recently: it was originally a club for classical Thai music and was made into a department under three of the leading student members of the club in the 1970s. A master's degree was instituted in 1989, but the department at that time was primarily oriented toward undergraduates, who could choose to concentrate in either classical Thai or Western music. Students who complete the major are qualified to teach music at the elementary or high school level once they pass the examinations required and administered by the Ministry of Education.

The department has two professors who teach Western art music and six who teach Thai classical music. In the Thai music section, the three professors who founded the department were in their early forties at the time of my research and had received their degrees at Srinakharinwirot University in other subjects (Thai language and literature and geography); the other three professors graduated from the music education department after its inception.[7] The most recent addition to the faculty at that time was an accomplished *piiphaat* performer in his mid-forties—my teacher, Nikorn—who went back to college late in life. Once he finished his degree, he was immediately hired by the department to teach performance.

Undergraduates at Srinakharinwirot University do not choose a major until their junior year, first completing the core curriculum and only then beginning concentrated study in their major. Music majors thus spend two intensive years in the Department of Music Education. All are expected to perform, and the required performance course is "Introduction to the Gong Circle (Music 336)," mandatory for both Thai and Western music majors.[8] Upon graduation, music majors who choose to become teachers (and who pass the government exams) apply for whatever positions are available, and Prasanmit music graduates are thus posted to public schools all over Thailand, from the tip of the southern peninsula to the mountains of the north. Others choose to make a living as performers, usually in the restaurant entertainment circuit. And some, of course, end up in occupations totally nonmusical.

Some students come from musical families and are already accomplished musicians when they begin the music major. Most simply enjoy making music, however, and know how to play at least one instrument. Young women are generally familiar with stringed instruments such as the *sau duang* and *sau uu* (two-stringed fiddles), the zither, or hammer dulcimer; every graduating class also has one or two women who specialize in singing. The male students gravitate toward the percussive instruments of the *piiphaat* ensemble: the two xylophones, the gong circle, and the various kinds of drums. Such gender boundaries are by far the norm, but there are a few exceptions every year: one young woman was quite accomplished on the lead xylophone and had little interest in performing on any other instrument; another young man tended to play hammer dulcimer most of the time.

Most students, though, play a number of different instruments to varying degrees. For one thing, basic competence in all instruments is required by the major (as public school teachers, the students will have to teach all of them), and male students in particular are often able to play the bowed instruments—often the first instruments they encountered as children in their homes. Only two instruments—the quadruple-reed oboe and the sacred two-headed drum—are strictly defined by gender. The oboe-like instrument called the *pii* is not off limits to women, but the basic technique of producing sound by puffing out the cheeks and blowing hard is considered so unattractive—and a refined demeanor is so important to middle-class Thai women—that, in reality, women simply never play it. The two-headed drum called the *taphoon* is another matter entirely; it is a symbol of the Old Father and is thus proscribed for women.

This introduction to the department and its students is necessary to understanding why the *wai khruu* ritual is an important annual event. One of the ritual's basic functions is to initiate musicians (and dancers) into higher levels of repertoire. The *wai khruu* ceremony at Prasanmit is held in February, toward the end of the Thai academic year (which runs from June through early March). At least one of its many purposes is to initiate the juniors into the next level of repertoire, ensuring that all music majors graduate with an ability to play a certain body of ritual music.[9] The ritual is necessary for basic spiritual reasons, but it also plays an important role in the department curriculum and the design of the music major. This incorporation of ritual into university structures is one of many late-twentieth-century changes in ritual practice and context.

The *wai khruu* ceremony at Prasanmit is always held on a Sunday in early February, and the reasons for this date implicate who leads the Prasanmit ritual, who has led it in the past, and who may lead it in the future. During the 1970s, when the department was still only a club, the students arranged for certain music teachers to instruct them after school hours. The most eminent of these teachers was Chin Silapabanleng (1906–1988), the daughter of the famous *Luang* Pradit Phairau (1881–1954). *Luang* Pradit Phairau is widely regarded as the most remarkable teacher and musician of the twentieth century, and he ritually empowered many of today's highly regarded *wai khruu* officiants (whom I discuss in detail in Chapter 6). Now honored as the paradigm of tradition, *Luang* Pradit Phairau was in fact extremely innovative and broke with ritual tradition by investing his daughter—a woman—with the right to lead the *wai khruu* ceremony; normally, only men are qualified to lead the ritual.[10] In all, he granted seven different musicians the right the lead the *wai khruu* ceremony, and one of these was his daughter Chin.

Chin was a noted teacher of music who taught at many schools and universities during her long and productive life. She was not, however, particularly active as a *wai khruu* officiant; Prasanmit is the only place I know where she performed the ritual on a regular basis. When I first saw the Prasanmit ceremony in 1987, she was already too old and frail to lead the ritual, but she still attended it and was given a seat of honor in the front row of spectators and participants. She was clearly much loved, and I was told many times that her kindliness and humility had endeared her to students of several generations.

When Chin first began to lack the stamina to lead the *wai khruu* ceremony, the professors at Prasanmit had to find someone else; at her suggestion, they invited *Khruu* Chüa Dontriirot to take her place. *Khruu* Chüa (b. 1918) also taught at Prasanmit on an occasional basis. He is from a distinguished family of musicians and had studied for a time with *Luang* Pradit Phairau, Chin's father, so he was an appropriate choice for several reasons: he was already associated with the Prasanmit music department, he was of the same pedagogical lineage as Chin, and he was highly respected as a musician. He has led the annual *wai khruu* ceremony at Prasanmit ever since, as well as at a number of other schools and universities.

The annual *wai khruu* at Prasanmit is held on the first or second Sunday in February, as close as possible to Chin's birthday on February 5th. Groups of disciples often schedule their *wai khruu* ceremony around a teacher's birth date, following the practice of making merit for respected persons (often deceased) on their day of birth. That is, disciples try to accrue continued good karma for their teachers through the *wai khruu*, to ensure their teachers' rebirth in better circumstances.[11] Thursday, considered "teachers' day," is the preferred day for *wai khruu* ceremonies, but Prasanmit, like many schools, holds its event on Sunday because more alumni are likely to be able to attend on a weekend.

Preparations for the ceremony began on Monday, February 6, 1989, with a general (but mandatory) organizational meeting at the music department. At 4:30 P.M. all the Thai music majors, along with a few Western music majors, gathered in an upstairs classroom. The meeting was led by Prateep Lountratana-ari,[12] though Kanchana Intarasunanont, the department chairperson, helped. Two other professors, Nikorn Chanthasorn and Chalermpon Ngamsutti, sat in the back of the room and were present throughout but did not actively contribute to the proceedings. Manop Wisuttipaet, the youngest professor in the department, first sat in back but later moved up to the front row in order to hear better: the classroom, like most in Thailand, was open-air, uncarpeted, and filled with the ambient noise of cars passing, students practicing downstairs, and the chatter of students in the room. About forty-five students were present, including nearly all of the third- and fourth-year music majors, and the small group of fifth-year students. The first two rows of seats were filled with girls who were involved and helpful but also made small talk the entire time, adding to the generally informal and lighthearted atmosphere. Since it was a school day, everyone was dressed in university "uniform," that is, black pants or skirts and white shirts or blouses with the university pin on their breast pockets.

The meeting was a beautiful example of Thai cooperation, which is a combination of coercion and volunteerism. Prateep stood at the head of the classroom for the entire hour and kept things moving by constantly asking who was going to "help" with each task. Seniority was evident among the students: the third-year students, who were new to the procedure, were slow to volunteer for anything, whereas the fourth-year students, who had participated in the previous year's preparations, volunteered with only a little prompting from Prateep, and the fifth-year students (many of whom were already teachers, working part-time toward a degree) offered help for various tasks with no prompting at all.

Prateep started out by explaining when and where the preparations, and the actual ritual itself, would take place. He emphasized that everyone would have to be responsible and help out in whatever way they wanted and that all they had to do was say what they would rather do. He added that everyone was, after all, a music major, and the ritual was an important part of the major. He then noted that I would be documenting the event for my research,[13] and he therefore wanted everything to be done right this year and all the offerings to be present. He then began writing on the blackboard some of the main tasks: making the food offerings, preparing all the equipment for the monks, making small iconic representations of Mount Meru from banana leaves filled with rice (*bai srii paak cham*), making food for the monks' meal and for all the guests, and so forth. He said he was expecting between two hundred and two hundred and fifty people to attend, mostly alumni and friends of the department.

At this point one of the fifth-year students stood up and offered the fifth-year students' services in buying and preparing some of the food for the guests' meal, mentioning chicken curry, deep-fried fish cakes, fruit, and several other things. This got things moving. Suriyaa, a particularly well-liked and responsible senior, suggested that the seniors provide one complete "set" of offerings. Everyone already knew that three nearly identical sets of food offerings are necessary for the ritual. More discussion ensued, and finally someone proposed that the juniors should get *all* of the animal offerings—three each of the pigs' heads, ducks, and chickens. Everyone agreed that this made most sense, but a short debate followed over where the items should be bought—everyone had their own opinion about where the biggest poultry could be purchased for the least money. Prateep figured that all nine animals should come to about seven hundred *baht* (U.S.$28—pigs' heads, a common offering, are fairly expensive).

By this time, the room was filled with excited conversation and jokes. Prateep had to cup his ears to hear what people were saying to him, but he never told everyone to quiet down. He wrote down a long list of things on the blackboard—serpent's-head fish, crab, shrimp, shellfish, seven kinds of fruit, taro, potato, sugarcane, banana leaf/rice mountains, flowers—and then began calling for volunteers. Two or three different students offered to get each thing, and Prateep asked me if I would help make the banana leaf/rice mountains, saying that they were hard to make but "high" (i.e., sacred) and important to know about. Of course I said yes, and several other young women offered to help too.

Someone asked how much the entire event would cost, and Prateep answered probably no more than 20,000 *baht* (U.S.$800), adding that the professors would all make donations (or, as he put it, "help each other"). Kanchana announced that she would buy all the flowers early on Saturday morning and asked who would like to go with her. Three girls volunteered immediately, because Kanchana was much admired for her taste and skill in flower arrangements. Prateep announced that preparing the ritual area—the main auditorium at the university—was a matter of great importance, and he asked that Manop (the youngest professor) and Nikorn (the performance instructor) supervise. He then told all the male juniors and seniors to come on Saturday to help set up the stage area, including all the sound and light equipment.

By then it was almost 5:30, and some final tasks were allocated in quick succession: preparing the monks' meal, looking after the schoolchildren who would attend, picking up and returning the monks to their temple, and so on. When the meeting broke up, everyone was talking at once and in very good spirits.

Saturday, the day before the ritual, was a day of intensive preparation. Early in the morning, Kanchana and her student assistants went to a well-known flower market near Chinatown and bought all the orchids and lotus buds that would decorate the altar and be used in worship. Others presumably did their market shopping as well. When I arrived at the university auditorium around 3:00 in the afternoon, most of the male students and Manop, Nikorn, and Chalermpon were already there, just beginning to set up the altar. All the musical instruments and dance masks had already been brought over from the department (which was just two buildings away) and were scattered around the stage; the dance masks were carefully set out on a low wooden table used as the main stage prop in dance-drama performances. The altar, made from five successively smaller levels of risers completely covered with white cloth, dominated the stage. When I arrived, only the first object had been arranged, a green glass Buddha image set at the very top on a small table.

Everyone was dressed casually (except for Chalermpon, who wore his customary professor's uniform), and was milling around, moving things or chatting. The three professors' relative status was very much in evidence: Chalermpon, the most senior, was standing back and watching, occasionally giving advice but not doing any manual labor; Nikorn, whose domain was the instruments and their care, was ordering students around and carrying things to where they needed to be; and Manop, the youngest, was the most active, always on hand to haul what needed to be hauled, and generally keeping things moving.

Several young women had already started making the banana leaf/rice mountains—Kanchana had left rolls of banana leaves, jasmine flowers, cutting tools, and staplers. One young woman (an alumna now working at the Educational Radio station) put herself in charge: she ended up spending over two hours on the objects, continuing to work even after the other girls had wandered off. I sat down and spent half an hour learning how to clean the banana leaves and cut them into the right shapes, rolling them into small tight cones and stapling them shut.

Once the presiding Buddha image was in place, the men started arranging all the *piiphaat* instruments on the altar. The big gold-painted arched frames of the Mon gong circles were put on the second level, and the other instruments were placed on the second to fourth levels; the xylophone keyboards were left rolled up but put carefully inside the bodies of the instruments. Everyone took their shoes off when they climbed up on the altar, mostly to keep the white cloth clean but also out of respect. When all the *piiphaat* instruments were in place, the dance masks were arranged in a long row on the fifth and highest level, just below the table with the Buddha image. The demonic characters were put on stage right, ranked according to status: two masks of Totsakan (Ravana), one green-faced and one gold, were closest to the center, followed by his demon son Inthaurachit and the astrologer Phipheek, and then by three demon soldiers. On the left, from the center outwards, were ten masks: five dance headdresses for refined characters, the golden deer headdress, the horse-head headdress, Hanuman, and two monkey soldiers. In the center, slightly elevated above the other masks on a pedestal, was the most important mask of all, the Old Father. Everyone helped to move the masks, but the Old Father was lifted into place by an older student who *wai*-ed to the mask before picking it up.

Several zithers and the curved gold frame for the Mon drumstand[14] were then put on the second level, and Manop came in with the framed picture of *Luang* Pradit Phairau that usually hung in the main practice room; out of several pictures of teachers,[15] this was the only one taken out of the room. He put it on the fourth level in the center, just below the mask of the Old Father. In the meantime, Chalermpon had several students climb up on tables and take down some big styrofoam signs suspended from the ceiling, left over from a computer conference held earlier that morning. By keeping certain words ("Srinakharinwirot University" and "February 2532"), judiciously cutting up other words, and running off to the university workshop for other letters, a new sign was assembled, reading "The Annual *Wai Khruu* Ceremony, 12 February 2532, Srinakharinwirot University–Prasanmit," suspended above the altar on strings.

While the letters were being rearranged, Manop and Nikorn set up a low platform to stage right for the *piiphaat* ensemble that would perform live during the ceremony. They unrolled green carpeting and set up a "paired" or "double" *piiphaat* ensemble (*piiphaat khrüang khuu*, i.e., an ensemble made up of two xylophones, two gong circles, the sacred two-headed drum, and two barrel-shaped drums). The oboe player would bring his own instrument. Someone produced snapshots of the previous year's ceremony, and the three professors gathered around, comparing what they had done so far with last year's arrangement of the altar. A brief, spirited discussion ensued about where the three knobbed, suspended gongs *(moong)* should be placed, and then Nikorn went back to the platform for the *piiphaat* ensemble to unroll the xylophone keyboards. Wichaa, a senior and a fairly talented gong circle player from a musical family, hung one xylophone keyboard and made sure none of the keys were touching, but Nikorn wasn't satisfied—the keyboard was hanging too low, so he retied the end to make it shorter and tighter. He showed Wichaa how to tie the knot, saying, "You have to know how to do this right if you're going to be a teacher."

By then it was nearly 4:30, and the banana leaf/rice mountains were coming along nicely though now attended to by only the one woman. Six small "mountains" stood in separate white bowls, and she was trimming jasmine flowers and placing one in the tip of each cone. Meanwhile, Chalermpon was trying to decide whether it was worth the trouble to have someone go off and get the necessary letters for the word "ritual"—there were divided opinions on whether the words "*wai khruu*" were enough.

Two piles of xylophone and gong circle mallets were placed on trays and put on the second level of the altar. Six colorful potted plants appeared out of nowhere and were dragged into place at the sides of the altar and the *piiphaat* platform. Two male students began arranging one of the most important and cumbersome objects, a long length of white string that had to surround the entire building. They carefully climbed up the altar to the Buddha image (trying not to knock over any instruments) and tied the end of the string around the green glass image, then looped it through all the refined masks and headdresses, through several of the large instruments on the left, and (under Manop's direction) went off into the left stage wing and outside through a door. They spent the next half hour threading the string around the outside perimeter of the building, taking care to loop it over the many doors.

In the protected overhang at the back of the building, food preparation was in full swing. Whereas most of the male students were inside making the altar, almost all the female students were busily washing bowls and plates, chopping, mixing, and generally creating a meal for several hundred people. Pranee, a senior, was washing a pile of lotus buds. Five young women were sitting and gossiping while rolling leaves around stalks of grass and then tying each little bundle closed with white thread; these auspicious objects (about the size of a cigarette) would be tucked behind the ear of each of the participants in the ritual, so the women had to make at least two hundred and fifty.[16]

Inside the auditorium, Prateep was putting the finishing touches on the altar. It was nearly 6:00, and he had spent the day running around the city doing a number of little errands for the ritual. He had brought a larger Buddha image of brass to replace the small green one dominating the altar. With the help of an older dance student, he climbed up, exchanged the images, and fussed with the tables until he had the effect he wanted, a three-level arrangement with the Buddha image at the top, the Old Father's mask directly below that, and a small model of a *taphoon*—the sacred drum, symbol of the Old Father—below the mask. He then moved the headdresses for Rama and Sida to either side of this central arrangement and put them up on pedestals so that they framed the Old Father.

The auditorium was now nearly empty; everyone had gone home or was out back, cooking and eating dinner. The final touches were now put on the altar, including eight huge flower arrangements of spilling purple and orange orchids, laced with fern fronds, that had taken Kanchana and her assistants all day. As Kanchana stood in the audience and shouted directions ("Move it more to the right! Now a little bit to the left!"), Prateep and a male student placed them on the altar. Two were put inside the gong circles to

Figure 2.5   Framed photograph of Chin Silapabanleng on the *wai khruu* altar at Srinakharinwirot University–Prasanmit in 1989. Photograph by Sarah Grew.

either side; one was placed in the center, hanging down over the photograph of *Luang* Pradit Phairau; the others were arranged symmetrically, filling the altar with color. After many adjustments, Kanchana was finally pleased.

Red carpeting was unrolled, covering the stage, and was meticulously swept with little hand brooms until it was spotless. Finally, Prateep and three recent alumni polished a collection of brass candlesticks and vases until they gleamed and put new orange candles in each one. The young woman who had now finally finished the banana leaf/rice mountains carefully prepared some lotus buds by folding back the outer petals and then arranged them in vases. Prateep placed two bottles of whiskey at either side of the altar and then showed me a snapshot of Chin, an official portrait in old age. "I found it last night in a bunch of other photos," he said; "I'll get it framed tonight and will put it on the altar tomorrow." (See fig. 2.5.)

It was now 7:00 P.M., and the altar was finished. "Not bad," Prateep said. "About eight hours from start to finish." When I left, there were still a number of students eating dinner out back, and Prateep and Kanchana were with them.

When I arrived at the auditorium on Sunday morning at about 8:00 A.M., most of the students and professors were already there. Nine monks had arrived in a minivan at about 7:00 A.M. and were ensconced in

Figure 2.6   Buddhist monks at Srinakharinwirot University–Prasanmit
for the *wai khruu* ritual in 1989. Photograph by Sarah Grew.

an empty carpeted room at the front of the auditorium building where
a small altar with a Buddha image had been set up (see fig. 2.6). The sacred
string tied to the Buddha image on the stage altar was also attached to this
statue. The monks were seated on the floor along two adjacent walls, with
the eldest and most senior monk next to the altar. Holding the string between their *wai*-ing hands, the monks had chanted morning prayers that
sacralized the entire area, paving the way for the *wai khruu* ceremony proper.

A big canopy had been erected outside the auditorium, and students
were serving coffee to guests who had arrived early and were sitting in the
canopy's shade at long tables. The eight musicians who would be performing in the ceremony, all men in their late thirties and early forties, sat here
too, joking and making small talk. They had known each other for years,
most having gone to elementary and high school together at the Department Fine Arts's School of Performing Arts. Nikorn had invited this group
and would himself be playing the gong circle.

It was still quiet inside the auditorium. The food offerings were already
in place on the altar and in front of the platform for the *piiphaat* ensemble.
Each kind of food—fish, poultry, fruit, sweets, and so forth—had its own
bowl or plate, and everything was arranged as colorfully as possible. The
pigs' heads were even decorated with flowers stuck in their mouths and ears.

At 8:20, the first musician, the sacred drum player, came in by himself and sat down at the instrument. The drum had a strip of white cloth wrapped around its middle, indicating that the imminent performance was a sacred event. The drummer spent several minutes kneading and attaching a small lump of wax to the left drumhead, trying out the sound by striking the drum repeatedly until he was satisfied. He put his bag of wax shavings away and fussed with the offering bowls clustered in front of the drum. A total of eight bowls, one for each of the musicians, had been provided, and each contained a garland of jasmine flowers, a small packet of incense, a candle, and a piece of white cloth. After spreading them further apart, the drummer chose a bowl for himself and opened its packet of incense.

Khruu Chüa, the elderly teacher who was to lead the ritual, arrived and spent half an hour inspecting and slowly rearranging objects on the altar. Still in his street clothes, he first went over the food offerings and moved them all around. Suriyaa, the senior who had been appointed *Khruu* Chüa's assistant for the day, stayed close by his side and helped. When he moved one of the banana leaf "mountains," it fell over and he saw that there wasn't yet any rice inside it so he went off, muttering to himself, to find some. Another student was sweeping the carpet yet again.

Meanwhile, the drum player had taken the candle from his offering bowl and attached it to the drum so that it stood upright. He lit it, then lit three sticks of incense from the candle, and silently began to recite a series of propitiary verbal formulas specifically for the drum and the deities of the *piiphaat* ensemble. He prayed with his hands clasped in a *wai* at his chest and the incense held between his palms, moving his lips as he prayed but making no sound (see fig. 2.7); he *wai*-ed at certain points in his texts by bringing his hands to his forehead, and also stopped periodically to knock ash off the incense. After reciting the prayers for several minutes, he finished and stuck the incense sticks into the lacing on the drum's body, spreading them slightly apart so that their smoke fanned out. His preparations over, he *wai*-ed three times on top of the drum: bowing deeply over it, then placing his hands, palms down, flat on its body and touching his forehead to them.

By now it was past 8:30 and getting busier. Students were going back and forth seeing to final tasks. Suriyaa returned with the *bai srii* (mountains), now filled with rice; he put them in place and carefully topped each with a hard-boiled egg, impaled on a long wooden skewer (see fig. 2.8). *Khruu* Chüa now inspected the offerings in front of the *piiphaat* ensemble and rearranged them with Suriyaa's help. Two of the musicians came in and immediately went over to *Khruu* Chüa, *wai*-ing deeply. They then went to

Figure 2.7   Taphoon player prays before the *wai khruu* ritual at Srinakharinwirot
University–Prasanmit in 1989. Photograph by Sarah Grew.

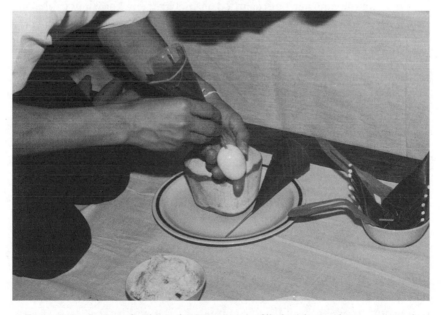

Figure 2.8   Suriyaa finishing the *bai srii*, now filled with rice, by topping each
with a hard-boiled egg impaled on a long wooden skewer.
Photograph by Sarah Grew.

chat with the drum player. Suriyaa and another student were sent up onto the altar to attach long strings of Christmas lights here and there, framing the photograph of *Luang* Pradit Phairau and outlining the inner frames of the Mon gong circles. A female senior arrived with a paper bag full of tiny red cloth squares, approximately an inch long and wide, each with a red thread loop; she and another student began hanging them on all of the altar instruments and masks—most already decorated with small flower garlands—as a sign of blessing.

By 9:00 *Khruu* Chüa had changed into completely white clothes and was seated in front of the altar, where he would remain for the next several hours. He was dressed as a *wai khruu* officiant must be, in a long-sleeved white dress shirt, a white *phaanung*—a length of cloth wound around the waist and pulled up between the legs as a pair of loose trousers, extending below the knees—and a sashlike piece of white cloth hung diagonally across his chest and tossed over his left shoulder. The rest of the *piiphaat* musicians came in and went up to *Khruu* Chüa to *wai* to him before sitting down at their instruments; a few *wai*-ed to the altar as well. The lead xylophone player, Natthaphong Soowat, was widely regarded as one of the best xylophone players in Bangkok; he taught part-time at Prasanmit as well as at several other schools.[17] The other xylophone player, Bunchuay Soowat, was best known as an oboe player but regarded as an extremely knowledgeable, all-round musician; he taught at Chulalongkorn University. All the musicians had, at one time or another, studied at the School of Dramatic Arts, and one—the drum player—was a full-time performer in the Music Division of the National Theater troupe. All of them performed regularly in *wai khruu* ceremonies: as professional *piiphaat* performers and teachers, they were among the select minority of male musicians who had received the right to play all the high sacred music used in the ritual.

ᢍ

In the last moments before the ceremony began, *Khruu* Chüa checked all of his ritual equipment (see fig. 2.9). Experimentally, he shook the short branch of leaves he would later use for scattering sacralized water. He re-arranged the candlesticks and incense holder and asked Suriyaa to replace the big silver bowl of water at his side with the earthenware urn usually kept on the altar in the main practice room. The audience of participants had begun to assemble, filling a number of the auditorium seats. Quite a large number of elementary school students were present, chaperoned by their parents. All were from the Prasanmit Demonstration School, an

Figure 2.9   Khruu Chüa Dontriirot sitting in front of the *wai khruu* altar at
Srinakharinwirot University–Prasanmit just before the ritual begins in 1989,
with student assistant Suriyaa to his right. Photograph by Sarah Grew.

elementary school on the grounds of the university. Its music and dance
program was taught largely by Prasanmit graduates, and all the children beginning music study were expected to participate in the university *wai
khruu* ceremony. Also present were a number of university alumni, most in
their twenties and thirties. The current music department students were in
and out of the auditorium during the ritual; as hosts, most were kept busy
with various tasks and duties. A small number of professional musicians who
played nightly at a local restaurant in a group organized by Chalermpon and
led by Nikorn also attended; these men sat together, off to the side.

At 9:10 the ritual officially began. Prateep and the vice president of
the university came up and knelt beside *Khruu* Chüa. Suriyaa lit a tall white
candle and handed it to the vice president who, on his knees, went up to the
candles in front of *Khruu* Chüa and lit the first of five. Poised to play and
watching closely, the *piiphaat* musicians immediately struck up the sacred
piece *Saathukaan* as the first candle caught flame (see fig. 2.10). Everyone in
the audience *wai*-ed as the piece began with four distinctive drum strokes
(da-DA, da-da) instantly recognizable to everyone. As the music continued,
the vice president lit the rest of the candles and then three sticks of incense
from the white candle used to light the others, placing them in the holder in

Figure 2.10   Piiphaat ensemble, led by Natthaphong Soowat on the lead
xylophone, playing *Saathukaan* at the beginning of the Prasanmit *wai khruu* ritual.
Photograph by Sarah Grew.

front of *Khruu* Chüa. He then prostrated himself three times in front of the
altar, his forehead touching the floor. Watching closely, the musicians (cued
by Natthaphong, the xylophone player) played the cadence and brought
Saathukaan to a close.

    In the silence that followed, the musicians all *wai*-ed the altar, and
Khruu Chüa began to utter silent prayers, moving his lips and sitting with
his hands in a *wai* at chest level. At the same time, Prateep and Suriyaa each
took a big bundle of incense and carefully lit them from the candles, making
sure that every stick was ablaze before finally shaking them out (see fig. 2.11.
The smoking bundles were handed to two students waiting at the foot of
the stage who then spent several minutes distributing one stick each to the
audience members. More incense was taken just outside the doors and stuck
into the grass to further sacralize the area (see fig. 2.12).

    Meanwhile, *Khruu* Chüa was sacralizing the water in the earthenware
urn. As Suriyaa watched, he took a small white candle, lit it from the main
candle, and then moved it in a circular motion over the urn while silently
reciting prayers. This took several minutes. He extinguished the candle in
the water and prostrated himself three times on the white pillow in front of
him. The water ready, he had Suriyaa pull the microphone closer to him
and turn it on. His hands in a *wai*, he turned to the microphone and softly

Figure 2.11   Prateep and Suriyaa lighting bundles of incense.
Photograph by Sarah Grew.

Figure 2.12   Lit incense sticks in the grass outside the auditorium doors.
Photograph by Sarah Grew.

said, "We will now say the *Namo* together," and prostrated himself three times again before reciting the following:

> Namo tatsa
> Phrakhawato
> Arahato
> Sama samphutthasat[18]

Everyone quietly recited this three times in unison. *Khruu* Chüa then leaned close to the microphone and said, "*Saathukaan Klaung*," letting the *piiphaat* musicians know that he now wanted this piece to be played. They immediately began playing, and the gestures of respect surrounding the performance of the piece were the same for each of the twenty-seven pieces played in the course of the ritual. As the piece began, *Khruu* Chüa prostrated himself three times on the pillow in front of him and then sat listening, occasionally taking a sip of tea, spitting into a tureen, or adjusting his clothing. When the musicians began to play a distinctive free-meter coda (called a *rua*, appended to each piece), he prostrated himself three times again. At the conclusion of the coda, the musicians all *wai*-ed, most still holding their mallets. Each of the pieces summoned a particular deity or group of deities, and the free-meter coda represented a salutation—in dance-drama, dancers would actually perform a stylized *wai* at this point. The piece *Saathukaan Klaung* expresses respect specifically for the ritual and its deities—unlike *Saathukaan*, an expression of respect for the Buddha, the Dharma, and the institution of the monkhood.[19]

Saathukaan Klaung* took two minutes to play. At 9:20 the piece ended, everyone *wai*-ed, and *Khruu* Chüa began to recite the special propitiary verses of respect called *oongkaan*.[20] Though some teachers keep their book of these verses open in front of them, *Khruu* Chüa recited them from memory, phrase by phrase, and everyone softly repeated each phrase after him. Each phrase was three or four syllables long, and most adults admit that they understand many but not all of the words, which are in a combination of Pali, the sacred language of both Buddhist and Brahman ritual in Thailand, and Thai. Each short text invited a specific deity or group of deities (just like the musical pieces) and was recited, start to finish, three times in succession. Everyone, including *Khruu* Chüa, held their hands in a *wai* at chest level as they recited, and it was hard to distinguish the words because everyone murmured them or even uttered them inaudibly, just moving their lips. Suriyaa and the *piiphaat* musicians followed along in the same manner.

At 9:21 *Khruu* Chüa finished the first set of verses and called for the *piiphaat* ensemble to play *Tra Baungkan*, a piece asking for general blessings from the deities called *theewadaa*. When the piece ended at 9:24, he began to recite the next set of ritual verses, which included the phrase, *"Srii srii— wan nii pen wan dii"* (*srii* is an auspicious word, followed by, "Today is a good day"). During these two minutes of recitation, Natthaphong was busy fixing one of the xylophone keys, whose lump of tuning wax, attached underneath, had come off; he heated it with a cigarette lighter and stuck it back on as the other musicians watched.

More pieces and recited prayers followed. At 9:41, *Khruu* Chüa called for a long succession of pieces by murmuring, *"Baatsakuunii—Samoe Khaam Samut—Hoomroong—Khom Wian"* into the microphone. These four pieces, always played without pause, took twenty-one minutes to perform, while *Khruu* Chüa sat quietly, sipping tea and waiting. The children in the audience became restless and began to talk, and the adults also began to relax a little, still solemn but not as attentive. The four pieces completed a series of actions in rapid succession. *Baatsakuunii* assembled some of the remaining deities such as Wisanuukaam (Vishnu), Pancasingkhaun (the deity of stringed instruments and singing), and Parakhonthap (the deity of *piiphaat*). *Samoe Khaam Samut* brought the deities into the area of the ritual. The *Hoomroong* (Overture), a series of pieces in its own right, brought the deities from the heavens down to the human realm. Finally, *Khom Wian* represented the figurative circumambulation of the ritual area with candles, making it an auspicious space.

As the *piiphaat* ensemble played the coda at the end of *Samoe Theen*, an elderly professor named Kamthaun Snitwong came up and seated himself alongside *Khruu* Chüa, accompanied by the vice president. When the coda ended, *Khruu* Chüa quickly said, *"Long Song"* into the microphone, and the *piiphaat* ensemble began to play the piece. *Long Song* means "to bathe" (i.e., to pour water over something to cleanse it) and in this case accompanied the bathing of a small Ganesha image placed in a small bowl in front of *Khruu* Chüa. As the person of highest status, the vice president came forward on his knees and was the first to pour water over the statue, a little bit from each of three bottles in succession. Kamthaun, a highly regarded professor of Western music, now retired, went next; he had been instrumental in establishing the music department at Prasanmit and was sometimes referred to as the *"Luang* Phau," or honored father, of the department. These two men *wai*-ed before and after pouring the water. Prateep came next, but he chose to prostrate himself and then poured the water with the extremely respectful and subordinate gesture of supporting his right arm in his left hand.

As two more pieces were played, *Khruu* Chüa prepared the powder mixture he would soon use to anoint the objects on the altar and, later, the participants in the ritual. He took a little glass full of the dried remains of powder from past *wai khruu* ceremonies at Prasanmit (usually kept on the altar in the main practice room) and poured in some of the sacralized water used to bathe the Ganesha image, mixing it together with a white stick.

When the two pieces ended at 10:16, Prateep and Suriyaa once again approached on their knees and began to light big bundles of incense. As they patiently held the incense in the candle flames, waiting for them to catch fire, *Khruu* Chüa announced into the microphone that *Phra* Phiraap (the demonic teacher of dance-drama) would next be invited to enter the ritual and that everyone should help invite him. He then lit three sticks of incense himself and held them in a *wai* while silently uttering a prayer; when finished, he sat waiting for the audience to be ready. The musicians were also waiting, talking quietly among themselves. Natthaphong was still trying to fix the troublesome key on the xylophone. Prateep and Suriyaa passed the now-smoking bundles of incense to four students and an alumnus, who distributed the incense to the audience. Some adults held their stick in a *wai* to their foreheads, silently praying; the children merely held the incense for a moment until the same students re-collected all the sticks. The students then took the sticks of incense outside and stuck them the ground at the four corners of the building.

Attending to the incense took almost ten minutes. At 10:23 *Khruu* Chüa looked over his shoulder to see whether the audience was ready and then said, "We will recite the *Namo* together" into the microphone. Everyone, including the musicians, grew silent and respectful—an air of deeper solemnity settled over the auditorium. After the third repetition of the *Namo*, *Khruu* Chüa began to recite the special prayer text for *Phra* Phiraap, calling on him by name and by his dangerous power *(itthirit)*. At 10:26, after the third repetition of this text, *Khruu* Chüa leaned into the microphone and called out, "*Phra Phiraap Tem Ong—Khuk Phaat*," and the *piiphaat* immediately began to play.

The audience was quiet and somber during this long (thirteen-minute) sequence of pieces. *Phra Phiraap Tem Ong* is the "highest" or most sacred of the pieces in the ritual repertoire: only men can perform it, and furthermore, only men who are over thirty who have already been ordained as Buddhist monks and been given the right to learn and perform the piece by a master teacher.[21] By specifying "*Tem Ong*," the "full deity" or "complete deity," *Khruu* Chüa specified that the piece would be played in its longest, most complete version, with none of the elisions that are sometimes made to save time. As *Phra Phiraap Tem Ong* drew to a close and the musicians were playing the coda before going straight into *Khuk Phaat*, the lump of tuning wax once again fell off the problem key on Natthaphong's *ranaat eek*, but he kept on playing—he had to, because it would have been

extremely inauspicious if not dangerous to stop in the middle of the sequence. The hand cymbal player, who noticed since he was sitting right beside the xylophone, quickly passed the cymbals to the barrel drum player
and began reheating the lump with the cigarette lighter as Natthaphong
played on, avoiding the key (quite a feat). By now all the musicians in the
ensemble were watching with concern as they played, and a moment later
a young man came up from the audience and took the cymbals from the
drum player so that all the instruments were covered.

After the coda that ended *Khuk Phaat*, the musicians began to play the
three short final pieces (*Pathom*, *Laa*, and *Rua Saam Laa*) that always con-
clude the sequence, creating the extra closure necessary for such an important piece. The instant *Pathom* began, five or six male students hurried
up on stage and began to ritually slice each of the food offerings, cutting a
small piece off each animal offering, opening the whiskey bottles, lighting
the cigarettes, slicing open the fruit, and so on. At 10:39 the music ended
as the students continued to prepare the food. Another bundle of incense
was lit and sticks of incense were inserted into each of the offerings. Meanwhile, a recent graduate named Tum, who came from a musicians' family
and was therefore particularly sensitive to musicians' problems, came up
and had a brief whispered conversation with *Khruu* Chüa. After *Khruu*
Chüa nodded, he took a rolled-up xylophone keyboard from the altar to
Natthaphong, who exchanged it for the keyboard that had been giving him
so much trouble. He hung it in place as several students began cutting up
the food offerings in front of the *piiphaat* ensemble.

Khruu Chüa announced that they would now present the food offerings to the assembled deities, asking everyone to recite the *Namo* with him
once again. This done, he began the special prayer for the food offerings as
informally dressed students dashed back and forth in the wings, carrying
lunch on trays to the waiting monks who had to eat their final meal of the
day before noon. *Khruu* Chüa then instructed the *piiphaat* ensemble to play
four pieces in succession: the first two pieces assembled the remaining demonic spirits, and the last two, whose names mean "Sitting to Eat" and "Offering Liquor," prompted the gathered deities to accept the food offerings.

While "Offering Liquor" was being played, twelve female students
gathered in the wings, dressed in matching pink traditional Thai trousers
(*phaanung*) and informal blouses. When the piece ended, *Khruu* Chüa gestured for them to come onstage; they hesitated, but Pranee, the most talented dancer and a senior, confidently led the way. They arranged themselves in two long lines facing the altar with their backs to the audience, the
six girls dancing female roles on stage right and those dancing the male roles

Figure 2.13   The dance offering called *Thawaai Müü* or "Offering the Hands,"
performed by undergraduate music majors at Srinakharinwirot University–
Prasanmit in 1989. Photograph by Sarah Grew.

on the left. They all prostrated themselves following Pranee's lead, and then
the *piiphaat* ensemble (without being told) began to play the piece *Kraao
Ram* (literally, "To Dance Together"); this part of the ritual, called *Thawaai
Müü* or "Offering the Hands," is a dance offering always accompanied
by this piece. This dance contains a number of basic dance movements—
walking, flying, and so forth—and is thus a symbolic enactment of dance
vocabulary (see figs. 2.13 and 2.14).

The dance offering ended with deep stylized prostrations by the
dancers; many of them also passed their hands over their heads after *wai-
ing*, transferring some of the auspiciousness of the gesture back into themselves. They exited the same way they had come on, smiling a little self-
consciously. As they left the stage, *Khruu* Chüa began the final short prayer
thanking the deities for their presence and blessings. He then called for two
pieces: "The Brahmins Go Out" and "Entering the Place," both representing the departure of the deities after a successful ritual and their return to
their heavenly abodes.

As they finished playing the *rua* following *Samoe Khao Thii*, the musicians looked expectantly at *Khruu* Chüa, who called out, "*Prooi Khao Tauk*"
("Scattering Popped Rice"). As the music began, he prostrated himself three
times on his pillow, lifted a bowl of popped rice above his head, silently

Figure 2.14   The dance offering called *Thawaai Müü* or
"Offering the Hands." Photograph by Sarah Grew.

uttering a magical verse. He then got to his feet and did what the name of
the piece indicated: he scattered the popped rice over the altar in generous
handfuls, first on the left side and then on the right (see fig. 2.15). Finally, he
went over to the musicians and threw two handfuls of rice over them as they
played. The piece ended but *Khruu* Chüa went back to his seat, picked up a
second bowl of popped rice, and scattered this over the altar in silence, going back to the musicians and now throwing quite a number of handfuls over
their bowed heads, careful to touch each man. They *wai*-ed very respectfully
as he did this, holding their clasped hands to their foreheads.

   Khruu Chüa then sat down, prostrated himself three times, and called
for the piece "Great Victory" (*Mahaachai*), which expresses gladness and
celebrates the success of a ritual. As the piece began, *Khruu* Chüa got to his
feet holding the branch of leaves; he dipped the branch in the urn and scattered sacralized water over first the left and then the right side of the altar.
One of the floodlamps on the altar burst with a popping sound when struck
by the water, but *Khruu* Chüa went on, unperturbed. He scattered water
over the musicians, who each stopped, quickly *wai*-ed, and then went on

Figure 2.15 *Khruu* Chüa scatters popped rice over the altar as student assistant
Suriyaa looks on. Photograph by Sarah Grew.

playing. Directing Suriyaa to place the urn of water beside his seat, *Khruu*
Chüa sat down and the musicians brought "Great Victory" to a close. One
final prayer text was recited, thanking the deities once more, and *Khruu*
Chüa then called for the final piece that sends the deities on their way.[22]

As this short, lively piece began, there was a burst of movement and
activity. Some ten male students rushed up to the altar and began cutting
and dividing up the food offerings in earnest; Tum came up with big rectangular pieces of banana leaf that were made into four trays, each bearing
a minuscule amount of all the different offerings. As they were doing this,
Khruu Chüa stirred the pasty mixture of scented powder and water in his
little cup and carefully anointed the Ganesha image on its forehead before
rising and going up on the altar; methodically, he went from instrument to
instrument, anointing each and silently uttering magical verses. The musicians were packing up, sliding their beaters into cloth bags and going outside to smoke and chat. The drum player, always conscientious, gathered the
musicians' offering bowls together and took them all over to *Khruu* Chüa's
empty seat.

The audience dispersed outside, but the stage was still humming with
activity. Suriyaa came up to me with a hard-boiled egg and, slicing a piece
off, said, "Here, eat this. It's good luck—it's from the 'mountains'; it'll make
you smart." *Khruu* Chüa sat down again; he had anointed only the lower

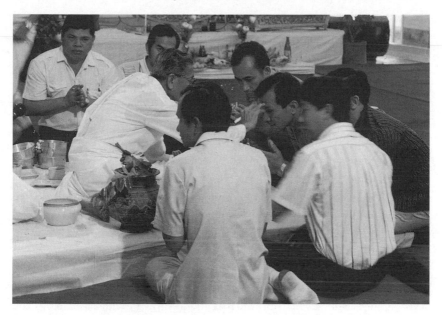

Figure 2.16   Khruu Chüa blesses the members of the *piiphaat* ensemble at
the beginning of the initiations following the *wai khruu* ritual.
Photograph by Sarah Grew.

levels of the crowded altar, the upper levels apparently requiring a balance
and coordination beyond his seventy-two-year-old frame. The banana leaf
trays, now fully assembled, were borne off to the four outside corners of the
building to join the incense, and the rest of the male students began to take
the food offerings away.

Suriyaa knelt by *Khruu* Chüa to ask for further instructions and was sent
over to the *piiphaat* platform, where he picked up the gong circle that Nikorn
had played and brought it over, setting it down behind *Khruu* Chüa's seat.
The *khraup* ("covering") ritual, or the ritual of blessing and transferring
spiritual power, began without preamble at 11:16, when some of the musicians from the *piiphaat* ensemble, along with several other male musicians
of similar age and status, came up to *Khruu* Chüa. All knelt in a semicircle
around *Khruu* Chüa with their hands in a *wai*. Starting on the right, *Khruu*
Chüa lowered the wetted branch over each of their heads, scattering water
and moving his lips as he silently uttered a magical formula. Chalermpon
hurried up at this point and squeezed into the circle just in time to have his
head wetted. Using a slim white candlestick dipped in the powder and water mixture, *Khruu* Chüa anointed their foreheads one by one, starting on
his right (stage left) and writing a sacred sign (a *yan*, from the Sanskrit *yantra*)
between their eyebrows (see fig. 2.16).[23] Rangsi, a young teacher at the

elementary school, dashed up as the third musician was being anointed and prostrated himself three times to the altar. Nikorn also hurried up and squeezed into the circle between Natthaphong and a musician friend from the restaurant, but he and Rangsi were too late to be included. *Khruu* Chüa gave a small leaf and grass bundle to each of the musicians in the circle, placing it in their waiting hands, and then they *wai*-ed deeply and backed away from him on their knees. Some took the leaf cylinder and stuck it behind their left ear; others put it carefully in their pocket.

The next group, consisting of Nikorn, Rangsi, Suriyaa, Tum, Kanchana's musician husband, and myself, pushed forward and formed a semicircle. As we were similarly wetted and anointed, Chalermpon went down to the microphone at the foot of the stage and announced that the ritual of being "covered" had begun and that everyone was invited to come up and participate; lunch, he added, was being served outside. As my circle of teachers and musicians was finished, the next immediately pushed into place, including the children of several professors. Chalermpon pressed in his two sons (aged six and seven), and Suriyaa made sure they had a place in the circle.

By this time, an outer ring of waiting students had formed. Most were elementary school children from the Prasanmit Demonstration School, wearing school uniforms (a white blouse with a rather nautical navy-blue bow and a full blue skirt for the girls, a white shirt and blue shorts for the boys). All of the children held stainless steel offering bowls, received at the foot of the stage from two music majors whose task was to hand them out; each bowl contained a stalk of orchids, a packet of incense, a handkerchief-sized piece of white cloth, a small yellow candle, and six *baht* in coins provided by the child (see fig. 2.17).[24] Circle after circle of children was blessed, with six to ten children in each group. Shy and unsure of what to do, the children were lined up by Suriyaa and another music major; *Khruu* Chüa would then say, "Two hands!," indicating that they should offer him the bowls with both hands as a sign of respect and humility. After accepting their bowls, he blessed them, anointed their foreheads, and then "covered" them by pressing one of a pair of small hand cymbals to the top of their heads while grasping the other in his left hand and silently uttering a magical formula. Group after group of children was "covered" quickly and efficiently. Suriyaa and another student took the offering bowls from *Khruu* Chüa as he received them, taking out the coins and recycling the bowls back to the table at the foot of the stage so they could be used again.

By 11:30 the schoolchildren were mostly finished, and older students and adults began to come up. A young dance teacher (a recent graduate, newly married and now pregnant) came up and was "covered" along with

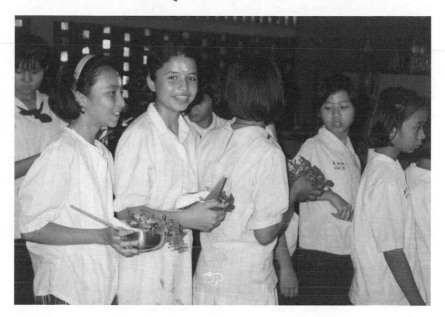

Figure 2.17   Schoolchildren from the Prasanmit Demonstration School in
line with their offering bowls, waiting to be initiated in the *wai khruu* ritual at
Srinakharinwirot University–Prasanmit in 1987. Photograph by Deborah Wong.

her husband; they knew *Khruu* Chüa well, and the ritual gestures were executed affectionately, with much smiling. Several music major juniors were
being done together when a teacher led up a group of elementary children.
Trying to keep appropriate age groups together, *Khruu* Chüa waved them
back while he did the young adults, and only then had them approach.
These children were to be blessed specifically for the two-stringed fiddle
(*sau duang*), so *Khruu* Chüa spent a minute tuning one even though it
wasn't actually played. He then had the first boy hold up the instrument
horizontally, in both raised hands. Cupping the child's hands in his, he
uttered a magical verse as the boy waited, his head bowed.

Meanwhile, the monks had finished their meal in the front room and
were chanting their final prayers. Each of the nine monks had been given
a yellow plastic bucket and a cellophane-wrapped basket, both full of soap,
tissues, toothpaste, and other small gifts. The chanting ended at noon. In the
silence that followed, the vice president and Prateep approached the head
monk on their knees as he pulled a large silver bowl of sacralized water close
and lifted a small straw whisk. He held the whisk to his forehead in a *wai*
while silently uttering a magical verse and then held the whisk in the water, pausing while reciting another verse. The vice president and Prateep
watched, their hands in *wai*-s. The moment the head monk lifted the whisk

and sprinkled the vice president with water, the monks burst into a final chant, and then everyone else in the room—other teachers and students, about thirty people in all—began crawling forward to be blessed.

The head monk got to his feet, still scattering water over the people in the room, as Prateep came forward and picked up the bowl of water. Escorted by Prateep, the monk swiftly strode into the auditorium where *Khruu* Chüa was blessing a circle of music majors. The head monk first scattered water over the altar and then turned to the people onstage. *Khruu* Chüa and the students immediately stopped what they were doing to *wai* deeply as the water touched them. The monk then went outside to bless the four corners of the building, Prateep following closely with the bowl.

Now that most of the children had finished, some of the more specific initiations began. One young woman "received the right" *(rap maup)* to be a music teacher: after being blessed with water and anointed on the forehead, she held a large tray stacked with gong circle and xylophone mallets, hand cymbals, and a fiddle as *Khruu* Chüa held the other side of the tray and uttered a magical formula. Five or six juniors watched closely as this was done —in a few years, they would probably be doing the same ritual. One senior girl was "covered" and then, smiling, asked *Khruu* Chüa to anoint the pick for her zither—a short pointed length of horn with a length of yarn used to tie the pick to the forefinger. He did so, anointing it with his finger, uttering a prayer, placing it in her open palms and closing her hands over it in both of his.

Nikorn came up while this was happening and knelt by *Khruu* Chüa to whisper a few words to him when he finished. The juniors who had been watching came forward on their knees, holding offering bowls. *Khruu* Chüa listened to Nikorn's request and then nodded. The juniors specializing in *piiphaat* all needed to "have their hands grasped" *(cap müü)*, or to be initiated, into the fourth level of the ritual repertoire (explained further in Chapter 4). When the group of nine students had all been blessed and anointed, they went and sat by the waiting gong circle as Nikorn helped *Khruu* Chüa get up.

The first student, a young woman, sat down in the gong circle and waited, looking nervous. *Khruu* Chüa came and stood behind her inside the frame of the gong circle. She raised her hands to her chest in a *wai* and he held the gong circle mallets to his forehead for a brief moment while uttering a prayer; he handed her the mallets, picked up a pair of soft, long-handled xylophone mallets, and bent over her to play the first phrase of the piece "Bird's Foot" *(Baatsakuunii)* on the gong circle (see fig. 2.18). She watched closely and then tried to play it but had trouble remembering how it went

Figure 2.18 Khruu Chüa initiating a music major into a higher level of ritual repertoire in the1987 Prasanmit *wai khruu* ritual. Photograph by Deborah Wong.

even though *Khruu* Chüa guided her to the right gongs by pointing with his mallets. He had to show her some parts several times, correcting her when she played two pitches successively instead of simultaneously, and making sure she got the rhythms right. She played the phrase three times, gaining confidence with each try. The other students sat around the perimeter of the gong circle, watching closely because they too would have to play the piece in a moment. When the young woman finished, she put the mallets neatly in the gong circle frame and then prostrated herself three times on top of the instrument.

The next student, named Ekasit, was probably the most talented student in the department; a virtuoso *ranaat eek* player, he came from a musicians' family. Once again, *Khruu* Chüa first played the phrase himself and then had Ekasit play—which he did perfectly, already seeming to know the piece. The next student, a young man, also played it perfectly. By this time the waiting students had been able to memorize the phrase, and *Khruu* Chüa no longer had to demonstrate the phrase but simply had each succeeding student play it three times. Three more students were initiated into the fourth level, including one more young woman.

Meanwhile, Kanchana and Manop were setting up an easy chair near the foot of the stage on the left, and several students were preparing a big bowl of flowers and a low table. As the *piiphaat* initiations continued near the altar, Kamthaun, the "honored father" of the department, was seated in the easy chair by several of the professors. He was smiling and making jokes, and everyone was similarly lighthearted as a "ritual of pouring water" *(phithii rot naam)* began. Kamthaun held his hands in a *wai* over the bowl of flowers, and the professors came up one by one to pour water over his hands from a small conch shell inlaid with silver. Each person *wai*-ed, poured the water over Kamthaun's hands, *wai*-ed again, and Kamthaun then *wai*-ed in response, usually passing his wet hands over his hair and head. He said something jovial to each person and smiled throughout. People came up in general order of status: first the various professors and older teachers, then younger teachers, and finally students. A few people prostrated themselves on the floor as well. Prateep stood at the microphone and announced each person's name as they approached Kamthaun; the line of well-wishers was so long that the ritual went on for almost half an hour, and Kamthaun's hair was soon dripping wet.

Meanwhile, five male music majors were being initiated for the sacred drum *(taphoon)* on the other side of the stage. The drum played during the ceremony was brought over and *Khruu* Chüa sat down facing the students with the drum between them. As with the gong circle, *Khruu* Chüa played the first phrase of the *taphoon* part for a piece and each student repeated it three times and then prostrated himself on the drum.

It was now 1:00. As *Khruu* Chüa packed up his equipment, Prateep approached and asked to be blessed. Unlike the others, he prostrated himself both to *Khruu* Chüa and then to the altar. His job completed, *Khruu* Chüa once more sat down at his prepared place and prostrated himself deeply on his pillow. He put his cigarettes back in his satchel and then slowly went backstage to change into his street clothes. A few moments later he could be seen outside, quietly sitting under the canopy, smoking and drinking tea while a student prepared a plate of food for him (see fig. 2.19). Back in the auditorium, a group of elementary children carrying violins trooped onstage to scattered applause from parents, the first of many informal performances that day. As the afternoon went on, a number of student groups would perform, mostly Thai classical music, each group faster and more skilled than the next.

When was the event over? The last performing group, some music majors running through *mahoorii* repertoire just for the fun of it, finished up at almost 5:00. Other people were still sitting around talking, though the schoolchildren and their parents had all left by early afternoon. Then there was cleaning up the area and taking apart the altar. Like most Thai ritual events, it had neither a clear beginning nor a clear end. Did the event begin

Figure 2.19 Food for participants and guests at the 1989 Prasanmit
wai khruu ritual. Photograph by Sarah Grew.

with *Saathukaan* and the lighting of the stage candles, with the monks'
chants at 7:00 A.M., with the construction of the altar the day before, or
with the organizational meeting earlier that week? Did it end with *Khruu*
Chüa's final prostration or when the last person went home?

The intensely overlapping activities that made the event successful (and
difficult to document) grew out of careful planning and the informal cooperation of many people, though Prateep was certainly the main manager of
the event. *Khruu* Chüa "covered" or initiated over one hundred and fifty
people and stayed onstage for almost five hours without a break—a formi-
dable task for an elderly man, but expected of a *wai khruu* officiant. Vast
amounts of food had been prepared and consumed. The elementary school
students were properly inducted into music study, the current college students were initiated into the necessary repertoire, and alumni renewed old
friendships with each other and past professors. No major problems or
hitches had arisen. Everyone agreed it was a successful event.

Conclusions

The two ritual events described above are contrasting examples of how
the *wai khruu* ceremony can be celebrated and by whom. Although the ritual procedures were essentially the same, the social contexts were quite

different. In class terms alone, there was no comparison. The ritual at the temple was widely perceived (by most performers) as an event for working-class musicians and dancers, whereas the university ritual was held for an extended circle of people sharing a relatively high status. In spirit and in principle, both events were inclusive, yet in practice, a street performer would never show up at the university event uninvited. On the other hand, any performer—even one perceived as having high status—could, and would, attend the annual *wai khruu* at Wat Phra Phireen.

The atmosphere—I would even say personality—of each event was profoundly different. The university gathering was unremittingly solemn and restrained, whereas the temple event was noisy and at certain points threatened to run out of control. Each was powerful and effective nonetheless. *Khruu* Chüa's and *Mom* Caruun's comportment were strikingly similar: all officiants carry themselves with a kind of grave humility and concentration. The participants' behaviors contrasted strongly, however. The display of emotion (including enthusiasm) is a Thai performative of class, so the university participants were generally quiet and restrained, whereas the temple participants made noise and showed their enjoyment in the spectacle of the event. Nor did this necessarily detract from the temple *wai khruu*'s efficacy.

Spirit possession was a key difference between the two ritual events. This was partly due to the focus of the university ritual (music) and the broad inclusiveness (music, dance, street drama, comedy, etc.) of the temple ritual. Quite a number of participants were "entered" by deities at Wat Phra Phireen, but none were at Prasanmit. This does not mean that more spirits were present at Wat Phra Phireen. On the contrary, some performers would say that this reflected particular *participants'* spiritual strength or weakness. Any *wai khruu* ritual is filled with the invisible presence of deities—that is the entire point of the undertaking. Participants' abilities to deal with such powerful presences is another matter. And while participants represent a wide field of strength, susceptibility, and understanding, officiants are the channel through whom they encounter the forces that make them performers.

Finally, the *wai khruu* at the university filled another function: it implicated the entire undergraduate music curriculum, which is structured around the proficiencies of the ritual repertoire. The levels and hierarchy of *piiphaat* music will be discussed in a later chapter, but the structural function that the *wai khruu* now fills in university and conservatory contexts is a late-twentieth-century development. The ritual technologies remain the same, but the reasons for directing them toward certain people have changed. I would venture to guess that more young women now enter the high levels of repertoire (discussed in Chapter 4), yet none will ever perform in a *wai khruu* ritual due to gender restrictions surrounding the most sacred repertoire.

I should also add that these two ritual events gave me the strongest sense of how participation creates connections to other people, or (actually) how each ritual event acts out and reaffirms such connections. The university ceremony involved *my* circle of musicians and showed me how the communal experience of helping prepare for the event is as much a part of its spirit as the ritual itself. At Wat Phra Phireen, meeting so many performers that I knew from so many different contexts and venues brought home how knowing musicians outside of one's immediate circle opens the way to other lineages. It was pleasing too to see that the social structure of lineages which creates different *wai khruu* events does not lead to isolation but rather to interpenetrating lines of affiliation and transmission.

My point here was to show how the event is "realized"—through cooperation between large numbers of people and as a performed ritual. Now that I have described the *wai khruu* as a performance event, I can turn to the deeper meanings behind its ritual technologies—that is, I can address the links between ritual praxis and Thai ideologies of knowledge and performance.

Three

Knowledge and Power in Thai Culture:
Teachers as Hermits

Ties That Bind: Teachers and Students

One cannot understand the Thai performing arts without understanding the centrality of teachers. Teachers of all kinds are given great respect and status in Thailand. They bring together all the things that children in Asia are socialized to hold in great regard: age, knowledge, and spirituality. They are the ultimate source of all knowledge in traditional Thai thought. Books are of course recognized as another great source, but (as will become clear in Chapter 5) books of sacred knowledge are never openly circulated, and in fact literacy carries connotations of power because of the access it traditionally granted to specialized texts (Tambiah 1968).

The Thai word for teacher, *khruu*, comes from the Sanskrit word *guru* and implies a person with mystical knowledge. University professors are referred to as *aacaan* (from the Sanskrit *achariya*), which in some ways denotes higher status since it indicates at least a college if not a graduate degree, while elementary school teachers are referred to as *khruu*. *Khruu* has a significantly different feeling, though, when used as a title of respect for practitioners of traditional knowledge. A Western-educated Thai friend once told me (with a dramatic shiver) that the word *khruu* was simply heavier and deeper for her than the word *aacaan*.

Teachers of music and dance are also addressed as *khruu*, and this defines the particular kind of teacher-pupil relationship involved. Students of the traditional performing arts, of arts and crafts, of healing, and so forth are called *sit* or *luuk sit*, which comes from the Sanskrit word *shishya* and translates as "disciple." Professors *(aacaan)* at universities have students, not disciples.[1] The bond between *khruu* and their *luuk sit* is deep and often lifelong. Even after a disciple becomes an adult teacher in his or her own right, the basic behavior between the two remains largely unchanged: the disciple will still hasten to hold doors, serve food, and defer to the teacher in every way. As Alan Guskin says, in "the traditional teacher-student relationship, the teacher is the transmitter of knowledge and deserves every possible deference and respect; the student is immature, passive, and ignorant—an empty vessel into which proper knowledge must be poured" (1966, 92).[2]

The Southeast Asian paradigm of the all-knowing teacher and the submissive disciple originated in classical India, where an esoteric model of knowledge left a profound impact on learning of all kinds. Many of the basic patterns and principles underlying the social organization of Indian musicians structure the Thai system as well, but what is often strict and codified in India has a softer focus in Thailand. It is worth looking at some of these similarities and differences with India. Although the similarities, which are the result of ancient cultural contact, are sometimes pronounced, I do not mean to suggest that the social organization of Thai musicians in Bangkok mirrors that of the musicians in Delhi described by Daniel Neuman (1990); instead, it bears clear family resemblances.

In the following discussion, I focus on the world of *piiphaat* musicians, which means that most of my comments refer to men. Women can and do participate in the system of *khruu* and disciples, but serious female musicians tend to study the feminine arts of singing—with female teachers—whereas the instrumental world of the *piiphaat* ensemble is by and large characterized by men teaching men. In short, this system of knowledge dissemination is gendered in particular ways.

Despite some differences, the fundamental relationship between teacher and pupil is strikingly similar to that in contemporary India. Teacher and disciple are ideally as close as, or sometimes closer than, father and son. In Thailand, in contrast to India, sometimes they *are* father and son: some of the most famous musicians in Thai music history not only had children who became famous musicians in their own right, but sometimes gave their children the right to act as ritual officiants.[3] Though the children of Thai musicians often become musicians themselves, not all performers come from musical families, and even those who do may later find teachers outside their family. When a student finds a teacher and forms a close relationship, the bond can become one of the most important in his or her life.

My own teacher, whose father was a musician, once told me, "When my father died, I grieved, but when my teacher died, I wept."

In India, true devotion to a *guru* involves obedience, submission, and respect; the disciple's devotion is returned by the *guru* as love, benevolence, and knowledge, though it may be years before the disciple is thus rewarded. Ideally, the disciple's devotion is total: he may live in his *guru*'s house and generally look after him like a trusted servant, bringing him his meals and generally trying to "make life as comfortable as possible for him" (Neuman 1990, 46). The same was, and to some extent still is, true in Thailand. Up until the mid-twentieth century, it was common for the household of a famous teacher to resemble a small conservatory. The home of *Luang* Pradit Phairau, who is widely regarded as *the* teacher, musician, and ritual authority of the twentieth century, had so many resident disciples that it actually became a conservatory after his death in the 1950s. It was reportedly full of the sound of students practicing day and night. An account exists of how one student joined the household: a boy from the provinces, holding nothing more than a bamboo flute, a small bag with his clothes, and some fruit appeared at the gate and asked if he could study with the great teacher. *Luang* Pradit Phairau absentmindedly told him to find a place to sleep with the other boys, and that was that. One of *Luang* Pradit Phairau's students, Subin Cankaew, has written about his life as a young disciple in this household: "Sometimes the Master would think of a new version of a piece in the middle of the night. At dawn, when it was still dark, he'd come up to where we disciples stayed, raise our mosquito nets, and wake us up so he could teach it to us right away" (2530/1987, 59).

With the rise of university music departments, this way of life is largely a thing of the past, but in 1989 I visited one teacher, Sakol Kaewpenkhaat, who had several young students living in his home. Mostly teenagers, these young men helped their teacher's elderly wife with housework and errands and managed to practice almost continuously. Whenever *Khruu* Sakol was mentioned by other musicians, his traditional lifestyle was always commented on as unusual and as the way it really *should* be; most musicians agreed that such close proximity is the best way to absorb a teacher's knowledge.

Formal study with a teacher traditionally began with a short ritual called "depositing oneself as a disciple." Uthit Naksawat, a musician admired for his attempts to bring Thai music to the general public as well as into the Thai public school system in the 1960s, calls this "the introductory *wai khruu*" and notes that, when he was a child (in the 1920s), his father always had him do this when he entered a new school of any kind (2530/1987, 192–93). In one of his most well-known books, Uthit describes how the new student was expected to bring flowers, incense, and a candle to the teacher, usually on a Thursday or a Sunday because these two days were (and still are) considered "teachers' days," i.e., days of the week when the Hindu-Buddhist deities of knowledge and learning were particularly receptive to being honored. The teacher then took the offerings, lit the incense and candle to honor the divine teachers, and then uttered propitiary formulas called *khaathaa*, with the student repeating each phrase after him. These utterances asked the deities to bless and protect the student and to help him or her achieve wisdom and skill. The set verses included a profession of respect for the Buddha and the institution of the Buddhist monkhood,[4] a *khaathaa* for all Hindu-Buddhist deities, a verse proffering the flowers, incense, and candle, and a verse inviting the major Hindu-Buddhist deities to come and listen.[5] The teacher then recited the following verse, with the student repeating each phrase after him:

> Namo!
> I would like to salute,
> I would like to partake of that which is wisdom,
> To be given intelligence and cleverness,
> To be able to fathom strummed, bowed, struck, and blown instruments
> And singing and dancing.
> I would like to be given wisdom and a steadfast memory for instruments
>   of every kind,
> To be made confident and not to lose or forget my way,
> To increase my thought,
> My perceptions,
> My knowledge,
> And for all these to flourish.
> Oh enlightened teachers:
> *Prasitthimee!*[6]
> *Ayu! Wanna! Sukkha! Phaala!*[7]
> *Mahaasukhoo! Mahaalaphoo! Mahaachaiyoo!*[8]

The teacher then held the student's hands and led him or her through part of a piece on the instrument they were to study. Uthit (2530/1987, 193) explains that this ritual established the student as a disciple of the divine teachers, with the human teacher as their substitute or stand-in.

Although this short ritual is less common than it once was, students still follow its model when approaching a highly regarded teacher as a potential disciple. It is common for a student to bring a teacher some kind of ritual gift (e.g., flowers or fruit). Nikorn Chanthasorn, my own teacher, once told me how he asked a famous gong circle player (Saun Wongkhaung) to be his teacher in the traditional way, even though they saw each other at school every day. By asking in the way he did, he made it clear that he wanted to learn more than was possible in an institutional setting; he was also putting himself in a position where it would be possible for him to in-herit the teacher's famous solo pieces, as he explains:

> When I was fifteen or sixteen I decided to ask Khruu Saun if I could be his disciple. I wanted to learn his solo pieces—I really wanted to learn them! I saw him at school every day, but I went to look for him at his house. I remember it was raining really hard, but I went to his house any-way, and bought some fruit on the way. I asked if I could be his disciple, and he said yes.
>
> After that I went to his house in the afternoon every day after school was over. I'd practice for a while and then sweep the yard or whatever. We'd all eat dinner together—there were several other students too—and then Khruu Saun would teach us for a few hours after that. I'd get home at nine or ten. Sometimes Khruu Saun would take us along when he was playing somewhere at night.

Teachers did not formerly expect their disciples to pay for lessons.[9] Aside from the ritual gifts at the beginning of formal study, disciples did not formerly pay their teacher but instead put themselves at his disposal. When he was invited to perform somewhere at night, disciples were expected to go along and help in every way possible, or if the teacher told a disciple to go perform somewhere, the student was expected to do so without complaint or objection, even if it disrupted his own plans.

In fact, even today a disciple shouldn't express personal opinions at all. When he is with his teacher, he should be reticent if not silent and should avoid drawing attention to himself. Even when directly asked a question by a teacher, most young disciples will blush, giggle, mumble an answer, or all three. Some teachers are more informal and affectionate than others and may talk more freely with their students, but a student should still be passive, deferential, and extremely respectful.

What, then, does a teacher get from the relationship, besides added household expenses? As in most of Southeast Asia, Thai social relations are to a great extent based on the "patron-client" relationship, which has much in common with the teacher-pupil bond. A patron is anyone who has more wealth, power, or prestige than someone else; clients are those who have less of all three and attach themselves to patrons by asking for their help or favors. Both persons in such a relationship benefit: the client "gets ahead" by being lent money or by having a good word put in for him, and the patron can then ask for a return favor or for the client's support at some later time. Powerful Thais, whether in politics, business, or intellectual circles, wield influence by acquiring a retinue of "clients." Such bonds can last for many years or even a lifetime; sometimes the debt of obligation is discharged fairly quickly. But it is probably safe to say that every Thai is, at any moment, both a patron and a client, and this basic dynamic is the glue that holds a great many social circles together.

Leaders of all kinds gather a group of followers around them called a *phuak* (literally, "group, party"). Circumstance dictates whether members of the group are seen as cronies, disciples, or friends with a similar way of thinking. The "group" is certainly of primary importance in Thai politics, but it is also openly used to describe the different intellectual circles of the Thai literary world (Phillips 1987, 16–17, 39–44). The word *phuak* is not generally used to describe a teacher's group of students (who are usually simply called his "disciples"), but the end result is much the same, and teachers take understandable pride in attracting students (though it is not considered good taste to admit it; see also Myers-Moro 1993, 105). Nearly every teacher is sure that his way of rendering repertoire is the best and most authentic; having a body of students to pass this on to is important (though some teachers hoard their knowledge, refusing to pass it on because they feel none of their students are yet worthy of it). In the music circles of Bangkok, a powerful following can make a real difference in advancing through administrative hierarchies at universities and conservatories. By the same token, primary disciples of leading teachers can also expect to one day inherit that teacher's administrative status, and this of course has everything to do with how postcolonial bureaucratic structures are linked to older structures of power and authority.

The scheming and planning implied in the alliances described above is real enough, but teachers do not simply use their students like pawns for their own purposes. Every teacher has two groups of students: his disciples and his primary disciples. *All* of his students are disciples *(luuk sit)*, but only a few are primary disciples *(luuk sit eek)*. In fact, a teacher may have only one primary disciple or even none at all. It takes years to become a primary disciple, and the transition from being simply a disciple to a primary one is not marked by ritual or any dramatic change; rather, the relationship of love and respect deepens over time. Eventually the teacher teaches—or, as Thai musicians may put it, "gives"—the disciple many of his most valued musical pieces; if he is a *wai khruu* officiant, the teacher will grant his disciple the

Figure 3.1   A young woman music major at Srinakharinwirot University–
Prasanmit practicing the supporting xylophone *(ranaat thum)* in 1988.
Photograph by Deborah Wong.

right to lead the ceremony. Although these bestowals usually occur pri-
vately, the disciple's position as the primary inheritor of the teacher's knowledge will gradually become clear to other musicians.

I have had trouble deciding when to use the present or past tense in some
of the above explanations, because the rise of university music departments
during the past twenty years has introduced changes into the teacher-
disciple relationship, while other traditional patterns have been maintained.
Few pupils now live at their teacher's home.[10] In many cases, the main rehearsal room at a college music department has replaced the teacher's home,
where teacher and students will spend many hours a day learning pieces,
making music, and generally spending time together. Few students formally
"deposit" themselves as a teacher's disciple. The gender balance of musicians is also changing. Traditionally, women sang and played string instruments, while men played struck and blown instruments in addition
to singing and playing string instruments. This meant that the kind of
ensemble central to ritual and dance-drama repertoire, the *piiphaat* (an ensemble of xylophones, gong circles, drums, and a quadruple-reed aerophone) was essentially male. In the context of university music departments, it is more and more common for young women to play the xylophone
and knobbed gong circle (see fig. 3.1). Women are, however, still forbidden

Figure 3.2   Nikorn Chanthasorn giving a lesson to two music majors in the rehearsal room in the Department of Music Education at Srinakharinwirot University–Prasarnmit in 1988. Note the altar in the back left corner of the room. Photograph by Deborah Wong.

to play the sacred drum (the *taphoon,* considered a symbol of the first teacher of music) that leads the *piiphaat* ensemble and never play the quadruple-reed wind instrument called the *pii,* though there is no proscription against it.[11] I have seen female and male music students initiated into high levels of sacred repertoire in *wai khruu* ceremonies held at university music departments, where initiation into successive levels of repertoire is part of the structure of the music major,[12] and approximately half of the initiates were young women. But the gender configuration of ritual musicians remains unchanged: those who perform publicly in *wai khruu* ceremonies are only male, and in music departments male students are most likely to spend extensive time with their teachers like traditional disciples (see fig. 3.2). In other words, the universities are producing both male and female music majors who are routinely initiated into the higher levels of the sacred dance-drama repertoire, but in actual practice, it is almost entirely the male students who perform it professionally.[13]

The strength and permanence of many teacher-pupil relationships is undeniable, but I do not mean to suggest that this system is without its tensions. While I never heard anyone openly accuse someone else of insincerity or opportunism as a disciple, identification with certain famous or powerful teachers can certainly make a difference in one's career and also in one's standing among other musicians. The latter is intangible but nonetheless extremely important since everyone knows everyone else in Bangkok's music circles. I knew one musician who was publicly slighted by an elder, highly regarded teacher and *wai khruu* officiant. This musician had studied with the teacher as a young man while still in school but had continued to run into his former teacher (as all Bangkok musicians do) in later years at performances and other events, and was proud to be able to say that he had studied with him. They encountered each other at a gathering in 1989, but when the musician went up to his old teacher to *wai* and pay his respects, the teacher deliberately acted as if he didn't know him and went so far as to ask him who he was. (I'm still not sure why the teacher behaved this way but think he may have been expressing disapproval of the musician's reputation as an excessive drinker.) The musician maintained a respectful demeanor at the time, but he fumed about the incident for days afterward, ranting about it to anyone who would listen; he had lost face but was also genuinely hurt and angry. A few weeks later, the teacher in question was designated a National Artist and his university sponsored a public ceremony in which anyone who wanted to could come and pour consecrated water over his hands as a sign of respect and celebration.[14] It was of course expected that all of his former students would go, but the slighted musician made a great show of saying that he wouldn't attend. His friends and fellow musicians prevailed upon him to go, and he finally did—in fact, he carried himself with great decorum at the ceremony, and any signs of conflict were quite absent. But he made it clear that he attended as a favor to his friends, not to the teacher.

Tensions like this never arise between young disciples and their teachers, and they are rare between older musicians and their teachers. When they do surface, they tend to issue from matters of group identification. Professional musicians are already part of a system in which getting ahead is quite openly a matter of who one knows. Almost all adult musicians have had more than one teacher and will maintain ties with all of them. A teacher doesn't stop being your teacher just because you no longer study with him or her: once your teacher, he or she will always be your teacher. But it is sometimes important or necessary to be associated (by others) with a certain teacher. For example, almost all university music departments (including the Department of Fine Arts) hire their own students when a position opens up, and the closest disciples are always chosen. This practice is seen not as inbreeding or favoritism but as the obvious choice, and as a way of maintaining lines of transmission.

The Teacher's Numinous Body:
Merit, Power, and the *Wai*

The habits and practices described above point to a Thai aesthetic of materiality and the location of teachers (actually, their bodies) in a physical present that opens up the material past. Teachers interact with students in wonderfully physical terms. When learning a piece, I (like any Thai music student) interacted not with a sheet of notated music but with my teacher's body: I followed his sounds and his movements in space as best I could with my hands—that is, with *my* body. In ritual performance, the teacher's body is occupied—no, *is*—the body of a being from the ancient past. Teachers put power into the bodies of students by touching them meaningfully—with writing objects, with instruments, with water and breath. Knowledge-as-power is material and materialized.

Other cultures too conceive of knowledge in physical terms. Johannes Fabian's entire study *Power and Performance* (1990) is an exploration of the Luba saying, "Power is eaten whole." Fabian traces the movement of power through people in metaphors of consumption, noting that Luba languages of Central Africa generally denote access to power with the verb "to eat." Considering the translation of the proverb into French and its exegesis by Zairean actors and friends, Fabian is led to the ontological "wholeness" of power in Luba thought and its unsharability: power is tied to "concrete embodiments, persons, and material symbols," unlike power in the West which is imagined as abstract and disembodied (25).

In *Sensuous Scholarship* (1997), Paul Stoller describes how Songhay sorcerers eat power and Songhay griots eat history. As Stoller extemporizes,

> flesh both *inscribes* and *incorporates* cultural memory and history. These memories may take the form of a scar that recalls a tortuous episode. They may be triggered by the stylized movements of dance, the melodic contours of music, the fragrant odors of perfume, or, perhaps, the rhapsody of song. Usually these sensuous modalities provoke memories—and histories—"from below," histories of the dispossessed that historians never recorded. These are memories of existential content: pain, hunger, abuse, struggle, mirth, pleasure—the very substance of a sensuous scholarship. As such, the elicitation and presentation of embodied cultural memories fleshes out the story of a people. (47)

Cultural memories of Thai music and dance, on the other hand, are sensuously enacted from above: teachers move/sound/confer spiritual power into their willing students. Teachers' command of those modalities described by Stoller as "sensuous" is the locus of their authority.

The reciprocal relationship of the Thai disciple's devotion and the teacher's bestowal of knowledge (and other intangibles made material) is a balanced dyad that is also the pivot of the relationship between parents and children and between monks and laypersons. Students and children should "give gratitude" to their teachers and parents for being raised, protected, and taught. This gratitude is seen as having two components. Students should "know" gratitude, deeply and sincerely, in an intellectual and emotional sense; this quality is called *kattanyuu*. But they must also demonstrate this gratitude with respectful behaviors that are seen as "paying back" *(sanaung)* the kindness received from others.[15] Like knowledge, gratitude must be acted out in the real world of social beings.

The connection between teaching and Buddhism is overt. Many elementary schools are still on the grounds of, or adjacent to, Buddhist temples, hearkening back to the times before 1921 when temples *were* the schools:[16] male (and some female) children learned basic literacy from Buddhist monks, and in fact some young men still enter the monkhood to get an education (Wyatt 1982, 228–29).[17] Teachers in public elementary school are responsible for teaching not only reading, writing, and math but also basic Buddhist chants, correct behavior with monks, and Buddhist ethics and morality.

Teaching and the transfer of intangible powers are deeply linked. Many kinds of knowledge are closely linked to morality, which is tied up with merit *(bun)*. Merit is an abstract substance that Theravadan Buddhists spend their lives amassing to ensure a better birth in their next reincarnation; it is intimately related to *karma* (called *kam* in Thai), that is, the lifelong series of checks and debits that determines the next life of all living beings, including animals. As Charles Keyes has written, "Throughout Buddhist Southeast Asia, . . . merit is conceived almost as a substance that can be possessed in variable quantities and that can be translated into this-worldly virtue or power as well as stored up to be used at death to ensure a good rebirth" (1983, 270).

Thai Buddhists make merit (*tham bun*, literally "do, make" + "merit") in any number of ways, including giving food to monks, making monetary donations to temples, freeing animals from captivity, being ordained as a monk or nun, participating in Buddhist ritual, and teaching. Teaching of all kinds is widely recognized as a merit-making activity because it alludes to the Buddha's teachings. Following his model, teachers thus make merit nearly every day of their lives, assuring themselves a better rebirth. Teachers themselves are quite aware of this: when a professor at the university in Bangkok where I studied heard that I was teaching a summer course in

English conversation for children, his pleased response was "So you're mak-ing a little merit!"

Thai Buddhists can also make merit by coming into contact with mer-itful beings. The pattern of giving *and* receiving is basic to the transfer of merit. Parents make merit by raising children and making all the selfless sac-rifices intrinsic to parenting; children, on the other hand, make merit by expressing respect and gratitude to their parents, and most importantly, they make merit *for* their parents when they are ordained as a monk.[18] Monks are extremely meritful beings. Thus, when laypersons give gifts to monks (e.g., food, new robes, and small gifts like soap and towels), they receive merit in return. Generous acts are, in a sense, far from selfless—they are an admired and responsible way of furthering one's karmic possibilities.

Birthdays are especially important merit-making days for Thai Bud-dhists. Most people's birthdays pass by without any fanfare or festivities; instead, the person whose birthday it is makes a point of getting up early and giving food to monks on their morning rounds. The birthdays of older people are celebrated as opportunities for expressing respect, especially birthdays marking the end of twelve-year cycles (i.e., the sixtieth, seventy-second, eighty-fourth, etc.).

Making merit is central to *wai khruu* ceremonies, which are often held on or near the birthday of a deceased teacher. This practice raises several issues. First, there is the apparent paradox of making merit not only for someone else, but for someone who (according to doctrine) may already have been reborn. The transference of merit from one person to another (usually family members) is, in fact, basic to Theravada Buddhism all over Southeast Asia. The doctrinal belief that one is morally responsible and accountable for one's own actions is contradicted by the popular belief that merit can be transferred between persons, usually from an extremely meritful person to a more needy one. Charles Keyes notes that merit-transference is most apt to be stressed in death and ordination rituals, specu-lating that this is when a "rupture in the social order" occurs (1983, 283).[19] He suggests that merit-transference is a way of reconciling the conflict be-tween "the demands of lay society and the demands of following the Path of the Buddha" (279). If laypersons didn't get something back from world-renouncers like monks, the social tension between the two could be con-siderable. As Keyes puts it,

> Why should anyone seek to sponsor a person in renouncing the world, since in so doing the person so patronized would not be in a position to repay his patron with tangible benefits? [The idea of merit-transference]

answers these implicit questions by stressing that all those who release a
man from his social obligations in order that he might become a member
of the Sangha [the monkhood] will receive transcendent benefits, a reward
of great merit, thereby ensuring a decrease in suffering in the future. (Ibid.)

But this functional explanation of merit-transference does not explain
why children make merit for dead parents and music disciples for dead
teachers. Teachers make merit by teaching, and disciples by honoring and
respecting their teachers; but at least one reason for holding a *wai khruu*
ceremony is for merit to be transferred back to a great teacher, usually dead.
The behaviors surrounding such practices suggest that ancestor worship,
concepts of power, and merit form a ritual constellation in which empowerment is the goal and motivation. As Keyes says, "The centrality of merit-
making to the practice of Theravada Buddhism has made of merit a complex
symbol to which many meanings adhere" (1983, 267). Empowerment is certainly one of its many meanings.

This brings me to the *wai* and its role in empowerment. The *wai* is a
physical gesture of bringing the joined palms and fingers to the chest or
forehead in greeting, leave taking, apology, and respect; it is also maintained
during Buddhist chants, both by the chanting monks and the listening laypersons (Anuman 1968). It is related to the gesture called *sembah*[20] in Malay
and Javanese and *sampeah*[21] in Khmer. Children are taught how to *wai* politely and gracefully, both at home by parents and again in school. The shape
of a pair of hands in a *wai* is described as "like a lotus bud," which is deeply
imbued with Buddhist symbolism of enlightenment. Laypersons may hold
an actual lotus bud, candle, and incense between their palms while *wai*-ing
in a Buddhist ceremony.

Two essential characteristics of the *wai* are (a) it must be responded to,
with another *wai* or some other gesture,[22] and (b) the manner in which it
is executed expresses the relative status of the persons involved. A *wai* is a
transaction begun by a person of junior rank, age, or status: when someone
of higher status is encountered, the junior person will *wai* by raising both
hands, palm-to-palm in a "praying" gesture, to the face. The higher the status or the respect being expressed, the higher the hands are raised: mouth or
nose level is most common, but as high as the forehead or even above the
head is also possible. Whenever a student encounters a professor outside the
classroom, the student *wai*-s with the tips of the fingers at about nose level;
the professor then *wai*-s back, usually in a fairly cursory manner since the
professor answers *wai*-s many times in the course of a day. The most deferential and submissive version of the *wai* is the gesture called *kraap*, when
a person prostrates him- or herself on the ground. Prostration is still

Figure 3.3   A group of students performing a unison, ceremonial prostration
(kraap) in a university-wide beginning-of-the-year *wai khruu* ritual.
Photograph by Deborah Wong.

performed before the King and Royal Family in some contexts and was
mandatory until the 1870s, during the reign of King Rama V (Wyatt 1982,
192). Many college classes begin with the students performing a unison *wai*
to the professor when a designated student utters the word "Prostrate!"
(kraap; see fig. 3.3).

    Although the *wai* is a physical gesture, conversational references to it
imply more than the actual hand movement—the bodily gesture is regarded
as synechdochic. I was frequently asked whether I had "*wai*-ed" at a particular *wai khruu* ceremony, in other words, whether I had participated, and laypersons will often talk of going to *wai* a monk *(pai wai phra)*, in other words,
to go make merit by giving a monk food or gifts. It is clear from both speech
and action that the *wai* is a transaction in which respect is expressed and
something is exchanged. Peter Vandergeest (1990) has suggested that the
wai "activates" an exchange of power. He notes that in rural southern Thailand marriage was formerly sealed when the couple went and *wai*-ed both
sets of parents and elders, receiving "blessings" *(hai phon)* in return. The

blessings would empower the couple in their new life and livelihood; without them, they would come to misfortune. Vandergeest suggests that *wai*-ing a teacher is a transaction in which respect is expressed and power is returned: "Parents and elders passed on a power which enabled children to constitute their livelihood, much as the *khruu* passed on enabling power in more specialized activities: the power was activated by the *wai*, and given through a 'blessing' which, unlike the powerless ritual implied in the notion of the blessing in the West, was treated as an act of transferring power" (12–13).

It is no coincidence that dancers and musicians—especially those involved with ritual performance and dance-drama—*wai* frequently. They *wai* when they meet, and careful attention is paid to generational rank, relative age within generation, and those regarded as important teachers. Dancers *wai* at the beginning and end of dances, and musicians *wai* at the beginning and end of musical pieces from the dance-drama repertoire. Performers *wai* when they speak of their deceased teachers, and they *wai* before and after handling or wearing dance masks. Keeping Vandergeest's comments in mind, power is constantly being transferred into and between performers—not only between human beings but between people and objects, people and music, and people and dance as well.

Thai Epistemology:
How Thais Talk about What They Know

Thai discourse about knowledge—its nature, its attributes, and its transmission—is rich in metaphor. The *wai khruu* ceremony is a ritual expression of the transfer of knowledge from teacher to pupil. Understanding how Thais conceive of knowledge is thus no footnote but rather the ontological basis of ritual and performance.

Before discussing the Thai concept of knowledge, however, I must first address Western notions of knowledge and how it is conceived of through language. In English, we talk about knowledge as if it exists in a physical way. Anne Salmond, an anthropologist who has written about culturally specific epistemologies, notes that in the West "our discourse about knowledge characteristically elaborates a series of metaphors about location in a physical landscape" (1982, 67). Phrases such as "a conceptual landscape," "the semantic sphere," "to focus on a point," "a flash of insight," "it's gone right out of my head," and "to sink to the level of the unconscious" portray knowledge as something that exists in three dimensions. In conversation and in writing, we tend to situate knowledge in space: our conceptions of highs, lows, insides, and outsides are expressed in phrases like "high minded," "a deep thinker," "short sighted," and "empty headed."

Several Thai words approximate our Western ideas of "knowledge." *Withayaa* implies knowledge of an orderly, scientific kind. Usually used in compound words, it is the equivalent of "-ology" in words like *cittawithayaa* (psychology) and *manutsayaawithayaa* (anthropology). *Withayaasaat* (*withayaa* + *saat*, from the Sanskrit *sastra*) means "the sciences." The word *panyaa*, on the other hand, is closer to our sense of "wisdom": it implies knowledge acquired through experience, as opposed to the orderliness of the sciences. But it is the simple word *ruu*, "to know," that has the deepest, broadest base of all. *Ruu* is frequently contrasted with the Khmer loanword *saap*, which means to know facts, such as to know what day someone is going to return to town.[23] *Ruu*, however, implies understanding as well as information, and when it is made into a noun (by attaching the bound stem *khwaam-*), it has an undeniable weight for Thais. *Khwaamruu* is the felicitous combination of factual knowledge and experiential understanding. Teachers and learned persons are often described by Thais as "having a lot of knowledge" *(mii khwaamruu maak)*, a formulaic phrase of respect.

I had a long conversation (over several afternoons) with a monk[24] about the differences between these words, and he described not only their etymology but also broke them down (as Thais love to do) into categories—though I should emphasize that these are his personal theories. *Withayaa*, he said, comes from Sanskrit, and *panyaa* and a similar word, *wichaa*, come from Pali, but *ruu* is truly Thai, as evidenced by its monosyllable and its straightforward Thai spelling. The three words borrowed from Sanskrit and Pali have the elegance and formality of Latinate words in English and carry associations of poetry and Buddhist scripture. *Wichaa* is the kind of knowledge acquired from study. Certain kinds of spiritual knowledge are *wichaa*, including particular ways to meditate that can lead to the ability to fly, to remember past lives, and so on. *Panyaa* is an especially complex thing: its two roots, *pa* and *anna*, mean "completely, widely" and "to know." There are three sources of *panyaa*:

1. *Sutamayapanna*,[25] the wisdom that comes from listening.
2. *Cintamayapanna*, the wisdom that comes from thinking.
3. *Bhavanamayapanna*, the wisdom that comes from meditation, prayer, and the development of numbers 1 and 2.

Sutamayapanna comes from listening to others, reading, and asking questions. It comes from outside yourself and thus constitutes worldly wisdom. *Cintamayapanna*, which comes from thinking, also comes from outside, but you make decisions yourself, based on what you have read and heard. *Bhavanamayapanna*, however, comes from inside and arises from practice—in other words, from meditation and contemplation. Crucial to *bhavanamayapanna* is experience: you cannot really understand it until you've tried to do it. An example of this is Einstein's realization that $E = mc^2$. His insight, the monk told me, was the result of working through *sutamayapanna* and *cintamayapanna* to *bhavanamayapanna*.

While he admitted that these three kinds of wisdom are esoteric categories, the monk said that the relationship between *wichaa, panyaa,* and *khwaamruu* is the important thing. You must have, and actively use, both *wichaa* and *panyaa* to achieve *khwaamruu*; you *use* the first two to get the third (cf. the three kinds of *panyaa* above). *Khwaamruu*, he said, is like a bright beam of light; this is what the Buddha attained and then taught.

The crucial connection at this point is to see that *teaching* the knowledge achieved through the synthesis of information, thought, and contemplation is, as another monk told me, "the pinnacle of knowledge." Several monks pointed out that the word *theet*, "to preach, give a sermon," really means "to teach" *(saun)*. Passing knowledge on to the world of people is the crux of the matter.

Stanley Tambiah has addressed the unity of knowledge and experience in Thai epistemology (1985, 120–22). "Knowledge," he writes, "implies and is wedded to practice"—that is, real knowledge is acted out and is not separable from the knower (as we in the West tend to believe) because of the intimate way it arises. It is literally embodied in people, and metaphors about its transmission permeate the Thai language.

A conception of intellectual activity as a journey is central to both Thai and Western epistemology.[26] Our English-language talk about knowledge is crowded with metaphors of exploration. Great thinkers, for instance, are described as pioneers. Thoughtful activity is seen as proceeding along a path toward a goal, and the traveler may be beset by "false trails," "detours," "blind alleys," and "pitfalls." Our knowledge about knowledge is, of course, culturally constrained, but Thai discourse about knowing is similarly tied to the metaphor of the journey—perhaps even more so than English.

Many of the Thai verbs surrounding knowledge imply searching.[27] One "looks for" knowledge *(haa khwaamruu)*. "To do research" *(khon khwaa)* is made up of two similar words: *khon* means "to search for, seek," and *khwaa* means "to snatch, grab, reach for." Thinking and remembering are directional, that is, they are done "toward" their object: the preposition *thüng* is necessary in expressions such as *khit thüng*, "to miss (to) (someone)," and *ralük thüng*, "to recall, recollect, think back on, bring to mind." A text, or the gist of a matter, is "the sought-for meat/flesh/gist/substance" *(nüa haa)*, in which the verb *haa*, "to look for," suggests that this core is something discovered only by those who seek.

Even closer to the heart of Thai epistemology are its many verbs detailing the passage or transmission of knowledge from a knower to other people. Their sheer number suggests that a high value is placed on the knowledge that flows from learned people. Expressed in its simplest form, teachers *hai*, "give," their knowledge to students. They are also said to *phoei phrae*, "propagate, spread out," their knowledge; *phoei* means "to reveal, make known, uncover, expose, open," implying the revelation of contained knowledge. Teachers *prasit prasaat*, "confer, transmit, bestow," their fund of knowledge on their students; the pleasing alliteration of this compound word as well as its component meanings (*prasit*, "success"; *prasaat*, "to confer, to take pleasure in giving") make it common in writings about teachers and students. Teachers also *thaai thaut*, "transmit, hand down (as to the next generation)," their knowledge; *thaai* means to let something flow or to transfer something from one thing to another, and *thaut* means to cast, lay down, or (a vivid image) for a plant to send forth roots. Put together, the compound word strongly conveys a sense of knowledge as a physical substance that can be sent out from the holder.

None of the words and phrases discussed thus far is especially musical, but all are common if not formulaic in Thai writings and talk about music. An idiomatic expression used to describe the transmission of dance choreography or musical repertoire, *tau*, is largely unknown to nonperformers, who tend to use the verb *saun*, "to teach," in its place. Musicians, however, would say that a teacher will *tau phleeng*, or literally "add on" a piece to a student. *Tau* is a verb found in a multitude of expressions. It means to join, connect, put together, continue, extend, or add on. In many ways, it sums up the salient concepts behind performers' teacher-pupil relationships, implying not only the slow, piece-by-piece accumulation of repertoire but also the fundamental tie between teacher and student. It almost suggests that the transmission of a piece or a dance results in a bond between the two.

The journey metaphor is also basic to discourse about music. The elegant word *damnoen*, "to proceed, walk, go," is used to describe the way a melody or rhythmic pattern proceeds. *Naew*, or "line, row, strip," is used in a similar way, as if to say that melody, rhythm, and tuning follow a path; two instruments that are perfectly in tune with each other, for instance, are said to have the same *naew (yuu nai naew dieo kan)*.

One word, *thaang*, not only epitomizes the journey metaphor but is utterly fundamental to Thai notions of musical style as well as to the social organization of musicians. *Thaang* has both musical and nonmusical meanings. Those nonmusical include:

1. Way, path, road, route, trail
2. Way, means
3. By way of, via; toward; in, through
4. Classifier for roads and such

I would go so far as to say that *thaang* is the paradigm of the journey metaphor in Thai and that this sense underlies its various musical meanings. Thai musicians use the word *thaang* when talking about musical style of all kinds, including the individual style of a musician, of a particular mode, or even the characteristics of a particular instrument (Montri 2530/1987). *Thaang* thus refers to several different registers of meaning all at once, including social ties as well as more "purely" musical matter—or perhaps it makes more sense to say that Thai musicians automatically connect the musical to the social. Whenever a musician plays a piece, the musician realizes all three meanings of *thaang*: musical mode, individual improvisational style, and the idiosyncrasies of that kind of instrument. In a tradition that is both oral and improvisational, it isn't hard to see why the concept of *thaang* looms so large—it is what makes every performance, musician, and instrument different from another.

Most importantly, *thaang* is used to mean the "line" or "school" of a particular teacher. Although musical style is inherent in this idea, passing along knowledge as if it were a substance being passed from one person to another—that is, from teacher to pupil—is at the heart of this metaphor. Contemporary musicians recognize three or four major Bangkok *thaang*, or stylistic schools, that originated in outstanding turn-of-the-century teachers. Although Pamela Myers-Moro (1993, 107–9) speculates that *thaang* essentially expresses musical differences,[28] my feeling is that this may well be secondary to its expression of the transmission of knowledge. The social construction of musical style via the vital teacher-pupil dyad is everything in classical performance traditions, though these dyadic links have undoubtedly weakened with the rise of university music departments. When a musician proudly asserts that she or he can play a solo piece in the *thaang* of Teacher So-and-So, a large part of that pride comes from the social fact that such pieces are "bestowed" by teachers only on worthy students, and the piece's exact transmission over generations is much emphasized. Playing a piece in a particular *thaang* expresses real, direct social ties with teachers who may now exist only in another dimension.

Connecting Power to Ancient India

I am laboriously, carefully building an argument—based on Thai aesthetics and poetics as expressed in language and behavior—that knowledge and power are related in Thai thought, especially for performers. But what, exactly, is this "power"? In his well-known essay on the idea of power in Javanese culture, Benedict Anderson says that "the Javanese see power as something concrete, homogeneous, constant in total quantity, and without moral implications as such" (1972, 8). Whether spiritual or political, power in Thai culture is conceived of in similar terms. It can be accumulated, and there is no apparent limit on how much power a person can gather; it can also be channeled into people and objects. Thais sometimes use electricity as an analogy for it. Like the Javanese, Thais believe the total amount of power in the universe is constant. While the total amount does not increase or decrease, however, power does constantly move between different beings and objects. Thus, its concentration, or the amount of power located in or possessed by a person, being, or object, is constantly changing.

The amorality of power is less clear in Thailand than in Java. First, merit *(bun)* and power are clearly similar and sometimes the same, and merit is the hallmark of morality. People who acquire a lot of merit are also powerful, as seen in political persons, from kings to revolutionaries.[29] Second, there are words for different kinds of power, and these reflect different moralities.

The most general and neutral words for power are *anuphaap* and *amnaat*, which both convey the meanings "power," "influence," and "authority." *Itthirit* or *rit*, on the other hand, refers to magical power of a violent, possibly destructive kind. Finally, *saksit*, often translated as "holy" or "sacred," refers to a kind of power usually channeled through deities and other divine beings.

The Sanskrit-Pali roots of the words *itthirit* and *saksit* suggest some differences between these kinds of power. *Itthi* comes from the Pali word *iddhi* (and the Sanskrit word *siddhi*) for mystical powers usually acquired through meditation. Tambiah explains *iddhi* as a this-worldly power: "The ascetic meditator by the very process of gaining control over his volition, senses, and consciousness liberates himself from the limitations and transitoriness of corporeal and sensory experience. Hence, this gain of control is literally a metaphysical victory. He, therefore, has mystical powers which transcend, so to say, the ordinary laws of 'physics' which pertain to the physical world" (1985, 90–91, 102, 108). *Iddhi* is a power wielded by humans in the human realm, though it can bring the meditation adept up to a level where they can even command deities. It is also the kind of power, however, that makes demons and ghosts dangerous—demons and ghosts who, unlike the unembodied divine beings, are intensely corporeal and are tortured by sensory desires because of their great lack of merit.

Saksit power is ubiquitous in daily life. *Saksit* is a compound word with two roots, *sak* and *sit*. *Sak*, or *sakti* (the *ti* isn't pronounced in Thai), means "rank, authority, status" and is the root of various Thai words referring to an elaborate system of conferred titles and land rights. But *sakti* is also the female cosmic energy that permeates the universe of Shaivite traditions and in Southeast Asia often refers to "the particular strengths that result from the union of opposites personified as male and female" (Becker 1988, 388). *Sit*, or *sitthi* (again, the *thi* is not pronounced), also from Pali and Sanskrit, means "a person of success," or "anchorite, hermit."

The nature of *saksit* has been left largely unexplored by Western scholars of Thai studies. In his huge inventory of the "supernatural" in a single central Thai village, Robert Textor merely notes that *saksit* is an "Indic loan word which pre-eminently signals a supernatural object or entity as having derived from the Indic tradition" (1973, 568):

> "And all things sacred" is a frequently heard phrase that epitomizes the repertory of miscellaneous deities with whom an actor or doctor might interact in order to secure a particular reward. Often I have received a blessing from a doctor, monk, or elderly layman, in which assistance or protection was supplicated on my behalf, first perhaps from the goodness of the Buddha, the Dharma, and the Sangha . . . ; then perhaps from certain Brahmanical deities mentioned by name; and finally from "all things sacred" *(sing saksit thaang laaj)*. It was as if the person pronouncing the blessing was unwilling to take any chances on leaving out any possible sources of supernatural power. ". . . And all things sacred" is, then, a sort of supernatural "et cetera." . . . Clearly, it is the Brahmanical sacred beings that are peculiarly subject to the "et cetera" notion. (Ibid.)

Vandergeest (1990) has described *saksit* as a kind of amoral power contrasted by Thais with merit, which is inherently moral. He notes that in the southern shadow-puppet plays *(nang talung)*, *saksit* is often obtained from hermits *(rüsii)* by both lords and demons. He suggests that *saksit* was "available to all males through the empowered teacher *(khruu)*," and even posits that this was the kind of power mobilized by peasants "to counter the fearsome [meritful] power of the ruling nobility" (20–21).[30] In fact, he found that men in rural southern Thailand continue to seek out *saksit* by learning power-laden verbal formulas from monks, though both monks and laymen "unhesitatingly labelled [these formulas] 'Brahmanism'" (22).

Brahmanism is a slippery category of ritual in Thailand. Thais frequently refer to various non-Buddhist ritual practices as "Brahmanism" *(saasanaa Phraam)*. Brahmanism probably entered Thailand through Cambodia, which had in turn received it directly from India. Whatever the case,

Thai kings had resident court Brahmins by the eighth or ninth century A.D. who oversaw court ritual, much of it centering on the Vaisnavite worship of the *devaraja* or god-king. Although descendants of these court Brahmins continue to maintain the royal rituals in contemporary Bangkok, elements of Shaivite Brahminism are widespread in both rural and urban Thailand (Daweewarn 1982).

Tambiah (1970) has described not only the classical Brahman priests of the Thai courts but also a kind of lay ritual expert called a *phaam* or *phraahm* in Thai. Although Tambiah's data are from northeast Thailand, these ritual experts are in fact found all over Thailand: nearly every village has a middle-aged or elderly man of this sort who owns powerful texts and who can lead certain empowering rituals—particularly a ritual called *tham khwaan* or *sukhwaan*. Tambiah says, "The *paahm* in [Tambiah's village of research] is a lay ritual officiant, a householder and a village elder, who performs auspicious rites in some ways reminiscent of the classical *brahman* priest. He is no blood descendant of the court *brahmans* of Thailand, but is in some ways a comparable entity" (254). More importantly, Tambiah sets up a complementary relationship between the village *phraahm* and the village monk. He notes that, "dynamically considered, the Buddhist monk in time *becomes* the *paahm*" (255)—that is, men who become *paahm* in later life were necessarily Buddhist monks as young men, when they learned asceticism and how to read esoteric texts while residing at the temple. As he puts it, this dynamic succession fulfills the life cycle in northeastern Thai villages.

In short, the Buddhist power of merit and the "Brahman" power of *saksit* are joined in certain men, and they are not mutually exclusive. If anything, the felicitous intersection of these trajectories seems to amplify power. The point of all this is that the master teachers who act as officiants in the *wai khruu* ritual hold a similar position: they are unanimously regarded as men of great personal merit, they "become" a *phraahm* or Brahmin in the course of the ritual event, and they encounter the dangerous power of *itthirit* when they do so. Officiants thus wield all three kinds of power, and they are able to do so as *performers*, in performance.

It is impossible to understand the emotional and aesthetic significance of the *wai khruu* ritual without some sense of these concepts—knowledge, teaching, and Brahminism. Knowledge implies access to spiritual efficacy of several kinds. Teaching implies social connections between people—indeed, bonds that are deep and politically as well as sympathetically binding. Brahminism in Thailand is not what it is in South Asia: it is historically imagined in the Thai present in particular ways, all imbued with an epistemological weightiness that stems directly from its origins in a mystical, mythical past. All these elements come together in Thai music and dance, and—even more specifically—they come together in performance. That is, knowledge/power is activated and passed on through ephemeral, efficacious, potent sounds and movements.

The Hermit in the Thai Performing Arts

The Old Father's protective powers frame every performance event. As the original teacher and the fountainhead of knowledge about performance, he is called upon (both formally and informally) by performers immediately before most performances, though such preparations seem to be shorter than they once were. The Old Father is a symbol and a paradigm of all teachers and is thus invoked along with performers' human teachers—but always first. I must stress that he is symbol, paradigm, and index all at once: he is the model for teachers in the here and now, but he is also a real being who continues to intercede in performers' lives.

Every kind of knowledge in Thailand has its patron hermit *(rüsii)*, its original teacher who continues to guide and protect contemporary practitioners. In the performing arts, a particular hermit is of paramount importance: he is worshipped as the origin and paradigm of specialized knowledge. For musicians, dancers, and actors, this hermit is not merely a symbol but a real being who periodically visits and walks among the contemporary practitioners of music and dance. He is quite literally the embodiment of this knowledge, because he is one of the seven hermits who received the Seven Kinds of Knowledge from the four original ascetics *(muunii)*.

The smiling face of this hermit is found in almost every practice room or stage area, either as a full-sized mask, a small papier-mâché replica of a mask, or even a photograph. Many musicians and dancers keep his image in the room at home where they teach or rehearse. Music and dance classrooms at universities and public schools usually have a small altar in a corner with his image, and everyone salutes him with a *wai* upon entering (see fig. 3.4). When the Thailand Cultural Center, the most modern performing facility in Thailand, was built in Bangkok in the late 1980s, a small room was installed in the stage wings for the hermit's mask and altar, and performers regularly pay their respects before rehearsing or performing.

Who is this hermit? There is no consensus among performers on his proper name or identity: he is simply called *Phra*[31] *Rüsii*, "the Lord Hermit," or *Phau Kae*, "the Old Father." Although I asked the contemporary hermit *Khruu* Nim many times what the Old Father's proper name was, he always laughed and either answered that the hermit had many names, or that it simply wasn't important—worshiping him and respecting him from the heart

Figure 3.4   Altar in the main rehearsal room at the Department of Music
Education, Srinakharinwirot University–Prasanmit in 1987. The lowest level
features dance masks and headdresses as well as a ceramic container that might
hold sacralized water in a ritual context; the next level up supports a small image
of Ganesha and a miniature drum *(taphoon)*; the next features the mask of the
Old Father and two headdresses; and the uppermost level features a green glass
image of the Buddha. Photograph by Deborah Wong.

was more to the point. Nevertheless, there seem to be two separate hermits
for music and dance, though they look the same, and performers do not
agree which is *the* Old Father. *Phra* Phrotrüsii or Pharotharüsii, which is the
Thai version of the Indian name Bharatamuni, is often regarded as the
hermit of dance. According to Indian belief, it was this hermit who witnessed Shiva's cosmic dance near Tillai in southern India and later compiled the definitive text of his 108 dance positions. Narot (the Thai version
of the Indian name Narada) is usually regarded as the hermit of music and
as a great musician who entertained the deities. Performers are not agreed
in this, however. For instance, one source (Sirirat 2530/1987: 36) explains
their relationship as follows: "One teacher is the closest of all to ordinary
musicians: the Old Father. There are nine deities of music *(theepduriyaang)*.
We are all most familiar with *Phra* Prohm the Creator, *Phra* Narai the Pre-
server, and *Phra* Isuan the destroyer. There is also *Phra* Phiraap, *Phra*
Parakhonthap, *Phra* Pancasingkhaun, *Phra* Khaneet, and *Phra* Narotrüsii.
Last is *Phra* Phrotmunii" (Sirirat 2530/1987, 36).

    Sirirat claims that the Old Father is *Phra* Phrotmunii: Narotrüsii, he says, was an actual deity *(theep)*, whereas Phrotmunii was made a deity later by the gods for his diligence. He was Rama's half-brother, conceived from the same batch of sweetmeats: as Sirirat tells the story, King Thotsarot made four sweetmeats and gave them to his three wives, one each to Kaosanlaya and Kaikesi, and two to Sumitra. Kaosanlaya gave birth to Rama (the hero of the *Ramakien*), Kaikesi to Phrot, and Sumitra to Lak (Laksmana) and Satrut. Later, when Rama was exiled to the forest, his half-brother Phrot tried to get him to return to no avail; finally, he placed Rama's shoes on the throne and installed himself as regent rather than king. He took vows and lived as a *yogi* for the fourteen-year period of exile, waiting for his brother's return.

Although the *Ramakien* explains how Phrot became an ascetic, he has no special associations in the epic with music and dance. Sirirat turns to Indian sources (ibid., 37), citing the *Natyasastra* of Bharatamuni, to find these associations. He admits that this source does not address Bharatamuni's origins, but relates that the many ascetics went to Bharata's hermitage *(asarom)* asking him to perform the great ritual dances *(natayaweet)* and to explain their origins and uses. Bharatamuni told them that Brahma created the ritual dances himself but that they weren't part of the divine magic *(phra weet)*, which was strictly off-limits to anyone not of the proper caste. There were four scriptures of the divine magic, and Brahma created a fifth—the *natayaweet* or ritual dances—to be available to people of any caste. He made this fifth kind of magic by combining parts of the four preexisting scriptures: the verbal arts came from the scripture praising the deities, the art of singing came from the scripture of chant, the dance positions came from the scripture of mantras, and taste or quality came from the scripture of aesthetics. The point, Sirirat says, is that Bharatamuni was clearly conversant in all these arts, and thus it makes sense to call him the Old Father of music as well as dance.

It is clear, at any rate, that although there is disagreement about the Old Father's ultimate identity, there *is* general agreement that Phrot is Bharatamuni, the Indian ascetic who received dance from the deities. Narot may be the hermit of music as opposed to dance, but the precise identity of the powerful Lord Hermit is not of great importance to most performers. The Old Father, whoever he may be, is recognized and worshiped as a figure of power and consequence but is cloaked in considerable mystery.

Representations of the Hermit

Masks and small medallions of the Old Father (and even photographs of these objects) are revered as objects of power. They are generally kept on altars, out in the open—the masks are never stored away in boxes but are kept in places of honor. Masks of the Old Father are worn only in the *wai khruu* ceremony. To my knowledge, these masks are never worn in dramatic performances. Amulets or medallions with his image are more private and are usually worn on a chain hung around the neck but kept under the wearer's shirt; if not worn, they are kept on an altar at home along with other sacred objects, usually high above floor level.

There are probably thousands of masks (and miniature replicas of such masks) of the Old Father in Thailand. Full-sized masks are generally owned only by the teachers who perform the *wai khruu* ceremony or by institutions like university music and dance departments. Professional performers often own a small replica for their home altars and may remove it only to have it blessed at a *wai khruu* ceremony.[32]

The craftsmen who make dance masks (*chaang hua khoon*) generally make the large masks of the Old Father only on commission, but may also make small mask replicas ready for instant sale. Most performers are far from well-to-do and tend to go to more humble workshops for these mask replicas. Costs vary, but a six-inch-tall mask cost between 150 and 250 *baht* (U.S.$6–$10) in the late 1980s. The workmanship of these craftsmen is often looked down on by more highly placed, institutionalized performers; when I told one musician that I had recently visited one of these shops, he said, "Oh, that stuff is like village work—you should go to so-and-so to get your own 'head.'" Both of the shops I knew in Bangkok were nonetheless run by families of artisans who had learned the craft from their parents. Some of their income came from tourists. In fact, one of the shops had a permanent stand at the Weekend Market, filled with cheap papier-mâché dance masks, but they also regularly received commissions and special orders from professional performers. One shop had a sign (in Thai only) hanging on the wall saying, "Order Your Old Father Mask Here." Another shop, called Padung Cheep, adjacent to the tourist district of inexpensive hostels, kept a large number of Old Father mask replicas on view along with other dance masks. They guarded them, however, with awkwardly lettered signs in English saying, "Not for Sale to Tourists."[33]

The great mask makers patronized by well-to-do performers are few in number but known by all. One of the most famous in the late 1980s was *Momrachawong* Caruunsawat Suksawat (called "*Mom* Caruun" by performers), a distant relative of the royal family who lives an hour from Bangkok in the old capital of Ayuthaya. His lineage as a mask maker and as a *wai khruu* officiant is quite distinguished. His masks of the Old Father are beautiful, well known, and expensive. In 1989 he and his assistants were making them

Figure 3.5   Four mask molds in *Momrachawong* Caruun's workshop in Ayuthaya in 1989. From the left, the first and third molds are for demons; the other two are for full-size masks of the Old Father. A poster of the Crown Princess is below. Photograph by Deborah Wong.

in three sizes: a full-size mask cost 6,000 *baht* (U.S.$240), a six-inch-tall replica was 3,000 *baht* (U.S.$120), and a four-inch replica was 1,500 *baht* (U.S.$60; see fig. 3.5).[34]

    Over the years, Caruun has arrived at a standard design for the Old Father (see fig. 3.6). The mask's face is entirely gold, either from gold leaf or paint. The face is broad and square and surprisingly Caucasian; the eyes are blue, adding to this effect. The Old Father always has white eyebrows and a white mustache (painted on), and the many wrinkles around his eyes, nose, and chin are painted in red and pink. Caruun says that the Old Father should always smile slightly (*yim noi*). The mouth is open and two teeth can be seen—two because the Old Father is, after all, an old man and has lost some. The head is crowned with the distinctive conical headdress of a hermit, which contains his uncut, matted hair, flaring at the top. Its base across the forehead is defined by a triple row of rhinestones. The Old Father's ears are framed by flame-shaped ornaments (known as *kaan ciak* or *caun huu*) that are a standard part of dance headdresses. The surface of the headdress is covered with painted spots representing tigerskin.

    Older masks share many of these characteristics, but with the personal variations of past artisans. A catalogue from a 1971 exhibition of dance

Figure 3.6 Momrachawong Caruun in his home and workshop in Ayuthaya
in 1989 with one of his finished masks of the Old Father.
Photograph by Deborah Wong.

masks at the National Museum (National Museum 2514/1971) contains
three photographs of Old Father masks, including one that probably dates
from the reigns of Rama I and Rama II (ca. 1782–1824). Possibly one of the
oldest Old Father masks in existence,[35] this mask has startling blue eyes
and a direct, rather commanding expression. Two striking differences from
Caruun's masks are a tuft of fur emerging from the crown of his headdress
and his brown skin color; brown-faced masks are still seen today but are
much more rare than the gold-faced are. The other two have gold faces,
though one (formerly belonging to *Phraya* Natthakanurak) is so old that
much of its gold is gone. Owned by Akhom Saiyakhom, the great dance
teacher and *wai khruu* officiant at the National Theater until his death in
1982, this mask was presumably used in *wai khruu* ceremonies, possibly
by both owners. The third mask, the only Old Father mask in the catalogue
whose maker is still known, was made by Cit Kaewduangyai, a famous mask
maker of the last generation whose children continue to run his workshop.
This mask has an old man's squint and an almost petulant expression; the
stylized cords wrapped around the tigerskin headdress are especially clear.

Masks of other characters may also employ hermit iconography. The
National Museum catalogue contains a photograph of a Hanuman mask,
also made by Cit, entitled "Hanuman is ordained" *(Hanuman buat);* the face

is Hanuman's, but the monkey wears a hermit's headdress. Another hermit, named Kalaikot, is usually depicted with the muzzle of a deer, the ears and eyes of a human, and the headdress and white eyebrows of a hermit. Caruun also once showed me a snapshot of a special hermit mask he had made, commissioned by a spirit medium *(khon song):* though wearing a hermit's headdress, this "hermit" was clearly a demon, with a demon's green face and fangs.

Varravinai Hiranmas, a contemporary mask maker who teaches at the College of Arts and Crafts *(Witthayakheet Phau Chaang)* in Bangkok, explained to me that there are 108 hermits and each has his own colors and traits. When performers order masks of the Old Father from him, he usually gives it a gold face, because this is the color of respect and worship, and makes the *Phra Rüsii* beautiful and dignified. His face can also be flesh-colored *(sii nua)*, pink *(sii kliip bua,* "lotus-petal color"), or purple *(sii muang)*, but gold is generally preferred. The Lord Hermit made for spirit mediums has a green face (like Totsakan and many other demons) to make him look cruel and fierce *(du)*. The Old Father of music and dance usually smiles a little, Varravinai explained, to help hearten performers before they go onstage:

> The Old Father has many faces. Some masks look severe or ferocious *(du)*, but performers tend to be fearful of these, and aren't brave enough to *wai* them. When they come order a mask from me, they usually ask that I make him smile a little so that they can look at him and feel calm and contented *(sabaaicai)*. We artisans will make him look like whatever the person wants. . . . But dancers like for him to smile and look kind. When they *wai* him, they want to be able to feel sure of themselves, so they can go out and perform well without feeling that the Teacher is severe or cruel *(du)*. Sometimes they go out and make mistakes, but then they come back and *wai* him and he smiles.

Not surprisingly, the process of creating Old Father masks is different from making other kinds of masks. The ritual process for creating this mask and that of the demon dance teacher *Phra* Phiraap involves special offerings and precautions because these two masks are the most sacred of all. The catalogue of the National Museum exhibit describes the making of these special masks as follows:

> Making the masks of the Lord Teacher Hermit and the Lord Teacher Phiraap, who are worshiped by performing artists, is like making other masks up to the point that the papier-mâché cast is removed from the mold

and closed up (*pit hun*). After that, the mask maker must observe the Five
Buddhist Precepts, dress completely in white, and arrange a table of food
offerings (*khrüang sangwoei buuchaa*). When the mask is completely finished, its eyes must be opened and the spirit (*winyaan*) of the Father
Teacher invited to enter. (6)

Varravinai gave a slightly different explanation, saying that making the
mask of the Old Father (and of the demon Phiraap) necessitates three separate rituals at successive stages of the mask's construction. On the day the
mask maker molds the mask, he must dress completely in white and observe
either the Five or the Eight Precepts as he sees fit. Food offerings must also
be set out: the meats for the Old Father must be cooked whereas those for
Phiraap are raw. No further ritual is necessary until the day the face is drawn
and painted on, when the same precautions are observed. The third and
last ritual is performed when the mask is brought to life and imbued with
a spirit (*winyaan*). This last ritual, called *boek phra neet* (literally, "opening
the eyes"), "brings the mask to life" (*mii chiiwit khün maa*); if not observed,
the mask will be as if blind and won't be able to see anything or to help the
performers who worship it. This final ritual is done only for masks that will
be worn in ritual, not for small mask replicas.[36]

Imbuing masks with life and power is part of a larger pattern of sacralizing objects, a practice that extends far beyond the performing arts.
Tambiah's study of amulets (1984) documents the manner in which images
of famous monks and of the Buddha himself are sacralized and become protective in their own right. Following the same principle, performers (and
some healers) sometimes keep small amulets bearing the Old Father's image. Made of metal or terra-cotta and worn on a chain, these amulets protect their wearers in the same way that Buddhist amulets help prevent accidents and misfortune. I bought four amulets of the Old Father from different
sellers at the amulet market around Wat Mahathat in Bangkok. Two are
terra-cotta pressings that are almost certainly from the same mold: both
show the Old Father looking off to the right, and his broad face, round
cheeks, and slight smile are especially pronounced. One is rectangular and
the other is oval. The oval one is covered with a patch of gold leaf, a sign
of respect possibly applied by a former owner. A third amulet is copper,
with the Old Father's face on one side and a *taphoon* (the sacred drum that
symbolizes the Old Father) on the other. Its shape is that of an upside-down
temple boundary stone (*bai seemaa*).[37] The side with his face is inscribed
with the words "Loving Kindness and Virtue" (*meettaa thii khün*) across the
top and "A souvenir of the *wai khruu* ceremony" (*thii ralük nai ngaan wai
khruu*) beneath his face. The other side is inscribed with the name of the

Figure 3.7   Amulets of the Old Father. Slide by Deborah Wong.

temple where the *wai khruu* ceremony was held (Wat Taku, Amphoe Bang Ban, Ayuthaya Province). A fourth amulet that I bought is not flat like the others but rather a small three-dimensional head of the Old Father, made of clay or terra-cotta and rubbed smooth from handling. I received a fifth amulet at an actual *wai khruu* ceremony,[38] where small ceramic amulets of the Old Father's face were handed out one by one to each participant during the blessing and initiation *(khraup)* section of the ritual. I was told that a monk had blessed these amulets sometime before the ceremony. (See fig. 3.7.)

The most well known and, many performers feel, most powerful amulets of the Old Father are the two sets commissioned by the Association for Assistance to Friends and Performers *(Samaakhom Songkhrau Sahaai Silapin)*. Founded in 1969 by a small group of concerned performers and sponsored by the abbot of Wat Phra Phireen, the Association is dedicated to helping performers out with small loans. In the previous chapter, I describe its sumptuous and well-attended *wai khruu* ceremony, held annually in September at Wat Phra Phireen in Bangkok. The history and efficacy of its amulets is described in an essay from a commemorative booklet distributed at their ceremony in 1973 ("Sit Buchaa *Khruu*" 2516/1973). The writer (who uses a pseudonym) claims that amulets of the Old Father were also made in 1939 (somewhat unsuccessfully) and 1959. He also claims that King Rama VI (r. 1910–1925) sponsored a batch of terra-cotta amulets with a full-body view of the Old Father on one side and the Buddha on the other and distributed them to all the performers in what was then called the Department of Entertainment (*Krom Mahoorasop*, the precursor of the contemporary Department of Fine Arts). There was, in other words, a precedent for such amulets, but they were still uncommon when the Association decided to sponsor the making of a batch for their first big *wai khruu* ceremony in 1970. The amulets were planned as a remembrance of the event, as an act of worship and respect for the Old Father, and as a fund-raising venture for the Association. Designed by several of the Association's founding members, five thousand amulets were minted (in silver, gold-dipped copper, and darkened copper) and then consecrated *(pluuk seek)*. Every single amulet was sold: after an initial investment of 10,000 *baht* (U.S.$400), the Association made a profit of 40,000 *baht* (U.S.$1,600). This success prompted a second batch of another five thousand in 1972, made this time of copper dipped in gold; some amulets from this second batch still remain, and I bought one at the Association's *wai khruu* ceremony in 1989 for 40 *baht* (U.S.$1.60).

The author of this essay (who is clearly an Association officer) then relates a number of stories, all told to him by various performers. Those wearing the amulets have been left miraculously unscathed after horrific car accidents and have survived drunken melees without scratches. Since performers tend to spend a lot of time traveling to engagements on the dangerous roads of rural and urban Thailand, the amulets' power to protect their owners from accidents is especially valued. The author himself relates two instances when his amulet helped him get money in times of need—when his sister died and when his mask of the Old Father was renovated. It is clear from his stories that the amulets have protective powers in their own right, but that it is ultimately the wearer's belief in the Old Father that is protective. He writes:

> I don't think it's important whether the Old Father amulets are actually powerful or not. Their importance lies in the fact that I believe I have to have one. . . .
>
> Why do I have to have an Old Father amulet? How has the Old Father helped me? Is what I've told you true? I'm not going to address any of that because I'm the one who best knows the taste of what I eat, and whether it's good or not—no one else. . . .
>
> We performers respect the Old Father, we worship him, so naturally he helps us. As I have experienced, if you keep your distance from him and don't worship him, and don't support and patronize him as you should, or are indifferent to him, and then just wait for him to help you—well, you'll

wait. When it comes to things like this, he who does something gets something; he who eats will know the taste. We artists hang amulets of the Old Father around our necks. Whoever says we're old-fashioned—that's all right! Whoever says we're crazy—fine! We're proud to say that we hold to our amulets as a reminder of the Teacher's virtue and goodness, as we have been taught repeatedly. And this teaching makes our calling as performers possible. We are not ungrateful, we think of the great Teachers, we hold to our amulets of the Old Father, we performers. We'll vouch for the fact that the Teacher protects us from danger.

Preperformance Invocations to the Hermit

The power of the male ascetic and his connection to Shiva is found in many parts of Indic Southeast Asia. The paradigm of the empowered hermit looms large, for instance, in the Tengger ritual of east Java, where the power of the Tengger priests (who were called *resi*) stems directly from Shiva.[39] Robert Hefner's description of a key Tengger ritual has strong, direct parallels to the Thai *wai khruu* ceremony: "Guru is Shiva as World Teacher. Here he is invited not only to descend to the ritual site but, according to the prayer appeal, to enter and possess the priest. This, then, is the source of the priest's ritual power; he is a vehicle for Lord Guru. . . . It is through Shiva's power, the priest proclaims, that the rite about to occur will take place" (1985, 177).

The connection between the empowered teacher-hermit and Shiva is not common knowledge among Thai musicians and dancers. Shiva and Vishnu are regularly summoned and worshipped in many Hindu-Buddhist rituals, but the identification of the Old Father with Shiva is part of the esoteric knowledge that officiants pass on to their students and that they never tire of discussing among themselves. Yet the signs of Shiva are everywhere. The mask maker and officiant *Momrachawong* Caruunsawat Suksawat has added the flamboyant touch of sitting on a tigerskin (a symbol of Shiva) as he conducts the ceremony (fig. 3.8); he also includes a small Indian statue of Shiva Nataraja at one point in the ceremony. When I simply asked another officiant[40] whether the Hermit was Shiva, he nodded and said, "The Lord Hermit is a manifestation (*paang*) of Lord Shiva."

In *nang yai* (the great shadow theater), the *wai khruu* sequence and the ritual scene "opening the stage" (*boek roong*) place the Hermit between contrasting powers: between Narai and Isuan (i.e., Vishnu and Shiva) and between the Dharma and evil (*tham* and *aatham*). The Hermit apparently stands between various kinds of forces, both literally (e.g., when his puppet is placed between that of Narai and Isuan) and figuratively, mediating and

Figure 3.8 Momrachawong Caruun's tigerskin in front of an altar at the
beginning of a *wai khruu* ritual over which he officiated in 1989.
Slide by Deborah Wong.

even bringing these forces together. He himself is neither one kind of power
nor the other, but rather the power implicit in such encounters.

The shadow theater traditions of the royal court and of rural southern
Thailand (extending into Malaysia) include long invocations that begin
an evening's performance.[41] Although often described as *preceding* the performance, in fact, these invocations are the source of the event itself. The
Hindu-Buddhist model for performance dictates a frame of metaperformance in which statements are made about the ultimate source and significance of the event that follows. All-night puppet performances in both
mainland and insular Southeast Asia seem to have especially long and formulaic invocations in which the Hermit figures prominently.

Nang yai, the great shadow play of the Thai courts (*nang*, "skin, leather";
yai, "big, great")[42] is now virtually extinct except for a troupe in Rachburi
province made up of elderly men. Its puppets were quite large (3–6 feet
tall), unjointed, and supported by individual men whose choreography reflected the character and its actions. Narration and dialogue was provided

by one or two chanters who stood to the side of the screen, accompanied by
the music of a *piiphaat* ensemble. The stories were almost entirely from the
Ramakien, though the *Inao* (Panji) stories were also occasionally performed.
Nang yai was first mentioned in a text dating to A.D. 1458, but the present
form of the texts used in performance are from the early Ratanakosin period (late eighteenth century), and may have been reconstructed from earlier Ayuthian texts (Smithies and Euayporn 1974,143).

As with the mask, making the puppet figure of the Hermit requires special preparations. Dhaninivat describes these ritual formalities as follows:

> The figures . . . of the gods of Hinduism, such as Vishnu and Shiva, and the
> *rishi*, must be made of the hide of a virgin cow and considerable offerings
> of articles of food by way of propitiation of the Master of the *nang* would
> be required. For the *rishi* however the hide of a tiger or a bear is some-
> times preferred. The artist who draws the patterns of these three exalted
> figures is moreover required to wear a ceremonial garb of white, and finish
> his work within the space of a day. (2531/1988, 9)

Nearly always performed at night, a performance of *nang yai* began
with a *wai khruu* ceremony involving numerous offerings and recited invocations. "The Three Teachers"—Narai, Isuan, and the Hermit—were
placed on the screen, with the Hermit in the center; candles were lit, the
piiphaat ensemble played, and the puppet master would recite the *wai khruu*
text.[43] Quite long, this text both salutes and explains the deities and teachers of *nang yai*. As Smithies and Euayporn have described it,

> The text is lengthy and the meaning at times obscure. It starts with an
> invocation to king Totsarot (Dasaratha) and the teachers of the art of the
> *nang* who were apparently skilled magicians. The making of the figures of
> Rama and Lakshana is described. The hermit and the Buddha are saluted,
> as are, for good measure, the animistic spirits of nature. The setting of
> the *nang* is next recounted—the screen, the supporting poles, the musi-
> cians, the figure. The audience is then invited to come and watch the
> shadow play, to listen to the tale that has been handed down through the
> generations. (1974, 144)

Once the *wai khruu* text was completed, a short section called *boek
roong* (literally "to widen, expand, open the stage") was performed (Pha-op
2520/1977, 25–26). This section always featured the Hermit and puppets of two monkeys, one white and one black. The Hermit would send
the white monkey to find the black one, the two monkeys would fight,
and the white monkey would win and bring the black one back to the Hermit. The white monkey supposedly represented good and the Dharma; the

black monkey, the opposite (26). This opening vignette was not related to the following story. Rather, it was a spirited prelude with fast music, a fight scene, and much taunting and joking, all of which showed off the skills of the puppeteers, the narrator, and the musicians. It was evidently a great crowd-pleaser and helped to attract an audience.

A similar opening sequence is used in *nang talung*, the shadow puppet theater of rural southern Thailand. Unlike *nang yai*, *nang talung* is still a vital tradition, supported at both the local and government levels: its performance at night is integral to ritual and festive events, and several master puppeteers have been named National Artists.[44] *Nang talung* has been extensively documented (especially in the Songkhla area), making it possible to look at the role of the Hermit in some detail.

As in *nang yai*, the puppet figure of the Hermit is accorded a special status. There are six character types in *nang yai*, and the Hermit is included in the group of sacred figures *(ruup saksit)* that includes deities. Vandergeest has noted that when the puppets are stacked and stored away, their order reproduces a hierarchy of levels of power, with the hermit placed on the top, above the Hindu deities (1990, 9). Somcai describes the hermit as follows:

> The figure of the *rüsii* is of primary importance. Every *nang talung* troupe must have this figure, and must use it before every performance in the *boek rong* sequence. There is a strong belief that this grants the troupe auspiciousness and blessings. The *rüsii* is cut from the hide of an ox or water buffalo that has all the characteristics of Lord Isuan's steed—that is, it must have mottled hooves, a tail like a flower, a dew's lap like pleated cloth, and a face shaped like a *bodhi* leaf. . . . In some places the *rüsii* is cut from the hide of a tiger. . . . This may have come about because, in Nakhon Srithammarat and Phattalung [cities in southern Thailand], it is said that the *rüsii* wears a garment of tigerskin; following this belief, some puppetmakers may have actually started making the *rüsii* figure from tigerskin in order to give themselves magical and auspicious powers and to further their craft. (2528/1985, 36)

The opening sequence that leads up to the actual story begins with a small *wai khruu* ceremony that the puppeteer and musicians perform for themselves. The musicians play a musical overture or *hoomroong*. As the puppeteers remove the puppets from their box, they make offerings and utter mantras. The performers follow this with the *boek roong* sequence. Previously, the white and black monkey fight (called *ling hua kham*, "The Monkeys at Dusk") was performed, but is now usually omitted;[45] some have speculated that the scene was originally taken from *nang yai*. The two monkeys would fight and then go find the Hermit, who would ask them the cause of their quarrel. The white monkey would explain that he caught the black monkey eating fruit from his trees and dragged him to the Hermit so that the Hermit would kill the black monkey for his misdeeds. But the Hermit would defer, saying that he (the Hermit) lived according to the Dharma, which expressly forbids the taking of life and the killing of animals. He would ask whether he could instead instruct the black monkey in proper behavior, and the white monkey would agree.

Interestingly, this entire sequence was performed without the Hermit being seen: only his voice was heard in conversation with the monkeys.[46] The Hermit made his entrance only after the quarrel was resolved. In contemporary performances, the Hermit's entrance (called *kan choet ruup Rüsii*) follows the overture and is one of the most important parts of the entire opening sequence. As the musicians play the piece called *Choet*, the Hermit brandishes his staff three times from the side of the screen, and then flies across it from right to left and then back again. He then walks across the screen leaning on his staff, starting out three times before finally reaching the middle; this takes about five minutes, as he starts out slowly and hesitantly and then gains assurance and speed. Once again he flies across the screen, but this time from left to right and back again, three times. The puppeteer then plants the figure in the center of the screen, sticking it into the banana trunk at its base, and the music stops as the puppeteer utters the Hermit's formulaic verses. This done, the musicians play *Choet* once again, and the Hermit flies from right to left and back again once more and then exits.

After the exit of the Hermit, Isuan (Shiva) appears mounted on his ox and goes through formulaic movements that show off the technical skill of the puppeteer (fig. 3.9). Following the three stanzas of invocational verses for him and his exit, the story gradually begins: three separate characters (usually clowns and a ruling lord) come out and explain what the story will be about.

Sutthiwong (2522/1979, 38–40) has pointed out that the Hermit, Isuan (Shiva), and the deity known as Betara Guru in Malaysia and Java are closely linked. He speculates that *nang talung* is a regional adaptation of shadow puppet forms originally from India and influenced by Javanese *wayang kulit*. In the *nang talung* of southern Thailand, the Hermit and Isuan mounted on his ox are an essential part of the *boek roong* sequence, or the "opening" of the performance; the verses for both deities are preceded by the sacred word *om*, signaling their primacy in the divine hierarchy. Just as there is a close relationship between Isuan and the hermit, Isuan and Betara Guru are identified with each other: *Betara* means "lord" and *Guru* is, of course, the

Figure 3.9   In a *nang talung* performance outside the city of Songkhla in 1987, a puppeteer holds a puppet of Shiva riding his ox against the screen; the puppet of the Hermit is on the lower right. Photograph by Deborah Wong.

Sanskrit word for "teacher" that is also the source of the Thai word *khruu*. Sutthiwong writes that "Lord Isuan is the great teacher of the arts in India, and is the equivalent of the Javanese puppet known as Betara Guru. This deity has the duty of washing away the sins of the world. In the Javanese shadow theater performed in Pattani (called *wayang yawau*), the figure of Betara Guru is brought out in a similar fashion, after the figure of Gunung Wilisamahara (which is a symbol of the four heavenly realms)" (38–39).

Singaravelu (1970) makes the most explicit connections between Betara Guru, the Hermit, and Shiva as Lord of the Dance (Nataraja). He writes that in Kelantan (Malaysia), Betara Guru is considered the "First of the Teachers and the First of the Actors" (48) and is regarded as the greatest of the Malay deities. In the invocations preceding the Kelantan shadow play, the *dalang* addresses him as *Sang Kala, Batara Kala, To' Maha Risi Kala*, and *To' Maha Risi Kala Yang Bermatakan Api* (the great sage Kala with the fiery eyes). Singaravelu claims that Betara Guru's titles contain the word *Kala* or "time" in reference to Shiva as the lord of absolute, eternal time, and as the all-destroyer (48–49). Other titles, such as *Yang Berdiri Kaki Tunggal* (the deity standing on a single foot) and *Sang Kaki Bentara Kala*, probably refer to Shiva as Nataraja, the king of the dance: in this role, Shiva stands on one foot as he dances the cycle of birth and destruction. Betara Guru is also invoked in the Kelantan area by Malay magicians, who recognize a wide number of Shiva's manifestations (Endicott 1985, 101–3).[47]

Javanese beliefs surrounding Betara Guru are similar to those surrounding the Thai hermit. A standard book on the characters of central Javanese *wayang kulit* opens with the figure of Betara Guru and states:

> According to Javanese beliefs, especially the beliefs of *dhalang* [puppeteers], Betara Guru is greatly venerated and considered the most sacred. The puppet of Betara Guru is thus considered different from other puppets. For example, only his figure is kept covered with a beautiful batik cloth. Furthermore, this puppet is held over incense before being used in performance, and people are afraid to step over the banana tree trunk [at the bottom of the screen] after it has been pierced by the figure of Betara Guru. . . .
>
> Manikmaya [another name for Betara Guru] is a deity, the son of Hyang Tunggal ("The One [God]"). He was born as a ray of light, along with Ismaya [Semar]. Manikmaya radiates a brilliant white light. Hyang Tunggal decreed that Manikmaya will later rule this universe because of his supernatural powers and appropriateness.[48] (Hardjowirogo 1982, 35–38)

Prayers and mantras to Betara Guru are common among *dhalang*, the puppeteers. At the close of his book on Hindu ritual among the Tengger of eastern Java, Robert Hefner includes the following prayer, given to him as a parting gift by a Tengger priest:

> Hong! *pekulun* [beautiful essence] I watch the *wayang* puppetry of Lord Guru. It is he who guides the puppet shadows, and heavenly spirits who play the *gamelan*. Holy shadows on the screen, hey! The audience is drawn tense with the movement. Yet there are no people at that moment, invisible are those who watch invisible. The movement is exciting and the handwork deft. The audience is drawn into the play, but what they see is invisible an illusion those who watch invisible those who watch invisible. (1985, 270)

Shiva as divine teacher is thus part and parcel of performance, especially shadow theater, in many parts of Southeast Asia. His framing presence is often referenced at the beginning of an event, and addressing him through prayer activates a transfer of power from him to the performer(s). In short, the beliefs that drive Thai music and dance are not unique but are, rather, part of a broader cultural pattern. In Thailand, however, the Indic origins of this pattern have been valorized to the extent that key icons—Brahmins, Pali vocabulary, and the use of Brahminic ritual technologies such as sacral water—immediately indicate the mysterious, the ancient, and the powerful. Knowledge as material power is central to this intricate aesthetic landscape: it moves through objects and between people in tangible ways. This field of esoteric materialism is familiar to all musicians, whether street performers or university professors. Control over the movement of knowledge-as-power is another matter. The following chapters address the technologies of the written word and performed music, as well as who gets to write, read, and make musical sound.

Four

··

Sounding the Sacred

Wai khruu rituals fill the air with sound. Latecomers can find the site of a ceremony by following the sound of the *piiphaat* ensemble. Whether amplified or not, the loud, brilliant sound of the xylophone and the deep thuds of the barrel drums carry quite a long way. In fact, filling the air in this way —creating a special space filled with special sound—is central to all Thai ritual and festive events. The blare of taped music broadcast over a public address system (often powerfully distorted) is nearly a given at such events. Once, early in my fieldwork, I was looking for the house where a *wai khruu* was to be held. Unfamiliar with the area, I knew only on what lane *(soi)* the house was located and had neither the house number nor any idea of how deep the lane was (and some can be quite long). A few houses past the entrance to the lane, I saw an elderly man standing in his front door and asked him if he knew the house I was looking for. He looked at me in surprise and said, "Can't you hear it?" And then I did. Accustomed to the din of Bangkok's traffic, I had filtered out—ignored—the "noise" of taped classical music amplified through the neighborhood from the house in question, which was a five-minute walk farther down the lane.

The *wai khruu* is full of music, and this chapter focuses on its musical repertoire. In some ways, this may seem the most musicological section of my study: I discuss questions of repertoire, its differentiation from other repertoires, and its implications for the social structure of Thai classical musicians. I will not, however, dwell much on its formal characteristics. Thai musicians simply don't think, talk, or write about the music in that way. Although discussion of "the music" means talking about "the elements" (pitch, meter, timbre, etc.) in the West, and although in Western scholarship this leads inevitably to matters of form, this is not the way that practicing Thai musicians conceive of their music. Thai scholars of music can (and do) address Thai music in this way, and their models are drawn entirely from Western art music analysis. That is, their methodologies focus on and construct "the music" as an object that can be discussed in purely musical terms. In discussing Thai music, I emulate Thai musicians' modes of talk, then; ultimately, I am interested not in "the music" but rather in how Thai musicians discuss the pieces that they play. This means following their lead. Indeed, I believe "the music" does not exist outside of their conceptions of it, and this above all marks my approach as that of an anthropologist/ethnomusicologist rather than a musicologist, music theorist, or acoustician. As a result, little musical notation, whether Thai or Western, appears here.

As a musician, I spent a lot of time learning this music and talking to other musicians about it. My own teacher, a gong circle and xylophone player, specializes in the ritual repertoire and had much to say to me about it. I also took ritual steps (described below) to delve deeper into this body of music, which in turn led me to consider broader patterns of sound and the sacred in Thailand. Certain kinds of ritually defined sound (e.g., music and recited texts) create a bridge between the human and sacred realms. The final part of this chapter moves away from music qua music and considers how sound, in sympathetic combination with other media, is regarded by Thai performers as truly performative—that is, as a force that changes the balance and composition of the human realm.

When the ritual repertoire is played in a *wai khruu* ritual, its sacred nature is at stage center. The *piiphaat* musicians, the ritual officiant, and knowledgeable listeners/participants mark the beginning and end of each piece with *wai*-s: still holding their mallets, the musicians bring their hands to their foreheads, and devout participants will listen with their hands in a *wai*, bringing them to their foreheads at the conclusion of each piece. This gesture of respect is not, of course, for the music itself—Thais have no concept of music as an object—but for the actions that the music completes, and in the *wai khruu* ritual this means deities in motion.

The Musical Repertoire of the
Wai Khruu Ritual: *Phleeng Naa Phaat*

I witnessed or participated in about twenty *wai khruu* rituals during 1988 and 1989 (and eight more during the 1990s), and at least half of each event was filled with the live performance of sacred instrumental works by a *piiphaat* ensemble. In other words, if a particular ritual took two hours to perform, over an hour of that time would be filled with *piiphaat* music and little else: while the *piiphaat* ensemble was playing, the officiant and participants generally just sat listening. Most officiants asked for the *piiphaat* ensemble to play anywhere from twenty to thirty pieces, depending on their individual practice and the amount of time available to them. The total repertoire of pieces that can be used in the ritual is considerably larger than the number usually performed at a single event—about seventy pieces in all (see the list of pieces in Appendix B): some are interchangeable, some are mandatory, and some may be omitted.

These pieces are variously called "teacher's pieces," "sacred pieces," or "high pieces" (*phleeng khruu, phleeng saksit,* or *phleeng suung*). They belong to a larger repertoire of two to three hundred pieces called *phleeng naa phaat* that are considered the oldest music in Thailand; Montri Tramote has speculated that they date to the late Ayuthaya period (early eighteenth century or before). Many of the names and melodies are clearly related to Khmer pieces still performed today in Cambodia (for more on these ties, see Miller and Sam 1995, 240–41). The Thai *naa phaat* pieces are used in various rituals (including the soul-tying and tonsure ceremonies) and to accompany the related performance traditions of masked dance-drama *(khoon)*, the great shadow theater *(nang yai)*, hand-puppet theater *(hun krabauk)*, and working-class dance-drama *(likee)*.

The name *naa phaat* is of unclear origin, though both Thai and Western musicians have speculated about its meaning. *Naa phaat* is certainly related to the word *piiphaat*. The syllable *-phaat* comes from the Sanskrit word *vadya*, which means "musical instrument" or "instrumental piece," as opposed to vocal music.[1] In Thai, *-phaat* means "instruments that are blown or beaten to herald or proclaim" (see Manit 2528/1985, 666). Sangat Phukhaothaung, a noted scholar of classical Thai music, writes that *naa phaat* means "voice" or "spoken words,"[2] and that the names of the Mon and Burmese musical ensembles—*pat* and *pataya*—reflect the same etymological roots (2532/1989, 213). *Naa* means "face" or "in front of, before"; the *pii* is the quadruple-reed instrument in the *piiphaat* ensemble. Thus, *naa phaat* may refer to the dances performed "in front of" the *piiphaat* ensemble (Myers-Moro 1988a, 436, fn.1), in other words, the instrumental ensemble featuring the *pii*. This makes sense since the *naa phaat* pieces and their corresponding dances are mutually referential: they have the same names and imply one another.

The traits of the *naa phaat*, or ritual, repertoire are most easily seen in contrast to another, complementary repertoire, the body of pieces called *seephaa mahoorii* that are used for entertainment.[3] The ritual repertoire is played *only* by the *piiphaat* ensemble, whereas the *seephaa mahoorii* repertoire is played by either the *mahoorii*, *piiphaat*, or string ensembles. All musicians are familiar with the *seephaa mahoorii* repertoire, whereas only a minority (mostly men) are well versed in ritual pieces. The *seephaa mahoorii* repertoire continues to grow as contemporary composers add to it, but the ritual repertoire is considered fixed and ancient. *Seephaa mahoorii* pieces are generally constructed out of symmetrical phrases and sections and have lyrical melodies; ritual pieces are often asymmetrical and are constructed out of a limited number of smaller motives, of which only a few are unique to particular pieces. Finally, the *seephaa mahoorii* repertoire is generally text-centered: a singer alternates verses with the *mahoorii* ensemble. The ritual repertoire, by contrast, is strictly instrumental. The *naa phaat* and *seephaa mahoorii* musical structures and performance practices can quickly be compared as shown in table 4.1.

The formal structure of ritual pieces is anomalous, especially when compared to *seephaa mahoorii* pieces. Following the symmetrical poetic structures of the lyrics, *seephaa mahoorii* pieces fall into neat sections *(thaun)*, lines *(banthat)*, and phrases or half-lines *(wak)*. Ritual pieces can be broken down into smaller units, but neither my own teacher nor other musicians that I asked felt comfortable talking about their structure in this way. Whenever I asked questions along these lines, I was told to go talk to Montri Tramote. Some ritual pieces do have "sections" *(thaun)*, but many don't. The most sacred and dangerous piece in the ritual repertoire, *Phleeng Ong Phra Phiraap*, has sections called "splinters" or "slivers" *(sian)* rather than *thaun*. The whole class of ritual pieces called *Choet* are constructed out of short phrases called "bodies" *(tua)* that end with the same phrase but begin differently; the short sections of the rubato, free-meter pieces called *rua* are each called "leaving" or "saying good-bye" *(laa)*. In short, the ritual repertoire is rife with specialized, idiosyncratic vocabulary about musical structure—vocabulary that musicians are neither comfortable with, nor agreed upon, nor particularly interested in.

In all my conversations and readings, I have come across only one description of the form of a ritual piece, and this is by Uthit Naksawat, from his well-known book on Thai music theory. The piece is *Ong Phra Phiraap*, the most sacred piece in the repertoire and unique in its alternation of

Table 4.1 Comparison of *Naa Phaat* and *Seephaa Mahoorii* Musical Structures and Performance Practices

	Naa Phaat	Seephaa Mahoorii
Social context	Ritual; sacred.	Secular; entertainment.
Use as dance accompaniment	Dance-drama of the court *(khoon)* and portions of working-class dance-drama *(likee)*.	*Rabam*, i.e., choreographed ensemble dances for women.
Performers' gender	Mostly men.	Men and women.
Instruments	Mostly struck instruments (drums, gongs, xylophones, cymbals) plus one wind instrument (double-reed oboe); no singing.	Struck, bowed, and wind instruments; singing.
Musical structure	Phrasing often asymmetrical.	Phrasing generally symmetrical.
Age	Very old (probably more than 200 years old, dating back to the pre-Ratanakosin era).	Both old and recent; new compositions still being added.
Composers	Unknown.	Both known and unknown; some composers (especially *Luang* Pradit Phairau) composed or arranged hundreds of pieces.

metered and unmetered sections—which is presumably why Uthit tried to describe it:

> *Phleeng Ong Phra Phiraap* is really a set of pieces *(phleeng chut)*. It begins with a *rua*, which is followed by a *sian* [splinter, sliver]. This is followed by *phan Phiraap* [the name of another section; *phan* = "thousand" or "to wind or wrap around"], and then the *sian* returns one more time. This ends the beginning of the piece. The alternation of the right and left hands on the gong circle is quite special, and different from any other piece. The rhythmic movement *(liilaa)* of the piece is strange and beautiful to listen to. The rhythm is slow, fast, it accelerates, and then backs up on itself—it's really interesting to listen to. The body of *Phra* Phiraap *(tua Ong Phra)* follows the beginning of the piece, and the musicians must *wai* before they go on to this section. After that, the *rua Phra Phiraap*—which is very beautiful—is played, followed once again by the *sian*. When this is finished, an abbreviated version of the *sian* called a *raun* is played. Finally, the ensemble returns to the beginning and plays that section twice. This completes the piece, which is immediately followed by the pieces *Pathom*, *Laa*, and then a *rua*. (2530/1987, 120–21)

I would venture to say that only a musician already familiar with the piece could make sense of this formal description. Its major sections seem to be the "beginning" *(ton)*, the "body" *(tua)*, and then the return of the "beginning"—that is, a large arch form. The "beginning" itself also follows an arch form *(sian—phan Phiraap—sian)*. I must emphasize, however, that such sectionalization is unusual for the ritual repertoire as a whole.

In short, formal analysis of musical structure is generally not a productive or meaningful approach to the ritual pieces, nor has it any emic base in Thai musical thought. The repertoire certainly includes categories of piece "types," but they pertain to a far more salient characteristic: each piece depicts a specific action or emotion.

The Performative Nature of the Ritual Repertoire

Each ritual piece embodies a particular movement, action, or emotion. I was tempted to use the word "represents" rather than "embodies," but these pieces do not mirror action as much as they *are* action. When Thai audiences hear certain pieces, they know that a character is traveling or weeping or sleeping even if the character is unseen or offstage. Action pieces are not unique to Thai drama; they are found all over Asia and other parts of the world as well.[4] Western writers frequently describe them as operating like Wagnerian *leitmotifs:* their melodies, or even fragments of their melodies, can create or modify the dramatic context. David Morton, for instance, addresses the Thai ritual repertoire only in passing, but notes that "Each composition has become identified with a certain action, event, stage movement, character, and so forth, and is used as background music to the drama in a manner comparable to Wagner's system of *leitmotifs* in his music dramas" (1976, 216). Pamela Myers-Moro also observes that "To indulge an analogy from the West, the melodies appear to function like leitmotivs [*sic*] in Wagner's operas: melodies are so consistently associated with specific actions and characters that informed audiences learn to 'follow a script' explicitly encoded in music" (1988a, 130).

Musicians' respect for these pieces suggests that they are not, as Morton says, mere "background music," but something far more. Performers also refer to the ritual repertoire as *phleeng prakaup kiriyaa*, or "pieces that perform actions" (*prakaup* = "to do, perform, consist of, join together"; *kiriyaa* = "behavior, manners, action"). The name of any ritual piece implies its dance and vice versa: the music doesn't simply accompany the dance movements but manifests them in a different medium. As mentioned above, the musical pieces and their dances have the same names, testifying to the mutual referentiality of ritual dance and music. The ritual piece called *Narai Banthom Sin* ("Narai Asleep in the Ocean"), for instance, has a corresponding dance that enacts Narai or *Phra* Ram asleep. When performers talk about *naa phaat*, they can be referring to either dance, or to music, or to both at once: if they really want to be specific, they can say *phleeng naa phaat* (*naa phaat* pieces) or *thaa ram naa phaat* (*naa phaat* dance positions), but performers are apt to refer to the two as a single reality.

There is a point, however, beyond which the two do not exactly align. If a ritual piece is played without a dancer, the implied action is still considered to have taken place, but the reverse is not possible: dance does not and *cannot* take place without music. Consider the following explanation of ritual pieces by Sangat Phukhaothaung: "The pieces that perform actions [*phleeng prakaup kiriyaa*] were implemented by musicians to *replace* actions, events, movements, or the expression of nearly anything: the animate or inanimate, people, animals, or objects, the corporeal or incorporeal, the real or the supposed, the past or present, and things of the imagination, such as deities and ghosts and demons" (2532/1989, 211). Sangat's use of the word "replace" *(thaen)* emphasizes the performative nature of these pieces. As he describes them, the musical pieces are clearly more than dance accompaniment. He even goes on to suggest that ritual pieces have a certain preeminence over their dance movements: "Dancers must follow the [notes of] these pieces—that is, they must hold onto the pieces as onto a post. This suggests that the musical works came first and the dance positions were devised later" (214).

In conversation, musicians emphasize the ability of ritual pieces to make things happen. Musicians do not say, as we might in English, that the pieces "reflect," "indicate" or "accompany" dramatic action; instead, they say that such-and-such a piece *is (pen)*, or *means (maai thüng)*, an action.[5] This is true not just in dance-drama but also and *especially* in ritual, wherein (to quote Tambiah quoting Austin) saying something is also doing something (1985, 128). The performative ability of the ritual repertoire is the heart of its efficacy, and its importance to the aesthetics of Thai ritual cannot be underestimated. In the *wai khruu*, these musical works literally bring or "invite" *(anchoen)* the teacher-deities of music and dance to the ritual event. They are the ephemeral doorway through which these deities can come and go, a frame of sound that *is* the sacred in motion.

Categories within the Ritual Repertoire

Thai musicians group or categorize the ritual repertoire in different ways depending on context. Myers-Moro (1993, 102) has commented on the delight that Thai musicians take in classifying repertoire and on the variation between individual accounts. I have come across three different ways of categorizing the ritual repertoire: by level of sacredness (discussed further in the next section), by performance context, and by the type of action depicted.

Sangat (2532/1989, 216–19) divides up the ritual repertoire by performance context, noting a considerable overlap between these categories. His categories are as follows: those used in dance-drama (*khoon* and *lakhon*), the *wai khruu* ritual, the *tham khwan* or soul-tying ritual, the recitation of the *Mahaachaat* (the story of Prince Wetsundaun, i.e., the Gautama Buddha's penultimate life), and other rituals involving Buddhist monks. All of these rituals require certain ritual pieces at certain points in the event, as Sangat details.

Uthit (2530/1987, 107–21) broadly divides the ritual repertoire into two categories, pieces for dance-drama and pieces for the *wai khruu* ritual, and then categorizes the pieces for dance-drama by their dramatic function, as follows:

1. Pieces for uttering magical spells and formulas *(khaathaa)* and for changing shape.
2. Pieces for exerting magical power *(itthirit)*.
3. Pieces for the mustering of armies and their troops.
4. Pieces for coming, going, and for travel.
5. Pieces for eating and drinking.
6. Pieces for sleeping.
7. Pieces for bathing.
8. Pieces for expressing pride.
9. Pieces for laughter or happiness.
10. Pieces for sadness and sorrow.
11. Pieces that summon deities and various sacred things.
12. Pieces for dance-drama *(lakhon)* characters' important dance positions.
13. The highest *naa phaat* piece: *Ong Phra Phiraap*.

Uthit discusses category 11, the "pieces that summon deities and various sacred things," in great detail because it includes a large number of pieces, essentially those used in the *wai khruu* ritual. Uthit doesn't enumerate them all, but instead explains why *Saathukaan* and all the pieces beginning with the word *Tra* are so important.

All performers, Uthit says, whether dancers or musicians, raise their hands and *wai* whenever they hear *Saathukaan*, because this piece invites the Triple Gem and "the many sacred things" into any ritual, so they can sit and listen to the prayers or sermons. There are two versions of *Saathukaan:* *Saathukaan Thammada* (the "normal" *Saathukaan*) and *Saathukaan Klaung* (*klaung* = "drum"), which is performed only in the *wai khruu* ritual for music. Uthit says that musicians who study *piiphaat* instruments must learn *Saathukaan* first, usually on the gong circle, because the piece contains the motives (Uthit says "notes," *luuk*) used in many other pieces; once *Saathukaan* is learned, all other pieces come more easily. Most importantly, *Saathukaan* is an extremely sacred piece, and most teachers feel that it should be learned first for that reason if no other.[6]

Uthit writes that *Luang* Pradit Phairau told him the story of *Saathukaan's* origin as follows: Shiva once challenged the Buddha to see who was the greater, saying that he would go hide somewhere in the universe and daring the Buddha to find him. He made himself into a grain of dust and hid himself on the floor of the ocean (literally, "the navel of the ocean"), but the Buddha, who sees all, quickly found him. When it was the Buddha's turn to hide, he also turned himself into a grain of dust, but then hid on top of Shiva's head. Shiva looked for him everywhere but couldn't find him, never thinking to look on top of his own head. He searched the universe but finally had to admit defeat. When the Buddha told him where he was, Shiva was extremely vexed and spoke sharply, telling him to come down. The Buddha refused to descend, saying that Shiva should speak more politely. Shiva realized he would have to comply, and therefore arranged for heavenly music to be played, inviting the Buddha to come down. The ensemble of divine musicians played *Saathukaan*, which has been considered sacred ever since, played to solicit the presence of the Buddha's auspiciousness and the many sacred things.[7]

Uthit also discusses the many pieces whose names begin with the word *Tra*, noting that performers *wai*, just as for *Saathukaan*, when they hear them played.[8] All *Tra* pieces, he says, are auspicious and should cause performers to think of their teachers—in fact, musicians' hair is likely to "stand on end" when they hear them, and some are struck by a feeling of intense joy that is "impossible to describe." All these pieces are from the "high level" of the ritual repertoire. *Tra Choen*, for instance, is performed to invite the high gods *(theewadaa chan phuu yai)* into the ritual; when one of Rama VI's compositions is to be performed, a special offering table is arranged and *Tra Choen* is played to invite him to come down and listen.

Performance Practice

Ritual pieces often have a distinctive sound in performance because they are the only repertoire for which *piiphaat* musicians use hard mallets. Unlike the soft, cloth-padded mallets used in the *mahoorii* ensemble, the harder mallets used in ritual and (sometimes) dance-drama contexts have a loud, brilliant sound. The xylophone mallets for this kind of playing are not padded at all, but end in small lumps of a hard, black, lacquerlike substance; quite light, they allow a musician to play extremely quickly. The gong circle mallets are of hardened leather, without the layers of cotton cloth padding that characterize the mallets used for *seephaa mahoorii* music. Hard and soft mallet performance is referred to as just that: literally "hard-" and "soft-" mallet *piiphaat* (*piiphaat mai khaeng* and *piiphaat mai nuam*).

The *rua*, a short free-meter piece played at the end of each featured piece (or at the end of a string of connected pieces), is in many ways the musical enactment of a *wai*. *Rua* are anomalous in the ritual repertoire. They are not usually included in any of the various organizational schemes for categories of ritual pieces, and they are the only free-meter pieces I am aware of in either the ritual or *seephaa mahoorii* repertoires. In performance, the xylophone player leads and the other musicians follow, with everyone arriving together at the ends of phrases.

There are two different kinds of *rua*, one whose form is in three sections (*Rua Saam Laa*) and another of a single section (*Rua Laa Dieo*). Their motives are closely related.[9] The *rua* made up of only one section (*Rua Laa Dieo*) is shorter and played in dance-drama performance when a character prostrates (*kraap*) him or herself to a superior, usually before leaving the stage. In the *wai khruu* ritual, this same short piece is played near the end of almost every piece or set of pieces to express respect to the deity or deities who have just arrived during the preceding piece. The *rua* in three sections (*Rua Saam Laa*) has a slightly different significance. Uthit (2530/1987, 109) writes that this *rua* is an expression of ferocious magical power (*itthirit*). It is used in masked dance-drama, for instance, when the monkey Sukhrip pulls up trees or when Hanuman yawns out stars. Trying to describe the sound of the piece, Uthit says that "it stops, it turns on itself, it steps on its own feet." This *rua* is used only twice during the *wai khruu* ritual: once during the *Evening Overture* (described below), after the piece *Tra Hoomroong;* and as a coda to the most sacred and dangerous piece in the ritual repertoire, *Ong Phra Phiraap.*

While the various *rua* are a mandatory coda to all the pieces performed in the *wai khruu*, other aspects of performance practice are more flexible. The lead musician in the *piiphaat* ensemble—that is, the xylophone player —constantly makes decisions during the ritual, deciding how long to play each piece (i.e., how many repeats to take) by keeping an eye on other activities (such as passing out incense or cutting up the food offerings). If the ritual starts late, the xylophone player may make each piece as short as possible in order to end, as the ritual must, before 11:00 A.M. Musicians speak of how they can *tii tat* a piece, "striking/playing and cutting" it, or sometimes of *tii khrüng*, "striking/playing it in half": both are ways of shortening pieces by not taking repeats. In any of the *Choet* pieces, the xylophone player decides exactly how many different short sections (*tua*, "bodies") to include (which can be anywhere from ten to over thirty). Some pieces, however, are less flexible. *Chamnaan* must be played twice, for instance. *Tra Hoomroong* and a number of other pieces cannot be shortened or the drum patterns won't fit correctly. I once asked my teacher Nikorn why officiants always asked their *piiphaat* ensemble to play *Ong Phra Phiraap* by calling out, "*Phra Phiraap Tem Ong!*" or "*Phra* Phiraap, the whole deity." Nikorn explained that asking for "the whole deity" meant that the entire piece should be played without any shortcuts or omissions. In the past, he said, it was possible to play a shortened version, called *Khün Ong* or *Ong Lek* ("the beginning of the deity" or "the small deity"), but no one shortens it anymore—in fact, he wasn't even sure how to play it this way.

Nikorn also had firm opinions about the appropriate manner for playing ritual pieces. Because they are "high" or sacred pieces, he said they should be played plainly or neatly *(riap)*, without the grace notes or little flourishes (*sabat* and *khayii*) that musicians can spontaneously add on. To perform them otherwise, he felt, was "dirty" *(sokkabrok)*. Even more importantly, he said, all ritual pieces should be played confidently and correctly: these are not works through which a musician should attempt to "feel" his or her way or to guess at. Nikorn's comments were yet another expression of musicians' beliefs that these pieces delineate powerful actions and that to complete these actions incorrectly or inadequately was to court disaster.

How the ritual pieces are played in the ritual, for how long, and in what manner are matters of great concern and interest to *piiphaat* musicians like Nikorn. But not all Thai musicians are empowered to play the ritual repertoire: *who* can play these pieces is as much a matter of performance practice as how they are played.

The Hierarchy of the Ritual Repertoire:
Secrecy and Initiation

The ritual repertoire is a closed, hierarchical system defined by ritual initiation. It contains five levels, each holding a successively smaller number of musicians. Most performers are never initiated any further than the first, most basic level; only those who will specialize in dance-drama accompaniment go on and are gradually initiated into increasingly powerful levels of repertoire. Competence in all five levels of the *naa phaat* repertoire also defines which musicians will be officiants: only those who undergo another initiation after achieving the fifth level of repertoire can lead the *wai khruu* and "covering" rituals.

Sangat (2532/1989, 215) recognizes three hierarchical levels rather than five. The "ordinary" or "common" ritual pieces *(naa phaat saaman)*, he says, are those used for ordinary characters such as lower-status monkeys and demons; pieces used for characters like these include *Samoe Thammaadaa*, all the "ethnic" *Samoe, Choet, Kraao Nauk, Kraao Nai, Ot, Laa, Pathom,* and so on. The "midlevel" ritual pieces *(naa phaat chan klaang)*, he says, are used for higher-ranking characters such as kings and various deities; such pieces include *Hau, Samoe Man, Samoe Theen, Tra Baungkan, Chamnaan, Tra Naun, Tra Nimit, Khuk Phaat, Tra Banthom Phraai, Tra Banthom Sin, Klom, Phraahm Khao, Phraahm Auk,* and so on. Finally, the "high-level" ritual pieces *(naa phaat chan suung)* depict high sacred beings like *Phra* Phiraap and *Phra* Parakhonthap. Here he lists many of the pieces used in the *wai khruu* ritual, noting that *Ong Phra Phiraap* is the most sacred piece of all. In short, Sangat sees the ritual repertoire as a reflection of social hierarchy, as seen through the mythic frame of the *Ramakien:* pieces depicting nonaristocratic beings (whether human, animal, or demonic) are at the lowest level, with an ascending hierarchy of pieces for rulers and then deities.

Montri Tramote (2527/1984, 124–25) has described the five levels of repertoire as a sacred hierarchy, noting that each new level is opened up to a student only after an initiation ritual:

1. *The first level is an abbreviated "covering" (initiation).* The student takes flowers, incense, a candle, and a designated amount of money to the teacher, who grasps the student's hands and plays the gong circle, playing the beginning of *Saathukaan* three times. When this is done, the student can then begin the study of *piiphaat* instruments, usually by learning the rest of *Saathukaan* (whether from the same teacher or someone else). The *Evening Overture* should then be learned, with the exception of the piece *Tra Hoomroong;* the teacher may teach other pieces as well.

2. *Being "covered" for the second level.* When the student has finished learning the *Evening Overture,* he or she can then learn the piece *Tra Hoomroong,* which was left out [of the *Overture*] at first. The teacher grasps the student's hands over the gong circle and plays the beginning of *Tra Hoomroong* three times.

3. *Being "covered" for the third level.* The student begins to learn the *Daytime Overture:* the teacher grasps the student's hands and plays the piece *Kra Baungkan.*

4. *The fourth level.* The student begins to study the high-level ritual pieces. For this level, the teacher grasps the student's hands and plays the piece *Baatsakuunii.*

5. *The fifth level.* The student begins to study the piece *Ong Phra Phiraap,* considered the highest piece of all.

The ritual of "grasping the hands" *(cap müü)* was described in Chapter 2, when *Khruu* Chüa initiated most of the seniors in the music department at Prasanmit into the fourth level of the repertoire by having them play the first phrase of *Baatsakuunii* on the gong circle.

Each successive level is thus opened up to a student through a certain piece: first *Saathukaan,* then *Tra Hoomroong,* then *Kra Baungkan* (sometimes called *Tra Baungkan*), then *Baatsakuunii,* and, finally, *Ong Phra Phiraap.* Between each level and each initiation, the student must learn and memorize a certain portion of the ritual repertoire before advancing further. Because of the highly sacred nature of such pieces, a teacher must consider the personal qualities of a student before passing the pieces on: Are they virtuous and disciplined? Do they have the ability to "preserve" *(raksaa)* the melodies or the dance movements correctly? If a student meets these basic requirements, he or she then goes through the ritual of "grasping the hands" *(phithii cap müü)* before learning the pieces, as described in Chapter 2. The first three levels of the repertoire are defined by three overtures (the *Evening, Morning,* and *Daytime* overtures), so it is important to pause here and take a closer look at the ritual and metaphoric role of the overture.

Threshold to the Sacred:
The Overture and the First and Second
Levels of the Ritual Repertoire

The concept of the *Hoomroong* or overture is central to the ritual repertoire, exemplifying the potential power of Thai music and dance. Three overtures are at the heart of the ritual repertoire, named for the times of day they can be performed. The *Evening Overture,* or *Hoomroong Yen* (*Hoomroong* = "overture, prelude"; *yen* = "evening") is literally played at night, preceding evening performances[10] and night ritual events such as ceremonies involving monks' evening chants. The *Morning Overture (Hoomroong Chao)* and the *Daytime Overture (Hoomroong Klang Wan)* are used for daylight ritual and performance.

The *Evening Overture* is a special medley of pieces played at the beginning of many Hindu-Buddhist rituals.[11] It is the gateway to the specialized ritual repertoire. Rather than being an obscure piece of music known only to a few, however, it is part of the basic equipment for many rituals, and its sound has strong spiritual associations for most Thais.

Uthit (2530/1987, 101) wrote that the three ritual overtures invite the deities and other sacred beings to congregate in the area of a ritual or performance and to confer their blessings on the host, the guests, and the performing musicians. Montri Tramote describes the *Evening Overture* as being "like a gathering of deities reciting magical formulas" (2526/1983, 2). He adds that the *Evening Overture* has a meaning and import beyond other overtures—it is, he says, "the foundation" *(pen lak)*. This phrase, "the foundation," is frequently used by musicians when talking about the *Evening Overture*, though they rarely explain what it is the foundation of. Similarly, anthropologist Pranee Jearaditharporn writes that the "*Homrong yen*, or the evening prelude, seems to be the basis or standard for all other preludes" (1973, 75). In fact, a number of different kinds of evidence point to the *Evening Overture* as both the core of and the threshold to the specialized ritual repertoire.

Three important words with closely related meanings underscore the guiding metaphors behind this music. The word *hoom* (the first word in the compound word *hoomroong*) is of Sanskrit origin (Jit 2522/1979, 101) and is strongly associated with the Hindu-Brahman ritual of purificatory fire worship. In ancient Cambodia and Thailand, this ritual was (and continues to be) part of several royal ceremonies conducted by the Court Brahmins, a small group of ritual specialists who have for centuries maintained the non-Buddhist ceremonies surrounding kings.[12] A Khmer inscription from the ninth century describes King Yasovarman conducting a ritual called *kotihoma* that involved the worship of fire (Wales 1931, 59), and a ritual called *homa* (or *kralahoom*) is also part of the contemporary Thai ceremonies surrounding the King's coronation and New Year's rituals.[13]

This purificatory ritual is also performed in Cambodia. Sam-Ang Sam, a contemporary Khmer musician, writes, "The word *hom* . . . originated in a religious sacrifice to god by the Brahmins, in which milk is sprayed into the fire. It has since been commonly used to signify a religious sacrifice or offering" (1988, 267). *Hoom* thus implies ritual purification. *Roong* means "building" or "structure." The compound word *Hoomroong*, or "overture," then, suggests sacralizing an area, but doing so with sound rather than fire.[14]

The words *piiphaat* and *naa phaat* both contain the Sanskrit root *-phat*, defined by the dictionary as "*khrüang prakhoom*," or "instruments that *prakhoom*" (Manit 2528/1985, 666). In fact, both *-phaat* and *hoom* are associated with the word *prakhoom*, which means "(1) to blow, sound (a trumpet),

(2) to beat (a percussion instrument), (3) to herald (with drum-beat or fan-fare), (4) to play a prelude, and (5) to proclaim" (Haas 1964, 302). *Prakhoom* thus has a cluster of related meanings, including to proclaim or herald some-one with the wind and percussion instruments reserved for royal or divine beings.[15] Significantly, *prakhoom* is defined by the dictionary of the Royal Institute in terms of the word *hoom* (Manit 2528/1985, 554). The words *hoom*, *prakhoom*, and *-phaat* thus have meanings that converge on purifying a ritual area and heralding or introducing high sacred beings with instrumen-tal musical sound. This metaphor underlies the words *hoomroong*, *piiphaat*, and *naa phaat*.

Entering the Ritual Repertoire:
Learning *Saathukaan* and the *Evening Overture*

Learning to play the *Evening Overture* on the gong circle was one of the most important processes of my fieldwork. It gave me firsthand, musicianly knowledge of the ritual and *wai khruu* repertoire, and it deepened my rela-tionship with my teacher Nikorn. I had already spent a year learning stan-dard *seephaa mahoorii* pieces on the xylophone. When I began my second year of study in 1988, however, I asked whether I could work on the gong circle because this instrument plays the melodic framework *(thamnaung lak)* on which all other instruments' parts are based. Nikorn agreed, partly because he agreed with my reasoning and partly because the gong circle is his main instrument. (See figs. 4.1 and 4.2.) By studying this instrument, I learned special parts for the gong circle taught to Nikorn by *his* teacher. Also, I gained access to Nikorn's specialty, the ritual repertoire—as a gifted gong circle player, he is regularly invited to perform in *wai khruu* rituals and is well versed in its repertoire. Last but not least, all knowledge in Thailand is wedded to practice (Tambiah 1985, 121), so it was essential that I learn about the *wai khruu* repertoire as a musician and not as a by-stander.

I did not immediately begin learning the *Evening Overture*. Nikorn first taught me *Saathukaan*—a long and (no doubt for him) painful process due to my inexperience on the gong circle and the difficulties of the piece it-self. Unlike the lyrical, symmetrical *seephaa mahoorii* pieces I was used to, *Saathukaan* had asymmetrical phrases that doubled back on themselves at several points, providing ample opportunity for me to lose my way. It took me nearly a month of daily two- to three-hour lessons to learn the piece, phrase by phrase. Nikorn usually sat across from me at another gong circle, played a phrase several times, and then had me try it. When he was sure I had it right, he would leave me to practice it and go teach some other

Figure 4.1   Nikorn Chanthasorn playing the gong circle
(khaung wong yai) in 1987. Photograph by Deborah Wong.

student in the room. Five or ten minutes later, he would come back and ask
whether I'd memorized it yet, literally, whether I was "sure of it" *(maen)* yet.
If I said no, he went off and left me to practice some more; if I said yes, he
would listen to me play it, and then usually said, "Not yet—keep practicing." With that, he would go off once more, leaving me to play it another ten
or twenty times. When he was finally satisfied that I had mastered the new
phrase, he would sit down and say, "Okay, from the beginning." Once I began playing, of course, I often had trouble remembering the phrases that
preceded the one I had just learned. The lesson wasn't over until I could play
the day's new phrases as part of the piece, from the beginning. Learning was
therefore additive, and a slow process of refining technical skill, as well as an
exercise in memorization. Nothing was notated, because gong circle parts
are simply too much trouble.[16] Instead, Nikorn allowed me at the end of
each lesson to tape record myself playing what I had learned (he refused to
tape it for me, though, until the eve of my departure). Initially, I learned
much more slowly than the other music students, but otherwise, my lessons
were like theirs. They too were left to practice and memorize new parts at

Figure 4.2   Nikorn Chanthasorn playing the Mon gong circle *(khaung wong Mon)* at a funeral in 1994. Photograph by Deborah Wong.

their own pace, and the more motivated (or desperate) students also tape recorded what they were given in each lesson.

After *Saathukaan*, Nikorn taught me a short suite of four pieces, called *Tap Ton Phleeng Ching*. This is one of the shortest such suites (called *rüang*) in the ritual repertoire and is often taught to beginning *piiphaat* musicians. Some of its motives are the same as those in *Saathukaan*, and the suite encompasses many of the most basic motives found in ritual pieces, introducing many of the more basic techniques on the gong circle (i.e., how to alternate the right and left hands in certain figures, and so on). As the motives became familiar, I began to learn more quickly, and the format of our lessons gradually changed. Rather than show me a phrase on the gong circle, Nikorn would play a gong circle phrase on the xylophone, giving me several phrases in a row before leaving me to assimilate them on my own. When he had me play the pieces back from the beginning, he would play along—playing not the gong circle part but the xylophone part, to see whether I was really sure of myself or not. This also approximated real performance practice, where other instruments play different versions of the same melody.

Two months later, I had learned the suite to Nikorn's general satisfaction and then had a brief hiatus while he didn't start teaching me anything new but simply had me play my total repertoire (*Saathukaan* and the suite) for him every day, to ensure that they really had a secure foothold in my

memory. After some consideration, I asked Nikorn if he would next teach
me the *Evening Overture*. I knew by then that the *Evening Overture* was the
gateway to the rest of the ritual repertoire, but I was hesitant to appear over-
confident of my abilities. On the contrary, Nikorn was pleased and immediately said yes. For one thing, he said, the *Overture* was perhaps beyond my
present abilities, but he assured me that by the time I finished learning it,
it wouldn't be (and I couldn't argue with this logic). Also, he thought it was
an immensely important thing to learn and felt it was a terrible shame that
so few young musicians today learn it; worse still, those who learn it tend to
forget it all afterward.

It took me almost four months to learn the *Evening Overture*. Once
again, the learning process was slow and additive, but in the end, I was initiated into the second level of the ritual repertoire. The experience was invaluable, making the music of the *wai khruu* ritual comprehensible to me in
a new way and bringing me closer to an understanding of the ritual repertoire's performative nature.

The *Evening Overture* has from twelve to twenty pieces (depending on
how they are counted) and can take from eight to forty minutes to perform
(depending on how much time the musicians have). It can, in other words,
be expanded or contracted—the number of pieces included in the performance may be changed, and sections of pieces can be repeated if desired.
The *Overture* is always played without break; some of the pieces are elided
through short bridge passages, and others come to a stop with a brief pause
before the next piece begins. All these pieces are regularly used in dance-
drama, where they have similar meaning, but their order in the *Evening
Overture* creates a series of performative acts strung together to form a
bridge between two separate realms. It literally brings (or "invites") a series
of Hindu deities and divine beings from the sacred realm down to ours,
where they oversee and sacralize a performance or ritual event.

Nikorn taught me the pieces of the *Overture* in the order they occur,
as follows:[17]

1. *Saathukaan:* Symbolizes the worship of the Triple Gem of Buddhism,
   paying respect to and calling to mind the Great Teachers.
2. *Tra Hoomroong:* An invocation to the deities.
3. *Rua Saam Laa:* The concluding act of salutation.
4. *Khao Man:* The entry of the lower-status deities into the presence of
   the high Hindu gods—they inform the gods of the invitation from the
   human realm and ask them to descend and give their blessings to the
   impending performance.
5. *Pathom-Thai Khao Man:* Two movements that represent the gathering

of the procession that will accompany the high deities to the earthly performance. *Pathom* is a march, and *Thai Khao Man* is the "end" of *Khao Man.*

6. *Laa:* The conclusion of the gathering-together.
7. *Samoe:* The exit of the high deities from their celestial palaces.
8. *Rua Laa Dieo:* The departure of the deities from heaven to earth.
9. *Choet:* The high deities' processional journey to the human realm.
10. *Klom:* The arrival of the deities and the divine teachers of music and dance.
11. *Chamnaan:* The assembly of deities blesses the event about to take place.
12. *Kraao Nai:* The arrival of the highest, most sacred demon deity.
13. *Khao Man:* The entry of the lesser deities.
14. *Laa:* The conclusion of the invocation, indicating that the deities are now assembled.

Looking at the *Evening Overture* as a narrative, its actions describe a journey from the heavenly realm down to the human world. First, the event is framed as Buddhist with the high sacred piece called *Saathukaan.* Then (in pieces 4 through 6) the divinities assemble in the heavens—both greater and lesser deities as well as demons (who represent an additional kind of power necessary to most rituals). The deities then form a procession and depart from the heavens in pieces 7 through 9, traveling the long distance to the area of the imminent ceremony. The great Hindu deities Shiva and Narai (Vishnu) arrive with piece 10, *Klom,* and give their blessings to the event with *Chamnaan,* piece 11. Finally, the great demons arrive along with the lesser deities in pieces 12 and 13 (*Kraao Nai* and, once again, *Ton Khao Man*). The *Overture* concludes with the entire divine host assembled during the final piece, and it is believed that they stay for the entire event.[18]

Nikorn generally didn't explain the meaning of the pieces unless I asked, but once he realized I was interested, he had much to say about them. Sometimes, even outside of our lesson time, he would remember something about the *Overture* and tell me to write it down in my notebook. He stressed and restressed that he was teaching me the "correct" version of the *Evening Overture;* some teachers, he said, didn't have it right. He also explained that he was teaching me its shortest and simplest version, omitting many repeats and thereby avoiding multiple endings by teaching me only the bridges from one piece to another. When it came time to teach me *Choet,* he deliberated over how many of its short sections to include, finally deciding on twelve out of the thirty or so that he knew. During lessons, he sometimes showed me how a repeat could be taken but was careful not to "confuse" me, having me memorize only one way of playing it, without alternate renditions. He also made a point of explaining that the length of each piece wasn't important: it didn't really matter, he said, whether all repeats were taken or not—the *Overture* was equally efficacious whether played in its shortest or longest form. What *was* important was that all the right pieces were included.

Nikorn admitted, however, that he did bend custom a bit by teaching me *Tra Hoomroong*, the second piece in the *Overture*, in its correct order. Ordinarily, teachers omit *Tra Hoomroong* when teaching the *Overture*. When a student has finished learning all the other pieces in the *Evening Overture* and in the *Morning Overture* (which has just five pieces, all duplicated in the *Evening Overture*), she or he can then be initiated into the second level of the sacred repertoire. Once again, the student's hands are grasped by the teacher, but this time the student is led through the first phrase of *Tra Hoomroong*, the second piece in the *Evening Overture*. *Tra Hoomroong* means "the divine overture" and is a single piece, not a set of pieces like the *Evening Overture*. With *Tra Hoomroong*, the first level of the repertoire is completed, and the student has entered the second. *Tra Hoomroong* is the link between the two levels: a student cannot play the *Evening Overture* in its entirety until he or she has been initiated into this piece and the second level. Nikorn broke with tradition by teaching me the piece before I had been initiated, but he told me to be sure and be initiated for it as soon as I could—he knew, of course, that I was constantly attending *wai khruu* rituals, and that I had ample opportunity to correct this inconsistency. He was more concerned, he said, that I learn the entire *Overture*, and he wanted neither to waste our limited time together nor to confuse me by initially omitting the piece.[19]

That another piece called *Hoomroong* serves as an entryway into the next level of repertoire supports the broader metaphorical meaning of *hoomroong* suggested earlier—that is, it heralds closer proximity to the sacred. A musical phrase found in both *Saathukaan* and *Tra Hoomroong* underscores this iconic association. As I mentioned above, the pieces of the ritual repertoire are constructed out of a limited number of motives arranged in different ways. Learning the ritual repertoire becomes both easier and more difficult the more pieces a student learns: the basic motivic material quickly becomes familiar, but remembering its configuration in different pieces becomes more and more challenging. It is not unusual for a student to start out in one piece but end up in another by taking a wrong turn. The motive found near the beginning of both *Saathukaan* and *Tra Hoomroong* (as played on the gong circle) can be seen in fig. 4.3. Nikorn noted many times during my lessons

Figure 4.3   Musical motive found in both *Saathukaan* and *Tra Hoomroong*.
Rendered in Western notation by Deborah Wong.

that the beginning of *Tra Hoomroong* is exactly like *Saathukaan*, the trick is
to remember where the two pieces part ways.[20]

The use of musical frames for ritual events follows an intriguing pattern
of embedding: an important musical motive in *Tra Hoomroong* is embedded
in *Saathukaan*, and *Tra Hoomroong* is embedded in a set of pieces collectively
called *Hoomroong*. Yet another embedding emphasizes the *Evening Overture*'s function as a ritual frame. The entire *Evening Overture* is, in fact, inserted into the *wai khruu* ceremony, contradicting both parts of its name: it
is played not in the evening (since the ritual is always held in the morning)
and not as a prelude to the ceremony but rather sometime during the first
hour, after the ritual is well under way.[21] When played as part of the ritual,
the *Evening Overture* is simply referred to as *Hoomroong*, and it took me several months of my fieldwork to realize that this was the *Evening Overture* performed in its most abbreviated form. When I asked one ritual musician[22]
why it was inserted into the ritual, he said, "It invites the many sacred ones
to descend to the ceremony. Besides, it's the basis, the foundation. Sometimes the *Morning Overture* is played before the ceremony starts, but you
still have to have *the Hoomroong* later on."

Here there are frames within frames: usually used as a framing device,
the *Hoomroong* itself is framed within the *wai khruu* ritual as one of the chief
expressive and performative agents of the *piiphaat* ensemble and its repertoire. In this context, it is both causative (it brings the deities to the ritual)
and is itself given prominence as it transports the divine earthwards, highlighted in a ritual that pays homage to the music and dance of power.

The Third and Fourth Levels of
the Ritual Repertoire

The third level is defined by the *Daytime Overture (Hoomroong Klang Wan)*,
the longest of the three ritual overtures. The *Daytime Overture* was formerly
performed in the afternoon, after the midday lunch break at all-day performance or ritual events. When people heard the overture being played, they

knew the performance was about to start up again, and the overture also functioned to reassemble the deities who, like Buddhist monks, do not eat after noon and were assumed to have gone back to the heavens for their last meal of the day.

The *Daytime Overture* is quite long and is open to more variation than the *Evening* and *Morning Overtures*. It can contain at least fourteen or fifteen of the following pieces:

Kraao Nai
Samoe Khaam Samut
Choet
Laa
Kra Baungkan
Prooi Khao Tauk
Pluuk Ton Mai
Ruk Lon
Chai Rua
Phlae
Hau
Khuk Phaat
Phan Phiraap
Tra Sannibaat
Choet–Prathom–Rua
Baatsakuunii
Kraao Ram

While the *Daytime Overture* obviously overlaps with the *Evening* and *Morning Overtures* (e.g., *Kraao Nai, Choet*, and *Laa* are in all three), it also contains a number of pieces that are not in the other overtures but are part of the *wai khruu* repertoire. These pieces are all from the third or fourth level of the ritual repertoire and can be played only by performers who have been initiated into the proper level.

Just like the *Evening Overture*, the *Daytime Overture* contains a single piece from the level above it: *Baatsakuunii* initiates musicians into the fourth level of repertoire. Once again, part of a higher level is embedded in a lower-level overture and is also the key between the two. The fourth level of the ritual repertoire contains almost all the "high-level" sacred pieces whose names begin with the prefix *Tra*. All the pieces from this level are played in the *wai khruu* ritual; some are performed virtually *only* in the ritual, and rarely in dance-drama.

Piiphaat musicians of a surprisingly young age can attain the fourth level of repertoire. As described in Chapter 2, some of the seniors in the music department at Prasanmit were initiated into this level in their annual *wai khruu* ritual. Their average age was about twenty. These students were, of course, all studying *piiphaat* instruments and most had been musicians since childhood. For the young women, the initiation into the fourth level represented a ritual boundary: only men can be initiated into the fifth and highest level of the repertoire, as described below.

The Fifth Level of the Ritual Repertoire:
Ong Phra Phiraap

The highest level of the ritual repertoire, *Phleeng Ong Phra Phiraap*, is a single piece of unusual form and meter. The piece welcomes *Phra* Phiraap, one of the major deities of dance, into the *wai khruu* ritual. This piece alone *is* the highest level of the ritual repertoire *(phleeng naa phaat chan suung sut):* it is a category unto itself. Anyone who aspires to learn this piece must have the appropriate knowledge, ability, gender, age, and must have been "covered," or initiated, specifically for it. Furthermore, only officiants who have themselves been "covered" for *Ong Phra Phiraap* can call for its performance during a *wai khruu* ritual. Quite long—it can take up to twenty minutes to perform—the piece is sometimes referred to by musicians as a "set" of pieces *(chut)* rather than a single piece *(phleeng)*.

    Whereas *Saathukaan* is the piece transmitted to young students in the first, most basic initiation, *Phleeng Ong Phra Phiraap* is the last. Both are extremely sacred, but *Saathukaan* is theoretically known by all musicians, whereas *Phleeng Ong Phra Phiraap* can be played by very few indeed. Only men can perform (or be initiated to learn) it, and they must also be over thirty years old and have been ordained as a Buddhist monk sometime in the past. Although *piiphaat* musicians do not usually reminisce about their lower-level initiations, they often make a point of mentioning which teacher initiated them for *Ong Phra Phiraap* and which actually taught them the piece, since the two may not be the same. Nikorn's teacher, *Khruu* Saun Wongkhaung, was a *wai khruu* officiant, so Nikorn both "received" *(rap maup)* and then learned it from him. (See fig. 4.4.) Nikorn recalled that he was thirty-five years old when this happened and that he brought along two of his friends, also *piiphaat* musicians, who received the piece along with him.[23] They all refrained from drinking or from having sexual relations for the day before receiving the piece and then again for the day before and after learning it. *Khruu* Saun insisted, in the traditional manner, that Nikorn and his friends learn the piece in a single day, feeling it unsafe to sound the piece for too protracted a time.

    Ong Phra Phiraap—both the musical piece and the dance—is regarded

Figure 4.4   Nikorn Chanthasorn's photograph of his teacher, *Khruu* Saun
Wongkhaung, ca. 1950s.

with fear and respect by performers. If there is any question that the members of a *piiphaat* ensemble lack the skill to perform the piece, *Khuk Phaat* is substituted. *Ong Phra Phiraap* is simply a dangerous piece, and to play it badly is considered worse than not playing it at all. Letting loose *Phra* Phiraap's anger can bring about illness, accidents, or death. When the piece is performed during a *wai khruu* ritual, the participants sitting in the audience stop chatting and sit silently. The mood is both solemn and somewhat tense. During the large *wai khruu* ritual at Wat Phra Phireen described in Chapter 2, quite a number of audience participants fell into trance or were possessed by demonic deities while the piece was performed; there was a real sense that anything could happen and that dangerous forces had been unleashed.

Phra Phiraap is the demonic deity of masked dance-drama *(khoon)*. His mask is dark purple (or sometimes gold) and is used in the ritual of "covering." If the piece is danced, its performer wears a purple brocade *phaanung* (dhoti-like trousers) and is bare-chested except for a long flower garland; he carries a long spear and a branch of leaves. *Phra* Phiraap is a minor character in the *Ramakien*, and most performers admit that they don't know why he is of small significance in the epic yet so important in the pantheon of performers' deities. In the *Ramakien*, *Phra* Phiraap was born as a demon *(yak)* and sent down to earth to guard an orchard at the foot of a mountain until he could fight *Phra* Ram, be killed in battle, and thus be reborn. All of this occurs in a short episode that today is no longer performed in dance-drama. Although performers are not usually aware of it, most officiants know that *Phra* Phiraap is a fierce manifestation of Shiva called Bhairava in Indian mythology (Orawan 2531/1988; Mattani 1975b). This explains his preeminence in the cosmology of Thai performance: *Phra* Phiraap and the Old Father—the benevolent, ascetic manifestation of Shiva—represent complementary kinds of power.

The music for *Ong Phra Phiraap* has never (as far as I know) been in danger of dying out, but the dance nearly came to a dead end in the chain of transmission—at least in the minds of the performers at the Department of Fine Arts. The dance for *Ong Phra Phiraap* throws a spotlight on the presence of different genealogies of authority that have a vexed relationship in Bangkok, and the measures that performers at the Department of Fine Arts were willing to take suggests that, for them, the stakes are high. More than one line of transmission exists for *Ong Phra Phiraap*'s dance, but by the 1960s, only one dance teacher in the Department of Fine Arts, *Khruu* Rongphakdi (Cian Carucaun), was qualified to initiate and then teach it to students. To prevent its disappearance from the Department of Fine Arts dance repertoire, in 1963 King Rama IX arranged for him to confer the dance ritually on four master teachers in a royal ceremony—and then the king himself "covered" the four teachers, imbuing them with unimaginable auspiciousness and power (Panya Nittayasawan 2523/1980, 11).[24]

Meanwhile, the dance was alive and well outside the Department of Fine Arts. While the line of transmission through the former dancers of the royal court was imperiled, the ritual dance for *Ong Phra Phiraap* was still taught in other pedagogical lines. In 1989 I witnessed a dramatic performance of the dance as part of a *wai khruu* ritual at Wat Nok in Thonburi. The performer, a middle-aged dancer, was the friend and disciple of the officiant, *Khruu* Somyot Pobiamlot. *Khruu* Somyot told me that his versions of the ritual dances are older and "purer" than those known and taught at the Department of Fine Arts. Whether *Khruu* Somyot's or *Khruu* Rongphakdi's version is "more" authentic is obviously not the question, as it begs the entire matter of how authority is constructed and maintained—and by whom. *Khruu* Somyot studied with teachers from outside the court/Department of Fine Arts lineages—in fact, some of his teachers had connections to *likee* and thus to working-class performance. While *Khruu* Somyot and the performers at the Department of Fine Arts may have nothing but disdain for each other, the king's intervention established the Department of Fine Arts's version of the dance as *the* version, even if it could not do away with the presence of multiple versions. In short, the continued vitality of *Ong*

Phra Phiraap's dance points to real struggles over status and authority in the world of dance-drama.

Though only a small number of dancers learn the movements to accompany *Ong Phra Phiraap*, it appears that the music has never been in danger of disappearing. *Ong Phra Phiraap* is an important and necessary part of the *wai khruu* ritual, but it is now rarely danced—the sound of the piece alone is enough in most *wai khruu* rituals. *Ong Phra Phiraap* is the prime example of music wherein saying something is doing something: the piece is never notated and is completely unavailable on commercial recordings of the ritual repertoire because the forces summoned by the piece are simply unmanageable in any context except the *wai khruu*.

The Musicians Who Sound
the Ritual Repertoire

The hierarchical nature of the ritual repertoire ensures that only a minority of all musicians is equipped to perform in the *wai khruu* ritual and that they are all men. Nearly every town in Thailand probably has at least one musician qualified to play the *wai khruu* repertoire, but one group of *piiphaat* musicians in particular is famed for its strong, efficacious performances. The full-time professional musicians at the *Kaung Kan Sangkhiit*, or the Music Division of the Department of Fine Arts, are considered experts in the ritual repertoire. Almost entirely composed of men (aside from a few female singers), these musicians are organized into three "teams" that are assigned a busy schedule of royal rituals and dance-drama performances in the National Theater. In 1989, I saw these men perform constantly: at Wat Phra Kaew, where the King observes Buddhist holy days, at the funeral of the Supreme Patriarch, and at many other major events. When the National Theater troupe went on a two-month performance tour of Europe, one team was sent along. From June until August—the rainy season and the most intensive period of *wai khruu* ritual activity—these musicians are kept almost frantically busy. Whenever Montri or Silapi Tramote go to perform the ritual at the provincial branches of the Department of Fine Arts, a team is sent along with them. During my research, nearly every *wai khruu* ritual that I attended in Bangkok was accompanied by some combination of these musicians, whose names, personalities, and family histories became familiar to me. Virtually every single university or institution sponsoring a *wai khruu* ritual arranged for them to perform, and quite a large number of private sponsors did so as well.

Most of these musicians were in their early or mid-forties. They had known each other for decades because they all attended the Department of

Fine Arts's School of Dramatic Arts together: most (like Nikorn) entered the school at the elementary level, when they were about ten years old. Most were hired by the Division of Music even before they graduated and were later made into full civil servants (*khaaraachakaan*). A few, like Bunchuay Soowat, who now teaches at Chulalongkorn University, were later hired elsewhere. Some maintain part-time posts at other schools, like Manat Khaoplüüm, who taught at the Witthayalai Khruu Baan Somdet (Ban Somdet Teachers College). Some, like Suwat Orropakarit, an oboe player who performs almost nightly at a popular restaurant with Nikorn, do freelance playing after hours. Most, however, find that their performance schedule through the Department of Fine Arts fills all their time.

Nikorn is on the outer circle of this group of musicians. Although he attended the School of Dramatic Arts and is close friends with many of these men, he never graduated from the college-level division of the school, instead playing at restaurants for years and working as a banker by day. Eventually he went back to school and received his B.A. in music at Prasanmit, where he was then hired. His training as a *piiphaat* musician is the same as these other musicians', and he is sometimes invited to play with them in *wai khruu* rituals; when Prasanmit holds its annual *wai khruu* ritual in February, he arranges for his old classmates to come and performs with them. But Nikorn is now a full-time teacher, whereas his old friends are full-time performers.

Almost all these men come from families of musicians, many from outside Bangkok. Chaiya Thangmisri, one of the leading xylophone performers, grew up in Rachburi and was a disciple of *Khruu* Ruam Phrohmburi before attending the School of Dramatic Arts. Nikorn grew up in Nakhon Pathom and came to Bangkok when he was eleven years old; his father was a *piiphaat* musician. Many of the other men, like Phat Buathang, are the sons of famous musicians and officiants. The ritual repertoire and its belief system are basic to the lives of these men.

Their friendships with each other are probably their strongest relationships: they grew up together at the School of Dramatic Arts and continue, decades later, to spend most of their time together performing. Although most have families, I am sure they live up to the classic Thai women's complaint that performers don't make good husbands. Performers are often out all night performing, and many of the ritual contexts where they are needed (funerals, ordinations, etc.) are alcohol intensive. Some drink too much, as they readily admit or even criticize each other for behind their backs. On the other hand, alcohol sometimes stimulates brilliant performances at all-night events.

While some of these musicians have had problems with alcohol or family life, others walk a narrower path, especially as they move into middle age. When it comes to performing in *wai khruu* rituals, all are consistently serious and careful. Bunchuay Soowat has written a short essay, "The Characteristics of the Musicians Who Perform in the *Wai Khruu* Ceremony" (2532/1989), where he lays out the ideal behavior and background of such men. All *wai khruu* musicians, he writes,

- Should have been ordained as a monk in the past,
- Should have superior ability in *piiphaat* performance,
- Should be recognized by other musicians,
- Should have a "complete" knowledge of the ritual repertoire (including, of course, *Ong Phra Phiraap),*
- Should have good manners,
- Should observe the moral precepts and rules of the Dharma,
- Should serve as good role models for younger musicians, and
- Should have received permission from their teacher to perform in the *wai khruu* ceremony.

Furthermore, Bunchuay says, *wai khruu* musicians should always help out when asked: if invited to perform in a *wai khruu* ritual, they shouldn't refuse. They are also responsible for teaching the repertoire and making sure it is passed on. When preparing to perform in a *wai khruu* ritual, they should observe the Five Precepts for at least the day of the ritual, should review the repertoire beforehand (making mistakes during the ritual is felt to be inauspicious for the performer), and "should keep their ability up to standard and be on the watch for anything less than that." When the ritual is over, each performer should give alms to monks on the following day in order to make merit for the teachers who gave them their knowledge of the ritual repertoire.

The fifth level of repertoire may be the highest, but it is not the last possible initiation: those who are initiated beyond the fifth level are transformed into ritual officiants. While Bunchuay's code of conduct is probably an ideal many *piiphaat* musicians do not live up to, it is a way of life for the men who eventually become officiants. Their access to texts as well as music means that they command several kinds of powerful sound, as addressed below.

Conclusions: Sound, Secrecy, and Power

Most of the master teachers in Thailand are men and are in late middle age if not elderly. By master teachers I mean dancers or musicians whose performance skill, personal and moral qualities, and memory for repertoire have led to their investiture as *wai khruu* officiants. I spent a lot of time talking (and sometimes only trying to talk) with such men and was impressed more than once by their distance and silence. Their resistance to conversation has been well described by Paul Fuller, who says:

> When I have asked weathered and prestigious musicians about things so long regarded as secret, privileged, and valuable, there has often been nothing but a wink, occasionally even disgust. Such matters are not to be bandied about. They may be sold. Usually they will not be published. There may or may not be much to be learned, but it is often guarded well—from foreigners to a degree, but mostly from competing musicians and threatening youth. One can walk on the surface quite easily, and be helped by any and all. But attempts to sink freely to details of music practice, subtleties, motives, concepts, cognition—especially with experts of advanced age—may often be met in silence. . . . I am talking about deliberate protective concealment. (1983, 152–53)

The ritual music is not veiled in deceptions, nor is it ever performed in inappropriate ways or by the wrong people. As far as I know, there are no sorcerer's apprentices of Thai music who dare to delve into matters beyond their capabilities.[25] On the contrary, the sacred repertoire that is transmitted during initiation is not secret in and of itself. It is played quite publicly in virtually every *wai khruu* ritual, and most of the musicians who are initiated into it have grown up hearing the pieces played. Rather, the right to *perform* the pieces, and the act of being given the pieces in initiation is the mystery, and although officiants are willing to talk about the ritual actions that complete the transfer, they will not discuss what it is, exactly, that happens.

Officiants are particularly unwilling to discuss the spoken formulas that are their sole right. Sound, and the right to make sound, drives this system of power. For musicians and officiants, there are two kinds of sounds: musical pieces and auspicious spoken formulas, and both are cloaked in mystery. The ritual texts uttered in conjunction with the sound of the sacred musical pieces literally bring deities into the *wai khruu* ritual, and officiants alone can grant the right to *other* officiants to sound the words. These manuscripts are restricted to specialists because they detail the precise combination of music, dance, and words that will empower performers.

What I am suggesting is that, at a certain point, the command of music and the command of powerful language converge. Musicians cannot aspire to be officiants until they have completely mastered the ritual repertoire, and being an officiant is, in many ways, all about sound: sounding powerful texts (i.e., reading them aloud), instructing the *piiphaat* ensemble when and what to play, and empowering students to make sound—especially the ritual repertoire.

The ritual texts are sacred objects, kept on altars and untouchable except by officiants. They are also scripts for the *wai khruu* ritual—"how-to" books that explain how music, dance, incense, food offerings, and many other elements should be efficaciously combined. And they are full of prayer texts, texts of invocation and supplication that shift easily between a sacred language of the past (Pali) and the language of the present (central Thai). Across the world, prayer is often performed as the central and most important act in ritual processes: its sounds, settings, and occasions are almost always distinctive. The anthropologist Sam Gill has emphasized that the performance of prayer signals "a special frame of experience" that goes beyond the pragmatic messages conveyed in its words, evoking "a network of images related to sense experiences, moods, emotions, and values" (1987, 97).

Language and music are intimately related in Thai musicians' minds. When talking about playing the *seephaa mahoorii* repertoire, musicians say they *tii klaun*, or literally "strike/play poetry." The whole body of music called *phleeng phaasaa* or "language pieces" is built around the idea that foreign (i.e., non-Thai) musical styles can be rendered by Thai ensembles using musical "dialects" called *samniang*, a word that means "the sound of speech, pronunciation, accent."[26] Music is sometimes talked of as a kind of language, or even as *based* on language. Once again, Sangat (2532/1989, 211) has some intriguing ideas along these lines, seeing music and dance as a late development in the evolution of language. He posits that humans first communicated with gestures and facial expressions, then with spoken language, and then with written language, which in turn evolved into the "language of the arts" *(phaasaa thaang silapaa)*, including poetry, literature, music, and dance. In other words, Sangat posits that the expressive arts grew out of other forms of language.

The question remains, Why do the ritual texts have to be sounded—in other words, spoken aloud? And why are they paired with musical performance, another kind of powerful sound?

To answer these questions, I want to explore some parallels with the Balinese tradition of reading texts aloud in group gatherings. Called *pepaosan*, these get-togethers revolve around the performance and discussion of literary texts and, as Mary Zurbuchen writes, highlight "the cultural value of group literary enjoyment in Bali" (1987, 88). Held at rite-of-passage and temple rituals, as informal events between friends and neighbors, or as formal, invitational competitions between literati, these literary performances are founded on the premise that certain written texts are meant to be socially sounded and received.

Balinese poetry is read aloud at these gatherings but is far from the only kind of Southeast Asian text intended for oral rather than silent reading. In Southeast Asia, literacy was traditionally associated with the ability to read sacred texts (Tambiah 1968). A close relationship between education and Buddhism persists today in Thailand, where most public schools are still adjacent to temples. Sacred texts often represent a marriage of orality and literacy, meant not for silent contemplation but for performance aloud. Ritual texts, like those for monks' chants, are treated as respected if not sacred objects, but their potential is most fully realized when they are declaimed aloud. Most classical Southeast Asian literature, almost entirely poetry, was intended for recitation aloud. In short, reading in the West may be a solitary, silent process, but in much of Southeast Asia "'literature' implies group activity" (Zurbuchen 1987, 91).

Furthermore, reading aloud is generally a matter of verbal art, not a straightforward rendition of the words on the page. Reading can mean heightened speech, chant, or even singing, as well as a creative manipulation of the given words. Reading as a performance is thus of-the-moment, like all oral traditions: the way a text is rendered at a particular event by a particular reader is always unique and one-time-only. A text may be fixed, but its social realization is always ephemeral: "the text represented by the manuscript is only one element of the text as experienced" (Zurbuchen 1987, 87).

The Balinese *pepaosan* follows all these patterns. The poetry read aloud at these gatherings can be from mimeographed sheets of paper, or, more often, is contained in *lontar*s, oblong palm-leaf books much like traditional books in Thailand. The text is placed (just as in the Thai *wai khruu*) on a low table along with small offerings and burning incense, and the reader "reads" by singing the poetry aloud. A good reader has a beautiful voice and a sure command of the formulaic melodies and motives appropriate to the form, meter, and genre of the poetry.[27]

The reader, however, is only half the performance: a second performer, the "translator," sits nearby, delivering an impromptu commentary or translation of each phrase as it is read. The total effect is overlapping and multivocalic, with the translator beginning his version of the phrase before the reader has ended his. Although the reader sings, the translator comments in heightened speech. While the reader may be singing in old Balinese, the translator speaks in contemporary Balinese, expanding on the text in the language of the present. A good translator is thoughtful, analytical, and

knowledgeable about many texts. While it is possible for a translator to utter memorized, formulaic responses, spontaneous and eloquent commentary is most admired. In fact, the translator is the expert's role: students and
beginners often perform as the reader, with an older, experienced teacher
acting as the translator.

Text and readers thus have a remarkable relationship in the Balinese
pepaosan. As Zurbuchen says,

> The Balinese experience of literature is multi-sensory, participatory, com-
> munal, and socially integrative in nature. For the participant in pepaosan,
> literature is more a process than an object. The literary performer experi-
> ences the interweaving of reading, sounding, listening, speaking, and con-
> templation, while for other persons present there is an immediacy of both
> musical and verbal meanings. . . . For all, the enjoyment of verbal art does
> not suppose a cleavage between sight and sound; the learned language [i.e.,
> old Balinese], rather than cutting people off from the spoken word through
> the distance imposed by writing, promotes the unfolding of an aesthetic
> experience that goes beyond the formal bounds of the medium. (92)

I have gone into detail about the Balinese reading group because it bears
strong and meaningful family resemblances to the interaction of texts and
music in the *wai khruu* ritual. Just as the Balinese reader and translator create the totality of the literary performance together, each section of the officiant's ritual text is paired with a particular ritual musical piece. Text and
music essentially execute the same ritual action: bringing a deity from there
to here. Each section of the ritual text summons a different deity or group of
deities. The officiant reads a section aloud three times, with the participants
repeating each phrase after him. The officiant then calls out the name of the
ritual piece he wants the *piiphaat* ensemble to perform, and they immediately begin playing. For instance, the officiant and participants might together recite the text inviting *Phra* Parakhonthap, the deity of *piiphaat*
instruments, to descend from the heavens and join in the ritual, and the
piiphaat ensemble then plays the piece called *Tra Phra Parakhonthap*.

Some officiants add yet another level and precede sections of the ritual texts with spontaneous (not read) explanations of why the deity they are
about to summon is important. One officiant in particular, *Khruu* Somyot,
emphasized this didactic aspect of the ritual. Before summoning *Phra*
Phikhaneet (Ganesha), for instance, he offered the following comments
at a *wai khruu* I attended:[28] "Now we will invite *Phra* Phikaneet, the deity
of success. Those who will study music must worship him, and truly worship him, or you cannot meet with success. It is therefore necessary to

invite him, all of us together in this *wai khruu* today. Let's say the *Namo* together."

The multivocalic nature of the *wai khruu* ritual is, if anything, even more pronounced than in the Balinese *pepaosan*. When the officiant and participants recite the ritual texts together, the texts are sounded in a thick, overlapping manner, with repetitions upon repetitions since each section is sounded three times and each phrase of each section twice (first by the officiant and then by the participants). In ritual performance, the ritual texts are thus realized many times through many voices: their affective, efficacious form is the sum total of multiple soundings. The officiant's voice, on the other hand, is also multiple: he can "speak" the ritual texts or speak didactically in spontaneous asides.

But the crux of the question is why texts and music are paired, since they carry out essentially the same ritual actions. Each section of text invites a specific deity, and text alone can bring the deities into the ritual, without the help of music. In fact, it appears that the inclusion of live music in the *wai khruu* ritual for musicians is an early-twentieth-century addition. Several older musicians and officiants told me that they first remembered witnessing live music in a *wai khruu* at the home of *Luang* Pradit Phairau, who hosted one of the largest annual rituals in Bangkok during the 1930s and 1940s. The *wai khruu* for dance has apparently long included dance performance and thus the ritual music to accompany it; a ritual text from 1914 contains clear directions for which ritual pieces are to be performed, and at which points in the ritual event (Dhanit 2494/1951). Why would the *wai khruu* for dance include music and dance performance, but the one for music not? The performers and officiants I asked simply said they didn't know. I will take up issues of ritual change in Chapters 7 and 8, but it is worth noting here that dance offerings *(ram thawaai)* have an ancient history in mainland Southeast Asia (Cravath 1986; Catlin 1987); vow-releasing ritual performances (called *kae bon*) are one of the most common contexts for dance-drama and shadow theater performance (Grow 1991a; Paritta 1982).

The use of dance and music as a ritual offering aligns with the Thai tendency to make ritual multivocalic and redundant. Dance, as noted above, is the physical realization of music in space: dancers hold onto the notes "as onto a post." The interreferentiality of ritual music and dance is fundamental: dance can take place only to the music, and the music implies the dance. The ritual repertoire is, by definition, multimedia—as is ritual itself. Furthermore, music plays an important reiterative role in the contemporary *wai khruu* ritual, repeating ritual texts in a different medium in a redundant manner. The music is the counterpart of the texts, just as the ritual music and dance are analogous.

When I stress the importance of statement and restatement in the performance of Thai ritual, however, I do not mean that reiteration in different media creates equivalent gestures. Each piece of music is more than just a paraphrase of a text. The music and the sounded text are separate, distinct speech acts. As Zurbuchen says of the Balinese *pepaosan*, the two components are "not necessarily equivalent either semantically or in intent" (1989, 269). The Thai ritual music "says" things that may be related to language in the minds of Thai performers, but its medium is not words but powerful, percussive melodies: it says things that language cannot, by virtue of its medium. The relationship is parallel rather than equivalent, or—better still—the same ritual gesture is transformed into two kinds of sound. Finally, there is a point beyond which text and music must be regarded as a performative whole, because this is how contemporary participants in most *wai khruu* rituals experience them. Their totality in performance creates, as Zurbuchen said above, "the unfolding of an aesthetic experience" that emerges from the *combination* of sound media.

Finally, it is worth considering prayer in cross-cultural context. If uttered text and sounded music are related gestures in the *wai khruu*, it is still important to remember that the *performance* of these gestures is the point. Gill (1987, 110) has proposed at least three approaches to studying prayer: looking at prayer as a text (its words), as an act (its performance in specific contexts), and as a subject (cultural statements about its nature, efficacy, etc.). In Chapter 5, I look at the ritual texts as both text and subject; here I stress their performance. In his work on Native American prayer, Gill learned that the Navajo refer to prayer as "a person, indeed, a kind of holy person," related to the sacred beings who formerly inhabited the earth along with humans (126). As Gill writes, "Bridging the gap between the earth people and the holy people is a crucial element in Navajo ceremonial practices. This is accomplished by uttering prayers who are thought of as messengers who have unique communication and travel abilities" (126). Thai musicians do not speak of the ritual texts or the ritual pieces as beings—I am not attempting to collapse Thai and Navajo ritual practice. Nevertheless, the "sound equipment" of the *wai khruu* has a strikingly similar role: the ritual repertoire in performance is in many ways musical prayer—formulaic, summarizing and justifying the rest of the ritual, invoking and supplicating deities (Metcalf 1989, 4, 10).

Sounded discursively in the ritual, the ritual texts and the ritual pieces come together and create an ephemeral, efficacious path between the human

and sacred realms. The trope of power-transfer that underlies both is strin-
gently hierarchical and carefully restricted: officiants, and officiants alone,
can read the ritual texts and call for the performance of the ritual pieces in a
ritual context. Officiants *summon* the sounds of power, and do so with a sense
of responsibility and a flair for the dramatic that does much to create an
experience of the sacred for those who participate.

Five

Inscribing the *Wai Khruu* Ritual:
Two Written Accounts

I chose the two written accounts described below because of their contrast. The first is prescriptive, written by *Khruu* Akhom Saiyakhom, a famous teacher of *khoon* (masked dance-drama), as a guide to the ritual. I never met *Khruu* Akhom: he died in 1982, before I began my research. The second account is an actual sacred text, given to me by *Khruu* Nim Pho-iam. I was honored by *Khruu* Nim's trust in giving me a sacred text.

These documents represent a spectrum of performative power and possibilities. The two teachers' manuscripts are actual ritual scripts. Such written texts are the heart of the *wai khruu* ritual: called *bot oongkaan*, or *oongkaan* texts. During the ritual, an officiant reads the text aloud, and the participants repeat his phrases. As Jit Phumisak, a great Thai phonologist, noted, *oongkaan* is a Pali word that came from the Sanskrit word *om* (2524/1981, 1). *Om*, and *oongkaan* too, represent the sounded form of the sacred and come from the names of the three great Hindu gods—Shiva (*a*), Vishnu (*u*), and Brahma (*ma*)—combined into the word *aum*.[1] The oldest known such ritual text in Thailand is the *Oongkaan Chaeng Nam*, or the Water Oath, dated by Jit Phumisak to the fourteenth century A.D. (7). This text is an oath of fealty that was sworn to the king while pouring water.[2] *Oongkaan*, or ritual texts, of which there are many different kinds, usually summon Hindu deities to the site of a ritual.[3] They belong to a class of written texts meant to be uttered aloud but are powerful objects even in their silent, inscribed form.

The authority of any *wai khruu* officiant lies largely in his right to read and own ritual texts. One cannot be an officiant without access to such texts: becoming an officiant is literally called "receiving the *oongkaan* texts" or "receiving the right to read the *oongkaan* texts," and this right can be conferred only by another officiant. Many officiants receive such texts from more than one teacher, though usually from no more than three. Officiants are keenly interested in comparing texts, and many borrow and insert sections from different versions. Thongchai Phothyarom of the National Theater troupe referred to this process as "doing research" and related many anecdotes about long afternoons spent with a friend (another officiant) discussing the relative merits of different versions. A high premium is placed on old texts passed down from respected teachers, and many officiants will proudly claim to "read the texts" (i.e., read them aloud in a ritual context) exactly as a teacher of a previous generation did, though I suspect this is rarely true in a literal sense.

The books of *oongkaan* texts are sometimes called *tamraa* and sometimes *khamphii*. *Tamraa* literally means a textbook, reference book, or manual, and suggests a book full of formulas or prescriptions. *Khamphii* (from the Pali and Sanskrit *khamphir*) means a scripture, or a sacred text. The books themselves are often beautiful objects, usually handwritten in flowing, stylized script. In the old days they were made out of long sheets of palm leaf paper that were folded in accordion pleats and pierced with a string to hold the folds together (Kaungkaew 2530/1987). Such books still carry the associations of esoteric knowledge, coming as they do from the time before printing, when all texts were prized and valuable objects. Until the turn of the century, officiants' texts were often written in the Khmer-derived script called *Khaum* reserved for sacred texts and taught in the temples. This is now rare, though one teacher, *Khruu* Nim, was proud of his ability to write and read *Khaum* script, using it for certain powerful phrases. Some books of *oongkaan* texts are decorated with drawings of deities and most contain *yan* (Sanskrit *yantra*), in other words, powerful drawn symbols, at certain points. One teacher had a handsome book of black paper, written in white ink and decorated with Buddha images constructed entirely out of *yan*. Although most modern books of *oongkaan* texts are now made out of normal paper, the oblong shape is usually retained and the texts are still handwritten. The distinctive shape and handwritten script of traditional books are iconic of esoteric, nonpublic knowledge; such objects are necessarily treated with a respect not given to modern, printed books.[4]

The books of *oongkaan* texts are also objects of worship. They are usually kept on altars, carefully placed on a tray in front of the Old Father or a
Buddha image. It goes without saying that no one except officiants is allowed
to read them, though some officiants are less secretive than others. Montri
Tramote wouldn't let me see his at all, whereas *Momrachawong* Caruunsawat
showed me his book with pleasure, turning its pages so I could see the
beauty of the handwriting and even reading passages aloud to me. For some
teachers, the inherent power of the books' words calls for absolute secrecy;
for others, the books are objects of beauty and respect that can be shared,
though of course with care. I was never actually allowed to hold one, and
for me to sound the words (outside of a ritual context, where I would be following an officiant) was unimaginable.

Nevertheless, certain parts of these sacred texts are available for public
scrutiny—though what is omitted from them speaks volumes about where
their power lies. The two manuscripts described below illustrate a range of
choices made about secrecy, respect, and the importance of transmission.

A Prescriptive Text:
Khruu Akhom's Script for the Ritual

Toward the end of my fieldwork, two teachers[5] gave me a collection of
manuscripts that they said would help me in my research; among these was
a long photocopied excerpt (pages 63–80) from a book, essentially an officiant's script on how to perform the *wai khruu* ritual. One of the teachers
had written "of *Khruu* Akhom Saiyakhom" beside the heading "*wai khruu.*"
When I asked these two teachers for the source of the excerpt, they replied
that it was unfortunately unavailable, but I assume that the text is an attempt
by the Department of Fine Arts to preserve the "correct" way of conducting the *wai khruu* ritual.[6]

This text is a detailed outline of what an officiant should say and do at
each point of the ritual for dance. It contains everything from instructions
on when to light incense (and how many sticks) to long obscure passages
in Pali, written in the Thai alphabet but spelled out phonetically so that the
words can be uttered aloud. Although the pages given to me begin with
page 63—the opening of the actual *wai khruu* ritual—an incomplete section carried over from previous pages (not given to me) contains the tail end
of a description of the "ritual" of the celebrant dressing himself, with detailed instructions on how to wrap the cloth around the torso into trousers
and where magical verses *(khaathaa)* should be uttered (though these are
not supplied).

This manuscript is an important document because *Khruu* Akhom

Figure 5.1   *Khruu* Akhom Saiyakhom (1917–1982) leading a *wai khruu* ritual, probably at the College of Dramatic Arts in the 1960s.

Saiyakhom (1917–1982) was the great dance teacher of his generation. Until his sudden death at the age of sixty-five, he led the most important *wai khruu* rituals in Bangkok and beyond, including the ceremonies at the National Theater, the College of Dramatic Arts, and Wat Phra Phireen. (See fig. 5.1.)] During the last part of his life, he received the book of ritual texts for the royal *wai khruu* ritual from *Luang* Wilatwong-ngam, another great teacher. His name, "Akhom," was also given to him later in life, and means "*khaathaa*" or "*mantra*." His version of the *wai khruu* was considered powerful and authoritative, and it is thus not surprising that the Department of Fine Arts would want to preserve it. Another reason, even more compelling, is that *Khruu* Akhom died without having given any of his disciples the right to lead the *wai khruu* ritual: like the teachers of old, he had stringent standards in these matters. At the time of his death, he didn't feel that any of his students were yet worthy of the honor or responsibility.

This published text is thus an effort to keep *Khruu* Akhom's ritual knowledge and practice from disappearing. Though detailed, it is by no means a "complete" text: the strongest, most secret magical verses that give any *wai khruu* ritual its performative power are certainly missing, though some verses for more general knowledge are included.

The portion of the manuscript given to me opens with the heading "The Beginning of the *Wai Khruu* Ritual" and proceeds as follows:

> The teacher who acts as the leader of the ritual (dressed top to bottom in white) is assumed to be a Brahmin who observes the Precepts. He holds a conch shell and proceeds to the end of the white cloth placed on the floor. He turns and faces the altar and calls to the *piiphaat* ensemble to play the piece *Phraahm Khao* ["The Brahmin Enters"], and then dances into the ritual. At the end of the piece he turns in a circle and scatters water from the conch shell in a circle. . . . He then goes up and seats himself in front of the altar.

The next heading calls for the ritual's sponsor or leader (not the officiant, but someone of high status) to come light three candles and nine sticks of incense and then return to his or her place. In the margin beside this paragraph, Manat (one of the teachers who gave the manuscript to me) wrote in, "The *piiphaat* ensemble plays the piece *Saathukaan.*" The text continues:

> The officiant lights nine sticks of incense (or sometimes thirty-six sticks— equal to the amount of money designated as the disciples' ritual offering), prostrates himself three times, and begins to worship the Triple Gem and then the Assembled *Theewadaa.*

A text meant to be read aloud follows, under the heading "The Spoken Words for Worshipping the Triple Gem." Entirely in Pali, the three lines refer to the Buddha (*phutthang*), the Dharma (*thammang*), and the Sangha (*sangkhang*, the institution of the monkhood) as follows:

> *Arahang sammasamphuttho phakhawa phutthang phakhawantang*
> *   aphiwathemi*
> *Sawakkhato phakhawata thammo thammang namasatsami*
> *Supadipanno phakhawato sawakasangkho sangkhang namami*

The next heading is "The Assembled *Theewadaa,*" followed by a text also meant to be read aloud. The direction, "Utter the *Namo* three times," is given in italics. Extremely repetitive, the text beneath takes no shortcuts but writes out long, repeated phrases every time they occur: five groups of deities are invited in five different stanzas, but each is preceded by a long phrase, invoking the Triple Gem of Buddhism as follows:

> Come, oh come, Lord Buddha, come; Come, oh come, Lord Dharma, come; Come, oh come, Lord Sangha, come; hermits, come, come. . . .

This phrase is followed each time by specific invitations to *Phra* Pharühat, "the Lord of the Nineteen Deities," *Phra* Siwali, "the Lord of the Nine Deities," *Phra* Rahu, "the Lord of the Twelve Great Deities," *Phra* Ket,[7] "the Lord of the Nine Great Deities," and finally "*Luang Phau*[8] Phumiphol Adulyadet" (i.e., King Rama IX, the present king), followed by "the magnificent bones of the Buddha who attained enlightenment by himself, come, come, all the Great Deities, please descend."

A long, two-page magical verse follows, entirely in Pali and called the *Itipisoo Ruan Tia*,[9] punctuated by the lighting of incense and two recitations of the *Namo*. Long instructions for sacralizing the basin of water come next, with directions for the officiant to attach a candle to the basin's lip and then to have the *piiphaat* play the pieces *Tra Theewa Prasit* and the *Hoomroong* (or, if preferred, just the *Hoomroong*). Five Pali texts follow, including the *Thooranii Saan Lek* (a special ritual text for sacralizing water), the *Itipisoo* for the Eight Sides, texts for the Lords of the Ten Directions and the Arahants of the Eight Directions, and a final set of purificatory texts (called *Phra Chinpanchaun*).

Next is an invocation and summons to the Assembled Deities, each of whom is called by name. The list is long indeed, and includes (of course) the Triple Gem, a number of sacred Buddhist objects and principles (the Rules of Conduct, the sacred *bodhi* tree, the Buddha's parents, etc.), Hindu deities (Isuan, Narai, Lakshmi, Indra, Brahma, Thorani, Khongkha [the Ganges], Mount Sumeru, the garuda [a magical bird and the steed of Vishnu], the *naga* or magical serpent, various *singha* or magical lions, etc.), characters from the *Ramakien* (Phiraap, Sukhriip, Hanuman, Ongkhot, Rama, Laksmana, Phipheek, Sadayu, Kumphakan, the *kinnarii* and *kinnaun* [magical creatures that are part-human, part-bird], Inthaurachit, Ramasuun, etc.), the deities of the air, the deities of the various levels of heaven (Daowadung, Dusit, etc.), the deities of the sixteen celestial mansions, and so on. The list is long and esoteric and slips into Pali near the end. After a recitation of the *Namo*, the officiant invokes and invites the teachers of *manooraa*—an ancient southern form of dance-drama—and then prostrates himself three times.

The next section is called "Inviting the Teacher to Enter Yourself." It begins with a recitation of the *Namo*. The officiant then invokes the Triple Gem and invites Isuan to come down and be his left eye, Narai his right, Khongkha his saliva, Phai his breath, the *naga* king his necklace, and Kala his heart. He then thanks them for this auspiciousness. After reciting this three times, he prostrates himself thrice and recites the *Namo*. Two verses in Pali follow, with instructions to recite the last verse twice normally and then a third time "as a melody," in other words, in a heightened style of chant closer to singing. The officiant prostrates himself three times and this ends the section.

The next section is addressed more particularly to the teachers of dance, music, and crafts. After reciting the *Namo* and invoking the Triple Gem, the officiant invokes the many teachers: those that are *theep* or minor deities, and those that live in the forests, mountains, or indeed anywhere—he invites them all, emphasizing that he wants none left out. After some short phrases in Pali, he calls for the *piiphaat* ensemble to play *Saathukaan Klaung, Tra Narai Banthomsin,* and *Klom,* followed by more Pali phrases and then the piece *Khuk Phaat.* After another recitation of the *Namo* and a magical verse in Pali, the officiant invokes *Phra* Wisanuukaam (Vishnu) as the great creator of instruments and things of the earth; *Phra* Pancasingkhaun, the player of the *phin* and *bandau;*[10] and *Phra* Parakhonthap, the "old teacher." He also calls on the 108 hermits to bestow their blessings and protect all present from sorrow, illness, and misfortune. Following an invocation in Pali to *Phra* Parakhonthap, the officiant calls for a series of pieces to be played one after the other: *Tra Phra Parakhonthap, Samoe Saam Laa, Hau, Khom Wian, Phleeng Chaa–Phleeng Reo, Phlae,* and *Lo.*

Once the officiant has again recited the *Namo* and invoked the Triple Gem, a series of Pali phrases invite several important hermits (*Phra* Pharataya [Bharata], *Phra* Narot, *Phra* Rüsii Kalaikot, and *Phra* Khobut) and, finally, King Rama VI himself, addressed as "*Phau Cao,*" or "Great Father." Another series of musical pieces follow—*Kraao Nauk, Ruk Lon–Samoe Khaam Samut, Baatsakuunii, Damnoen Phraahm, Kraao Nai, Samoe Man,* and *Samoe Phii*—and then the important texts for *Phra* Phiraap begin.

Boldface letters instruct the officiant to have the "disciples" light incense and candles to worship *Phra* Phiraap, and then to recite the *Namo* once again. Unlike the texts for the other deities, the ritual text for *Phra* Phiraap contains numerous internal repetitions, most built around the Triple Gem and all in Pali; *Phra* Phiraap's name is also invoked many times, though he is summoned as "Ong *Phra* Phirathang," the Pali form of his name. This long text is followed by the pieces *Phra Phiraap Tem Ong* and *Tra Sannibaat.*

A series of prose instructions comes next, directing the officiant to put on the mask (literally "invite on the head") of *Phra* Pharot and then dance into the "circle" (*monthon,* from Sanskrit, *mandala*) of the ritual along the path of white cloth, accompanied by the piece *Samoe Then.* The text then tells him to ask the gathered participants, "Are you disciples, old and new, quite ready?" The disciples are to answer, "We are ready," and, the text says, "from that moment the officiant is assumed to be *Phra* Pharotrüsii." He goes and sits in front of the ritual area, takes or "invites" the mask off his head, and invites the many deities and "magical ones" to descend onto a tray; water is poured over them from the conch shell, and the ritual's sponsor comes up to pour water as well, followed by other teachers and disciples. As this goes on, the officiant is to recite magical verses and call for the piece *Long Song.* Further instructions direct him to invite the deities *(theepacao),* the *theewadaa,* the teachers of *khoon* and *lakhon,* the teachers of music, the teachers of crafts, the teachers of the many arts, deceased teachers, the deity of the city, and the deity of Siam to remain in the prepared area of the ritual. He then calls for the piece *Samoe Khao Thii.*

The next set of instructions tells the officiant to have all the disciples take up the food offerings, and he then dances, presenting the offerings to the deities, accompanied by the piece *Thawaai Khrüang.* The instructions then tell the officiant to have the offerings returned to their places but turned toward the altar, with each piece of fruit cut so that its flesh can be seen and the alcohol poured out into glasses. The manuscript then returns to text meant to be read aloud, beginning with another recitation of the *Namo* and an invocation to the Triple Gem. Then the officiant says:

> We would now like to present the food offerings: alcohol, rice, main courses, and sweets, raw and cooked, along with many kinds of fruit. We would like the deities and all things sacred to accept our offerings and to partake of them. May it be auspicious and perfect in every way.

Some phrases in Pali reiterate these requests, followed by the musical pieces *Nang Kin* and *Sen Lao* ["Sitting and Eating" and "Drinking Liquor"]. A "footnote" adds that

> If there is to be a circumambulation with candles *(wian thian),* the circle can be formed at this point.

The next heading directs the officiant to perform the ritual of "covering" and of conferring ritual rights. The directions continue:

> Put on the mask of *Phra* Pharot and dance *Samoe Saam Laa,* and then go sit on the large, overturned basin *(sip saung naksat).* (If there isn't such a basin, you can go back to your seat before the altar.) The ritual of "covering" begins at this point. The disciples who will be "covered" should be ready with offering bowls, which they should present to the teacher. You should "cover" them with the masks of *Phra* Pharot, *Phra* Phiraap, and the *soet* headdress, and then sprinkle them with sacralized water and anoint their foreheads, covering them with auspiciousness. Do this for each disciple until all who want to have been "covered." If a disciple is about to

end his or her study with you (literally "go out from you"), you can confer the arrow, the double-bladed knife, the club, the trident, the discus, and
the mace,[11] giving them permission and the right to be a teacher themselves. While this is going on, the pieces *Mahaarit* and *Mahaachai* should
be played. After this should be the *Ram Thawaai Müü* ["Offering of the
Hands"], or the conferral of ritual dances—for refined heroes and heroines, demons, and monkeys—on the disciples.

The officiant is then directed to go up to the altar and begin leading the
dance in which popped rice is cast as a blessing, with the disciples following
him; he should call for the piece *Prooi Khao Tauk* to accompany this. The instructions tell him to put on the mask of *Phra* Pharot and to stand, uttering
a blessing that confers good results and enlightenment, release from failure,
the seven-storied celestial mansion of diamonds, and riches; he asks that the
Lord Buddha help lead everyone, and that the Dharma be the lord of their
legs and descend into their hands—into all of his disciples, every one. The
instructions go on:

> From there, dance *Phraahm Auk* ["The Brahmin Leaves"]: turn and dance,
> leaving the ritual area following the path of white cloth, as the *piiphaat* en-
> semble plays *Phraahm Auk* and *Phra Cao Loi Thaat*. Then stand and lead
> the disciples in dance, calling for the pieces *Kraao Ram* (to send the teach-
> ers out) and *Choet*. Bid farewell to the food offerings and invite the *theep* and
> teachers to depart.
>
> This ends the *wai khruu* and "covering" rituals.

A final, pragmatic "footnote" adds:

> When calling for the ritual pieces, you can add to or delete some pieces in
> order to fit the time.

To summarize, this is a remarkable example of a private text made
public. Although it is esoteric and meant to be read and performed by a select few, the Department of Fine Arts evidently decided that its preservation and transmission was more important than the power of its silence. I
even suspect that this text and Dhanit Yupho's collection (2494/1951) of
wai khruu texts were the ones in question when a university music major at
Prasanmit noted in her thesis that "another view . . . is that the texts should
not be disseminated and published in various books," in other words, in the
eyes of some teachers, public dissemination was akin to disrespect (Sombat
2532/1989). The most powerful magical verses are certainly missing from
this text as published, so *Khruu* Akhom's deepest secrets remain a mystery.
All the same, this manuscript is the closest thing to an actual *wai khruu* text

that a nonofficiant would ever be allowed to study in detail. If I have erred
in including it here, I must ask forgiveness.

Khruu Nim Pho-iam's Lesser Ritual Text

Khruu Nim was essentially a contemporary hermit. He was probably born
in 1907,[12] and in 1949, after working as a policeman and performing in
likee, he decided to live the life of an ascetic. He retreated to Wat Phra
Phireen and pledged to follow the Eight Precepts: after that, he always
dressed completely in white, slept on a hard bed, and was celibate. He spent
his days in worship, but when he was not performing his private daily *wai
khruu*, he did woodwork and carpentry and committed his ritual knowledge to paper.

  Khruu Nim told me that he always enjoyed writing, even though he
stopped going to school after the equivalent of the fourth grade. As he saw
it, preserving what he had learned from other teachers was of paramount
importance. A cupboard near his simple bed was full of his handwritten
essays on the cosmology and sacred world of music and dance. All of these
manuscripts were titled "A Commemorative Book, Written before Death"
(*Anusaun kaun Taai*). *Anusaun* are commemorative books that usually honor
someone recently deceased and are often collections of essays by the students, family, and friends of the honoree; they are a kind of *festschrift* distributed at the person's funeral (Olson 1991b). That *Khruu* Nim planned a
commemorative book *before* dying, and wrote it himself, was unusual to say
the least—but completely in character. He felt strongly that the *wai khruu*
and the entire belief system surrounding teachers and their ascendancy was
too important, too essential, to be left in the hands of a few, or in fact to be
known to only a few. Writing down what he knew was, for him, an act of worship, and he clearly regarded the growing pile of papers in his cupboard as
a body of knowledge that should be assembled into a book upon his death.

  I visited *Khruu* Nim at Wat Phra Phireen every few weeks during 1988
and 1989 and had many long conversations with him about the hermits and
deities of music and dance. He occasionally gave me bits of his writing that
he thought would help answer my questions—sometimes photocopies of
his handwritten manuscripts and sometimes the originals. He knew that I
would be writing my dissertation on the *wai khruu*, and when he gave me
the text described below, he said I should include it if I could because it was
the "basic" ritual text.

  The manuscript (Nim 2530/1987b) consists of three photocopied
pages (8½″ × 14″) completely covered with *Khruu* Nim's handwriting (see

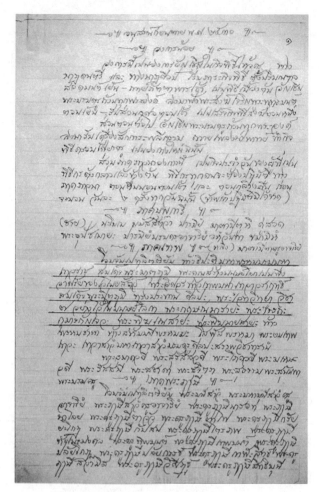

Figure 5.2   The first page of *Khruu* Nim's "A Commemorative Book, Written before Death, B.E. 2530," containing the *"Oongkaan Noi,"* or "Lesser Ritual Text." Slide by Deborah Wong.

figs. 5.2, 5.3, and 5.4). The title, "A Commemorative Book, Written before Death, B.E. 2530" (*B.E.* refers to "Buddhist Era"; B.E. 2530 is thus A.D. 1987), is followed by the heading, *"Oongkaan Noi,"* or "Lesser *Oongkaan.*" Both headings are bracketed with *unalom*s, a symbol that represents the word *om*, often placed near a mark to indicate its power and sacredness (Terwiel 1979, 88). The first three paragraphs explain the meaning and use of the text as follows:

> This ritual text is an invitation to the *wai khruu* ritual for *likee*[13] and
> dance. The ritual begins with the Evening Chant *(suatmon yen)* and the

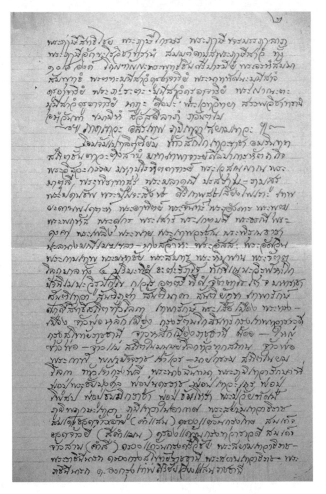

Figure 5.3 The second page of *Khruu* Nim's "A Commemorative Book."
Slide by Deborah Wong.

morning offering of food; these rituals are the preliminaries to inviting all
the great divine teachers. They come down and listen to the monks chanting the evening prayers, and receive their teachings in the morning. This
ends the monks' part of the ritual.

After this is the invitation to all the great divine teachers, who come
down and receive the food offerings; they are offered the ritual musical
pieces, and the ritual of "covering" is done with the teachers' masks. This
is the Greater *Oongkaan* Text.

This Lesser *Oongkaan* Text is for prayer and meditation and is done
daily by those who are celebrants. Every celebrant should pray or medi-

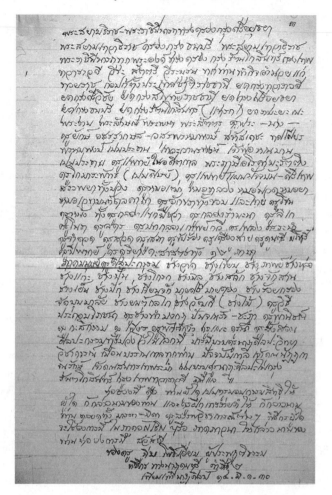

Figure 5.4   The third page of *Khruu* Nim's "A Commemorative Book."
Slide by Deborah Wong.

tate upon rising in the morning and before sleeping at night—that is,
twice a day, every day (I do this without fail).

This first section is in everyday Thai, though the spelling (as it is
throughout the text) is sometimes idiomatic and incorrect according to
standardized "dictionary" Thai. The next short section, only two lines
long, is titled *"Phaak Bup Karii,"* or "The Section for Parents and Men."
This section is meant to be recited by male officiants, indicated by the word
for "male" *(chaai)* in parentheses; that gender is "marked" by this explicit
reference is, I think, an indication that the *wai khruu* was not always the exclusive domain of men, as discussed further in Chapter 7. Entirely in Pali,

these two lines even contain the Pali diacritic of a small open circle placed over end consonants, representing an *-ang* sound. The paragraph runs as follows:

> *Namo me namassattawa paramiyang matapithi susuat Phra Upatmauya*
> *paramiyang barom khruu acariyang ahangwantha khamamihi.*[14]

The following sections are a compendium of the deities with whom officiants—and through them, all performers—must maintain contact. Though long, the list has a clear order and logic, beginning with the highest, most important and powerful deities, and proceeding down through the hierarchy. To summarize, the first section invokes the major deities of the Hindu pantheon (Brahma, Isuan, Ganesha, Uma, Saraswati, etc.), followed by the Hermits, who are one sacred level below the major deities but paramount in this cosmology as the source and fount of all kinds of knowledge. The third section covers a wide range of deities, from Indra and Vishnu to the specific deities of music, the days of the week, the Hindu deities of nature, and finally the specific place or guardian spirits of Thailand, including all the capitals through Thai history and their kings and queens. This leads straight into an invocation of the characters from the *Ramayana*—a telling proximity, pointing to Rama as the ancestor and prototype for Thai kings. Next are the Hermits and teachers of the healing arts, which leads directly into the teachers of magic and writing; again, these kinds of knowledge are intimately connected in the traditional Thai belief system. After this, the teachers of the performing arts are invoked, providing a breakdown of Thai performance genres. Finally, craftsmen and artisans are saluted, from those involved in the arts (as we in the West conceive of them) to cooks, merchants, farmers, and mechanics.

References to the teachers of performance are included throughout, even apart from the section devoted especially to the teachers of music and dance. They are invoked in the first section addressed to the great Hindu deities (i.e., "Great *theewa sawang*, great teachers of the arts and every kind of knowledge"). Even aside from the specific hermits for the performing arts, "dance" and "the arts" are invoked in almost the same way that auspicious Pali phrases are added on.

This list begins with a section titled "The Section for the *Theep*" *(Phaak Theep)*. The title is followed by the word "female" *(ying)* in parentheses and then the words, "Mother, father, and teachers." *Khruu* Nim meant for this section to be read by female officiants. The paragraph runs as follows:

> *Om campethulittiyam.*[15] Great King Brahma, the great *devaraja*, lord of
> the motherland, the lord who created the human realm, [illegible phrase].

Lord Isuan, the king of the great magical *theep*, lord of the fatherland, who bestowed the arts, the great science of magic, and the seven kinds of knowledge on the world of humans. Lord Karotsanumaraya.[16] Lord [illegible] Kumanrakancewa. *Phra* Phikhanesaiya.[17] *Phra* Phikhanaisaiya. King Brahma Chada. King Sahambadi Brahma.[18] Solot Brahma.[19] Lord Yomtheep Theewaa.[20] Great *theewaa sawang*, great teachers of the arts and every kind of knowledge.

Lady Umatwadi.[21] Lady Suratsasawasdi.[22] Lady Phokwadi.[23] Lady Mahesawadi.[24] Lady Rassami.[25] Lady Suchada, Lady Sucitra, Lady Sutham, Lady Sunanpha.[26] Great teachers.[27]

The next section is called "The Section for the Lord Hermits" and would presumably be read by either a male or female officiant. It begins near the bottom of the first page and continues to the top of the second page in a single paragraph:

> *Om campethulittiyam.* Lord Muunii *sawang.* Great Lord Muunii *sawang*, teachers, *acariyang.* Lord *Rüsii sawang*, teachers, *acariyang.* Lord Teacher *Rüsii* Naraut.[28] Lord *Rüsii* Nalai. Lord Teacher *Rüsii* with the eyes of an ox. Lord Teacher *Rüsii* with eyes of fire. Lord Teacher *Rüsii* Karaiyakot.[29] Lord Teacher *Rüsii* Kapsop. Lord Teacher *Rüsii* of the three worlds. Lord Teacher *Rüsii* who sees auspiciousness. Lord Teacher *Rüsii* Phipmon [?]. Lord Teacher *Rüsii thepmon.* Lord Teacher *Rüsii* Plaikot. Lord Teacher *Rüsii* Plaitham [?]. Lord Teacher *Rüsii* Kapha Sitthi. Lord Teacher *Rüsii* Sawamit. Lord Teacher *Rüsii* Wisit. Lord Teacher *Rüsii* Sitthimuni. Lord *Rüsii* Sitthichai. Lord *Rüsii* Kraisaun. Lord *Rüsii* Khacaunbandalat. Lord *Rüsii* Akkaro, the knowledge of *samang.* The hermits, the Lord *Rüsii sawang*, all 108 deities. *Kondanna Phra Phut chim sri baramiyang. Phra arahang samma samphutthang.*[30] Pharotthamuni[31] *sawang khruu acariyang.* Lord Natthasanamuni *sawang acariyang.* Lord Pharathamuni[32] *sawang khruu acariyang.* Lord Yanatamuni *sawang khruu acariyang.* Dance. The arts. The magical arts. Knowledge of all kinds. *Ahangwantha. Khamamihang. Sawatdilaphang. Phawantame.*

The next section is called "The Section for the *Theewaa* [Deva], the Demonic Deities, Place Deities, and the Deities of Siam" *(Phaak Theewaa Asuun Theewaa Phuumi Theewaa Sayaam Theewaa)* and is essentially a long list of names that continues to the middle of the third page as follows:

> *Om campethulittiyam.* King Sakko *devaraja.* Amarinthra who lives in the Daowadung Level of Heaven.[33] The great deity and teacher of the arts and crafts, Lord Wisanuukaam.[34] Lord Wesunuyan. Lord Matusi.

The demon Lord Phiratha.[35] Lord Mulatni. Protsaram—Ramasun.[36]
Lord Parakhonthap, Lord Pancasingkhaun, the auspicious *theep* of beau-
tiful sounds. The deities of the planets and the days of the week:[37]
Lord Athit, Lord Can, Lord Angkhan, Lord Phut, Lord Pharuhat, Lord
Suk, Lord Sao. Lord Ketumadi.[38] Lord Thorani.[39] Lord Khongkha.[40]
Lord Phloeng.[41] Lord Phai. Lord *Theep* Worachun. Lord Phirunthara.[42]
The soft Lady Mani Mekkhala[43]—Lady Sawaha. Lord Assa.[44] Lord
Assawin.[45] Lord Kammathep.[46] Lord Mahachai. Lord Samut.[47] Lord
Himphan.[48] The Lord of the First Four Worlds. *Phisang.* The builder and
ruler of the realm. The pure [?] Wirulahako.[49] In the west, Wirupakkho[50]
and Kuwero[51] in the north. *Phisang.* The might of the four great kings:
peace to the *theewaa*, peace to the eyes of the earth [?], peace to the *naga*,
peace to the demons.[52] The *theewaa* who preserve things sacred all
over the world. The *theewaa* who preserve the Lord Tiger of the Land.
Lord of the Realm. Honored Father, the City Pillar.[53] The city of
Ratanakosin.[54] The city of Dvaravadi. The city of Sukhothai Rachathani.
The honored City Pillars of the capitals, both lesser and greater. The
honored Fathers and Mothers who reside all over the human realm.[55] The
Honored Father Lord Kala Phaya Matcuracha,[56] the lord of bad deeds
and *karma* who resides in the realm of death. The honored ruler of the
city of Phli. The Lady Chanthana. The Lord Guardian Spirits who protect Lord Grandfather Chaiyamongkhon, the Honored Grandfather of
the city of Raachaa, the Honored Grandfather divine hermits, the Honored Grandfather of the rice,[57] the Honored Grandfather Thammi-
kracha, the Honored Grandfather Thamhora. Lord Puai Thatsani. The
guardian spirit Phritkasa.[58] The guardian spirit of the air. The divine
Lord and ruler of Siam, Honored Great-Grandfather (Kham Saen), who
ruled the city of Thai. The second Great-Grandfather (Si Kham Maen),
who ruled the city of Dvaravadi. The third lord (Kham Si), who ruled the
city of Srivijaiya. Divine King and Queen of Siam who ruled the city of
Sukhothai Rachathani. Divine King and Queen of Siam who ruled Krung
Thep Srivijaiya Saen Rachathani.[59] Divine King and Queen of Siam who
ruled the city of Ayuthaya. Divine King of Siam who ruled the city of
Thonburi. The divine Kings and Queens of Siam who ruled the city of
Ratanakosin.[60] The deities of Dvaravadi. Heroes. Warriors.[61] Ancestral
heroes. All who toiled for the King and the realm, who saved or established the country, the nation, the capital, who raised the city of Dvaravadi, who raised the city of Srivijaiya, who raised the city and capital of
Sukhothai, who raised the city of Ayuthaya, who raised the city of Thonburi, who raised the city of Ratanakosin, (insert),[62] who raised the *Ra-*

mayana,[63] Lord Ram, Lord Lak, Lord Phrot, Lord Satrut, the teachers of refined heroes and heroines, the teachers of demons—the lowest levels of demons, the demons in the Brahmin scriptures. Power. Totsian.[64] The divine monkeys. Honored Father Hanuman. The teachers of the healing arts in the past. Lord *Rüsii* Arosamaratting. *Khruu* Komaraphat (his disciple). The teachers of the healing arts in the present and those who are now *theep* in heaven. The old doctor-teachers. The royal doctors. The doctors of pain. The doctors of medicine. The doctors of the magical arts who created the magical verses. The teachers of written letters, both *Khaum*[65] and Thai. The teachers of masked dance-drama. The teachers of the shadow puppets. All the teachers of the Indian [*khaek*] drum and the *pii chawaa* [Javanese double-reed woodwind].[66] The teachers of the frame [*ramanaa*] drum.[67] The teachers of *likee*. The teachers of Southern Thai dance-drama [*nooraa*].[68] The teachers of dance-drama [*lakhon*].[69] The teachers of the dramatic poetic texts and of spoken poetry. The teachers of musical pieces. The teachers of dance. The teachers of comic characters. The teachers of chant. The teachers of chanted poetry [*seephaa*].[70] The teachers of singing. The teachers of stringed instruments. The teachers of *mahoorii* music. The teachers of *piiphaat*. The teachers of the musical arts in all twelve languages.[71]

The final section is called "The Section for the Human Teachers of the Arts and Crafts" *(Phaak Manut Khruu Sinlapakaam)* and is directed toward artisans and teachers of the nonperforming arts:

Painters. Drawers. Photographers. Casters. Carvers. Plasterers. Dyers. Perforators and punchers.[72] Sculptors. Artists of wickerwork. Needleworkers. Embroiderers. Cutters and trimmers. Artists of banana-leaf ritual objects.[73] Threaders of flower garlands. Mechanics. Carpenters. Teachers of food preparation. Teachers who make the *mongkut*, the *pancuret*, and the *chada* [three kinds of dance headdresses].[74] Teachers of commerce. Teachers of agriculture. Teachers who persevere. Teachers whose knowledge and memory were taken while they were at rest.[75] Teachers who advise—teachers who guide. Teachers who teach all the arts in this world. Mighty and glorious teachers of dance from every age. From the present age, the honored Natthakanurak and the honored Sunthauntheep Rabam,[76] the great teachers of dance in the city of Ratanakosin, Krung Theep Dvaravadi, etc.[77]

This ends the Lesser *Oongkaan*, but a short final paragraph gives instructions on how the text can be passed on if desired:

At this point, any teacher who wants to grant ownership [of this text] to someone else can do so by uttering his own name, the names of the teachers who taught him dance, the name of the person receiving it, his mother and father, the teachers of various kinds of knowledge, the names of any officiants who may use this ritual text either for the actual invitation [of deities] or for prayer and meditation. Farewell.

[Signed] *Khruu* Nim Pho-iam: performer and officiant in the *wai khruu* ritual for *likee*.[78] Scripture 2 of Dance, 14 March 30 [1987].

This remarkable text, though obscure in places, is the cosmological landscape in which an officiant lives. Compared to *Khruu* Akhom's text, the lack of a Buddhist frame in *Khruu* Nim's Lesser *Oongkaan* is striking. The Triple Gem of the Buddha, the Dharma, and the Sangha is evoked again and again in *Khruu* Akhom's text, framing nearly every section and subsection of text: it places the invocations—almost entirely to Hindu-Brahmin deities—in a Buddhist frame or envelope. This frame is missing from *Khruu* Nim's Lesser *Oongkaan;* not a single mention of the Buddha is made. *Khruu* Nim's text is also more listlike than *Khruu* Akhom's, with nearly no phrases of entreaty or invitations for the deities to descend or bestow blessings; instead, deities' names are piled on, one after the other. The cumulative effect of the many names has a solemn, mystical effect that *Khruu* Nim and other officiants are quite aware of, and in fact emphasize in their delivery when they read the texts aloud.

Khruu Nim died in July 1994. I went to visit him at Wat Phra Phireen and instead found his small dwelling (uncharacteristically) locked tight. When I asked a monk where *Khruu* Nim was, I learned he had died less than two weeks before and had been cremated at the temple. A "disciple" of his, a middle-aged *likee* performer, unlocked *Khruu* Nim's door for me and showed me his meager belongings. In one corner, part of a wooden sleeping platform and cabinet were burned; the disciple said that *Khruu* Nim had been writing by candlelight several years earlier, fell asleep, and awoke with the furniture in flames. He was lucky: several monks came and helped put out the fire. The disciple showed me some of *Khruu* Nim's remaining papers, including fewer handwritten manuscripts than I expected and a pile of old black and white photographs. The photos showed *Khruu* Nim at *wai khruu* rituals and (in one startling snapshot) dressed and made up as a young woman: he had specialized in female roles when he still performed *likee*. I asked where the papers would go, and the disciple said to the Association for Assistance to Friends and Performers. The elaborate altar, still filling the room with dusty splendor, would probably be dismantled.

Conclusions

Khruu Nim's Lesser *Oongkaan* and *Khruu* Akhom's Greater *Oongkaan* (as *Khruu* Nim would call it) have certain marked differences. *Khruu* Akhom's text was designed for public performance, for an "I" greater then one person: the invitational phrases meant for repetition by an audience of participants are integral to the text as a whole. Also, it is the public face of this text that is available for scrutiny. *Khruu* Nim's text, however, was quite openly intended for private prayer and meditation, as stated at the outset: he twice uses the word *phaowanaa*, "to pray, meditate," to describe how the text should be used. It contains no magic formulas: in other words, the text is meant not to transform or to change, but rather to invoke as an expression of respect. His text is a verbal map of the cosmological hierarchy within which an officiant operates, the scheme that gives the Thai performing arts meaning and efficaciousness.

These two texts, so different in intention and authority, raise important issues about the sacred *wai khruu* texts and the community of readers/performers. The slash between "readers" and "performers" is in many ways the gist of the matter, since the social authority of any officiant lies in the right to "perform" texts like these, in other words, to sound them aloud or even to utter them in the silent course of prayer. Ritual texts are meant to be sounded—sounded in the broadest sense of realizing them in the human realm, through a person. This can be done silently, but bringing the texts out of silence into sound is the prerogative and central function of officiants.

The relationship of these texts to the community of performers (both officiants and everyone else) points to the vitality of ritual in the Thai arts. There is a basic tension between the multiplicity of ritual texts and performers' feelings that some texts (and the officiants that utter them) are more powerful than others. The *wai khruu* derives much of its vigor from the competing facts that (1) each text ought to have been passed on *verbatim* from one officiant to another, and (2) every officiant tinkers with his text, cutting and pasting from other texts to make his script for the ritual performance as strong and efficacious as possible. Officiants themselves will stress the unchanging nature of the ritual texts and the *wai khruu* ritual: I was told many times that the *wai khruu* has existed unchanged "since ancient times," done in exactly the same way. In the next breath, officiants then usually discussed how the ritual has been adapted to suit contemporary needs and performance environments. Officiants are clearly aware of the difference between change and adaptation: for them, the important thing is that the basic thrust and technology of the ritual (spoken texts, food offerings, etc.) have remained the same, constituting the "unchanging" nature of the *wai khruu*. More importantly still, the affirmation of unbroken, uninterrupted links with the past is essential to ritual efficacy.

Paul Ricoeur's thoughts in these matters help put the Thai ritual texts in perspective. Pondering the sacred texts of the Christian Church, Ricoeur says, "I am intrigued by the question of the response of the community whose text has been 'critically edited.' Of course when this is done, it no longer *is* a sacred text, because it is no longer the text which the community always regarded as sacred; it is a scholars' text. So, in a sense, there can *be* no such thing as the critical editing of sacred texts" (1979, 271). He suggests that such self-conscious alteration results in "texts which are not texts of *any* community," that bringing such texts into the present (or, as A. L. Becker might say, making them speak the present) decontextualizes them.

Quite the opposite is true of the Thai ritual texts. As I have pointed out, the process of editing them is central to their transmission (though downplayed by officiants). In the largest sense, there is no canon of sacred texts: this tradition insists on *texts* (in the plural) rather than their collective unity or similarity. Instead, each officiant's ritual text is a unique gathering-together of other texts, a special edition of the most personal kind, although its authority still hinges on overt identification with particular officiants of the past. Walter Ong's comments about the noetic history of the Bible pertain equally well to the Thai ritual texts: "The Bible is made up of various works, composed in a variety of ways . . . , but as it has grown, it has always folded back on itself in memory, the later parts building a later history out of later states of consciousness but also building onto and out of and into and through the earlier parts" (1977, 231).[79]

Ricoeur, however, has more to say regarding authority, pointing out that a sacred text lets a community see itself because such a text constitutes the "founding act" of the community, in other words, both the community's origin myths and its *raison d'être*. As he puts it, "It is a hermeneutical act to recognize oneself as founded by a text and to read this text as founding. There is a reciprocity between the reading and the existing self-recognition of the identity of the community. There is a kind of reciprocity between the community and the text" (1979, 272). Each officiant re-creates this founding act when he edits and alters his ritual text, bolstering his own "self-recognition" and, by extension, the ritual participants'. Participants' sense of "community"—that is, their connections to particular teachers and to those teachers' teachers—thus remains strong.

Against a background of multiple performers' communities and multiple ritual texts, certain institutions persistently try to create a canon of authoritative texts. These institutions—notably the Department of Fine Arts and the College of Arts and Crafts (i.e., the contemporary shape of what were once the court circles)—have tried to canonize certain ritual texts reputedly used or even written by royal patrons, including King Rama VI himself. This has created a new tension. The pull toward the sacred center is nearly irresistible to many Thais, but the attempt to establish certain texts at the center of the tradition (by publishing them, no less) perturbs some performers. Others see this as necessary, as a way of buttressing the inevitable flow of power and knowledge away from the core.

Competing attitudes toward the control of sacred texts is further addressed in Chapter 6, where I discuss the confluence of kings, nation, and performative power in regard to the aesthetics of the state. My point has been to propose a Thai approach to sound and the sacred that includes both uttered words and music. It is no accident that music and the spoken word complete the same actions in Thai ritual: this poetics of sacred sound is central to Thai epistemologies of performance-as-ritual.

Six

Inheritance and Nationalism: The Social Construction of *Wai Khruu* Rituals in Bangkok

Ritual practice is not just a matter of *how* a ritual is done but also of who does it. This chapter addresses what makes great musicians great by examining a lineage of great officiants. Certain teachers in every generation are recognized as outstanding, and they are almost always officiants. Some have been so extraordinary that they have changed the shape of the tradition's music and its social landscape. When an eminent teacher dies, his deification begins to take place almost immediately in the *wai khruu* rituals led by his disciples, and other performers begin to seek links with him, often through other teachers.

At any given moment, the social structure of performers in Bangkok (or indeed anywhere in Thailand) is made up of multiple, overlapping lineages; the lineage or line is a fairly loose concept, especially since performers often study with more than one teacher in their lifetime.[1] Lineages do not have names, nor do disciples undergo any special ritual binding themselves to their teacher. Like most social relationships in Thailand, renegotiation is always a possibility: a student may seek instruction from other teachers but will regard all of his or her teachers with respect and devotion.

Studies of musical lineages are scattered despite their all-encompassing importance in certain traditions. The South Asian *gharana* and the Japanese *iemoto* system have already been referred to. Victoria M. Clara van Groenendael's remarkable study of *dalangs* (shadow puppet masters) in central Java contains an unusually detailed account of twenty-three *dalang* families and their genealogies (1985). She notes that the connection between esoteric knowledge and lineage is key: the power of particular kinds of knowledge leads to an exclusivity of transmission (in this case along family lines) that is similar to the behaviors of Thai officiants. Van Groenendael provides a transcript of one *dalang*'s reflexive dialogue from a *wayang kulit* performance in which he declares his right to perform a ritual puppet play by citing five preceding generations of *dalangs* in his family (52–53). Thai lineages of officiants are sometimes, but not necessarily, based on blood relation. Common to both Thailand and Java, though, is the matter of inherited permission to lead ritual *and* the inherited connection to a royal court. Performers' social systems and their relation to a state power are thus intimately related.

The Thai language has no single word for "officiant" or "celebrant." Performers do not speak of a teacher "leading" the ritual as we do in English. An officiant is commonly called "the person who reads the ritual texts" (*phuu aan oongkaan*), or even "the person who performs, or is an essential part of, the *wai khruu* ritual" (*phuu prakaup phithii wai khruu*).[2] Some performers simply refer to the officiant as the *phithiikaun*, a general word for "announcer" that could also be used for a game show announcer or a master of ceremonies.

What qualities and personality should an officiant ideally have? I first had a conversation about this with my teacher, Nikorn Chanthasorn (who is not an officiant), the day after we had both attended a *wai khruu* ritual at another school. He asked me what I had thought of the event, and when I said it was impressive (intended as a safe answer), he disagreed. In his opinion, the officiant had such a "little" voice that he could scarcely be heard. An officiant's voice, Nikorn said, should be "big and grand." Intrigued, I asked him what other characteristics an officiant should have, and he launched into a description of his own teacher, *Khruu* Saun Wongkhaung, a fairly well-known officiant until his death in 1975.[3] Nikorn emphasized *Khruu* Saun's moral qualities—that he was a devout Buddhist, and so on. He also stressed his celibacy, saying that an officiant shouldn't sleep with anyone the day before performing the ritual, but that *Khruu* Saun had gone a step further, and slept in a different bedroom from his wife once he became an officiant. I then asked him about several other teachers, finally inquiring whether a particularly famous and much loved woodwind teacher had been an officiant. Nikorn said no, he hadn't been: his temperament wasn't right for the role, he liked joking around too much. Half-seriously, I asked Nikorn if he thought *he* would ever be an officiant, and he laughed out loud, saying, "No way! I'm too fond of having fun, and it's far too late for me to change."[4]

This conversation was revealing in several ways. For Nikorn, a good— or perhaps I should say effective—officiant was a convincing performer (i.e., with a suitably loud voice) and also a moral role model. Furthermore, not everyone aspires to this responsibility; for some, being a performer to the best of their ability is enough, and in fact not all master teachers are officiants.

At least one musician has written about the qualities an officiant should have—a man who I know to be deeply concerned with standards of performance and behavior in Thai music. He has received the right to act as an officiant but is still too young to do so. The writer, Bunchuay Soowat, teaches at Chulalongkorn University and is an accomplished performer on the *pii* and other wind instruments. His short essay "The Reader of the Ritual Texts of Thai Music" (2531/1988) was included in a booklet commemorating an annual *wai khruu* ritual at Chulalongkorn University.[5] In it, he lays out five qualifications that any officiant should meet, including: a certain amount of life experience, an appropriate level of musical expertise and repertoire, morality, greatness, and having been initiated into the inner circles of esoteric musical knowledge.

Bunchuay opens the essay with his outlook on an officiant's responsibility. Such a teacher, he says, is given the power *(amnaat)* to "govern" *(pok khraung)* other musicians, and it is his duty to see that they "advance in an orderly and systematic fashion." Moreover, the means to such advancement was laid down by the teachers of old and is a matter of "believing in and observing tradition." The officiant is the keeper and protector of such tradition, but Bunchuay makes it clear that only a minority of musicians can take on this task: "It is not any person that can be a reader of the *oongkaan* texts for the *wai khruu*—everyone who studies music to completion and wants to become an officiant isn't able to. One must be ready and have certain qualities."

The first quality, he goes on to say, is that an officiant must be at least fifty years old. This ensures that "he has already lived the life of an artist for a long while." He must have been ordained as a Buddhist monk at some point in his life, and, in addition to experience and skill in music, he must be "thoughtful and circumspect." Second, the officiant must be a ritual musician who has been initiated not only into the highest level of the sacred repertoire (i.e., *Phleeng Phra Phiraap*) but also have been initiated as a teacher and officiant. In other words, he must have gone through seven different initiations, each more exclusive than the last, before he can even be considered as an officiant (being initiated as an officiant does not necessarily mean that that person will act as one).

The third and fourth traits concern moral qualities. An officiant must have *khunnathaam*, a concept not easily translated into English. *Khun* means good, virtue, value, or quality; *thaam* is the Dharma. Together they are the closest thing in Thai to a word for "morality." Bunchuay outlines this characteristic as follows:

> A person who reads the ritual texts . . . should "live in the Dharma" and always speak the truth. The teacher granting the right to be an officiant should therefore carefully consider whether the potential reader of the ritual texts has true virtue and goodness, to ensure that he will not cause sorrow, trouble, or damage to other people or to Thai music circles.
>
> There is yet one more standard of behavior that must be followed strictly: for one day before he is to perform the ritual (or for longer), the person who is to read the ritual texts must observe the Eight Precepts[6] in order to purify himself of desires and sadness, and to make his mind and heart clean and pure. Then he will be ready to perform the ritual on the appointed day and time.

The fourth quality is also foreign to the English language: an officiant must have *baaramii*, which could be translated as "greatness" or "virtue."[7] Great men have *baaramii*, and it makes them into leaders and role models. It is the aura that comes from taking right action and leading by example, and it accumulates with age and experience.[8] Kings must have *baaramii*,[9] but only some normal people acquire it. Bunchuay is succinct in this matter:

> In this case, having *baaramii* means having the ability to inspire faith and confidence in others. It takes a long time to build up *baaramii*. One must have extensive knowledge and technical ability, and various kinds of goodness must come together in such a person, until it is a matter of general agreement [i.e., it is evident to others]. Anyone considered for performing the *wai khruu* ceremony absolutely cannot lack this quality.

Finally, Bunchuay notes that even if these qualifications have been met, an officiant still should not perform the ritual until the teacher who granted him the right is no longer "sound of body and mind" or has specifically given him the duty of replacing him from time to time. In other words, having received the right (in the seventh and final initiation) is not the final step:

actually performing the ritual is essentially a matter of replacing one's teacher, either before or after his death. Bunchuay concludes: "When the reader of the ritual texts has these five good and beautiful qualities, he instills faith and confidence and belief in Thai musicians. He is then a person who is worshipped and respected and to whom everyone willingly wai-s and whom everyone remembers."

These standards are not merely an ideal. I met many officiants in the course of my fieldwork, and all lived up to these criteria. They were serious, self-contained men who lived morally upright lives and led by example. Many were reserved and loath to discuss their ritual responsibilities in any detail, but others saw such discussion as important. Some were quite distant, but others were relaxed, kindly, and pleased to help me understand their work. All were strikingly humble and quick to defer to older officiants; to a man, they all claimed that their teachers knew far more than they.

The *Wai Khruu* and the State

Although never explicitly described as such by Thai performers, the *wai khruu* delineates the political economy of Bangkok's performance institutions. The court traditions of music and dance most spectacularly maintained by the *wai khruu* have always been tied to ruling institutions, whether the Thai monarchy, dictatorships, or the erstwhile parliamentary system in place since 1933. Since 1932, particular *wai khruu* officiants have emerged in tandem with changing ideas about the Thai nation-state. In other words, the construction and maintenance of musical authority is closely tied to the construction and maintenance of the Thai state.

The emergence of the conservatory system in 1934 is key to understanding why particular men lead the *wai khruu* ritual at present (and might in the future). The government-sponsored College of Dramatic Arts (*Witthayalaai Natthasin*) and its changing relationship to different regimes has shaped and reshaped the authority of the *wai khruu* and who leads it. Some musicians have navigated the politics of their times better than others, rising to their positions as *wai khruu* officiants not only through musical skill and musicianly knowledge but also through skill in furthering their bureaucratic careers.

Performance is often shaped by its relationship to a state; quite a few studies have illuminated how certain traditions have been elevated, reinvented, or conveniently forgotten in the service of state ideologies. J. Lawrence Witzleben has shown how a particular ensemble tradition (*Jiangnan sizhu*) was celebrated as a Chinese regional treasure yet "improved" by Shanghai Conservatory musicians in ways distasteful to local amateur musicians—who in turn are regarded by the conservatory musicians as "hopelessly conservative, unable to appreciate anything new, and unwilling to see their music develop" (1995, 29). By the same token, Witzleben found that few conservatory musicians had any interest in becoming experts in the tradition. The conservatory's administrators, however, were dedicated to the tradition's status as a regional treasure while determined to "raise" the level of its music (140–41). Witzleben notes that "what is being promoted is a revisionist version of the tradition in which the more traditional groups are an anachronism" (140). Similarly, Sally Ann Ness examines a regional Philippine dance (the *sinulog* from Cebu City) and charts how it is transformed (choreographically and ideologically) to speak "Filipino-ness" rather than "Cebuano-ness." She compares a local, low-status version of the *sinulog* through its metamorphosis into parade choreography, where the weight of "big government" and nationalism interacts with local identities (1992, 206–7). These two examples of regional performance traditions on the geocultural periphery of centralized governments shed light on the process through which a regional Thai complex of performance at the geocultural center of the country was made to speak Thai nationalism. As the conservatory system was reproduced in regional branch campuses as well as in the burgeoning university system, the conservatory system came to represent the nation-state where it had once represented only the monarchy. In much the same way, Yvonne Daniel describes the "promotion, manipulation, and appropriation of rumba" in Cuba: rumba may have emerged from Afro-Cuban society, but it now "expresses the essence of postrevolutionary Cuba and its efforts toward egalitarian organization" (1995, 145). The (often postcolonial) manner in which localized traditions come to speak for collectivities sheds light on how cultural capital is constructed through performance.

Marta Savigliano takes such examination further, pointing out that the mechanics of state formation are deeply rooted in colonialism. Considering the tango and its "economy of passion," she suggests that "the" tango is the result of imperialist power play:

> Tango represents a particular sector of argentinos at home, but it assumes national representation abroad. Argentina becomes a nation and tango its symbol when the question of identity is at stake owing to international negotiations that involve issues of representation, legitimacy, and sovereignty (self-determination). Thus, tango shapes and mobilizes Argentineness when confronted with imperialist maneuvers and is activated as a symbol of national representation as it crosses over lines of identity formation. (1995, 4–5)

Similarly, changing conceptions of Thai performance as cultural capital have been shaped by self-conscious commitments to modernization, which is directly (and often problematically) linked to Western economies. Although Thailand was never colonized by a Western power, its experiments (by kings, dictators, and prime ministers) with new bureaucratic structures have everything to do with transnational and colonial movements of capital. In the past century, several Thai leaders have been anxious for Thailand to measure up as a modernized nation, and the performance of everyday life, including citizens' dress, has been shaped by decree. Like the tango, the old court traditions have localized associations that speak differently under the gaze of transnational cultural capital. The politics of Thailand's educational systems implicates who gets to lead the *wai khruu* ritual in different institutions, and those systems are themselves directly linked to ideas of modernity.

Three ethnomusicologists addressing Javanese *gamelan* traditions have written about the formative role of government policies and bureaucratic ideologies. R. Anderson Sutton's extended study of Javanese *gamelan* in twentieth-century Indonesia stands out for its consideration of "formal education," in other words, the conservatory system, and its effects on earlier behaviors and attitudes. Looking at the formation of particular government-sponsored performing arts schools, their curricula, and their administrators, Sutton outlines the tug-and-pull of regional versus national identities in the maintenance of different Javanese *gamelan* traditions. Considering the rise of conservatories outside the urban centers of Yogyakarta and Surakarta, he points to the construction of institutional authority in the politics of the conservatory: "It may seem preposterous, but, in the eyes of bureaucratic administrators not especially familiar with the arts, a formally educated traditional musician is a wiser choice for a government-sponsored teaching job [in a regional conservatory] than someone with no formal credentials, regardless of his regional artistic expertise" (1991, 179–80).

Sumarsam's examination of cross-cultural interactions in the formation of *gamelan* scholarship also addresses the cultural politics of educational institutions. By showing how Javanese, Dutch, and multiracial Javanese intellectuals interacted in the scholarly construction of Javanese studies, Sumarsam illuminates the mechanics of nation-building through scholarship and institution-building: "In the search for the identity of Indonesian culture, the question was: Should Indonesians retain and cultivate their indigenous cultures . . . , such as gamelan music? . . . Gamelan schools . . . inherited the same problems the nationalists had to confront. That is, the schools had to justify the relevance of their gamelan curriculum in a modern and pluralistic Indonesian society" (1995, 242). Sumarsam posits that the cultural role of *gamelan* in late-twentieth-century Indonesia (as opposed to Java) is a complex creation, produced by Javanese intellectuals and administrators responding to the scholarly construction of "Javanese culture" by Dutch and other Western scholars.

In his detailed study of how central Javanese *gamelan* musicians "know" the music they make, Benjamin Brinner scrutinizes the micropolitics of how musical competence is differently constructed by "traditional" and conservatory musicians. He muses in an aside that "the role of educational institutions in the formation and alteration of competence in twentieth-century Java deserves far lengthier discussion than I could provide here. The experiences of the many non-Indonesian musicians who have turned to the study of Javanese music have likewise been shaped by educational and political agendas and institutions that are probably completely invisible for many of the participants" (1995, 10). In short, the impact of bureaucratic, centralized educational institutions on central Javanese *gamelan* musicians has been addressed by more than one scholar, providing a picture of how Javanese epistemologies of music have changed through their contact with state ideologies.

Bureaucracies are dedicated to replicating themselves, and this often means creating (and then maintaining) authorities. Martin Stokes's work on the arabesk debate in Istanbul provides a detailed look at how a constellation of cultural influences has shaped the Turkish music now known as arabesk. Showing how the government has controlled the formation of conservatories, research institutes, television, and the radio, Stokes argues that these cultural institutions were quickly identified with preexisting political factions that implicated their attempts at music reforms. "For the most part," Stokes writes, "the reforms only succeeded in creating a new élite (defined in opposition to an old élite) of musicians sustained by and sustaining in turn the State Conservatory and [Turkish Radio and Television]" (1992, 47). Similarly, lineages of Thai officiants are now coterminous with state university and conservatory administrations, and I will show how these bureaucracies are, and are not, replications of the older court systems of performers' authority. In his participant-observation research on American funding panels for scholarly research, Donald Brenneis considers his "own situation as that of becoming a 'nonce bureaucrat,' or, more generally, of being socialized through negotiation with both standardized and more human interlocutors in how to carry out certain types of social practice" (1994, 33). Unlike the many studies focused on moments of social resistance, Brenneis's work considers the construction of "accommodation, complicity, and seduction" (26). In other words, he suggests that a close examination of bureaucrats and bureaucratic structures may well show us something about the mechanics of socialization. Looking at the patterning of Thai performers' bureaucracies after older systems of authority is thus a way to make visible the meeting ground of the court and the modernized nation-state.

The tie to the past, to a time when musicians were more talented and officiants more knowledgeable, dominates every officiant's outlook. Even more than other performers, officiants are tremendously conscious of their own ties to this past, particularly through their teachers, their teachers' teachers, and extending back into "ancient times" *(samaai booraan)*, a phrase that is never far from their lips. Yet the present configuration of authoritative teachers represents turbulent attempts to reconcile the court system with the emergent bureaucracy of the post-1932 Thai nation-state. A close look at one lineage of officiants will provide a vivid window onto the social and musical politics behind high-status *wai khruu* rituals in Bangkok.

Luang Pradit Phairau and the *Wai Khruu* for Music

Many officiants in Bangkok (and beyond) trace their status to *Luang* Pradit Phairau, widely regarded as the musician of the century.[10] Although he died in 1954, *Luang* Pradit Phairau is still seen as the genius behind Thai classical music as it is known today. His compositions are not only known and played, but are also attributed to him—the only corpus consistently identified with a composer. His playing techniques apparently transformed performance practice. Most of the great officiants in contemporary Bangkok were initiated by him, so his "line" is worth detailed examination. Rather than present this lineage of officiants in chronological order, I will start with *Luang* Pradit Phairau himself, a musician of the previous generation who is the source of these contemporary officiants' power and the crucial link with great musicians and officiants of the past.

Luang Pradit Phairau (1881–1954)

Luang Pradit Phairau, the name by which he is known today, was not the great musician's birthname. He was named Sorn ("arrow") when he was born on August 6, 1881, in Samut Songkhram province.[11] His father, Sin,[12] was a well-known musician in his own right and a disciple of *Khruu* Mi Khaek (*Phra* Pradit Phairo), a great court musician during the mid-nineteenth century.

Various accounts state that the young Sorn was able to play pieces on the gong circle at the age of five without having been taught but that his interest in studying began only when he was eleven years old. The event that drew him to music was apparently his own tonsure ceremony, a life-cycle event in traditional Thailand when a child's topknot was shaved off, marking their entrance into puberty and young adulthood.[13] A number of different *piiphaat* ensembles came to play for this celebration at *Khruu* Sin's invitation, and Sorn "suddenly felt the beauty of the music for the first time" (Sumonman 2524/1981, 264). He then began serious study with his father and was soon able to play with his father's ensemble and to perform in music competitions.

Although he spent his childhood far from Bangkok, Sorn was constantly exposed to aristocratic circles through his father's playing engagements. He was apparently well known by the time he was a teenager: his performances on the xylophone at aristocratic functions led to recognition by members of the royal family.[14] Competitions were of central importance for musicians during this period: reputations were made and broken at such meets, and (as in Sorn's case) careers begun. When he was about nineteen years old (ca. 1900), Sorn performed in the annual music competition in Rachburi, and the course of his life was changed.[15] Prince[16] Phanuphanthiwong Woradet, an enthusiastic amateur musician, was touring nearby Rachburi at the command of King Rama V; he had heard about the young Sorn's playing and went to the competition to hear him.[17] When the Prince listened to him play, he was so impressed that he asked Sorn's father, *Khruu* Sin, whether he could take the boy to Bangkok and make him a royal page.[18] (See fig. 6.1.)

Sorn's father agreed, and from then until 1932 (when the absolute monarchy was abolished), Sorn was a court musician. In addition to the court of the King himself, the sheer size of the extended royal family meant that numerous smaller courts and palaces flourished, and many supported music and dance troupes.[19] Court performers were professional and full-time: musicians not only played at their patron's official functions but were also on call for his personal listening pleasure at all hours of the day and night. They lived at their patron's palace and were often taken along to his summer home or on official tour. Court musicians were usually completely supported by their patron: food and housing were provided, and they drew a small salary as well. Many were given civil servant rankings commensurate with established levels of salary: Sorn was made a page *(mahat lek)*, a standard entry-level position for boys and young men. He eventually advanced to the rank of a *Caangwaang*, one of the highest positions among the royal pages.

Figure 6.1   Luang Pradit Phairau as a young man. Slide reproduced
with the permission of Malini Sagarik.

Prince Phanuphantiwong Woradet took his role as patron quite seriously and gave his performers special attention. He arranged for Sorn to be
ordained as a monk at the royal temple of Wat Boworniwet Wihan with the
Supreme Patriarch himself as his overseeing abbot.[20] He also arranged
Sorn's marriage. The Prince was a great music lover and went to considerable trouble to seek out the best teachers for his performers. One of these
teachers was *Phraya* Prasaan Duriyasap (birthname Plaek Prasaansap), a
leading court musician during the reigns of Rama V and VI and the head
of the Royal Department of *Piiphaat* during the entire reign of Rama VI.[21]
(See fig. 6.2.) Sorn became one of his close disciples and probably received
from him the right to lead the *wai khruu* ritual sometime after 1911 (when
Sorn turned thirty) and before *Phraya* Prasaan's death in 1924.[22]

The Prince apparently took pride in his troupe of musicians and was
determined that his palace be known for high musical standards. He was
quite strict and insisted that his musicians practice constantly (Phunphit
2529/1986, 135–36). He got what he wanted: the Buraphaa ("Eastern")
Palace had so many good performers and did so well in competitions that

พระยาประสานดุริยศัพท์
(แปลก ประสานศัพท์)

Figure 6.2 Luang Pradit Phairau's teacher, *Phraya* Prasaan Duriyasap (birthname
Plaek Prasaansap), a leading court musician during the reigns of Rama V and VI
and the head of the Royal Department of *Piiphaat* during the entire reign of
Rama VI. Slide reproduced with the permission of Malini Sagarik.

its name became synonymous with the best music. Sorn served the Prince
for several decades and evidently became the lead xylophone player of
the Buraphaa *piiphaat* ensemble—which meant he was the leader of the
ensemble—early on.

Aside from his ordination and marriage, I can find little mention of any
outstanding events in Sorn's life until 1925 (between the ages of nineteen
and forty-four), but it is safe to assume that he spent these years starting
a family, refining his performance technique, and making the Buraphaa
Palace *piiphaat* ensemble famous in Bangkok and beyond. The palace itself
was an elegant place, styled after the great mansions of Europe. In an
English-language account, Kumut Chandruang, who served as a page under the prince during this period, describes the palace as follows:

> The magnificent Eastern Palace was built on an estate as large as five
> or six city blocks. Four armed, uniformed guards at the gate stood mo-
> tionless like statues, to keep out intruders and to preserve the dignity of

the Prince. Behind the iron gate, outsiders might observe a single open hall where the Royal Orchestra [i.e., Sorn's ensemble] occasionally played before the Prince. The main palace was built in Roman style, with huge pillars, marble steps, and black and white tile floor. At the steps were two life-size statues of lions, grinning at oncomers. The main hall was decorated with a magnificent Persian carpet, European furniture, a huge chandelier, and a few large paintings by European artists. Up the middle of the marble stairway leading to the second floor was laid a soft scarlet rug.

Within the estate, there were a summer palace, a Japanese house, a swimming pool, a tennis court, the kitchen quarters, the junior quarters, the maids' quarters, a small barracks for the guards, a fruit garden, and a flower garden. Trees grew everywhere. (1970, 157–58)

This kind of European luxury was common among the Thai nobility during the reigns of Rama V, Rama VI, and Rama VII. As a page, Sorn probably lived in the junior quarters mentioned above. The Prince himself is also mentioned in Kumut's memoir, referred to as "Prince Pitula, commonly known as the Royal Uncle":[23] "The Royal Uncle was an old man with a Kaiser Wilhelm mustache. He walked with a cane, limping, for in his youth he had fallen from a horse. He spoke loudly, plainly, decisively—most of the pages trembled at his call" (ibid.).

At some point, Sorn was given the title *Caangwaang*, one of the highest positions among the pages. He and his family probably took up residence in a house "outside the wall of the Eastern Palace" sometime after this (ibid., 161), as described briefly by Kumut: "The location of the house . . . was not desirable. It was surrounded by three factories, an ice plant, and two sawmills" (163).

In 1908, the Prince went to Indonesia on official business, bringing Sorn and the *piiphaat* ensemble along with him. Sorn was by then already known for his ability to adapt and elaborate existing melodies, and he did this with several Javanese pieces.[24] He was also intrigued by the West Javanese instrument called *angklung*—bamboo rattles with fixed pitches played in interlocking patterns. He brought a set back to Thailand with him and had one of his students adapt the instruments for Thai classical music by creating one for each of the seven pitches of the Thai scale. Now called *angkhalung*, these instruments are widely used in elementary schools to teach Thai children classical music.[25]

Sorn was certainly known to the inner circles of royalty by 1915, when he arranged a piece in honor of King Rama VI and played it for him. The King had just completed a tour of southern Thailand, at one point traveling around the perimeter of Nakhon Srithammarat, an old capital of the south. Following a common compositional procedure, Sorn took an existing melody called *Khameen Khao Khieo* ("The Green Mountain," in Cambodian style) and rearranged it in *thao* form,[26] naming the new piece *Khameen Liap Nakhon*, or "Going around the Edge of the City." Moreover, Sorn played the new piece on xylophone using a technique of sustaining pitches by trilling or rolling the mallets, known in Thai as *krau*; this technique was at that time not common on the xylophone, but after Sorn's public performance of this piece for the King (and his consequent use of *krau* in other pieces), the technique eventually passed into standard performance practice. Sumonman notes that the King was so pleased that he gave Sorn a medallion with both his and Rama V's images on it, to commemorate his awareness of Sorn's talent from the time when he himself was still Crown Prince (2524/1981, 266).

The last year of his fifteen-year reign, in 1925, King Rama VI, an ardent supporter of the performing arts, conferred a title and a new name on *Caangwaang* Sorn.[27] One of his first acts after being crowned in 1910 was to organize a Department of Entertainment *(Krom Mahaurasop)* and to grant its more well-known performers nonhereditary aristocratic titles *(bandaasak)* with commensurate salaries and honorific names *(rachathinanuam)*. By the end of his reign, Rama VI had created fifty-nine honorific names for his musicians alone, all Sanskrit- or Pali-derived, polysyllabic, mellifluous, and descriptive of musical sound or skill (Myers-Moro 1988b, 84). In 1925, *Caangwaang* Sorn thus became *Luang* Pradit Phairau, as he is known today; at the same time, Rama VI gave Sorn's family the hereditary surname of Silapabanleng.[28] Although the conferral of a name and title on a performer was not unusual during this reign, Rama VI's choice of name —Pradit Phairau—was a great honor. Unlike most of the other honorific names, "Pradit Phairau" was not invented by Rama VI himself but originated during the reign of Rama IV, and three other musicians (during the reigns of Rama IV, V, and VI) had also borne the name, though with the title *Phra* (one level higher than *Luang* in the hierarchy of aristocratic titles).[29] *Pradit* means to invent, make, or devise; *phairau* means beautiful sound (e.g., speech, music, etc.). Sumonman (2524/1981, 266) notes that Rama VI gave Sorn the new name and title after hearing him play only once.[30]

King Rama VI died in 1925 and was succeeded by his younger brother, who was crowned as Rama VII. Prince Phanuphantiwong Woradet, *Luang* Pradit Phairau's patron, died a year or so later in 1926 or 1927,[31] and as Kumut notes in his memoir, "the death of the Royal Uncle brought a great change to the inhabitants of his estate" (1970, 161): the Eastern Palace and its estate were turned over to the Royal Treasury, and the many pages and servants had to look for work elsewhere. *Luang* Pradit Phairau was given a position in the Royal Department of *Piiphaat* and *Khoon* in 1926. Though left without his patron, *Luang* Pradit Phairau's eminence was such that he was immediately taken up by the Ministry of the Palace and became the King and Queen's private teacher. Also, his teacher, *Phraya* Prasaan Duriyasap, had died in 1924 and *Luang* Pradit Phairau was the likely successor to his position as head of the Royal Department of *Piiphaat.*

The performing arts departments were, in fact, in some disarray following the reign of Rama VI. An active and enthusiastic patron of the arts, Rama VI had reorganized all the royal music and dance-drama ensembles, placing them under the auspices of the Department of Entertainment *(Krom Mahoorasop)*: all crafts, *khoon*, *piiphaat*, dance-drama, hand puppets, the Royal Pages' *Phinphaat* Ensemble, the Western String Orchestra, and so forth, were put under its administration.[32] In previous reigns, these performance forms were all separate departments under the Ministry of the Royal Palace *(Krasuang Wang)*. When Rama VII assumed the throne in 1925, the "bankrupt condition of the Privy Purse" (Mattani 2525/1982, 155), caused largely by Rama VI's huge expenditures for entertainment, led the new king to consider closing down the Department of Entertainment; it seems that its various sections were returned to the control of the Ministry of the Royal Palace. As Mattani relates, "Many court dancers [and musicians] began to find new patrons in private troupes or palaces. This period has been described as *"ban taek saraek khat"* (that is, a period of severe disruption of home and family) for the members of the royal khon and lakhon troupes. It was reported that khon and lakhon properties, masks and costumes were left unattended. Many were stolen or destroyed" (ibid.). Unlike many less fortunate performers, *Luang* Pradit Phairau was apparently highly enough placed that he not only survived the change in reigns and administrative structure, but prospered and was placed even closer to the new king than in the previous reign.

He was then forty-five years old, and the reign of Rama VII (1925–1932) proved the apex of his career as a court musician. During this time he "helped" the King compose three pieces still popular today.[33] He also established two palace *mahoorii* ensembles, one for the King's personal listening pleasure (see fig. 6.3) and one made up entirely of women.[34] Kumut's memoir once again contains interesting anecdotes from those years: with the death of the Prince, the young page Kumut was sent by his father (a music lover) to live with *Luang* Pradit Phairau in his home near the Eastern Palace. Kumut provides a portrait of the teacher and his family:

Figure 6.3 A palace *mahoorii* ensemble playing at the king's seaside residence in Hua Hin, led by *Luang* Pradit Phairau, probably during the reign of Rama VII (1925–1932). Slide reproduced with the permission of Malini Sagarik.

The music master was a handsome, middle-aged man, with intelligent eyes, a well-kept moustache, and a light complexion. He was always well-dressed, and wore a huge diamond ring on his little finger. He was rather strict to his pupils—he even whipped the lazy ones. . . . He gave lessons to Their Majesties, the King and Queen, for he was recognized as a master mind. Siamese songs were recorded not in notes, but in the memories of the masters, and *Luang* Pradist [*sic*] remembered more ancient songs than anyone else in the land. (1970, 161–62)

Kumut also describes his wives and children:

He had two wives who were sisters.[35] I called them Aunt Chote and Aunt Foo. . . . Aunt Chote had three daughters and one son, Aunt Foo, three sons and one daughter. . . . Sister Chinn [*sic*], seven years senior to me, loved me as her own brother. She had graduated from Rajini School for Girls, and taught there now, and she could help me in my English, French, and mathematics. All the daughters of the music master were schoolteachers. (162)

Kumut's portrait of *Luang* Pradit Phairau's three eldest daughters provides a picture of the milieu in which the teacher and his family moved. Although technically a royal servant, *Luang* Pradit Phairau provided his children with an upper-middle-class upbringing and excellent educations. Kumut's description of Chin as a young woman of twenty or so is particularly poignant, because it was she who carried on her father's legacy and eventually acted as an officiant in the *wai khruu* at Srinakharinwirot University:

> Sister Chinn had a tragic romance. She was in love with a poor musician and writer. He did not have a general education, but he was intelligent. Her parents showed a slight prejudice against him. I was sympathetic and hoped they would marry. But Sister Chinn made him wait too long for her decision. He became disappointed and married someone else. Second Sister, Banleng, was a debutante, popular among the men. The Third Sister was married at nineteen to a lieutenant of the Royal Guards. (162–63)

Kumut's impressions of *Luang* Pradit Phairau's son Prasidh are also valuable, suggesting how personality can play an important role in the transmission of the right to be an officiant. As the oldest son, Prasidh would have been the obvious choice to inherit his father's ritual rights, but, in fact, Chin received the right to lead the *wai khruu* ritual and Prasidh did not. In time, Prasidh became a well-known Thai composer of Western-style art music, but not without some tension between him and his father:

> Aunt Chote's son [Prasidh] was a pessimistic character. His father wanted him to be a great musician like him, but the young son had a radical attitude. He slightly looked down upon Siamese music, but praised Occidental music, and this hurt his father's feelings. We called him Empty Basket, because he was full of dreams and wild imagination. He believed that Beethoven, Chopin, and Tchaikowsky were greater than his father, and he caused many quarrels in the family. The music master wanted the Empty Basket to practice on the native bamboo xylophone, but he sneaked away to practice his Occidental violin. (163)

King Rama VII kept *Luang* Pradit Phairau close to him, taking the musician along to his seaside resort in Hua Hin and even to Cambodia in 1929–1930. The trip to Cambodia, which included stops in Phnom Penh and Angkor Wat, has been described by Prasidh in a short anecdotal account (1975) that brings out both the honor and the obligation of being a royal servant. The King was making a royal tour of mainland Southeast Asia and decided, while in Cambodia, that he should have brought along some of his court musicians; he sent to Bangkok for *Luang* Pradit Phairau, who in turn commanded his eighteen-year-old son Prasidh to accompany him. After a long journey (first by train to the border, and then by officer-driven car to Phnom Penh), they reached the Cambodian capital and were set up in the finest hotel in the city. The King sent word that *Luang* Pradit Phairau was to perform the next night at Angkor Wat following a reception, which he did, playing several solos. The next day, *Luang* Pradit Phairau was invited to join the King's retinue for a tour of the ruins, while Prasidh, as "a minor member of the group," humbly remained outside. Back in Phnom Penh, *Luang* Pradit Phairau was commanded by Rama VII to perform a private *ranaat eek* recital for the King of Cambodia "as a return of hospitality." The Cambodian King, Srisawat Maniwongse, was so impressed that he asked Rama VII if *Luang* Pradit Phairau could stay to teach his own musicians. As Prasidh describes it, the King answered, "If Your Majesty would like to have *Luang* Pradit stay here and teach, I should be most happy to lend him to you for a month."

So stay they did, both *Luang* Pradit Phairau and Prasidh. After a few days *Luang* Pradit Phairau asked the King whether he could stay in the musicians' quarters rather than the expensive hotel, and he and Prasidh were instead set up in a smaller hotel near the palace. The month that followed was evidently a period of intense interchange between *Luang* Pradit Phairau and the Cambodian court musicians, whose instruments and ensembles were nearly identical, with much overlapping repertoire as well. *Luang* Pradit Phairau taught every day until noon and also learned a number of Cambodian compositions that Prasidh helped notate. Even before he left, *Luang* Pradit Phairau was apparently adapting and arranging these pieces, as Prasidh relates: "The Cambodian melodies were used mostly in "middle versions" (*song chan*), which my father arranged in the longer or 'extended' version (*sam chan*) or else composed both an extended version and a 'short version' (*chan dio*), making a full *thao* composition."

Back in Thailand, *Luang* Pradit Phairau continued to tinker with the Cambodian material, and some of these pieces (e.g., *Nok Khao Khamae*, "The Cambodian Dove") have since become standard repertoire for Thai musicians. Prasidh's account of this unplanned month-long trip offers a rare glimpse of the eminent court musician's social position. While put up in the best hotels and included in royal sightseeing trips, he was still "lent" out for a month, with no forewarning and probably without consultation.

Upon his return to Thailand in 1930, *Luang* Pradit Phairau was made the deputy director of the Royal Department of *Piiphaat* and *Khoon* in the Ministry of the Palace, receiving a monthly salary of 150 *baht*.[36] The events of 1932, however, when a coup led by young military officers led to Rama VII's abdication and the end of the absolute monarchy, brought dramatic changes. Many members of the royal family went into exile abroad, and the courts began to vanish almost overnight. Performers' lives were again disrupted, though *Luang* Pradit Phairau probably remained in the King's service until he finally abdicated in 1935. The new government established a national conservatory in 1934, and the newly formed Department of Fine Arts recognized the plight of court performers a year later in 1935. The teachers and performers formerly with the Ministry of the Royal Palace (including *Luang* Pradit Phairau) were reassembled as "The Dance and Music Section of the Fine Arts School," and their instruments and costumes went with them (Department of Fine Arts 1949, 1). The new government essentially replaced the royal family as the patron of court-style performance: performers changed from royal to civil servants, though this transition was not made without some tensions.[37]

Although the Department of Fine Arts was formed soon after the change of government, it lay almost completely dormant until after the end of World War II. *Luang* Pradit Phairau was named one of the senior teachers in the music section, but in reality he retreated to his home outside the walls of the old Buraphaa Palace. He was fifty-four years old in 1935 and one of the most famous musicians in Bangkok. The dissolution of the courts and the establishment of the National School of Dance and Music marked a hiatus in his life (as in all performers'), but it came at a point when teaching naturally begins to dominate most performers' lives. By then middle-aged and covered with honors, *Luang* Pradit Phairau's attention shifted to his students. Whereas his earlier years were marked first by intensive performing and competitions and then by royal service and teaching, the final twenty years of his life are largely undocumented except for numerous anecdotal accounts by his students of what it was like to live at his house as his disciple.

Subin Cankaew, now a well-known *khaung wong* player, lived at the house for a few years as a boy.[38] He remembers his lessons with the teacher as follows:

> *Khruu Luang* Pradit Phairo didn't teach his solo pieces the same way to each student—he took each student's individual ability into consideration. If a student had the skill to play a part as soon as it was taught to him, the master would modify it in order to show off the student's special skills. But if a student tried two or three times and still didn't get it, the master would change the part and make it easier. Likewise, if a student couldn't remember a part and had to ask the master to show him again, it usually wasn't exactly the same as before. It was like this because the master was always thinking up new ways to do his solo pieces.
>
> Whenever a disciple was called on to play a solo piece but wasn't brave enough to do it, the master would get extremely angry. (2530/1987, 59)

Another *piiphaat* musician, King Phloiphet (d. 1989), studied with *Luang* Pradit Phairau as a boy.[39] He lived at the musician's home from 1933 on and had similar recollections. Here he relates how he came to live at the house after his father, a *piiphaat* musician, had died:

> The teacher [*Luang* Pradit Phairau] asked us where we'd come from, and my mother told him exactly what our situation was. He asked me, "Can you play or not?" I said, "I can, a little." He said, "Let's hear you, then." I sat down and played a little bit of *Saathukaan* on the gong circle and then stopped. He didn't say anything until my mother asked if she could leave me there. He nodded and said, "I'll take him, though I don't want to—there're so many kids here already." (Sathian 2532/1989, 77–78)

The young King settled into the routine of the house, sleeping under the stairs and usually going out to eat with the other disciples at the many Chinese food shops in the area; he swept the yard and helped with other household chores, but mostly he practiced. Many students lived elsewhere, arriving early in the morning to practice. King says that *Luang* Pradit Phairau spent most of his time at home: he usually sent his disciples to play at the various engagements to which he was invited.[40] In fact, King notes that even more often than having lessons, he was sent to play at events or followed *Luang* Pradit Phairau along to such engagements, which were constant. It also seems that *Luang* Pradit Phairau was a night person—like Subin, King recalls being woken up by his teacher to practice:

> Sometimes I'd have to get up in the middle of the night and go play the gong circle as he listened. He wouldn't give me the next part until I'd played it over and over, nor would he let me go to sleep until I was absolutely sure of my part. (Naowarat 2532/1989, 70)

After the boy had lived at the house for a year or two, *Luang* Pradit Phairau's daughter Chin realized that the young King had never gone to school, so she enrolled him at the newly formed School of Dramatic Arts, where he received a general education as well as music lessons.[41] Since he received no money from his family or from *Luang* Pradit Phairau, he frequently cut classes to make money by playing. This got him into trouble with his teacher at least once:

> One time he was really stern with me—instead of going to one of his playing engagements, I went to someone else's. He was really mad. He and his son Prasidh caught me and tied my hands behind my back, sat me down in the middle of the yard, and poured a big jar of water over me—but only one! Then they opened the gates to the house so that people

passing by could see me. Ha! I was a teenager then, and was I ever embarrassed. (Sathian 2532/1989, 79)

King stayed until he had finished grammar school and was about to begin high school. Following an older friend's example, he decided to join the Navy as a musician. As he put it, he was tired of being poor: *Luang* Pradit Phairau provided him with food, housing, and lessons, but no pay—feeding the number of students that he did was already generous. King lied about his age and was accepted into the Thai music division of the Navy after his friend, also a disciple of *Luang* Pradit Phairau, pulled some strings. *Luang* Pradit Phairau was, as he relates, not pleased:

> When my teacher heard what I'd done, he was very angry. He felt that I should have come and told him, so that he could take me there and set me up in a more orderly fashion. As he saw it, I was running away from him, almost as if I were running to *Caangwaang* Thua, who was then the leader of the Navy ensemble [and a rival]. But I did it because I wanted to be in the Navy, and the salary was five *baht* a month, which at that time was pretty good. I didn't go back to my teacher's house at all—the Navy was very strict, we had to work every day.
>
> Before my teacher died, I went back to visit him. I was still in the Navy then. I brought him the coconut shell body of a *sau uu*. It was the first time I'd been back to visit him. He didn't say anything, but just nodded. I didn't speak, either—I just prostrated myself before him and then left. (Sathian 2532/1989, 80)

The last ten years of *Luang* Pradit Phairau's life (i.e., the mid-1940s to 1954) were probably the period when he was most active as a *wai khruu* celebrant, though he began to pass on the right to lead the ritual to certain students even earlier, in the mid-1930s. In deciding who would receive the right, he essentially determined the social landscape of musicians for the next generation, so it is important to look closely at which disciples he chose and why.

As noted above, he had probably received the right to lead the ritual sometime between 1911 (when he was of sufficient ritual age) and 1924, when his teacher *Phraya* Prasaan Duriyasap died. *Luang* Pradit Phairau's father (Sin Silapabanleng) was also an officiant and his granddaughter Malini Sagarik thinks it likely that he also received the right from him, even though he studied with his father when he was still quite young. *Luang* Pradit Phairau's father was "of the provinces" whereas *Phraya* Prasaan was "of the palace," so it would not be surprising if *Luang* Pradit Phairau sought the right from *Phraya* Prasaan Duriyasap: receiving the right from some-one close to the center of royal power is, and was, the preferred source for the ritual privilege to lead the *wai khruu*. Whether *Luang* Pradit Phairau received the right to lead the ritual from anyone else remains a mystery. He may well have been invested by Rama VI himself, as *Luang* Pradit Phairau was active in his court and the king was personally involved in the court *wai khruu* rituals for music and dance. This would help explain *Luang* Pradit Phairau's decision to pass on the right to a large number of disciples (and their attraction to him), as described below.

Luang Pradit Phairau probably first acted as an officiant in the mid-1930s, well after *Phraya* Prasaan died in 1924; he was just forty-three in 1924, still a bit young to lead the ritual. One of *Luang* Pradit Phairau's students, Sakol Kaewpenkhat, recalled attending a major *wai khruu* around 1923 or 1924 where *Phraya* Prasaan Duriyasap was the officiant and both *Luang* Pradit Phairau and *Caangwuang* Thua assisted with the initiations. Sakol also remembered that *Luang* Pradit Phairau was holding *wai khruu* rituals at his house by 1939. This was where he himself received ritual rights in 1939 or 1940 and where he first heard live *piiphaat* music included in the ritual between sections of the recited ritual texts.[42]

The earliest known photograph showing *Luang* Pradit Phairau leading the *wai khruu* ritual was taken at the School of Dramatic Arts in the late 1940s (Department of Fine Arts 1949, 6). He is seen sitting before a table of food offerings, dressed in white, his hands in a *wai* at chest level, eyes closed and obviously reciting the ritual texts. About ten men can be seen, all *wai*-ing and mostly middle-aged; to the left, part of the *piiphaat* ensemble can be seen.

Luang Pradit Phairau passed on the right to lead the *wai khruu* ritual to an unusually large number of students—thirteen that I know of and possibly more that I don't. These students were Montri Tramote, *Phraya* Phuumiseewin (Cit Cittaseewin), Oongkaan Kliipchüün, Sakol Kaewpen-khat, Phim Nakranaat, Ruam Phrohmburi, Wan Canaun, Samruai Kaew-sawaang, Prasit Thawon, Subin Cankaew, Choot Duriyapraniit, and Uthit Naksawat; at some point, *Luang* Pradit Phairau also granted ritual rights to his daughter, Chin Silapabanleng.[43] Some of these grantees are discussed in more detail below, but the order and circumstances of their conferrals (as far as I have been able to reconstruct them) are worth summarizing here.[44]

Montri Tramote, considered the greatest musician of his generation (that is, the generation after *Luang* Pradit Phairau), was the first student to whom *Luang* Pradit Phairau granted ritual rights, in 1934 or 1935—a tumultuous time for all Thais, but especially for court performers. Montri

Figure 6.4   Sakol Kaewpenkhat (b. 1909) leading a *wai khruu* ritual
at his home in 1988. Photograph by Deborah Wong.

was thirty-four or thirty-five years old at the time and a member of the Royal
Department of *Piiphaat*. He had just been transferred to the newly-formed
Department of Fine Arts along with *Luang* Pradit Phairau and all the other
performers from the Ministry of the Royal Palace. It is not clear how
closely Montri actually studied with *Luang* Pradit Phairau, but it was a high
honor for him to be the first disciple to whom the teacher granted the right
—and, as will be made clear, this honor helped make Montri the great
teacher of the next generation.

The second student to receive ritual rights from *Luang* Pradit Phairau
(according to Montri Tramote) was Oongkaan Kliipchüün (1912–1977).
The third student was Sakol Kaewpenkhat. Born in 1909, he studied with
Luang Pradit Phairau for about four years (1939–1943) and received ritual rights during that time. (See fig. 6.4.) Sometime after Sakol, Ruam
Phrohmburi (1912–1986) was given the right to lead the ritual but was
never one of *Luang* Pradit Phairau's closest students. Although he was a
musician in several palaces as a young man, he spent most of his life teaching and playing in the provincial capital of Rachburi, now two hours from

Bangkok by bus. Since *Khruu* Ruam would have been at least thirty years old when the conferral took place, it must have occurred after 1942.

The next student known to have been granted ritual rights was Prasit Thawon, in 1946. Prasit is an important link in the chain of conferrals. He has also written about the events that led *Luang* Pradit Phairau to grant him the right to be an officiant in a short memoir called "The Teacher Who Was Like My Father." He relates that *Luang* Pradit Phairau was invited to perform the ritual at the home of a *piiphaat* ensemble leader, and he, as a disciple, was taken along:

> [The host] sent his own car to pick *Luang* Pradit Phairau up on Wednesday [i.e., the day before the ritual]. My task was to help my teacher out in every way and to make things as convenient for him as possible. Whenever he had to go someplace, he usually didn't sleep at all the night before. At about 2 a.m. on Wednesday, he said, "*Cao* Sit,[45] I'm really old. If you're going to have it, you should have it all. Tomorrow morning, dress yourself cleanly—I'm going to confer the book on you." . . . I listened to him and said, "Yes, sir. Yes, sir." At dawn I changed my mind: I decided to leave music and to sell all my instruments. If I was going to leave music, why should I receive the book? When it was almost time to perform the ritual, my teacher was severe: "Why haven't you bathed?" I prostrated myself to him three times and then said, "I am still not ready. . . ." But in the end, I had to accept the knowledge that he gave me; it has raised and supported me ever since. (At that time, I was twenty-five or twenty-six years old.) (2531/1988, 42–43)

Prasit's account has an almost exaggerated humility: he makes it sound as if *Luang* Pradit Phairau decided to confer the ritual texts on him in a fit of elderly pique and anxiety, without considering his student's substantial talents. Prasit also emphasizes his own sense of inadequacy—common to officiants when they speak of their teachers—to melodramatic effect.

Probably the last disciple to whom *Luang* Pradit Phairau granted ritual rights was Uthit Naksawat, an economist and gifted musician who was instrumental in opening up classical Thai music to the middle classes through television and radio shows. Born in 1923, he studied closely with *Luang* Pradit Phairau from 1945 until 1954. He received ritual rights in 1954, the year of *Luang* Pradit Phairau's death, just before he left Thailand to study abroad at the age of thirty-one. He was one of *Luang* Pradit Phairau's last disciples and in many ways the most idiosyncratic, with a flair for public speaking and a willingness to experiment. Some would say that, by breaking with tradition in certain ways, he followed *Luang* Pradit Phairau's example more than other disciples. He and Prasit Thawon were also the

Figure 6.5   Prasidh Silapabanleng with his father, *Luang* Pradit Phairau.
Slide reproduced with the permission of Malini Sagarik.

teacher's closest disciples, coming to him as young men and staying with
him for years.

   Luang Pradit Phairau's decision to confer ritual rights on one of his children but not others is intriguing. Prasidh, as the eldest son of his first wife,
was the obvious choice, but "the Empty Basket" of Kumut's memoir was apparently too committed to Western art music to be an officiant.[46] Despite
their differences, father and son were apparently close, as Prasidh's memoir about the trip to Cambodia attests; he also arranged some of his father's
pieces for Western instruments.[47] (See fig. 6.5.) Prasidh's younger sister
Chin had extensive training in both Thai and Western art music, studying
not just with her father but with many eminent teachers of the time. Her
commitment to both preserving and extending the Thai music tradition (as
well as her kind and generous nature) led her father to entrust her with his
book of ritual texts and the right to read them aloud in performance, and she
in turn passed on the right to at least eight other musicians.[48] A photograph
from the early 1950s (Chin 2531/1988, 12) shows *Luang* Pradit Phairau

Figure 6.6   A photograph from the early 1950s showing *Luang* Pradit Phairau
leading the *wai khruu* ritual at his house, with his closest disciples around him,
including his daughter Chin Silapabanleng (front row, second from
left) and Uthit Naksawat (front row, far right, partially cut off).
Slide reproduced with the permission of Malini Sagarik.

leading the *wai khruu* ritual at his house, with his closest disciples in a ring
around him; Chin and Uthit Naksawat are among them (see fig. 6.6).

Luang Pradit Phairau died in 1954 at the age of seventy-three. His children, and now his grandchildren, continue to run the *Luang* Pradit Phairau
Foundation and the Phakavali Institute out of their home—a school of
music and dance that fills the compound with children on weekends. The
Foundation sponsors an annual music contest for children[49] and hands out
its awards at a large annual *wai khruu* ritual led by Prasit Thawon and some
of *Luang* Pradit Phairau's other disciples. Like *Luang* Pradit Phairau, his
grandchildren run the Foundation with a dual emphasis on high standards
(as evinced by their annual contest) and innovative teaching techniques,
which now include the use of computers and an extensive Internet site.[50]

Luang Pradit Phairau's fame and perceived accomplishments were so
extensive that, in some ways, he "froze" tradition for the following generation. Almost all Thai written sources laud his commitment to tradition and
its preservation, but *Luang* Pradit Phairau actually extended existing performance and compositional practice in ways that were sometimes radical.
Although my emphasis here is on the social connections between teachers

and disciples, and on the patronage system that supported Bangkok musicians, it must not be forgotten that great teachers and officiants are first recognized for their musical skill and technical expertise. That is, they are first and foremost excellent musicians, with a special talent for performing and remembering repertoire. *Luang* Pradit Phairau and the great teachers of the generations preceding and following him were also composers, adding hundreds of pieces to the repertoire.[51] Preservation and innovation, so often at odds in the Western musical tradition, are intimately connected in classical Thai music because a key compositional practice involves expanding or contracting existing melodies.[52] *Luang* Pradit Phairau was a master of this technique *(thao)*, a skill that almost certainly grew out of his talent for improvisation in competitions.

The reigns of Rama V and VI were the golden age of music competitions. As described above, *Luang* Pradit Phairau was "discovered" by his princely patron in a competition. The entire basis for competitions was the ability to improvise—instantly and elegantly—on any melody, whether as an entire ensemble or as a solo performer. The impulse toward competition was so keen that musicians or even entire ensembles would sometimes spontaneously "compete" when they found themselves in close proximity, for example, by playing the piece that the other group had just finished playing but in a different and more interesting way. Competition, whether formal or informal, was a serious business, sometimes leading to fights. Aristocratic patrons often took great delight in their musicians' ability to deal with such confrontations; musicians were even sometimes rewarded for "defeating" other groups. Sumonman (2524/1981, 265–66) relates an incident at the Buraphaa Palace, when visiting noblemen arranged for a singer to perform a Burmese piece that, of course, *Luang* Pradit Phairau's group had never heard. It was common for competing groups to spring obscure pieces on one another in an attempt to show off knowledge of repertoire, and noble patrons thoroughly enjoyed the ensuing musical displays of fast thinking. The vocalist from one group would simply start singing, and it was up to the rival group to figure out what piece the singer was performing and to come in correctly—or, if they didn't know the piece, to absorb its melody on the spot and to play it back with interesting variations. *Luang* Pradit Phairau's ability to come in correctly and on the appropriate pitch—no matter how much a singer wandered—was well known, so these noblemen decided to take things a step further by having a singer perform a foreign piece that any Thai musician would find strange. Sumonman says that despite some "clattering" from the rest of the ensemble, *Luang* Pradit Phairau came in correctly and then played a variation of the singer's melody after hearing it only once.[53] The noblemen "admitted defeat," but the Prince (*Luang* Pradit Phairau's patron) graciously wouldn't accept it since the ensemble as a whole hadn't been able to handle the surprise. Afterward, *Luang* Pradit Phairau complained that if the noblemen insisted on pieces like that, of course the ensemble would get confused. Still, he had the last word by remembering the piece and rearranging it, and it is still played today.[54]

Luang Pradit Phairau's skill for appropriating pieces—hearing them and then internalizing them so thoroughly that he could recreate them in an idiosyncratic way—was born in the crucible of competitions and led into his ability to compose. Listing *Luang* Pradit Phairau's musical accomplishments, Sumonman emphasizes his innovations (2524/1981, 268–70). Most extend preexisting ideas. *Luang* Pradit Phairau was the first *ranaat eek* player to sustain pitches by trilling (called *krau*), a now-standard technique that he almost certainly developed while competing and searching for virtuoso surprises. He is regarded as the first musician to realize consequent repetitions of a musical section in different ways (never playing it the same way twice), the first to begin pieces with a short introductory phrase,[55] and the first to write in a programmatic fashion, imitating the sounds of nature, and so on. His appropriation of Cambodian and Javanese pieces is frequently cited by musicians as a sign of his compositional genius. He transformed performance practice for the xylophone, creating flashy pieces in which he played two xylophones at once and, more importantly, came up with different ways of holding the xylophone mallets to create different moods, styles, and timbres. Challenged by Prince Boriphat, he expanded the most expansive metrical framework, 3 *chan*, to 6 *chan* and rendered an existing piece in this way.

I do not mean to suggest that such innovations, some quite radical, were instantly admired and imitated. When *Luang* Pradit Phairau began to experiment publicly with new mallet techniques, at least one listener said that he "played like a dog shaking off water" (Sumonman 2524/1981, 270). Older or more conservative musicians, no doubt, always had criticisms. *Luang* Pradit Phairau probably pulled these departures off through a combination of sheer virtuosity and his secure position in aristocratic circles. Clearly a different feeling surrounded the court musicians of these reigns than accompanies the musicians of the 1980s and 1990s—my sense is that the court musicians were characterized by a brashness, even a cockiness, and a willingness to take chances that were the delight and pride of their patrons.

Luang Pradit Phairau's transformation into the paradigm of tradition, as he is now seen, is thus somewhat ironic, but it is built into the historiography of classical Thai music. (See fig. 6.7.) Tradition is everything:

Figure 6.7   Luang Pradit Phairau in old age, mid-1950s, dressed as an officiant,
sitting before an altar with his book of ritual texts in front of him.
Slide reproduced with the permission of Malini Sagarik.

the idea of a monolithic past, passed down from teachers to disciples over
the centuries, permeates its aesthetics. The only musicians who can inno-
vate are, therefore, those most steeped in the tradition, who can manipulate repertoire in a masterful way—and their innovations become the new
paradigm of tradition. The great teachers, all *wai khruu* officiants, are sometimes the greatest innovators of all and paradoxically—necessarily—the
symbols of unchanging tradition at the same time. The extent to which
innovation is allowed changes from generation to generation: *Luang* Pradit
Phairau represents certain radical departures now tempered by the passage
of time. His students, even those whom he made officiants, have been less
bold but no less remarkable in their own ways.

Luang Pradit Phairau's Disciples

The contexts and institutions of musical authority were dramatically different for *Luang* Pradit Phairau and for his disciples. The means by which

musicians were recognized as authorities changed in the mid-twentieth century, and with them, the means by which officiants were defined. The courts and proximity to high-ranking aristocrats delineated great musicians before 1932; after that, classical musicians looked to government institutions, universities, and mass media for support and prestige.

Montri Tramote (1900–1995)

Montri Tramote was unquestionably the great teacher of his generation. He served as a court musician during the reigns of Rama VI and VII (from 1917 to 1935) and was of just the right age in 1935 to move immediately into a position of importance in the newly formed Department of Fine Arts. He was the head of the Thai Music Division at the Department of Fine Arts for decades and was the foremost *wai khruu* officiant of Thai classical music in the country until his death in August 1995: from the 1950s on, he led the ritual for music at the School of Dramatic Arts (as well as at its branches in various provinces) and at most leading music institutions in Bangkok.[56]

Montri's status as a distinguished teacher stemmed from his abilities as a composer and music historian, to some extent from his talents as a performer, and from two important investitures as an officiant, first by *Luang* Pradit Phairau and, much later, by King Rama IX (the present king). Musicians' respect for Montri cannot be underestimated. It was he who, every year at Chulalongkorn University, ritually "covered" the Crown Princess in their *wai khruu* ceremony, an honor that set him apart from other musicians. His great age and high status gave him an almost otherworldly aura.

Montri did not come from a musical family: his father was a mechanic and engineer.[57] His birthname was not Montri but Buntham, and the family had no surname until 1942.[58] He grew up in the provincial capital of Suphanburi, a town famed for its performers and musicians, and was drawn to music as a boy; a temple near his house had a resident *piiphaat* ensemble whose sound was a constant part of his boyhood. By the time he was thirteen, he had moved into the home of a musician and was studying both Thai and Western music, as well as composition. In 1917 (at age seventeen) he applied and was accepted as a civil servant in the Royal Department of *Phinphaat* of the Department of Entertainment and the Department of Royal Pages in Bangkok. He studied a variety of Thai instruments with famous court musicians, including *Phraya* Prasaan Duriyasap (Plaek Prasaansap), the head of the Royal Department of *Phinphaat*, mentioned above as one of *Luang* Pradit Phairau's teachers. Montri received a position in one of the palaces (Cankasem) and played in the *mahoorii* ensemble that accompanied

Figure 6.8   Montri Tramote during the reign of Rama VII.
Slide reproduced with the permission of Silapi Tramote.

Rama VI wherever he went. In 1925 he was initiated for *Phleeng Phra Phiraap*, the highest and most sacred ritual piece.[59]

Montri began studying with *Luang* Pradit Phairau in 1926 (Panya 2527/1984, 136), and his talent on the supporting xylophone *(ranaat thum)* led him to be the great teacher's first choice on this instrument. Whenever *Luang* Pradit Phairau had to play for important occasions, he led the group on xylophone and generally asked Montri to play supporting xylophone. As mentioned above, he liked to render repeated sections in a different way each time, and he liked Montri's ability to follow his lead (Phlaisupradit 2527/1984, 146–47).

During the reign of Rama VII (1925–1935), Montri began to compose many 3-*chan* and *thao* pieces (based on existing melodies) for radio stations and was also involved in an ambitious project to notate a large body of classical pieces.[60] (See fig. 6.8.)

With the establishment of the Department of Fine Arts in 1935, Montri became a teacher in the Music and Dance Division. At about the same time, *Phra* Chen Duriyang, a German musician who had overseen Western music activities at the courts,[61] opened a school of Western music and Montri entered it to study performance and Western notation. He became adept at composing in a style known as *phleeng Thai saakon*, or Thai pieces in a Western style, as well as in traditional classical style. In 1936 he entered a contest for a song celebrating Constitution Day and received first prize for both lyrics and music, which was in the Westernized Thai style mentioned above.

In 1940 Montri was made the head of the Thai Music Division at the Department of Fine Arts, a position he held for the next twenty-odd years. With his background in Western music, he was well suited to weather the ideological changes of 1938 to 1944 under the first government of Prime Minister Phibul Songkhram. A charismatic and controversial leader, Phibul's policy of Thai nationalism constituted a cultural revolution that had serious repercussions for the traditional Thai arts. During these six years, "Siam" became Thailand, central Thai became the official language of the country, the Western calendar was adopted, and laws were passed enforcing certain Westernizations in personal dress. (Western dress styles in shoes, hats, suits, dresses, etc. were required, and women were urged to abandon their traditional short hair.) Thai classical music was denigrated and Western music emphasized.[62] (See fig. 6.9.) The arts were radically affected. Between 1939 and 1942, twelve Cultural Mandates were issued (Wyatt 1982, 255), including the Decree of Cultural Determination for the Theater Arts in 1942 (Surapone 1980, 91–93). The decree was written by intellectuals with a background in Western theater who divided Thai drama into three categories—"opera," "spoken drama," and "dance-music" —and directed that all drama had to fit squarely into these categories.[63] The Department of Fine Arts was put in charge of overseeing and enforcing the new laws, and Montri was made an official government censor. All performers had to have an "artist identification card," which, Surapone claims, "was, in essence, a license to perform," obtained by undergoing an examination administered by the Department of Fine Arts.[64]

In the midst of these changes, Montri received the right to lead the *wai khruu* ritual for music from *Luang* Pradit Phairau in 1941 (Phlaisupradit 2527/1984, 151), the first student to be thus honored by the great teacher. One source (Panya Nittayasawan 2527/1984, 136) claims that a number of people asked Montri to perform the *wai khruu* ritual, so he asked *Luang* Pradit Phairau to grant him the right, and he did.[65] Even at this relatively young age (for an officiant), Montri was evidently held in high esteem by other musicians.

Figure 6.9 Photograph of Prime Minister Phibul Songkhram with the lyrics to *Saen Kham Nüng* (A Hundred Thousand Sorrows) superimposed over it. This piece, written by *Luang* Pradit Phairau, was a protest against the prime minister's musical reforms. Slide reproduced with the permission of Malini Sagarik.

Montri was busy during these years, regularly attending performances in his official role as a government censorship officer and also composing a large number of pieces. He was also on the government committee whose task was to standardize the Thai vocabulary for Western music terms. During this same period, working closely with the director of the Department of Fine Arts and with the choreographer of the National Theater dance troupe, he wrote the music for a number of "historical" or "archaeological pieces" (*phleeng prawatsaat* or *phleeng booraankhadii*); based on evidence from art history (mostly murals and some written inscriptions), these dances, their costumes, and their music were an imaginative *tour de force*—fascinating examples of self-consciously created history.[66] Montri also wrote the music for a large number of dances in the styles of other countries, most commissioned by the government in honor of visits by international delegations. In addition to his creative work at the Department of Fine Arts, Montri composed a piece for National Day *(wan chaat)* and entered it in a government contest, once again receiving first prize: his background in Western music served him in good stead, enabling him to write in the Westernized-Thai style promoted by the Phibul government.

Unlike his Thai pieces, which were often based on existing melodies, his Westernized-Thai works were newly composed and fully harmonized. Montri has commented that composing everything from scratch is simpler than the traditional procedure of basing works on other melodies ("Samphaat Rachabandit" 2524/1981, 8–9). He has also said that, when taking Thai pieces and adapting them, the original melody shouldn't be cut down or reduced but kept and cited.

Despite his background in Western music, Montri was essentially a classical Thai musician fortunate enough to have other talents during a difficult period of Thai history. His prominent career as a civil servant in the Department of Fine Arts was founded on his successful negotiation of the politically dangerous years of Phibul's first government, but I have never heard any criticism of the decisions he made. Many performers' careers were ruined during those years, and those who weathered the period were considered lucky. Most returned to, or tried to revive, traditional performance practices once it was all over.

Montri's work from the 1950s and 1960s included an extraordinary number of compositions. In many ways, he was the official composer of the Department of Fine Arts, always on hand to create pieces for whatever projects were at hand—new dances, special works commemorating diplomatic visits, international tours by the department's troupes, officials' anniversaries and birthdays, and so on. At the time of his death, he had composed about two hundred works, which he divided into several categories: 3 *chan* and *thao* pieces based on existing melodies, historical or archaeological works, dance pieces, and miscellaneous works (many composed for special occasions). Unlike many composers, Montri was also an accomplished poet and wrote most of the lyrics for his pieces. These lyrics are in a variety of traditional Thai verse forms, and his treatment of them is much admired.

His talent for writing extended far beyond poetry. Unlike musicians of earlier eras, Montri was also a music historian. His impulse to write about music, in prose and as a historian, issued from a desire to create a uniquely Thai history. His scholarly output was also the product of its time: much of it could have been written only following the intense Westernization of the Phibul years. Montri's writings of this kind are extensive. His major books are *Thai Music History* (1938), *Thai Entertainment* (1954), *Music Terminology* (1964), and *Explanations of the History and Meaning of Thai Musical Pieces*.[67] He also wrote various encyclopedia entries on Thai music and compiled an invaluable list of all the musicians given titles during the reign of Rama VI (Montri 2521/1978). He has contributed to the journal *Silapakorn* [Fine Arts] for years, including a piece transcribed into Western notation in nearly every issue, accompanied by historical information and analysis.

From the 1960s on, Montri was recognized as a national treasure. He received medals from the government and received at least two honorary degrees from leading universities. In 1985 he was named one of the first National Artists (along with Kukrit Pramoj). Although he retired as head of the Thai Music Division at the Department of Fine Arts in 1962, he held a special position as "Thai Music Expert" for many years, and, until his death, was still in his office most mornings by nine or ten o'clock. He was a "Special Teacher" of Thai musical arts at the College of Dramatic Arts and at Chulalongkorn University through the 1980s and served on a number of government committees regulating and standardizing the music curriculum for elementary schools and universities (Panya 2527/1984, 141). Up until his death in 1995, though he became physically rather frail, he remained extremely active, and his circuit of annual *wai khruu* rituals was quite demanding.

To put Montri and his achievements into a Thai perspective, it is worth quoting one of his disciples (Phlaisupradit 2527/1984, 141):

> Thai musicians can be divided into two kinds: those who are technically skilled, and those who are knowledgeable. There aren't many who are both, but Montri Tramote is among those few. He is one of the best *ranaat thum* players in the country and his knowledge of music is wide and extensive. He has received the highest accolades, and is seen as the most qualified musician of our times. Some music teachers have been exceptionally skilled in performance, knowledge, and composition. During the reigns of Rama III, IV, and the beginning of the reign of Rama V, *Khruu Phra* Pradit Phairau (Mii Duriyangkun), was the greatest *pii* player of the time and the composer of *Phleeng Choet Ciin, Thayoi Nauk, Khaek Mon An Lu Lan*. After his death, the honor went to *Khruu* Choi Sunthaurawathin (famous during the reigns of Rama IV to the middle of the reign of Rama V), a blind musician

Figure 6.10 Montri Tramote leading a *wai khruu* ritual in 1954,
the year of *Luang* Pradit Phairau's death. Slide reproduced with
the permission of Silapi Tramote.

skilled on *ranaat eek* . . . , who composed *Hoomroong Aiyareet, Khaek Lopburi
3 chan*, and *Khaek Ot 3 chan.* At the end of the reign of Rama V and during the reign of Rama VI, *Khruu Phrayaa* Prasaanduriyasap (a disciple of
Khruu Choi) held this honor. After him came *Khruu Luang* Pradit Phairau
(a disciple of *Phrayaa* Prasaanduriyasap and a "grandchild" disciple of *Phra*
Pradit Phairau as well). During the present reign, *Khruu* Montri Tramote
holds this honor: he has both performance and compositional skill.
(Phlaisupradit 2527/1984, 141)

The earliest photograph that I have found showing Montri leading a *wai
khruu* ritual dates to 1954, taken at the Association of Thai Performers, a
group that no longer exists (Seerii and Sucit 2527/1984, plate; see fig. 6.10).
This was the year of *Luang* Pradit Phairau's death and was probably the
first year (or one of the first few years) that Montri acted as an officiant:
then in his fifties, he was "of age" to be an officiant and would not have
been very active until after his teacher's death. The photograph shows
Montri seated in front of a table of offerings, flanked by two unidentified
men.[68] All three are *wai*-ing and are dressed in white Western-style suits,
rather than the traditional Thai dress now worn by nearly all officiants, including Montri himself. A row of monks can be seen to their side, and

Figure 6.11   Montri Tramote initiating American ethnomusicologist David
Morton on the gong circle at the College of Dramatic Arts in the early 1960s.
Slide reproduced with the permission of Silapi Tramote.

the other participants, all adult men and women, can be seen in the background. (See fig. 6.11.)

∽

In the mid-1980s, Montri was re-invested by King Rama IX as a *wai khruu*
officiant, an immense honor with a long history behind it. (I will address
this history in detail in Chapter 7.) With the death in 1982 of the leading
officiant for the dance-drama *wai khruu* (*Khruu* Akhom Saiyakhom), the
Department of Fine Arts appealed to the King to personally invest several
teachers as officiants; he did so in a special royal ritual and re-invested
Montri at the same time. To receive such spiritual power from royalty is
incomparable. Thai performers say it is the "highest" *(suung sut)* power of
all, and the performers who receive it are in a category all their own. (See
fig. 6.12.)

   Montri personally "covered" the Crown Princess every year in the
annual *wai khruu* ritual at Chulalongkorn University, the Princess's *alma
mater*. A patron and performer of classical Thai music, the Crown Princess
makes a point of attending this ritual and is always the first to be "covered"
at the end of the *wai khruu* ritual and the beginning of the initiation cere-

Figure 6.12   Montri Tramote being reinvested as a *wai khruu* officiant by
Rama IX. Slide reproduced with the permission of Silapi Tramote.

mony. When I attended this ritual in 1989, she knelt before Montri like any
disciple. Rather than touch her head (far too sacred to be touched by non-
royalty), however, Montri anointed the palms of her hands, writing the
secret sign of blessing there instead of on her forehead. (See fig. 6.13.)

After 1954, Montri's round of *wai khruu* rituals became quite extensive. The power and status surrounding him gave any *wai khruu* ritual over
which he presided a special efficaciousness. (See fig. 6.14.) His primary link
with *Luang* Pradit Phairau and the added power of his investiture by King
Rama IX granted him a palpable aura of *baaramii*, that elusive air of greatness described at the beginning of this chapter as a necessary quality for
officiants. Montri was a living monument—not just one of the last surviving court musicians, but the only living officiant for music to have received
royal investiture. Montri was the primary source of spiritual power for
classical musicians—a power that necessarily diminishes with each link in
the chain of officiants—and no musician since him has been similarly recognized by the King. Montri has given ten disciples the right to lead the
wai khruu ritual for music: Prasit Thawon (also invested by *Luang* Pradit
Phairau, as described above), Camnian Srithaiphan, his son Silapi Tramote,
Sangwian Thaungkham, Yongyot Wannamaat, Sirichaichan Faakcamrüün,
the brothers Natthaphong and Bunchuay Soowat, Cit Phoemkusol, and

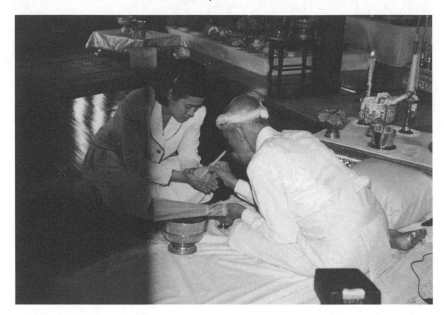

Figure 6.13   The Crown Princess (partly in shade) being "covered" by Montri
Tramote in the annual *wai khruu* ritual at Chulalongkorn University in 1989.
Photograph by Deborah Wong.

Prasit Thawon's son Thongchai Thawon. The reasons for his choices are
fascinating and will be examined at the end of this chapter.

Prasit Thawon (1921–present)

Prasit Thawon is a fascinating example of an officiant whose right to lead the
ritual crosses generations: as a young man, he was ritually invested by *Luang*
Pradit Phairau, and then re-invested later by Montri Tramote. His special
concentration of spiritual power may well have implications for the redis-
tribution of status and power following Montri's death in 1995.

Prasit was born in Ayuthaya, the former capital of Thailand (now about
an hour from Bangkok by bus). Neither of his parents was a musician, and
Prasit was the only one of his five siblings to become one. As a child, he first
studied music with a relative and quickly became accomplished on the
xylophone. Prasit attended elementary school and then entered the newly
formed School of Dramatic Arts in 1934 at the age of thirteen. During his
first year of study, one of the music teachers recognized his talent and took
him to the home of *Luang* Pradit Phairau, asking that the boy be accepted
as a disciple; after hearing him play a little bit of *Saathukaan* on the xylophone, the teacher immediately agreed. A few days later, Prasit and *Luang*

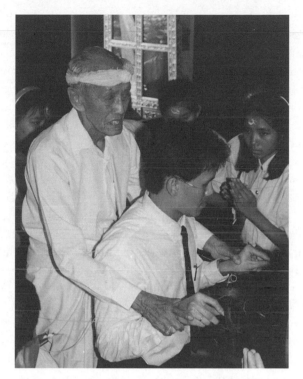

Figure 6.14   Montri Tramote initiating music majors at the annual *wai khruu* ritual at Chulalongkorn University in 1989. Photograph by Deborah Wong.

Pradit Phairau performed the ritual of "depositing oneself as a disciple" *(phithii faak tua pen sit)*, attended by Prasit's mother, his first teacher, and his present teacher. Prasit lived at *Luang* Pradit Phairau's home on and off until the teacher's death in 1954 and became one of his closest disciples. As described above, he received the right to lead the *wai khruu* ritual in 1946.

Prasit taught at various elementary schools and helped with his family's business until 1950, when he was hired at the Department of Fine Arts in the Music Division *(Kaung Kaan Sangkhiit)* as a full-time performer. He worked there for twenty-three years, gradually rising through the ranks of civil servants and eventually teaching at the School of Dramatic Arts.

Prasit's skill as a xylophone player is legendary. The xylophone was *Luang* Pradit Phairau's main instrument as well, so Prasit is the major transmitter of his teacher's style. He absorbed *Luang* Pradit Phairau's method of using the mallets in different ways to create different effects and also inherited his famous solo arrangements for the xylophone.

Prasit has never been especially active as a composer, but he created several pieces that have become well known, particularly one for the funeral *piiphaat* ensemble.[69] His major innovation (first assembled in 1972) was the "Great Musical Ensemble" *(Wong Mahaduriyang)*, a *mahoorii* ensemble consisting of anywhere from one hundred to four hundred musicians. Traditional ensembles usually have no more than fifteen musicians, with no instruments doubled, but the Great Ensemble had multiples of each instrument. The resulting sound is "great" indeed. Prasit claims that the idea actually came from *Luang* Pradit Phairau, who once had two *piiphaat* ensembles play together after the *wai khruu* at his home, just to revel in the sound (Prasit 2531/1988b, 43–44, 62).

While still at the Department of Fine Arts, Prasit organized a remarkable series of cassette recordings (over one hundred tapes in all) that covers many of the major pieces in the *piiphaat* and *mahoorii* repertoires. Intended as a historical record, the cassettes are plain and unadorned (unlike colorful commercial cassettes); they list only the names of the pieces and the name of the ensemble, *Khana Sit Thawon*, the "Sit Thawon Troupe," which was actually a revolving group of musicians drawn entirely from the Department of Fine Arts. The cassettes contain a wide variety of Thai music: pieces from the ritual repertoire, solo pieces for nearly every instrument, Montri Tramote's "archaeological pieces," *Luang* Pradit Phairau's piece for seven xylophones, the Department of Fine Arts's interpretations of rural musical genres, and so on. It is an eclectic and impressive collection and nearly the only place to find recordings of pieces from outside the old favorites of the *mahoorii* repertoire.

Prasit retired from the Department of Fine Arts in 1982 at the age of sixty-one and was immediately made a special teacher at Chulalongkorn University, where he helped establish the curriculum for music students. He has also opened his own music shop, selling classical Thai instruments of superb quality for fairly high prices, and is actively involved in various music contests for children. In general, he has been part of a movement to open up classical Thai music to nonspecialists, encouraging its inclusion in elementary and college curricula. He was named a National Artist in 1988 in recognition of his skill as a performer and his commitment to pedagogy.

Prasit may well be regarded as the next great teacher once Montri Tramote has passed on. His links to *Luang* Pradit Phairau are closer than any other living performer, and he has also received ritual rights from several different quarters. He was the first person to whom Montri granted the right to lead the *wai khruu* ritual, and he subsequently received the right from Chin Silapabanleng as well as from another famous officiant, *Khruu* Saun Wongkhaung. In other words, he received the right to lead the ritual from four different teachers, including *Luang* Pradit Phairau. (See fig. 6.15.)

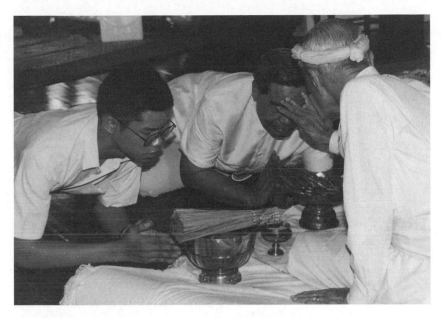

Figure 6.15   Prasit Thawon (and possibly his grandson) being blessed by Montri
Tramote in the annual *wai khruu* ritual at Chulalongkorn University in 1989.
Photograph by Deborah Wong.

He also requested ritual rights to ritual texts from two teachers, *Luang*
Bamrungcitcaroen and Chin Silapabanleng herself—whose texts came, of
course, from her father. Prasit therefore represents a concentration of *Luang*
Pradit Phairau's ritual power and expertise, received from the teacher him-
self, from his daughter, and from Montri Tramote, the first disciple to whom
Luang Pradit Phairau granted ritual rights.

At present, Prasit leads the annual *wai khruu* ritual held by the *Luang*
Pradit Phairau Foundation, a large ceremony held mostly for children taking lessons at the Foundation. (See fig. 6.16.) When he reads the ritual texts
in the course of this ritual, he invokes *Luang* Pradit Phairau and invites him
to enter the ceremony. I was told that he has passed on the right to lead
the ritual to his son, Thongchai Thawon, who teaches music in Chiang
Mai; Prasit is quite reserved about these matters, but I suspect that he has
already conferred ritual rights on several other disciples as well.

Compared to *Luang* Pradit Phairau, Prasit is fairly conservative: his in-
stincts run toward preservation more than innovation. He even attributes
his major experiment, the Great Ensemble, to an idea of his teacher's. He
has sought out ritual authority with acuity and has tried to counter the inevitable loss of spiritual power inherent in successive conferrals by linking

Figure 6.16   Prasit Thawon after leading the annual *wai khruu* for the *Luang*
Pradit Phairau Foundation in 1989. Photograph by Deborah Wong.

himself not only to *Luang* Pradit Phairau but to *Luang* Pradit Phairau's disciples as well. Whether he can follow in Montri Tramote's footsteps remains to be seen.

Chin Silapabanleng (1906–1988)

A remarkable woman, Chin Silapabanleng was from the first generation
of Thai women having access to education and seemingly tried to make
up for lost time by becoming fluent in French and English and becoming a
teacher herself. A poet, she wrote a huge body of song lyrics in classical
Thai meters. She was a capable performer of Western as well as Thai music,
playing the violin, singing soprano, and becoming conversant with Western
notation at an early age. She also carried forth her father's legacy by teaching Thai music at a large number of different schools and universities.

Chin was born in her father's house, just outside the walls of the
Buraphaa Palace. Her mother, Chot, was the first of *Luang* Pradit Phairau's
two wives, who evidently lived together quite amicably. Chin first began
making music at the age of eight on a homemade fiddle *(sau)* that her mother
made from an old milk can. After that, she studied with her father, learning
the cipher system of notation, with which he was already experimenting.

She was so good in school, however, that she didn't seriously intend to pursue music. As she entered her teens, her studies with her father intensified, and she also began studying Western violin and Western notation with another teacher. As a young woman, she played in an all-female *mahoorii* ensemble in the household of King Rama VII. A photograph from the time shows her, a slender young woman in traditional Thai dress, playing the *sau saam saai* (three-stringed fiddle; Surachai 2524/1981, 18). By 1926 she was the ensemble's leader, playing xylophone and *sau sam sai*.

After finishing school, she began teaching foreign languages and Thai music at a number of elementary schools. Chin was an extraordinary teacher by all accounts, and biographical essays on her achievements are essentially long prose accounts of all the schools at which she taught (see *Khunying Chin Silapabanleng* 2530/1987; "Chiiwit thii kieo" 2529/1986).[70] When the Department of Fine Arts was established in 1934, she was invited to head the Music Division, where she taught both Thai and Western music; she also organized and led performance tours by the school's students in Japan and elsewhere. In 1934, with her brothers' and sisters' help, she organized the Phakavali Troupe, made up of her father's disciples; after his death in 1954, they established the Phakavali Institute of Dance and Music, a school and performing group that was eventually renamed the *Luang Pradit Phairau Foundation*.[71]

Chin's involvement with student performance tours and the family troupe led her to experiment with different kinds of costumes and dramatic material. She adapted Western stories like "The Little Mermaid" and was constantly writing new song lyrics for old melodies to make them topical and immediately relevant to contemporary audiences. The Phakavali Troupe performed a weekly variety show at a tourist restaurant, so she constantly had to think up new and colorful ways of presenting Thai music and dance, borrowing freely from other Southeast Asian dance traditions (e.g., Lao and Burmese) and adapting Western subject matter. In this, she was very much her father's daughter, borrowing and appropriating other materials to great dramatic effect.

This is not to suggest that she flew in the face of tradition. In fact, Chin clearly had a deep and abiding respect for tradition. Her grounding in tradition enabled her—again, like her father—to extend it, usually by reworking existing pieces. Reaching adulthood during the years when the courts began to disappear, she helped create an entirely new context for performing and teaching music, bringing classical music into the schools and creating music clubs at universities (such as Prasanmit). Unlike court musicians, who generally spent young adulthood intensely active as performers and

Figure 6.17   Prateep Lountratana-ari teaching a class in Thai music
appreciation at Srinakharinwirot University–Prasanmit in 1988.
Photograph by Deborah Wong.

then middle and old age as teachers, Chin was a teacher throughout her long
and busy life—the change in music patronage created a different kind of
career, and a different progression through the life cycle.

Chin had a serious disposition even as a young woman and was known
as both kindly and modest. I don't know when her father granted her the
right to lead the *wai khruu* ritual, but I would guess that her suitability for
the role was evident from an early age. While mindful of tradition, she was
less concerned with maintaining the status quo than with the spirit of classical music. She told her students more than once that all you really need
for a *wai khruu* is your two hands (to form a *wai*) and your heart. She was
not particularly active as a celebrant: Prasanmit is the only place I know
where she regularly led the ritual. In the 1970s or 1980s, she granted
Prasit Thawon her father's book of ritual texts, thus recognizing him—
with customary modesty—as *Luang* Pradit Phairau's chief musical and
ritual heir. Also in the 1980s, she granted one of the Prasanmit students,
Prateep Lountratana-ari, the right to lead the ritual; now a professor in
the music department, Prateep told me that Chin was concerned that
someone of her father's lineage be able to lead the Prasanmit ritual once
Khruu Chüa, the present officiant, became too old. (See fig. 6.17.) She also
granted the right to lead the ritual to her nephew Chanok Sagarik, who is

Figure 6.18 Photograph of Chin Silapabanleng from the cover
of a booklet commemorating her eightieth birthday in 1986.
Slide reproduced with the permission of Malini Sagarik.

active in the administration of the *Luang* Pradit Phairau Foundation. In 1994, I was told that she had also conferred ritual rights to two other men, Sawit Thapthimsrii and Uthai Kaewla-iat, about whom I know nothing. In 1998 another one of her students, Narong Khianthongkul, said that she had also given the right to Somphop Khamprasoet, Suraphon Canthabat, and Subin Cankaew. Chin may well have passed on the right to other students too; as one account notes, "it has been said that Bangkok is full of her disciples" ("*Khunying* Chin Silapabanleng" 2530/1987, 60). Unlike the teachers of old who carefully chose a few close disciples, Chin disseminated what she knew to as many students as possible—and in this, too, she was like her father, who taught many students and made no less than thirteen of his disciples into officiants. (See fig. 6.18.)

Chin's legacy includes the lyrics for 192 songs and an edition of her father's collected works. This book presents his compositions in cipher notation, handsomely illustrated with photographs and drawings and was . published on the hundredth anniversary of his birth (Chin 2525/1982).[72]

But Chin's most telling achievement was her impact on hundreds if not thousands of students over several decades of teaching. The *Luang* Pradit Phairau Foundation is now run by her sister (Mrs. Banleng Sagarik) and her niece and nephew (Malini and Chanok Sagarik).

Kings, Officiants, and Power

The period of magnanimous royal support of the arts, and of performers' close proximity to the King, ended abruptly with King Vajiravudh's death in 1925. With the Royal Treasury in disarray from the King's excesses, the new King, Rama VII or King Prajadhipok, immediately disbanded the centralized Department of Royal Entertainment and plunged performers into a period of hardship by suddenly withdrawing royal patronage. Many of the masks and costumes used by the royal troupes were lost or stolen at this time, and court performers were forced to explore employment possibilities with private troupes. No royally sponsored *wai khruu* rituals were held during this reign. Then the entire institution of royal patronage came to an end in 1932 with a military coup and the King's abdication.

When the new government created the Department of Fine Arts in 1934, it gave the former court performers a new patron. Created expressly to support these performers and to preserve their expertise, the Department of Fine Arts institutionalized the court arts and made the performers into civil servants. This change in administrative structure had several effects. One was that authoritative teachers—that is, officiants—were installed as bureaucratic division heads and became administrators as well as teachers. In other words, their status as performers and as ritual experts gave them powerful positions in the hierarchy of the civil servant system, and very different kinds of social authority thus converged on certain people. Another effect was on ritual practice. Although performers had held small *wai khruu* rituals for their specific genres (*piiphaat*, singing, *khoon*, etc.), often at their homes, it was common for large *wai khruu* rituals to include all the performing arts. As the different divisions of the Department of Fine Arts became larger and more specialized over time, the *wai khruu* rituals for music and dance were celebrated separately and continue so today.

The former court performers' relationship to the royal family did not, however, end with the abolition of the absolute monarchy. In fact, the performers at the Department of Fine Arts continue in many ways to see themselves as court performers: many of today's performers are the children or grandchildren of court artists, and their orientation toward the King and his family is still basic to their perception of spiritual power and

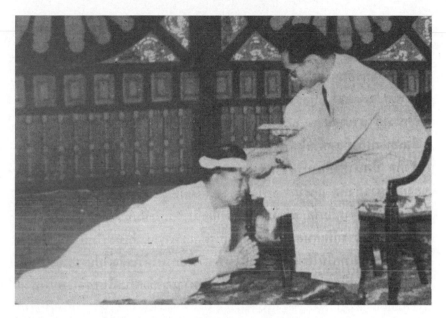

Figure 6.19   Akhom Saiyakhom being given the right to confer the dance of
Phra Phiraap by the present king, Rama IX in 1963.

their own efforts to "locate" their traditions. These matters came to a head,
first with a problem in the 1960s and then with a crisis in 1982.

The arrival of the demonic deity Phiraap is the high point of most *wai
khruu* rituals, and it is up to the officiant to control his savage power. By the
early 1960s, only one teacher at the Department of Fine Arts was ritually au-
thorized to dance as Phiraap, but he himself was not an officiant and did not
have the right to pass the dance on. After much deliberation, the head administrators took the problem to the King and asked that he personally invest several teachers with the right to dance as Phiraap and to pass the dance
on. The King agreed, and at a royal ritual *(Phra Raachaa Phithii)* held in 1963,
he invested four teachers and then watched as they "learned" the dance.[73]
(See fig. 6.19.) Without the king's intervention, Phiraap's dance (and possibly his presence in the ritual) would have died with the elderly teacher.

The decision to involve the present King reveals much about the Department of Fine Arts performers' beliefs in royal power. King Rama IX, or
King Bhumibol Adulyadej, is not an absolute monarch: Thailand has been
a constitutional monarchy since 1932, and Kings Rama VII and VIII lived
abroad for most of their reigns. The present king is Western-educated.
Despite ascending to the throne in 1946, he continued to live abroad until
1951, when he returned to Thailand and assumed his royal duties. In other

words, there was no royal presence in Thailand between 1932 and 1951 except for the actual coronation ceremonies and brief visits by Kings Rama VIII and IX. Nor is King Bhumibol a particularly enthusiastic patron of the traditional arts. His interest in music is confined to jazz, especially big-band music: an avid performer on clarinet and saxophone as a young man, the King has composed a number of songs and once invited Benny Goodman to perform at the palace. He never received any training in the traditional Thai performing arts and has never been very interested in them. When the Department of Fine Arts asked for his help, they were appealing to neither his personal involvement in classical performance nor to his actual political power (which is largely informal) but rather to his role as the spiritual center of the Thai kingdom.

In 1982 Akhom Saiyakhom, the leading teacher and officiant of *khoon* and *lakhon* at the Department of Fine Arts, died suddenly and unexpectedly the night before he was supposed to lead the *wai khruu* ritual in Chiang Mai. The Department of Fine Arts was left with a real problem of ritual authority: Akhom had not yet passed on the right to lead the *wai khruu* ritual to any of his disciples. He was only sixty-five years old and had been in good health. Furthermore, Akhom represented the Department of Fine Arts's last real link to royal investiture: he had studied with and received ritual rights from leading teachers from the court of King Rama VI who had been "covered" by the King himself [74] *and* he had been invested by Rama IX with the right to lead the *wai khruu* (in 1978). Although Rama IX's initiation of the five dancers for *Ong Phra Phiraap*'s dance in 1963 had addressed that particular crisis of dissemination, those teachers were not able to lead the *wai khruu*— as specialists in demonic dance roles, it was inappropriate, whereas Akhom specialized (as do all dance officiants) in the role of Rama. Although there were other dance officiants in the Department of Fine Arts, none had Akhom's stature. With Akhom, the last close link to royal spiritual power was broken, and it was this concern that led the administrators of the Department of Fine Arts to ask the King personally to invest five dance teachers as officiants. He agreed. (See fig. 6.20.) Photographs taken at the ritual in 1984 show the King, dressed in a gray Western-style suit, seated in a tall ceremonial chair and "covering" the teachers' heads with the masks of the Old Father, the demon Phiraap, and the *soet* headdress as they kneel on the floor below. Montri Tramote, already an officiant and the head of the Thai music division at the Department of Fine Arts, was also "covered," confirming his status as the most honored music officiant in the country.

Several of the five teachers were fairly young and were chosen to ensure that they would have time to pass the right on to their disciples. One

Figure 6.20   Ritual of royal "covering" at the court of Rama IX in the mid-1980s.
The five dance teachers include Thongchai Pothayarom.

of these men, Thongchai Phothayarom, explained to me why it was such
an honor to be invested by the King. The spiritual power instilled in them
that day is unequaled, he said. When they later pass on the right to certain
disciples, some of that power will be passed on, but not all of it; the direct
link to the King grants "the highest kind of power":

> The King gave the right to five people. I don't know what will happen af-
> ter this reign, but I don't think [this power] is all used up. And those who
> received the right are still fairly young—fifty or sixty years old. I'm fifty
> years old, and I'll pass the right on. But as I said before, I won't be able to
> pass on the strength of the auspiciousness *(mongkhon)* I've received. I
> won't be able to pass this thing on exactly—this is the highest. I can give
> my book of sacred texts away, but I can't give my auspiciousness away.
> Take *Aacaan* Montri: he was given the right at the same time I was. He
> was already a great teacher *(khruu phuu yai)*, and was already able to lead
> the *wai khruu* ceremony. But then he received the auspiciousness of the
> King, at the same time I did: the highest right of all, and no one else could
> equal that. *Khruu* Silapi [Montri's son] can't, even though his father gave
> him the right. He has the right, but it's not from the King. He's got per-
> mission to perform the *wai khruu*, as do I, but he doesn't have the auspi-
> ciousness that I do.

In other words, Thongchai (and presumably his fellow officiants at the Department of Fine Arts) feel it necessary to return periodically to the ultimate source of spiritual power, the king himself, since the strength of what a king confers diminishes with each transmission. Working in traditions that revolve around issues of power and royal legitimization, these performers have deliberately revived a relationship that languished after 1932. Following the model established by Rama VI, they looked to the King for empowerment, even though this King does not go through the dramatic motions of transforming himself into the hermit.

For Montri Tramote, the proximity is even more telling. Montri was already established as the great teacher of his generation. He also had close ties to the Crown Princess, a staunch supporter of classical music whose photograph is the frontispiece of most books on Thai music. She presides over the *wai khruu* ritual at Chulalongkorn University every year, where Montri "covered" and anointed her by writing a magic symbol on the palms of her hands (as mentioned earlier, no one, not even an officiant, can touch the head of a royal person). For a short time in the 1980s, rumors circulated that the King was considering making her the heir apparent, but such talk died when her older brother the Crown Prince was appointed, in keeping with tradition. Still, there is a strong feeling— especially among performers—that the Crown Princess too has the kind of auspicious power held by kings. Montri's close contact with both the Crown Princess and then her father put him in a class by himself among musicians.

In short, classical performance is still a royal art, at least for the performers at the Department of Fine Arts. Although the government is their real patron, none would ever consider asking the Prime Minister, for instance, to grant them ritual rights. And although their actual performances legitimize, and are an instrument of, the Thai government, there is no question in the minds of these performers that the King and his family are still the ultimate source of their empowerment.

The Nation-State at Work in the Practice of the *Wai Khruu*

When classical dance and particularly music were made part of the curriculum at schools and universities,[75] a number of changes in the ritual practice of the *wai khruu* gradually followed. Traditionally performed only on Thursday, considered "teacher's day," the modern Monday-through-Friday workweek dictates that most institutional *wai khruu* rituals are now held on Sunday so as not to disrupt school schedules. This, however, is the least of the changes involved.

Even in court circles, the *wai khruu* ritual was usually fairly small compared to its celebration in today's universities and public schools. Traditionally, a student looked to his or her teacher for the *wai khruu*, or to the teacher's teacher, and the ritual was celebrated among a close (and closed) circle of teachers and disciples. In public schools, however, where large numbers of students take music classes at any given time, the annual *wai khruu* can involve over one hundred students; at a university, which usually serves not just the professors and majors in the music department but also an attached elementary school and all the private students who take lessons after hours, the ritual must accommodate even more people. This presents the officiant with the logistical problem of how to "cover" all of the students without making the ritual into an all-day affair. Since most officiants are older if not elderly, the teacher's stamina must also be considered.

Traditionally, the *wai khruu* ritual itself was quite long, with a large number of deities and past teachers invited one by one into the ritual by reciting extended sacred texts. The initiation ritual that followed was usually fairly short since a limited number of students were involved. Today, the inverse is necessary. The initiation ritual can go on for several hours because of the sheer number of students, even with shortcuts such as "covering" children in groups of five (as is now common) or connecting a group of ten or more students with string and then initiating them all at once on *Saathukaan* (Montri did this in old age to save his strength). Since the *wai khruu* must end and the initiation ritual begin before noon (or even 11:00, according to some teachers), the *wai khruu* itself has been shortened: only the major deities are now invited into the ritual, and the sections of the sacred texts recited aloud have been shortened. This means that many of the lesser deities' names are now unfamiliar to many performers and that *piiphaat* musicians are seldom called upon to play the sacred pieces that summon them. The end result may well be a diminished pantheon, a more streamlined cosmology, and a reduced sacred repertoire.

At one point in my follow-up fieldwork, I was telling a young American graduate student I had just met about my research and he responded, "Oh, is that one of those fake ceremonies created by the government?" The *wai khruu* is no fake, but his question was understandable given the self-conscious efforts of various ministries to maintain certain "traditional" practices in the pursuit of Thai national identity. I know of two government-sponsored *wai khruu* rituals in recent years that were essentially public displays of Thai-ness. The Office of the National Culture Commission has sponsored large annual public *wai khruu* rituals for music and dance at the Thai Cultural Center since at least 1988 (when I attended one). Craig J. Reynolds (1991, 12) has described the evolution of this government office, tracing it from the National Cultural Maintenance Act of 1940 through the National Culture Acts of 1942 and 1943. These acts led to the establishment of the National Culture Council, headed by the Prime Minister himself during and just after World War II. In the 1950s, Prime Minister Phibul Songkhram established the Ministry of Culture, which has shifted between "a stream of commissions, councils, boards and bureaux charged with national culture policy since then" through subsequent governments (12). In a press announcement inviting the public to its annual *wai khruu* ritual in 1998, the Office of the National Culture Commission provided a page-long description of the ritual and its importance, couched in much the same language and terms that performers themselves would use, such as respect for teachers. There were also, however, a number of key phrases that few performers would use. At the end of the first paragraph, for instance, the Office stated, "but at present, this custom, the *wai khruu* for dance-drama and music, is a thing that is difficult to find and see, and in not too much time will vanish." Describing the ritual as something rare and in danger of disappearance is apparently a strategy to emphasize its rarity as well as the Office's supposed key role in maintaining it—a completely spurious role, in my experience.

Furthermore, the 1998 *wai khruu* (led by Silapi Tramote) was one of several events held April 2–5, during the Office's conference on "Thai Culture in Relation to a Dangerous Economy,"[76] in which they responded to the financial crisis of 1997–1998. The bulletin states that the Office sponsored it "in the hope that this beautiful Thai ritual might bolster the willpower of those who work in arts and culture so that they will have a stronger heart and spirit in this economic situation." In short, the *wai khruu* was pulled into the larger bureaucratic project of responding to the threat of the economic crisis.

Another government-sponsored *wai khruu* was held in the summer of 1994 during the annual Festival of American Folklife in Washington, D.C., sponsored by the Smithsonian Institution. Thailand was one of two cultures chosen for that year, and the External Relations Division of Thailand's National Culture Commission worked closely with the Smithsonian staff to come up with a number of "living exhibits," featuring over seventy-five Thai craftspeople making pottery, silver, silk, ceramics, food, lacquerware, and so forth. Sixteen "court performers" demonstrated music and dance-drama, and at one point, a public *wai khruu* was held. In *Smithsonian Talk Story*, the newsletter of the Center for Folklife Programs and Cultural Studies, curator Richard Kennedy wrote,

> People often ask why the Center "chooses" certain programs for the Festival. The process is never as simple as that. Festival programs develop in different ways with varied institutional collaborations. The Thailand program is one example.
>
> Discussions about this Festival program began in 1991, when Vichai Malikul of the Smithsonian National Museum of Natural History introduced me to the Thai government spokesperson Suvit Yodmani. Dr. Yodmani grasped the potential importance of the Festival as a platform for a national conversation on cultural identity in Thailand and took a proposal back to various ministries and the Thai cabinet. (1994, 1)

Kennedy went on to describe the slow process of bringing the National Culture Commission on board and of explaining the longtime aims of the Festival to showcase cultures in an interactive manner. Noting that the leader of the Thai delegation "understood that the Smithsonian Festival could be used as a model for future research-based educational programs in Thailand" (1994, 4), Kennedy alluded to the ways that both of these emblematic culture-preserving/producing institutions, one Thai and one American, viewed the Festival as part of on-going projects. The *wai khruu* at the Festival was thus one exhibit-spectacle among many, as well as an active attempt to construct a Thai public culture.

If the long arm of the nation-state is certainly felt in such government-sponsored events, its effects are experienced both broadly and specifically in the public school and university systems. When the educational system replaced the courts as performers' primary benefactors, everything changed. The shift in patronage to the Thai educational system has several implications, the most important being the very nature of the teacher-student relationship—that is, the cornerstone of the *wai khruu* paradigm. The officiant in most institutional *wai khruu* rituals is rarely the personal teacher of any of the participating students; he is often an elderly, prestigious teacher related in some way to the pedagogical line of the school's teachers, but brought in from outside. Students thus experience the ritual as an expression of respect to teachers in the generic sense; they usually do not have the personal experience of being "covered" or initiated by their own teacher who, for the moments of the ritual, literally becomes the tradition itself. Teachers may still embody the tradition, but not in the absolute performative sense that was once more common.

Conclusion

This chapter has charted out four generations of a single extraordinary lineage of officiants, but many loose threads remain. Besides *Luang* Pradit Phairau, to what other disciples did *Phraya* Prasaan Duriyasap grant the right to lead the *wai khruu* ritual? Did *Luang* Pradit Phairau honor even more disciples than the thirteen described here? And which disciples did they appoint in their turn? The pedagogical tree in fig. 6.21 lays out the relationships described in this chapter, but it is a composite picture assembled from conversations with many musicians; I met no one with identical understandings of the lineage because any individual understanding of it is based on one's personal connection to it. This tree is necessarily incomplete and in process; it may well be incorrect in places, but is based on what some twenty musicians told me over many years' time.

Luang Pradit Phairau dominated the music of this century, first, in his own right and then through his many disciples. He rose from a humble rural background to command music in the courts of the last two absolute monarchies of Thailand; he was, as one Thai writer put it, "a flame, a beam of light, a bright star" in the history of Thai music. His innovations—new compositions, new playing techniques, and new musical forms—are pervasive in what is now known as classical Thai music. *Luang* Pradit Phairau is the source of today's most honored ritual officiants of Thai music: an elite inner circle of these men can trace the source of their empowerment directly to him, and it is, in fact, these men who guide and direct contemporary music institutions like the Department of Fine Arts and leading university music departments.

One basis for Montri Tramote's authority was that he was the first student to whom *Luang* Pradit Phairau granted ritual rights: there is a general feeling that the first student so recognized receives the greatest amount of the teacher's spiritual power. Montri was long revered as a great musician and a great teacher, but he was also the last of his kind—the last great court musician. He was a venerable and highly honored relic of a former era. And although no one talked about it openly during his last years, the question was: Who would be the next great teacher when Montri died?

There are several contenders for the honor, though I must add that defining what "the great teacher" of a generation *is* isn't entirely straightforward. It is a matter of general consensus, not a formal position in a hierarchy. In some generations there may be more than one, or none. In some ways, the great teacher is identified with the head of the Thai Music Division at the Department of Fine Arts, but this is a bit circular since Montri

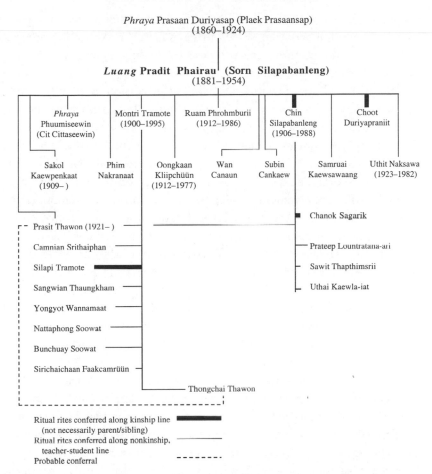

Phraya Prasaan Duriyasap (Plaek Prasaansap)
(1860–1924)

Luang Pradit Phairau (Sorn Silapabanleng)
(1881–1954)

Phraya Phuumiseewin (Cit Cittaseewin)	Montri Tramote (1900–1995)	Ruam Phrohmburii (1912–1986)	Chin Silapabanleng (1906–1988)	Choot Duriyapraniit

| Sakol Kaewpenkaat (1909–) | Phim Nakranaat | Oongkaan Kliipchüün (1912–1977) | Wan Canaun | Subin Cankaew | Samruai Kaewsawaang | Uthit Naksawa (1923–1982) |

Chanok Sagarik

Prasit Thawon (1921–)

Camnian Srithaiphan

Silapi Tramote

Sangwian Thaungkham

Yongyot Wannamaat

Nattaphong Soowat

Bunchuay Soowat

Sirichaichaan Faakcamrüün

Prateep Lountratana-ari

Sawit Thapthimsrii

Uthai Kaewla-iat

Thongchai Thawon

Ritual rites conferred along kinship line
(not necessarily parent/sibling)
Ritual rites conferred along nonkinship,
teacher-student line
Probable conferral

Figure 6.21 Transmission of ritual rights from *Luang* Pradit Phairau to
his disciples and beyond.

held the position for decades. Age also has a lot to do with it, as do the
respect and accolades of other musicians. Finally, such a teacher must (of
course) be a *wai khruu* officiant.

Prasit Thawon is the most obvious candidate to take Montri's place.
Born in 1921, Prasit represents the generation following Montri, too young
to have been a court musician himself but trained by teachers steeped in the
courts' standards and attitudes. Prasit's status is unique not only because of
his closeness to *Luang* Pradit Phairau as a disciple but also because he inherited the great teacher's book of secret ritual formulas. Prasit was also the first
student to whom Montri granted the right to lead the ritual. Prasit has subsequently sought out master teachers from outside *Luang* Pradit Phairau's

pedagogical lineage and received *their* ritual permission to lead the ceremony as well, thus acquiring some of their spiritual power in the process.
Whether Prasit is seen as respectful or as calculating, he may well be recognized as Montri's logical successor.

But Montri himself confused the line of succession by ritually investing two other musicians who could make strong claims to inherit his power.
In 1985, Montri passed on the right to lead the *wai khruu* ritual to his son
Silapi. Silapi, born in 1936, helped his father perform the ritual for years,
and began to take over Montri's ritual responsibilities in the late 1980s. Father and son sometimes even performed the ceremony together; although
Montri "led" such ceremonies, Silapi sat beside him and actually uttered
the ritual invocations. (See fig. 1.2.) Although Montri still went into his
office at the national conservatory every day until his last few years, Silapi
became the head of the Thai Music Division. In short, Montri arranged for
Silapi to take over both his administrative duties at the Department of Fine
Arts and his ritual responsibilities. As head of the music division, one of
Montri's major duties was to travel to all of the conservatory's regional
branches (outside Bangkok) every year to lead their *wai khruu* rituals, and
Silapi began to substitute for him in the late 1980s. Montri's personal choice
of successor was rather clear.

But at some point—whether before or after Silapi I'm not sure—Montri ritually invested a third student, Sirichaichan Faakcamrüün. Sirichaichan
was born in the mid-1940s and is highly regarded for his knowledge of
Thai music history. A number of people urged me to seek him out, whereas
no one suggested that I go talk to Silapi (at least partly, I assume, out of deference to his father). Sirichaichan has already served as the director of the
regional branch of the School of Dramatic Arts in Lopburi, a provincial
capital three hours north of Bangkok by car, and after Montri's death was
named head of the entire Music Division at the Department of Fine Arts
(thus making him Silapi's superior). Sirichaichan also teaches in the music
department at Chulalongkorn University. By 1994, he was leading the *wai
khruu* at the elementary school on the grounds of Chitlada palace, the home
of the royal family, and musicians were saying that his connection to the
Crown Princess was stronger than ever. (See fig. 6.22.) At the time of this
writing, most of Montri's other conferees were not yet acting officiants, but
it will indeed be interesting to see where and when they begin leading rituals. Although it is presumptuous of me to speculate, I would guess that
Montri was juggling competing loyalties as he chose his ritual heirs. Naturally, he wanted his son Silapi to carry his ritual knowledge, but he was
also expected to further the lineage of the Department of Fine Arts and

Figure 6.22 Sirichaichan Faakcamrüün initiating a schoolboy in the annual *wai khruu* ritual at the Chitlada Palace School on the grounds of Chitlada palace in 1994. Photograph by Deborah Wong.

he did so by recognizing Sirichaichan. He also recognized the abilities of other disciples, even though he knew that they aligned themselves with Chulalongkorn University, a competing institution. So he balanced loyalties of kinship, employment, and personal disciples by passing on the right to lead the *wai khruu* to all of these and essentially allowed the situation to resolve itself rather than trying to engineer it through narrow conferrals of ritual rights.

The question of authority is complicated by the recent rise of a strong music department at Chulalongkorn University and its connections with royalty. The Crown Princess is a great patron and performer of classical Thai music; she is also a graduate of Chulalongkorn University (not in music but in education) and has sponsored a number of major projects at the university—including the enlargement of the music department. In addition to Sirichaichan, Prasit Thawon now teaches at Chulalongkorn, as do several other important musicians. Significantly, this is where the Crown Princess goes when she attends her annual *wai khruu* ceremony, and Sirichaichan has led it several times since Montri's death in 1995. At the Department of Fine Arts, Silapi has led the *wai khruu* for music. Whereas Montri was unquestionably the ritual center of classical music for so many decades, a new period with multiple sites of ritual authority may have begun, and it is hard to say how it will end.

It may be that the former court musicians in the Department of Fine Arts no longer have exclusive access to royal patronage and power. I say this somewhat cautiously, because the fragmentation of power between the Department of Fine Arts and Chulalongkorn University is still unfolding. The Department of Fine Arts's authority is still unchallenged, and the Crown Princess is a woman of grace and diplomacy who has close, long-term relationships with several teachers there. Nevertheless, she has made her own patronage quite clear, and royal preference has important implications for a tradition that relies on royalty for spiritual empowerment.

At any rate, it is clear that the institutional structure of the Department of Fine Arts and of university music departments has everything to do with ritual authority. Moreover, the present balance of ritual and institutional authority is on the verge of change. With the loss of Montri Tramote, the enclosed world of classical music is without its longtime figurehead. Montri's son Silapi is a competent man who has had firsthand access to a wealth of esoteric information, but whether he has the authority to fill his father's shoes in the eyes of other musicians remains to be seen.

Writing this chapter, I frequently found myself unsure how best to depict the power dynamics of *Luang* Pradit Phairau's lineage. As a student of Thai music and musicians, I am compelled to describe these exemplary teachers as a Thai musician would, in unequivocally respectful terms. Stepping back to consider (publicly) their ambitions and motivations is not a move that any Thai musician would feel comfortable with. Commenting on an early draft of this manuscript, an American colleague asked whether I could find a way to write about these men that might afford them more depth than mere idealized types.[77] This suggestion challenged me considerably, forcing me to think hard about the praxis of respect and its performative function for Thai musicians. Talking and writing about officiants in certain ways moves them away from their status as ordinary men and closer to their social role as sacred conduits. This chapter has moved back and forth between different discourses, one emulating that of Thai musicians and the other more self-consciously that of an American ethnomusicologist. I hope that my respect and admiration for *Luang* Pradit Phairau and his many disciples is evident. As Martin Stokes has written, "Any field-worker is prone to absorb and replicate the dominant ideologies of the society they study [as an ethnographer]. One is obliged to seek the advice and guidance of people who have most successfully absorbed these discourses: media experts, highly published academics, and so on. Legitimate academic language is controlled by these people to such an extent that it is difficult to think in any other way" (1992, 2). Indeed, I hope I *have* "successfully absorbed" the respect practices of Thai musicians into my writing—if saying something is doing something, then it means that I have acquired some measure of understanding.

Contemporary Thai musical authority emerges from the confluence of three things: ritual knowledge, royal patronage, and institutional affiliation. I am reminded of Henry Kingsbury's (1988) description of the social organization of Western art music conservatories around individual teachers and their students; these "studios" are grounded in pedagogical lineages and often have rather tense relationships with the centralized administrative structures that run the conservatories. In Thailand, on the contrary, administrative structure grows out of the transmission of ritual rights between teachers and students. The pedagogical and ritual links across generations that are revealed in life histories such as those described above are thus far more than genealogical curiosities; they are the replication and maintenance of the tradition itself.

. . . .

Seven

The *Wai Khruu* as a
Gendered Cultural System

According to tradition, the presiding teacher who leads in the homage and performs the actual initiation must be a man. It is believed that the female touch will not bring success to an initiation: only misfortune will befall either the initiated or the initiator or both.

—Dhanit 1990, 6

Learning Gender

This book is largely a study of how patriarchy defines Thai music making. As the comments above, made by Dhanit Yupho (a past director of the government's Department of Fine Arts) makes clear, women have an explicitly limited role in the *wai khruu* ritual: they can be initiated up to a point but (officially) cannot lead it. I have seen countless women of note sit off to the side of the officiant, helping distribute incense and offering bowls, but I have never seen a woman directly assist the master teacher: a man, usually a close disciple, fills that function. Women can dance the "Offering of the Hands" *(Ram Thawaai Müü)* but are otherwise behind the scenes, busily preparing lunch, sometimes for hundreds of guests, while men and male authority sit squarely at the center of the ritual. I suspect that this development is only some seventy years old. Women have been marginalized in the *wai khruu*, but some continue to carry on ritual activities off to the side of the constitutive institutional *wai khruu* rituals. I believe that they also carry on a bodily response to the patriarchal norm now in place. Even as I write this, however, I hesitate because the historical specificity of "resistance" must be acknowledged, and I must wonder whether the intimate relationship between at least two women and the Old Father is a kind of parallel ritual activity rather than opposition or insurgency.

When I planned this fieldwork, as I lived it, and when I wrote it up
as a dissertation, I wasn't yet reading gender studies or feminist theory
and hadn't yet immersed myself in scholarship on difference. All that has
since changed. But even while I lived in Bangkok, I was keenly aware that
I couldn't behave as I had at home in the United States. Although I self-
identified as a feminist, I realized once I started spending time in the middle-
class environs of a Thai public university that I needed to change my body
language, the way I talked and dressed, and who I sat with. Middle-class
urban Thailand is deeply gendered, and it took me quite a while to stop
making mistakes.

One thing I knew before starting my fieldwork was that central Thai
builds gendered identification into speech. When speaking politely, for
example, to someone of higher status, people frequently add an untranslat-
able participle onto the end of their sentences: men say "*khrap*" and women
say "*kha.*"[1] I knew about this and understood how to use it, but I didn't understand how important it is to do so until I was halfway through an intensive advanced Thai program at Chiang Mai University in northern Thailand, my entree to Thai society. One of my American classmates, a white
man who had already spent a lot of time in Thailand and who was clearly
liked and respected by our Thai instructors, pulled me aside at one point and
said I should use *kha* a lot more than I was. He said it was one of the hardest
things for Americans to get used to but that it meant a lot to Thais. After that,
I started listening for it and realized that those gendered, polite participles
were everywhere in everyday Thai speech. People even used them as an
answer to a question, to mean "yes." And once I used it, people responded
more warmly to me.

One's speaking timbre is as cultural as everything else we do, but I had
never had to think about it before going to Thailand. A proper Thai woman
should speak softly and her voice should be rather high-pitched. The Thais
thought my "natural" speaking voice was quite gruff. I learned this when
I was teased about it, because Thais are rarely direct with their suggestions. This was my personal introduction to the aesthetics of *khwaamwaan*,
"sweetness," a guiding principle behind the arts as well as the practice of
everyday life. To me, Thai women sounded like little girls. When a young
woman would respond to an older man with a respectfully near-inaudible
girlish mumble, I would feel an intense feminist irritation. After I made a
point of emulating these speech patterns, however, I suddenly found that I
sounded, well, *Thai*, both to myself and to the people around me. Everyone seemed to understand better what I was saying. This was both satisfy-
ing and infuriating.

Changing my habitual body postures was much harder. In public, women never sit cross-legged even though they spend as much time on the floor as men. Instead, women sit *phap phiap*, with their legs off to one side, knees bent gracefully, the soles of the feet carefully angled out of sight. Women shouldn't hurry and should incline their heads slightly to communicate modesty and humility. Furthermore, women at the university dressed in a self-consciously feminine manner, always wearing skirts or dresses (never pants) and tending toward the frilly (lots of ribbons and lace). All of this is class-bound, is indeed part of the cultural performance of class: working-class women are more apt to talk loudly and stridently, to sit cross-legged, and generally to have, in Western feminist terms, more freedom in everyday Thai society.

Furthermore, I had chosen a dissertation project based on men and male performance. Indeed, the entire system of artistic and ritual authority is based on patriarchy, quite explicitly. I had given this no thought whatsoever —I had no framework for it—and simply proceeded, talking to men through most of my fieldwork. I know some of the male musicians thought it strange that I went to *wai khruu* rituals by myself, as most young women would prefer to attend public events in the company of women friends. I never found a woman colleague or assistant who had the time to attend events as doggedly as I did, so I just went ahead, often by myself. A young middle-class woman who goes around alone raises certain questions, but I think that my *farang*-ness (Western-ness) helped to mediate questions about my morality, because *farang* are regarded as a little odd, a little off, in any case.[2]

Without thinking about it, I gravitated toward instruments traditionally played by men—the gong circle and the xylophone. Women generally play stringed instruments or sing. I now wonder if I missed out on important ways of being a woman through music by not taking singing lessons, though I did take lessons on the *sau duang*, two-stringed fiddle, for some months during 1986–1987. I wanted to learn the gong circle and the xylophone because they are central to the *piiphaat* ensemble that plays ritual music, and I explained as much to my teacher Nikorn. He never tried to redirect me; indeed, he seemed to accept and to understand my interest. I am certain that he approved of my desire to understand the *wai khruu* repertoire as a musician, and I am also fairly certain that he thought this was really the only approach to the matter. In short, I learned two instruments usually played by men in order to understand a repertoire (mostly) played by men, which is part of a patriarchal system of authority and knowledge.

Writing about the *wai khruu* as a gendered system of ritual knowledge thus comes late in my interpretive process even though it was intimately part of my lived experience of the ritual and of Thai music generally. In some four extended visits to Thailand, I never saw a woman lead the ritual, though I know of three who did. I am of two minds about putting these remarkable women in a chapter by themselves—making a consideration of "women" equivalent to thinking about "gender" is an obvious mistake, and I don't mean to enact it here. As Sherry Ortner has written (1996), the "problem" of women as an analytic category is that posing questions via that category naturalizes "women" as a cross-cultural group and obscures issues of gender relations. On the other hand, I venture outside of Thai discussions of the *wai khruu* in creating this chapter, as I know of no Thai writings that discuss either the ritual or Thai court music in terms of gender. In this chapter, then, I depart most self-consciously from Thai representations. Nor do I want to create a chapter on "women" rather than "gender," because isolating women from broader questions of the construction of gendered social relations is of little use.[3]

Women and Thai Historiography

The Thai historian Thongchai Winichakul has reflected on Thai historiography and the emergence of "new histories" since 1973. Their close connection to the continuing formation of the nation is part of what Thongchai refers to as "the local political economy of Thai scholarship" (1995, 99). He also outlines the Thai emphasis since the 1980s on local histories that often contest the relationship between the state capitals, such as Bangkok and Ayuthaya, and outlying regions. He describes the formative role of the historian Nithi Aeusrivongse in critiquing the overwhelming influence of royalist histories (102–4) and feels that Nithi's revisionist work dismantled a Thai history that "was nothing but a political chronicle of the royal/national great men (and a few women)" (102). Critiquing the overweening role of state formation through histories of rulers thus opened the way for considering class, region, gender, and so on, as crucial kinds of social difference that help define new kinds of historical work.

Be that as it may, scholarship on music and performance in Thailand is markedly untouched by the intellectual foment that has marked Thai historical and anthropological work since the late 1970s. Work on performance traditions in the regions outside Bangkok is often characterized by transparent attempts to raise rural traditions to the status of aristocratic traditions in the capital. As Thai court music (*dontrii Thai doem*, the "original" Thai music) is inherently linked to the central Thai aristocracy, and since much of its history has been written by the performers most invested in that link, those histories, both written and oral, are deeply marked by the elitist, centrist ideologies described by Thongchai. Questions of difference are generally subsumed into royalist nationalism, and issues of gender completely drop out of consideration along with other issues that might present a more differentiated picture.

Gender studies and feminist theory have a limited presence in Thai scholarship. Much of the existing work focuses on women and development, as I think it must at this point; in this sense, it resembles first-wave feminist work in the West, where the creation of a strong body of work on women irrefutably establishes the necessity of considering gender. Several scholars have made important contributions to Thai gender studies through the lens of performance. Ubonrat Siriyuvasak's work linking women's listening habits with issues of class and labor is particularly valuable (1990). Two scholars working in performance studies, Paritta Chalermpow Koanantakool and Narumol Sriyanond, point toward emergent Thai scholarship inflected by Western cultural studies. Paritta's edited collection (2541/1998), *Revealing–Masking the Body*, offers new Thai scholarship on the body and issues of embodiment, and her own ethnographic work on *lakhon chaatrii* performers at the City Pillar in Bangkok addresses how dancers' bodies become sites for the politics of the time. Narumol's dissertation-in-progress (at New York University) focuses on Thai women's efforts to create community in diaspora through dance classes. Both her work and Paritta's is closely ethnographic and draws on anthropology and feminist theory.

Quite a few writers have examined the relationship between women and Theravada Buddhism. One of the most compelling books I have yet encountered is Chatsumarn Kabilsingh's *Thai Women in Buddhism* (1991), an openly feminist consideration of discrimination against women in Thai Buddhism and their exclusion from certain roles, particularly from the institution of the monkhood. Chatsumarn argues for a reexamination of both Theravada and Mahayana Buddhist texts in order "to determine the ways that women are supported and the ways they are repressed by the institutional structures of Buddhism" (1991, 22). During the lifetime of the Buddha, women could be ordained. Chatsumarn details the exclusion of ordained women *(bhikkhunis)* from the first gathering of the Sangha (the institution of the monkhood) as early as months after the Buddha's passing (ca. 543 B.C.). Looking closely at the actual texts of Theravada Buddhist doctrine, she finds that the "core teaching" of the Buddha is "free from contextual and gender bias by its very nature" (24), that is, the spiritual path leading to enlightenment is open to everyone regardless of gender. She concludes nevertheless that some texts, including some by the Buddha himself and other, secondary texts by monks, act out certain kinds of "gender bias" in accordance with the values of their time, and she thus argues that "the Buddha was an historic person, born into a specific social and cultural context that influenced his life. He retained some social values that appear to be strongly prejudiced from a modern standpoint" (25). Chatsumarn demonstrates that much standard contemporary Buddhist practice, both Theravada and Mahayana, is based on late additions to the Buddhist canon that are often deeply sexist for cultural and historical reasons. As she writes, any such doctrinal work "reflects how the Buddhist texts are primarily andocentric—male-centered. They were recorded for monks, in the interest of monks" (25). Ultimately, she encourages "concerned Buddhists" to read the scriptures critically, "to glean from them the pure message of the Buddha, which is otherwise clouded by the imposition of cultural values and gender bias" (34). In short, she argues that the exclusion of women in Buddhism is historically specific, standing apart from the spiritual importance of Buddhism.

The rest of Chatsumarn's book is devoted to the question of whether women can be ordained as monks—a key matter disallowed by Theravada Buddhism. She describes the plight of Buddhist nuns (*mae chii*, though she transliterates it as "mae ji"), in other words, women who choose to leave their worldly lives to devote themselves to worship. Since they cannot be ordained, most simply give up their possessions, shave their heads, and wear white robes. They are not supported by the Sangha as monks are, however, and many are therefore quite destitute. Some choose to live at temples, where they often look after the monks' daily needs. Laypersons do not make any more merit by giving to nuns than they do in giving to anyone else, whereas they make significant merit when they give to monks, so there are neither religious nor social reasons to take care of nuns or to sponsor their activities. Certain temples have become home for substantial communities of nuns (as many as several hundred), almost always because the resident (male) abbot is supportive. A few monks have even defied the prohibition by ordaining particular women, though this inevitably causes trouble for all parties. Chatsumarn recounts how her own mother, Voramai Kabilsingh, sought ordination but ultimately had to go to Taipei in 1971 for it, to a temple in a "sub-sect" of the Theravada tradition (1991, 52), and Voramai continues to attract controversy because of the ordination. *Bhikkhunis*, the female equivalent to monks, have thus never existed in Thailand as this Theravadan institution ceased to exist several thousand years ago. Some devout Thais are aware of this; *Khruu* Nim, for instance, showed me *wai khruu* texts he had written that included references to *bhikkhunis* and said he always *wai*-ed them as well as the Sangha.

Similarly, Charles Keyes (1984) has written that Thai women have specific options: they can be a mother or a mistress but never a monk. Keyes also explores the question of whether *karma* provides a complete argument for the subordination of women in Thai Buddhism. Mayoury Ngaosyvathn argues that the introduction of Buddhism to Laos over a thousand years ago carried important implications for class and gender relations, first affecting the upper class of feudal rulers and from there working down into the lower classes. Not mincing her words, Mayoury states: "Outrageously discriminating against women, the Buddhist religion introduced into Laos its world of male domination and female exclusion, separated with a meticulous insistence" (1990, 7). She outlines Lao women's crucial support of the Lao monkhood, particularly in terms of donating food on a daily basis and thus making important merit simultaneously for herself and her family. Furthermore, the "principal channel" through which women make merit is by offering up a son for the monkhood, as the substantial merit from this life cycle event goes entirely to the monk's parents, thus ensuring the mother's rebirth into a better life (15–16).

Work on Thai women by scholars from outside Thailand offers a useful frame, one that allows me to move beyond relativist acceptance to critique. Penny Van Esterik's work in particular is strongly feminist, based on anthropological research addressing Thai women, labor, and development. In an essay on the cultural politics of beauty contests in Thailand, she writes that "one of the means that has been used to keep Thai women—both rural and urban—in their place is beauty" (1996, 203). She traces the history of government-sponsored beauty contests since the 1930s and finds that social attitudes toward women's physical beauty have changed from a belief that it reflects a strong moral character to the commodification of surface beauty. Van Esterik worries that "Beauty contests probably have a greater influence on young Thai women than feminist writings" (216).

Historian Hong Lysa, however, critiques Van Esterik for her valorization of prostitutes' construction of a self-identity apart from the body, arguing that this view "glosses over the fundamental exploitation of the economic system that positions women as servants to the sexual demands of men, and the cultural values that condone such a system" (1998, 349). Indeed, Hong's critique is far-reaching: she decries the general "neglect of issues of race and gender" in Thai historical scholarship while acknowledging that the material conditions of Thai women's existence are the real problem. Hong argues that, since the 1980s, the cultural politics of the changing economy (from boom to bust) have resulted in scant change for Thai women: "The emergence of the middle class and the decentering of Thai national identity hence basically reinforced *sakdina* [traditional feudal] gender relations, typified by the prevalence of polygamy and prostitution" (335).

Thailand has, of course, developed prostitution as a major industry (for both international and domestic consumption), and this has important implications for alternative women's roles, both socially and in terms of the labor force. Cleo Odzer's remarkable ethnographic study of prostitutes in Patpong, Bangkok's famous red-light district for tourists, provides a reflexively conflicted picture of prostitutes' simultaneous social freedom and oppression. She writes,

> I believed Patpong prostitutes had advantages over nonprostitute Thai women who didn't belong to the rich upper class. They had more independence and opportunities. They were more worldly. They met and maintained contact with people from around the globe. . . . They became daring. Having broken one of society's taboos, they dared to break more. They went out alone at night and traveled on their own. . . . They developed skills to obtain what they wanted. Becoming deft at hustling, they recognized their ability to influence their environment. . . . Most importantly, they had money. Money allowed them to fulfill familial obligations while providing freedom of movement. (1994, 302)

Odzer thus argues that prostitutes' social position outside the virgin/ mother trajectory offers real freedoms. One might say that the binary is really a triangle—virgin/prostitute/mother—that leaves no space for women of spiritual power. Indeed, nuns *(mae chii)* are not even part of this picture, really, as their life choice carries no status (if anything, is seen as a bit eccentric), leaving them pious but little better than servants for monks.

Three Dancers and the Old Father

I met Rachani Phimthon (now Rachani Siri) in 1989 when I saw her play an integral role in the *wai khruu* at the central office of the Bangkok Bank (at the intersection of Rachadamnoen Klang and Phra Sumeru Roads). The ritual was led by Camnian Srithaiphan (a well-known double-reed player and a sometime member of Bruce Gaston's famous group, Fong Nam), but at one point, Rachani stood up and was entered by the Old Father in a spectacular extended moment of female authority. I have witnessed only one other woman act out this intimate connection to the Old Father, and I cannot help but feel that I was seeing something from out of the past, something discouraged since the reign of King Rama VI. Furthermore, Rachani carries the historical memory of other such women—an alternative history

Figure 7.1   Rachani Phimthon *wai*-ing as she sits in the audience listening to
Camnian Srithaiphan lead the *wai khruu* at the Bangkok Bank's Music Center
in 1988. Photograph by Deborah Wong.

of the *wai khruu* that is neither written nor recognized by the institutions
that have since absorbed the *wai khruu* into their apparatus of authority.

∽

The *wai khruu* at the Bangkok Bank was held in the Music Center *(Suun
Sangkhiit),* a small auditorium in the upstairs offices of the bank where free
public arts events have been featured every Friday afternoon for years; the
poet Naowarat Phongphaibun directed the series for a time and has long
been associated with the center. I have seen any number of music and dance
events at the center, from a presentation of the history of the Thai double-
reed oboe *(pii)* by the noted musicians Piip Khonglaithong and Bunchuay
Soowat to a military wind band playing traditional pieces to a dance presentation by schoolchildren. The *wai khruu* was led as usual by a man (Camnian
Srithaiphan[4]) who was part of the *Luang* Pradit Phairau/Montri Tramote
lineage (see Chapter 6). He led the ritual in the customary manner, wearing
traditional white clothes and sitting in the middle of the stage facing the
altar; the *piiphaat* ensemble was an ad hoc group of famous elderly musicians, including Bunyong Ketkhong on the gong circle and his brother

Figure 7.2 Rachani dancing as she is entered by the Old Father.
Photograph by Deborah Wong.

Bunyang Ketkhong on supporting xylophone *(ranaat thum)*. Camnian alter-
nately read the ritual texts aloud and called the ensemble to play the usual
pieces. At one point, four women got up from the audience and danced the
"Offering of the Hands" *(Ram Thawaai Müü)*; all were in their thirties or
forties and wore *phaanung* (draped dance trousers) and everyday blouses.
They sat down again in the audience when they were finished, and I noticed
that one of them was particularly focused and intent as she sat with her
hands in a *wai*, reciting the ritual phrases after Camnian (fig. 7.1). This was
Rachani: she was about forty years old and wore a simple white blouse with
a red *phaanung* like those worn by students and graduates of the College of
Performing Arts (Witthiyalaai Natthasin).

When the ritual arrived at the point where the hermits are invited to
join it, Camnian called for the musicians to play *Phraahm Khao*, and as the
music got underway, Rachani stood up and danced from her seat out to the
open area at the foot of the stage (fig. 7.2). Her face contorted and her body
bent; she suddenly looked like an old man, and I realized with a thrill of surprise and wonder that she had become the Old Father—that he had entered
her while Camnian sat waiting. (See fig. 7.3). Her face took on the smile of
a toothless old man as she danced over to the musicians and listened to them
play, nodding her head with pleasure. When they finished, she went over and

Figure 7.3   Rachani/the Old Father in front of the altar.
Photograph by Deborah Wong.

sat on the stage by Camnian, who *wai*-ed her and then went on reading the ritual texts. Neither he nor the musicians seemed surprised by this new presence.

As the ritual went on, Rachani/the Old Father listened to the music, always smiling and sometimes wagging her/his fingers along with the xylophone part or pretending to play the oboe, puffing out her/his cheeks in a comical way (fig. 7.4). S/he simply seemed like a good-natured, whimsical old man. When the musicians played *Nang Kin–Sen Lao*, s/he leapt up and, as assistants cut up the offerings and poured glasses of the whiskey, s/he started grabbing fruit, tossing it out to members of the audience. The three women who had danced with her pressed forward, reaching out and smiling, encouraging him/her to throw something to them. S/he pitched like a man, overhand and hard. A bit intimidated, I hoped s/he wouldn't throw anything at me. Everyone was laughing and moving forward; the room suddenly had the atmosphere of a party or a carnival. Rachani/the Old Father stopped launching fruit and stepped forward to the edge of the small stage, addressing everyone present in an old man's hoarse voice, smiling and saying, "I would like to wish everyone here good fortune—my blessings! Today is a good day. I invite everyone to come up now and receive my blessing." Camnian knelt at her/his feet and was the first to be blessed. One of

Figure 7.4   Rachani/the Old Father sitting on the altar, listening to the *piiphaat* ensemble play and tapping out its rhythms. Photograph by Deborah Wong.

Rachani's dance companions came forward with the bowl of fragrant powder and sat beside her/him holding it so that s/he could dip a stick in it. Rachani/the Old Father then wrote a blessing *(coem)* on Camnian's forehead and blew over his head, transmitting her/his spiritual power into him. Camnian *wai*-ed on the floor *(kraap)* at Rachani/the Old Father's feet and then made way for others. In fact, the moment that Rachani/the Old Father had finished speaking and turned to Camnian, the musicians and audience members rushed forward as one to get in line for her/his blessing. I did too. When my turn finally came, s/he wrote the sign on my forehead, and said, "I give you my blessing," and blew a sharp puff of air over me. (See fig. 7.5.)

When the time came to scatter flower petals and popped rice over the altar in blessing, Camnian held up the bowl so that s/he could reach in and then throw the mixture out in colorful handfuls (fig. 7.6). At the end of ritual, the musicians played *Phraahm Auk*, and Rachani/the Old Father danced out of the ritual; at the edge of the audience, Rachani paused, shook her head as if clearing it, and returned quietly to her seat (fig. 7.7). The musicians played *Mahaachai* as usual as Rachani sat, looking tired, and her woman friends attended to her, offering her a handkerchief and a glass of water. The ritual was over. People started milling around talking to each other,

Figure 7.5   Rachani/the Old Father blessing the dancers as *Khruu* Camnian
looks on. Photograph by Deborah Wong.

Figure 7.6   *Khruu* Camnian offers popped rice and flower petals to Rachani/
the Old Father, who tosses handfuls over the altar in blessing.
Photo by Deborah Wong.

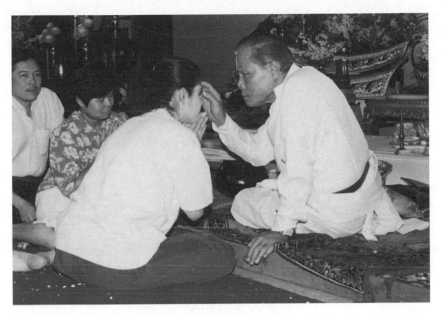

Figure 7.7   Rachani being blessed by *Khruu* Camnian after the Old Father has
left her. Photo by Deborah Wong.

catching up with old friends; I did the same after packing up my video camera. A little while later, I went over to where Rachani was still sitting with her
friends and introduced myself. She was very welcoming and, without any
prompting, said to me, "The Old Father is here to help all of us. We need
only worship him."

I never had the chance to speak with her again at any length, though,
as related in an earlier chapter, I later ran into her at Wat Phra Phireen on
the day of another *wai khruu* in 1989. During that ritual also, I witnessed her
become the Old Father. Later, she greeted me effusively when we met during that evening's musical performances, and she told me that she had encountered the Old Father many times and felt it was a good thing. I tried
to find her in 1998 when I returned to Bangkok, feeling that she was a major loose thread in my research and wondering why I hadn't sought her out
nine years earlier, but I was unsuccessful.

Nevertheless, as I made the rounds of friends and acquaintances asking
whether anyone knew how to contact her, I discovered that she wasn't as unusual as I had thought. At the National Theater, I was introduced to two different women, both dancers for the national troupe, who had been entered
by the Old Father during different *wai khruu* rituals. One didn't want to
talk about it, though I saw her entered twice in the course of the *wai khruu*

for the dancers at the National Theater in 1998, first by the Old Father and then by *Phra* Phiraap. The other woman was willing to tell me about her experiences once we had the chance to sit alone. I cannot use her name, as she was worried about what people would think of her; nor would she let me tape record the conversation, saying that she wouldn't feel at all comfortable (*sabaaicai*) if anyone else heard it, as most people would think she was crazy (she used two different words for this, *prasaat* and *baa*).

She told me that the Old Father had entered her many times. She was probably in her late forties; she had graduated from the School for Dramatic Arts next door, as had most of the dancers in the National Troupe, with the equivalent of a high school diploma. Afterward, she had taught for seven years "outside," as she put it (for these professionals, there is only "outside" the National Theater and "inside" it), before returning to the National Theater as a performer. She had been there for twenty years, since the late 1970s. She knew Rachani but hadn't seen her in many years; they had gone to school together though Rachani was a few years older. She related a long story about one time when she ran into Rachani outside school and was taken along to a house full of deities (*ong*), a *baan song*, literally a house of spirits. This house was dense with deities, not common ghosts (*phii*), and she saw Rachani entered by Brahma himself. She said that this experience made a strong impression on her, and after that she paid more attention when she saw people entered by deities during the *wai khruu* ritual; at school, she even saw *Phra* Phiraap enter a young woman. At that time, *Khruu* Akhom Saiyakhom was her teacher at the School for Dramatic Arts. Referring to him as Father Khom (*Phau* Khom), she said she and Rachani asked him about this matter and he helped them, though she didn't say how.

She was about eighteen when the Old Father first entered her, and she didn't understand what was happening. Since then he has come into her many times, though she never remembers it afterward. When it is about to happen, people have told her that she looks like she is about to faint, and then he enters her. She knows it's him because he has come to her in her dreams, and he looks just like his mask. I asked if he had a gold face and she said no, it was flesh-colored, just like some masks. He didn't smile as constantly as the masks do, but it was him. Before she goes to a *wai khruu* ritual, she eats only vegetarian food for a day, but otherwise cannot prepare herself to be entered and certainly cannot invite him to come into her: he comes when he comes, and she never knows when it will happen. At one point many years ago, she maintained a vegetarian diet all the time in an effort to remain pure, but once she had a family it was too difficult to continue. The Old Father still comes into her sometimes anyway, and people have told her that her voice and her face change when it happens.

Women, Spirits, and the Matter of Choice

Having met three women who are entered by the Old Father, I wonder whether there are others and suspect that there are. None of these women lead the *wai khruu* ritual as the invited officiant, yet Rachani's role at the Bangkok Bank in 1988 was more than that of a possessed participant: for a time, she led the initiation ritual, taking over for Camnian, the official celebrant, as evidenced by him asking for her blessing. She took over the central, crucial role of transmitting the Old Father's spiritual power into people of the present.

Whether "spirit mediums" can be discussed as one category of Thai social roles is an open question. Thais certainly talk about different kinds of mediums, both in terms of the beings that they access and in terms of class. Thongchai Phothayarom of the National Theater is clear on this point, saying that he invites the Old Father into him whereas ordinary mediums are seized or grabbed by spirits. Furthermore, the Old Father is a deity *(ong)*, not a spirit *(phii)*. These two distinctions were important to him. When I related this to two leading Thai anthropologists (who had best remain unnamed), they both laughed and said that it was all a matter of *phii*, really. Refashioning certain *phii* as *ong* was part of the apparatus of authority and legitimacy created by Rama VI, who related everything he considered important in Thai culture to India and Brahmanism. They said that it is really the spirits *(phii)* of deceased dance and music teachers that are worshipped in the *wai khruu* ritual.

Thongchai and my anthropologist friends raise two challenging issues. First, I must address the human construction of different kinds of social status for different kinds of spirits, and second, the matter of who those spirits enter and why. Deities are obviously higher-status beings and are literally higher up on the karmic hierarchy of reincarnation, whereas the thousands of different kinds of spirits range from ancestral spirits to legendary historical figures to the spirits of the recently departed. Deities and spirits enter both men and women,[5] but men of power and position are more apt to claim deities as their exclusive right—even though this is not always the case. Men like Thongchai may also bolster their right to a deity's higher status by arguing that choice—"inviting"—the being into them is a significant difference, but even this is not always the case. Some other examples from Thai ritual practice are in order.

Although she is outside the Thai Hindu-Buddhist pantheon, the Chinese deity Kwan Yin is present in Thailand. Her name is Thai-ized as "Kuan Im" by her followers, who are mostly but not entirely ethnic Chinese. A huge flamboyant temple to Kuan Im was built in northern Bangkok (off Lard

Phrao Road) in the early 1990s, and one of its regular features is scheduled appearances of the deity herself through two ritual practitioners. One is a woman and the other a man. Visitors to the temple can buy cassette recordings of past rituals, featuring the voice of the deity herself, speaking at length through her human conduits. Whether Kuan Im is a deity (*ong*) is a matter of context. Many Thais refer to her as such, but Thongchai and other followers of the Old Father would consider her a marginal figure because she is located in the ethnic Chinese community. On the other hand, that community in Bangkok is so large as to be nearly uncountable. Many Thais in urban areas are partly if not entirely ethnic Chinese and are at least third-generation Thai citizens. These ethnic Chinese were "assimilated" into Thai culture during the nineteenth and twentieth centuries via a number of discriminatory government policies that forced ethnic Chinese to adopt Thai names, closed Chinese schools, and so forth. Kuan Im's status as a deity is thus tied to the very definition of "Thainess" and cultural authenticity. As a deity from the Mahayana Buddhist tradition, she might be respected by a Thai Theravada Buddhist but is inevitably seen as Other.

The practices of mediums in northern Thailand have been studied extensively, and widespread participation by women is readily evident. Ruth-Inge Heinze notes the dominant role of woman mediums in the spirit lineages of Chiang Mai in northern Thailand (1988, 282–88). Anthropologist Marti Patel (1984, 1992) writes that women usually fill the key roles in Mon trance possession rituals in the Lampang area, invoking and "inviting" key ancestral spirits into the ritual and then dancing in order to bring different spirits into them. It is clear that the women dance as a means to voluntarily instigate possession—that is, they are themselves when they begin dancing, and the bodily invitation through movement encourages the spirits to enter them.

Anthropologist Mary Beth Mills (1995) suggests that the presence of widow ghosts (*phii mae maai*) throws a light on northeastern Thai anxieties over gender and labor migration. For a two-month period during the dry season in 1990, villagers in a region of northeast Thailand came to believe that they were under attack by these female spirits who seduce and kill men while they sleep; men who had worked in the Middle East on temporary labor contracts, as so many poor farmers in this region do, were considered particularly at risk. Mills suggests that the phenomenon had everything to do with gender relations, not only in terms of the obviously sexualized ghosts but also regarding the ways gender relations in the northeast are changing as women go to Bangkok in search of jobs as factory workers, maids, and so on. The gendered shape of labor migration—men to the

Middle East and women to the capital—introduces uncertainties as women become independent and mobile in new ways; away from their families when in Bangkok, they acquire lives and histories outside the knowledge of the village, and this is particularly troubling for men. Trying to interpret the widow ghost scare as a response by villagers to central Thai narratives of modernity and progress, Mills decides that it was more a window on "cultural struggle" than an example of peasant resistance (266–67). She concludes that "Widow ghost beliefs offered at best only a temporary and largely implicit critique of the political and material disparities that mark Northeasterners' experiences in contemporary Thai society" (267), a "momentary break" (268) that illuminated the relationship between changing labor practices and gender relations.

Conversely, the push toward modernity during the reigns of Rama V and VI spelled the end of women's spiritual authority at court. When the Inner Court was closed and *lakhon nai*, women's dance-drama, was allowed to decline, women's place in the *wai khruu*, and thus their relationship to the Old Father, was irrevocably changed. The authoritative discourse of the *wai khruu* has defined and changed gender relations in specific ways over time, and changing ideas of the royal court in relation to the modern nation-state have framed these changes to both the *wai khruu* and to gender relations.

Women as Court Performers

Now found in universities, public schools, and restaurants, classical music and dance was not so long ago the exclusive property of aristocracy and royalty. The court arts were cultivated as symbols of political legitimization, not just in Thailand but all over mainland Southeast Asia. The often violent relationships between the four kingdoms of Thailand, Laos, Cambodia, and Burma resulted in striking similarities between their court performance arts of music, dance, and shadow puppetry. As James Brandon comments, "The carnage was appalling, but the theatrical story makes fascinating telling" (1967, 26). When Thais destroyed Angkor Wat in 1431, they took Khmer court dancers and musicians back to the Thai capital of Ayuthaya along with other spoils of war (Morton 1980, 712). Ayuthaya in turn fell in 1767 to the Burmese, who carried off Thai court performers to Ava in similar fashion. In the early nineteenth century, royal Khmer dance-drama was said to have been revived by King Ang Duoung (r. 1796–1859) after lying dormant for some four hundred years, and was modeled after Thai dance styles originally borrowed from Angkor but by then much modified. As Brandon wryly notes, "It is popular to claim that the dance style of Angkor's apsaras of the twelfth century is perfectly preserved in the Royal Cambodian Ballet dance style. Unfortunately, this is romantic nonsense. A world of difference separates the elaborately costumed, chaste, and refined Cambodian dancers of today from the bare-breasted, hip-swinging beauties of Angkor" (1967, 59).

Despite such modifications and adaptations, these performing arts were continuously supported over the centuries because they were cogent symbols of political and spiritual power. The transportation of dancers and musicians over hundreds of miles, from one capital to another, is dramatic evidence of their importance. The kings of Southeast Asia (then and now) were seen as conduits between this world and the supernatural world of gods and spiritual power, sitting both physically and spiritually at the center of their realm. As the sacred or exemplary center of the kingdom, the king, court, and capital city were conceived of as a microcosm of the supernatural order. The ritual life of the court, as Geertz has said, was "thus paradigmatic, not merely reflective, of social order" (1980, 13). The pomp and ceremony of the court was not simply spectacle but actually helped maintain cosmic and political order. Not surprisingly, ceremonials became especially important at times of succession and ascension. Political legitimization was brought about by ritual as well as by military or political maneuvering, so that going through the motions of kingship by enacting kingly ritual was not mere gesture but rather a necessary way of establishing order (Chandler 1983). In the worldview of ancient Southeast Asian kings, to mirror a reality was to become it. As Geertz wrote, "It was an argument, made over and over again in the insistent vocabulary of ritual, that worldly status has a cosmic base, that hierarchy is the governing principle of the universe, and that the arrangements of human life are but approximations, more close or less, to those of the divine" (1980, 102). The theater state thus existed at several levels. While cosmic rituals of kingship, court, and state were generally enacted to "image" an ordered reality, music and dance literally enacted this image as theater. In a sense, a king was the hero of his own drama. Tambiah has referred to such ritual as "performative acts" (1985, 317), suggesting that the cosmic rituals of Southeast Asian kings constructed reality in much the same way that performative speech acts are the "doing of an action." One of the major ways that kings maintained order and legitimacy was through the patronage of organized religion (Hinduism or Buddhism) and the arts: kings expended considerable amounts of energy and revenue restoring temples and—especially—keeping large numbers of dancers (mostly women) and musicians (mostly men) at court.

These performers were far more than entertainers. Music and dance have deep indigenous connections with the supernatural world in Southeast

Asia, and there is compelling evidence that dance as a ritual offering pre-dates Indic influence on the mainland. In Thailand, *lakhon chaatrii*, the old-est form of Thai dance-drama, is still performed as an offering for place spir-its (Grow 1991a, 1991b; Brandon 1967, 61–62). Paul Cravath suggests that Khmer *robam*, or "pure dance," has an indigenous origin in fertility rites, originally associated with funerals, large bronze drums, and an ancestor-spirit cult (1986, 189–99). The association of *robam* with another world is preserved in the vocabulary of contemporary Khmer dance: "There is a very strong feeling that the dancers, who are considered in many *robam* to em-body live spirits, come from a sacred place into a space which is in turn sanctified by their presence. The Khmer word for entering the stage is *chaen* ("to go out") whereas leaving the stage is *chol* ("to enter")—as though sug-gesting that the dancer goes somewhere in performance and upon her exit from the stage reenters this world" (190).

The kings of Thailand, Laos, and Cambodia kept large personal troupes of female dancers in their inner courts. These dancers acted as royal consorts and even queens, representing, in a ritual sense, the female energy of the cosmos *(shakti)*. Twelfth-century records state that King Jayavarman VII of Angkor installed 615 female dancers at a temple honoring his mother, 1,000 dancers at a temple for his father, and 1,622 dancers at other temples (Catlin 1987, 28). Several kings of the Chakri dynasty in Thailand main-tained female *lakhon luang* (royal dance) troupes, including King Taksin, the general who drove the Burmese back out of Thailand. Reunifying the coun-try after the destruction of Ayuthaya in 1767, he established the new capital of Thonburi. According to a noted historian of Thai dance-drama, Mattani Rutnin, King Taksin then attempted

> to restore the traditional *khon* and *lakhon* within the royal court, both with the cultural aim of continuing the tradition of classical dance-drama of the Ayuthya period, and with a political aim of establishing himself as the rightful successor to the throne, the founder of a new dynasty. Socially, it was also necessary for him to set up his own royal court complete with its *Lakhon Luang* in the tradition of the Ayuthya kings; for to have possession of a *Lakhon Luang* troupe, particularly a *lakhon phuying khong luang* (female dance-drama of the royal court), was a privilege appertaining only to the monarch. (1978, 1)

During the reigns of Kings Rama I and II (1782–1809 and 1809–1824), the female performers in the *lakhon phuuying* or *lakhon nai* (dance-drama of the inner court) were also the kings' consorts and attendants. Rama III (r. 1824–1851), however, disapproved of dance-drama and disbanded the royal performers. King Rama IV (r. 1851–1868) reinstated the royal troupe, and his son, Rama V (r. 1868–1910), also maintained a large number of performers for both female dance-drama *(lakhon phuuying)* and male masked dance-drama *(khoon)*.

The earliest surviving record of a royal *wai khruu* ritual is from the reign of Rama IV, known in the West as King Mongkut. In 1854, three years after his ascension to the throne, the King inaugurated his new female dance troupe with an elaborate *wai khruu* and initiation ritual. Mattani Rutnin translates a description of the royal decree for the event as follows:[6]

> Phraya Hamroephak has received the royal command that the *Mom Lakhon* (king's consorts who were *lakhon* dancers) in the Royal Palace will come out to perform the Ceremony of *Khrop Wai Khru Lakhon* (Initiation of dancers and invocation to the dance teachers of *lakhon*) at the raised platform of the Dusit Mahaprasat Hall, and that seven monks will chant the Buddhist prayers at the *Thim Dap Khot* site in the palace on Wednesday, the 14th day of the waning moon, the fifth month, in the afternoon. On the next day, Thursday, the first day of the rising moon, sixth month, in the morning, after the monks have taken their meal, the [dance] teachers will initiate the *Mom Lakhon* by putting over their heads the sacred masks and head-dresses: that of the Bharata Rishi, Phra Phirap, and the *soet* head-dress of the *nora chatri*. (1993, 89)

King Mongkut also had the sacred texts edited and reassembled as *The Royal Book for the Khon and Lakhon Initiation Ritual [Phra Tamraa Khraup Khoon Lakhon Chabap Luang]*. Although ostensibly written by King Mongkut himself, the text was more likely put together by teachers and scholars and submitted to the King for his approval (Mattani 1978, 87). Edited yet again and published in 1951 by Dhanit Yupho (then the director of the Department of Fine Arts), it is clear from part of the text that this ritual was specifically for the female dance-drama performers.

The acting officiant is not named, but Dhanit has written elsewhere that one of the most renowned woman performers in King Mongkut's court was *Khruu* Keet, a dancer who performed as Rama and who also led the *wai khruu* and initiation rituals for the female performers of the inner court: "*Khruu* Keet led the initiation ritual for *khoon* and *lakhon*, both royal and amateur troupes, almost all over the city during the reign of Rama IV. *Khruu* Keet's book of *wai khruu* and *khraup* texts for *khoon* and *lakhon* is now in the National Library, and I edited it and had it published in 2494 [1951]" (2526/ 1983, 57). *Khruu* Keet was a lady-in-waiting during the reign of Rama III and evidently taught dance outside the court. She is said to have begun leading the *wai khruu* ritual for dance during the reign of Rama III and was most famous as an officiant during the reign of Rama IV and part of the reign of Rama V (Sombat 2532/1989).

King Rama V, or King Chulalongkorn, retained the performers from his father's troupes for the first thirteen years of his reign (1868–1881). After 1881, however, dance-drama troupes from outside the palace rose to prominence, and the remaining female dancers left over from the royal court of King Mongkut, increasingly elderly, performed at only a few isolated state occasions. King Chulalongkorn did not replace them with younger dancers, and the centuries-old tradition of female dancers and the inner court ended with his reign. If the King sponsored any major *wai khruu* rituals during his reign, they were not recorded.

Performers now look back on the fifteen-year reign of Rama VI (1910–1925), or King Vajiravudh, as the golden age of classical music and dance. An enthusiastic patron of the performing arts, King Vajiravudh completely reorganized the departmental structure of the various royal troupes and transferred them from the Ministry of the Royal Palace to the Department of Royal Pages *(Krom Mahaatlek)* under his direct command. During previous reigns, the Royal Departments of Masked Dance Drama, *Piiphaat*, Arts and Crafts, and the Western String Orchestra were under the direction of the Department of Entertainments *(Krom Mahoorasop)* within the Ministry of the Royal Palace; King Vajiravudh brought them under his own supervision and allocated them a larger budget than ever before.

The King's patronage of *khoon* (masked male dance-drama) represented a final, complete turning-away from the traditional royal emphasis on female dance-drama. The King even funneled additional boy performers into his troupes by assigning special battalions of the Royal Pages and the Wild Tiger Corps (two paramilitary organizations) to train as monkey soldiers in Rama's army for large productions of *khoon*. Favored male court officials and aristocrats were also encouraged by the King to become involved with these semi-military divisions, and then to participate in frequent and elaborate dance-drama productions. As Mattani has noted, "The King purposefully centralized all royal entertainment and dramatic activities around his own person in order to use them, not only for his own pleasure and entertainment, . . . but more so for his political schemes and ideas, and as a means to strengthen and glorify the institution of the absolute monarchy and to propagate concepts of national unity and patriotism with a great pride in Thai cultural heritage" (2525/1982, 134).

King Vajiravudh's nationalistic reforms have been described in detail by the historian Walter Vella (1978), who has documented the King's efforts to create a modern Thai nation through careful control of the media, the military, and education, as well as by introducing a new flag and various

patriotic holidays. The King also wrote (and rewrote) numerous plays and
dance-dramas promoting Thai nationalism and nationhood, seeing to it
that his ideas were literally acted out on stage. He himself performed in
Western-style spoken dramas as well as in Thai dance-dramas—unheard
of for a Thai king, and the subject of criticism from his own mother and
many Thai subjects as well.[7]

King Vajiravudh's efforts to link the absolute monarchy to the idea of
the Thai nation led to his close involvement with the *wai khruu* rituals of his
performers. Mattani notes that he acted as officiant in the royal *wai khruu*
and initiation rituals more than once, personally initiating his *khoon* performers (2525/1982, 130). He did extensive research in Sanskrit sources, including the Bharata Natyasastra (150–51), and either originated (according
to Mattani 1978, 86) or simply made explicit the idea that the Old Father
was Bharata Rishi, the Indian sage who received the classical dance positions
from Shiva. The leading Thai intellectual and social activist Sulak Sivaraksa
has noted Rama VI's fascination with classical Indian literature and suggests
that this "pav[ed] the way for young scholars of his generation to associate
Siamese culture and literature with ancient India" (1991, 44). Locating certain practices in a Sanskritic India was a legitimizing gesture and an attempt
to refocus Thai cultural origins. Mattani speculates that the King's research
on Shiva Nataraj, the Creator and Destroyer, led him to insert a symbolic
gesture into the *khraup* ritual in which he, dressed as the hermit, "acted as a
god, pretending to cut off the head of a leading dancer, and then sparing his
life upon the plea of the *khoon* and *lakhon* head teacher" (2525/1978, 150).

Dhanit Yupho's 1951 publication contains a detailed description of a
royal *wai khruu* ritual[8] held in 1914 for the royal performers of male and
female dance-drama and *piiphaat*. The ritual was held on Wednesday and
Thursday, May 13–14, and included elaborate food offerings and an even
more elaborate altar, all listed in detail. The *wai khruu* was apparently led by
the leading teachers *(khruu yai)*, but the King himself anointed all the masks
and performers and then enacted the little drama described above. The
King personally initiated the leading teachers and performers, holding the
masks of the Old Father, *Phra* Phiraap, and the *soet* headdress over each of
their heads, and he then presided over the rest of the ritual as the teachers
initiated the students.

◦∽◦

These ritual-dramatic flourishes accomplished what the King hoped. For
the royal performers, he was (as officiant) the source of the spiritual power

Figure 7.8   Drawing (probably from the 1920s) of Rama VI costumed as the
Old Father, from a dancer's home altar. Slide by Deborah Wong.

necessary to them; he was also the King and thus effected a power transfer in the style of the ancient *devaraja*. The impact of the King-as-officiant
on the court performing arts continues to be seen on contemporary performers' altars, where photographs of Rama VI costumed as the Old Father
are common, and in the sacred texts of many dance officiants, which specifically invite King Vajiravudh into the ritual (see fig. 7.8).

   The emphasis on royal power was felt in the *wai khruu* ritual for the
arts and crafts as well. King Vajiravudh opened the Phau Chaang College of
Arts and Crafts in 1913 and appointed his full brother Prince Chudadhuj
Dharadilok its royal advisor. The Prince arranged for an elaborate *wai khruu*
for artisans "in the ancient style" to be celebrated at the school in 1920
(Manat 2530/1987) and gave the school a book of sacred texts that the school
has used ever since. Referred to by the school's contemporary professors as
"royal scripture" *(Phra Khamphii)*, the book has been used so continuously
that it has begun to show signs of damage, prompting the present director
to order in the late 1980s that replicas be made. The facts that the book has

Figure 7.9   Copy of the *Phra Khamphii* or "royal scripture" used in the annual
wai khruu ritual at Phau Chaang College of Arts and Crafts in 1989; the
dark oblong object is the book, reproduced in the style of a traditional
Thai book. Video still by Deborah Wong.

a royal origin and that it is still used in the school's annual *wai khruu* and
initiation ritual are of great significance to the teachers. (See figs. 7.9 and
7.10.)

King Vajiravudh created the contemporary shape of the *wai khruu*
ritual in Bangkok. First, his preference for *khoon* and male forms of performance almost certainly led to the present emphasis on male ritual power and
male officiants; only two generations before his reign, female dance-drama
performers dominated the inner palace, and a woman, *Khruu* Keet, dominated *wai khruu* rituals all over Bangkok. Second, the King carefully and
self-consciously restored the ancient emphasis on the spiritual power of the
absolute monarch, personally "covering" his performers in the initiation
ritual and collapsing the male roles of King, hermit, and officiant. Literally
the hero and, in fact, god of his own drama, King Vajiravudh created a powerful patriarchal paradigm for court musicians and dancers.

Coexistence, Reinscription, Resistance

All this—the place of women in Theravada Buddhism, women's potential as
spirit mediums, their former importance at the royal court, and contempo-

Figure 7.10   Close-up of the *Phra Khamphii* or "royal scripture" used in the
annual *wai khruu* ritual at Phau Chaang College of Arts and Crafts in 1989.
Video still by Deborah Wong.

rary feminist critiques of Thai patriarchy—raises the problem of reinscription: do Thai woman performers collude in their control by men? If so, how
and why?

Aihwa Ong's work on Malay factory women and spirit possession (1987)
offers a useful counter-example to the gendered practices of the *wai khruu*.
Ong has written at length about the bodily resistance of Malay women working in factories: she argues that their possession by dangerous spirits carries
them beyond the reach of the men who control their labor. But Ong writes
agency in and out of her ethnographic narrative via troublesome choices of
vocabulary, arguing on the one hand that the factory workers "resist" capitalist control through trance and, on the other, that spirit possession is a
"hallucination" (9) and "a mode of unconscious retaliation against male
authority" (207). She thus frames their behaviors with the vocabulary often
used to describe unthinking, hysterical women. The workers themselves described their possession as involuntary: without any warning, they would
sob, scream, go rigid, or flail as they struggled against the marauding spirits.
Ong wonders whether the mass possessions were "the unconscious begin-
nings of an idiom of protest against labor discipline and male control in the
modern industrial situation" (207), though she also notes one management
decision to sack any worker after her third possession. Some managers
relied on medical or psychological explanations for the widespread phe-
nomena; others turned to traditional exegesis. One worker described a
coworker's affliction as follows: "She did not know what happened . . . she

saw a *hantu* [spirit], a were-tiger. Only she saw it, and she started scream-
ing. . . . The foremen would not let us talk with her for fear of recurrence.
She was possessed, maybe because she was spiritually weak. She was not
spiritually vigilant so that when she saw the *hantu* she was instantly afraid
and screamed. Usually, the *hantu* likes people who are spiritually weak,
yes" (207). This explanation, offered by a woman about another woman, is
strikingly like Thongchai Phothayarom's: the afflicted worker was entered
because she was weak and spiritually susceptible. Possession is thus a marker
of vulnerability, inevitably linked to women by their very nature.

I cannot know whether there were always some woman dancers who
were entered by the Old Father; whether woman officiants like *Khruu* Keet
had an exclusive relationship with him remains an open question. Perhaps
Rachani and other contemporary woman dancers carry on their intimate relation with the Old Father in a defiant attempt to maintain a direct female
link to performers' source of spiritual power; perhaps the Old Father himself favors male authority less than contemporary officiants think he does;
perhaps Rachani and her friends know the Old Father in ways that both men
and women always have.

These women who still have a close material relationship with the
Old Father are regarded as unusual by Thai performers and by Thais generally. They are a bit suspect, not in terms of morality but of sanity. The
two eminent woman musicians who have led the *wai khruu* in my own lifetime—*Khunying* Chin Silapabanleng (discussed in Chapter 6) and *Khunying*
Phaithuun Kittiwan[9]—stand in slightly different relation to all this, I think.
Their relationship to the Old Father was more abstract and sedate; as for
all officiants for music, they were regarded as "representatives of" or "re-
placements for" him *(phuu thaen)* rather having him enter them and absorb
their bodily selves as he does the officiant in the *wai khruu* for dance. *Khunying* Chin's and *Khunying* Phaithuun's social standing was also beyond question: as daughters of the most eminent musicians of the century *and* as
khunying, in other words, wives of men with the conferred political rank of
phrayaa, they were both of a certain class that put them beyond discussion.

Furthermore, their place in officiants' lineages fit broader regional
patterns for gender relations and cultural conceptions of women. Sherry
Ortner posits a broad area of hierarchical "prestige" cultures extending over
South Asia, Southeast Asia, and Oceania, where social status is linked to "criteria of social or religious value that theoretically transcend immediate political or economic 'realities'" (1996, 60). In such cultures, prestige is usually
considered innate or is inherited, or both. The "hegemonic ideologies" of
these societies are often based in constructions of aristocratic superiority,

and all this has implications for gender relations vis-à-vis kinship systems. Drawing on Goody's and Tambiah's work, Ortner outlines two mutually exclusive kinds of kinship systems, "patriliny, exogamy, and dowry on the one hand, and . . . cognatic descent reckoning, endogamy, and female inheritance on the other" (109). The hierarchical prestige cultures mentioned above almost always fall into the latter system. Ortner argues that the two systems "give radically different significance to marriage," as well as different ways of defining women. In the endogamous societies that practice female inheritance, women are viewed "more in terms of kinship than of marital roles" (111). This matter of relative emphasis is borne out through Thai beliefs about the transmission of performers' ritual rights. Officiants' prestige often bears no relation to their material wealth, and the transmission of rights is based on endogamous reasoning (if I can map this concept onto matters of ritual): gathering together a group of disciples is all about maintaining insiders, not about drawing in outsiders (exogamy). The inheritance of ritual rights is most ideally passed on to a leading male disciple, who may be a son. If such a candidate is missing or if the stakes are high enough, however, a daughter may receive the inheritance.

I must stress that *Khunying* Chin and *Khunying* Phaithuun are extraordinary cases—or rather, their fathers were, and that is the heart of the matter; although both women were remarkable musicians and teachers, the weight of their respective fathers' knowledge was at issue more than the daughters' abilities. Had the daughters been mediocre musicians, their fathers would not have taken these measures, and both men made a point of passing ritual rights to other male relatives (sons and grandsons) in addition to their daughters. I would argue that the value placed on ritual endogamy and on inherited prestige overrode gender, or at least placed gender further down in priority. *Khunying* Chin and *Khunying* Phaithuun were treated by their fathers as if they were valued sons, and neither the historical nor the anecdotal record indicates that either *Luang* Pradit Phairau or *Caangwaang* Thua ever openly addressed stepping outside the accepted bounds of gendered transmission.

The women who are entered by the Old Father during the ritual, who have no special status and whose bodily takeover occurs involuntarily, are another matter. They believe strongly in the power of what happens to them but know they may well be regarded as odd. Most importantly, their activities do not line up with the authority of the institutions created by bureaucracies of the nation-state: they may encounter the Old Father during a *wai khruu* sponsored by a college or a bank, but their intimate public moments of entering do not raise their status or bring them any closer to directing those institutions. If anything, their vibrant presence is a brief interruption, a few moments of the unexpected.

I believe that the presence and control of woman performers' bodies is also implicated. The Old Father (generally) does not enter musicians, and this may be a significant difference, at some level, for eminent male teachers making decisions about transmission. Neither *Khunying* Chin nor *Khunying* Phaithuun would ever be entered by the Old Father; their role was to pass on their fathers' spiritual power (prestige). I know of no male teachers of dance who appointed their daughters as officiants. At some level, the materiality of the body and its relationship to the Old Father is implicated, though no performer ever put it that way to me.

I should make it clear that no woman dancer or musician has ever complained to me about the restrictions placed on women in the tradition; rather, many have matter-of-factly told me that women don't have the strength to play the *pii nai* (double-reed instrument) or that they cannot initiate new performers because they cannot become monks. Indeed, all the self-identified Thai feminists that I have met are intellectuals or academics. The success of patriarchy often lies in drawing women into its terms and thus convincing women to reproduce its values. Chatsumarn Kabilsingh writes, "Women born into such a gender-stereotyped society will tend to internalize these beliefs and accept them as valid. Commonly held prejudices of women's mental and physical inferiority, handed down through cultural tradition and sanctioned by religion, have profoundly affected Thai women's self-image and expressions of self-worth" (1991, 19–20). Chatsumarn thus notes that patriarchy inscribes its values on both men and women. Similarly, Kornvipa Boonsue writes that Buddhism has been wielded "as a state ideology to anaesthetize women" (1989, 4). Van Esterik considers the politics of reinscription, writing that "Beauty contests set the tone for the way Thai women are evaluated and thought about and how they evaluate and think about themselves" (1996, 216). After much struggling with questions of cultural relativism, I feel able to discuss the *wai khruu* ritual in terms of gender restrictions rather than (more neutrally) gender definition partly because I think this was less true in the past and especially because I see Thai feminists discussing their own society in a critical way, with an eye toward change.

Cleo Odzer writes that "prostitutes are pioneers in advancing women's autonomy by breaking from the mold of suppressed and passive females" (1994, 309). The performers I know will be appalled to find me discussing prostitutes and master teachers in the space of the same essay, but I ask their understanding as I make the point that woman officiants disappeared from the *wai khruu* for particular social and historical reasons that surround the contemporary form of the ritual. The movement of the ritual into institutional government settings occurred just at the point when women's palace dance-drama had virtually disappeared and when a particular king created a court focused on the preeminence of the masculine, defined in ritual, military, and social terms. Watching the Old Father dance and hearing him speak through Rachani in 1989 was thus a window on a past when women empowered other women but also a moment when the overwhelmingly male technologies of the *wai khruu* were briefly resituated.

Eight

Conclusions: Thoughts on Change

The *wai khruu* says so many things about Thai culture, all at once. It is about kings and patriarchy; it reflects the maintenance of tradition yet is a vehicle for the machinations of the Thai nation-state; it defines performers' institutions and social systems; it outlines a syncretic and multifaceted cosmology; it constitutes a Thai theory of performance and ritual; it evokes powerful responses, ranging from solemnity and joy to poignancy. I would like to offer some final thoughts on the place of change in the *wai khruu*, but I also want to address change more broadly, in terms of writing. Considering the future practice of the *wai khruu* prompts me to reflect on how critical theory enables or renders invisible different ways of thinking about cultural change, and this in turn leads me to a final consideration of the experiential effects of this research on my own worldview and its impact on my writing. That is, I find it necessary to address the changes that this research effected in my own subjectivity.

(Not) Changing

Officiants almost always assert that the *wai khruu* has existed unchanged
since ancient times, ever since the Old Father gave music and dance to

humankind. From the sacred texts to the food offerings to the ritual music, they say everything has remained the same. Nevertheless, the *wai khruu* has changed a great deal during the twentieth century, and the same officiants who insist on the ritual's continuity over time also talk about changes with consideration and concern. Like all craftspersons, they are intensely interested in the details of their art. Most see no contradiction in asserting that the ritual has been passed down unchanged since time immemorial and in then immediately discussing the many modifications necessary for the ritual's performance in educational institutions. For them, the salient point is that the *wai khruu* is still performed and still fulfills the same important transformative function. At the very least, I know that "tradition" implies stability but not stasis for Thai performers.

The *wai khruu* is in no danger of disappearing. It is no museum relic or folkloricized practice; on the contrary, it is vital because it remains central to performers' belief systems. Globally, folkloricization is one of the main ways that nation-states control the meaning of the arts, often through a combination of coercion and persuasion. For instance, Thomas Turino shows how Andean highlanders who migrate to urban centers voluntarily reproduce the "legitimizing devices provided by the government (the stage, the emcee, the label 'folklore')" (1993, 231). He sees this as the success of hegemony: the highlanders' "reliance on sanctioned performance frames" is central to their subjugation by the dominant urban *criollo* culture. Redefining certain practices as "folklore" is really about redefining groups of people vis-à-vis one another. The *wai khruu* in Bangkok has long been linked to the nation-state—one could say that it is always already part of the complex of power relations and the play of representational practices that define the Thai nation-state, so there has been no *need* to folkloricize the ritual. I would extend the folkloricization argument further by suggesting that such processes do not always occur top-down but that these kinds of redefinition are often dialogic—that is, without privileging an utterly functional model of practice, I would argue that the framing gesture of "folklore" is potentially empowering even as it moves certain practices into new spaces of social control. The *wai khruu* has sometimes been performed in such contexts, but I see those instances as extensions of its practice rather than indications of profound change and redefinition.

Nor is the *wai khruu* an invented tradition, despite the popularity of such identifications since the early 1980s. Eric Hobsbawm's powerful idea (1983) reflected an early poststructuralist turn in historical work and has left many scholars confusing invention with cultural construction. Hobsbawm defines invented traditions as cultural practices *self-consciously* linked to the past, as distinct from "custom," and as (often) emerging at

historical junctures when a society is rapidly undergoing change (1–4). He
does not discuss colonialism and postcolonialism per se, though he notes
that nationalism (in the broadest, most general sense of the term) is often
at work in invented traditions (6, 12). Certainly the *wai khruu* has been
redefined more than once by specific circles of court performers in the last
one hundred and fifty years, but this process suggests the necessity of considering cultural change in close and specific terms (which I hope I have
done). Hobsbawm regards the reconfiguration of old and new "materials"
as invention (6), but this in itself is not remarkable, nor does it locate the
wai khruu as invented.

Among other things, the *wai khruu* is "about" the state, but it is focused
on the monarchy, whereas the Thai nation-state is now that and more. The
extent to which the *wai khruu* can encompass modernity's redefinition of
that state remains to be seen. Lisa Lowe's and David Lloyd's thoughts on
nationalism and modernization are helpful here. They argue that nations
become modern states by transforming the ways that subjects and social
spaces are defined and produced, and that the "discreteness" of those definitions is immediately challenged by the lived conditions of its subjects (e.g.,
poverty, racialization, etc.; 1997, 7). Nonetheless, modernization is often
inexorable. Lowe and Lloyd write, "The entry of the nation through the
medium of the modern state into the global world system requires the mas-
sive conversion of populations and their cultural forms into conformity with
the post–World War II project of universal modernization. Civil society
must be reshaped to produce subjects who might function in terms of
modern definitions of social spaces" (7). Court musicians thus became
civil servants, virtually overnight. Contradictions and incommensurabili-
ties still abound, however, as the categories of modern cultural forms remain
responsive to competing needs and histories; in many new states, such contradictions are part of decolonization, but in Thailand, nationalism is more
complicated and open-ended. "Tradition" in Thailand is thus not related
to anticolonial struggle, nor is it necessarily a gesture of antimodernity.
Lowe and Lloyd note that nationalism often "repeats the very distinction
between tradition and modernity that colonialism institutes to legitimate
domination," and that "forms of postcolonial modernity are modified to
accommodate a fetishized version of tradition" (9). While Thailand does
not define its modernity through the frame of colonialism, the *wai khruu* is
a form of cultural maintenance that has proven extraordinarily responsive to
changing ideas of the nation-state in the twentieth century. The *wai khruu*
has changed repeatedly and will probably continue to do so: when women's
dance-drama declined as a result of several kings' engagement with new
forms of modernity, the ritual was refigured as patriarchal; when public

schools replaced the court as a patron, ritual practice moved from Thursdays to Sundays. And so on. Its traditionality is valorized by the state (via the Ministry of Culture, etc.), but remains unfetishized by its practitioners because an ideology of custom and tradition has always been foregrounded.

One might ask why Thai performers stick so single-mindedly to a belief system centered on a court that no longer exists. Geertz's examination of Javanese land ownership led him to theorize "involution," the exhaustion of a cultural form. Whether the *wai khruu* represents a similar form of stasis and preservation remains to be seen, but I think not. Geertz argues that agricultural involution in Java was the result of a static economy, a burgeoning population, and Dutch colonial interference in Javanese laws defining control over land, leading to overtaxing agricultural resources and relentlessly dividing land rights up into smaller and smaller units. He describes it as an "ultimately self-defeating process," and broadly characterizes involution as "cultural patterns which, after having reached what would seem to be a definitive form, nevertheless fail either to stabilize or transform themselves into a new pattern but rather continue to develop by becoming internally more complicated" (1963, 80–81). Geertz suggests that this cultural pattern is aesthetic as well as material in its coherence, describing its realization in Java as a "'late Gothic' quality of agriculture" distinguished by "increasing tenacity of basic pattern; internal elaboration and ornateness; technical hairsplitting; and unending virtuosity" (82). He takes it further, arguing that the effects of this culturally defined agricultural pattern could be discerned more broadly in Javanese village life (103), even calling it "the Indonesian malaise" (154); he suggests that involution characterized not only agricultural practices specifically but also Javanese village life generally, using words such as "vague," "indeterminate," and "flaccid" to describe village culture (103). He writes, "The involution of the productive process in Javanese agriculture was matched and supported by a similar involution in rural family life, social stratification, political organization, religious practice, as well as in the 'folk-culture' value system" (101–2). In short, Geertz posited an interrelated system of effects, and I should address why I think the *wai khruu* is *not* an example of cultural involution despite its practitioners' focus on preservation on the one hand and their elaboration of detail on the other. In a way, the theory of involution argues against the dynamic nature of cultural production, gesturing back toward Ruth Benedict's models of cultural personality and coherence (1934); indeed, one might say that Geertz continued to work in that vein in his later books, constructing a model of culture in which each of its components lends itself to the coherent whole in seamless and mutually-supporting fashion. Change in any part of the culture ostensibly leads to a process of adjustment throughout the system, and involution could be said to start anywhere, though its effects would inevitably spread everywhere. The theory begs the question of subjectivity: according to whose terms has a given culture ground to a halt and given in to lethargy? At what point can a practice be pronounced exhausted of possibility? Javanese farmers probably didn't feel that their rural society was "flaccid" in the late 1950s, but then Geertz was not working in a mode in which his subjects' interpretations mattered. Thai performers' responses to state bureaucracies could be seen as analogous to Javanese farmers' reactions to Dutch interference, wherein any outside influence is theorized as damaging and intrusive. Instead, I see a long history of change in Thai performers' lives and social conditions. Where Geertz might see involution, I see dynamic response and flexibility, if within certain limits. I don't think that the *wai khruu* complex is capable of open-ended change and adaptation, but the theoretical models driving my understanding of culture lead me to focus on agency, innovation, and difference rather than on consistency and congruity. In short, I question the possibility of involution in any culture.

I am not saying that the more things change, the more they remain the same. Rather, the continued vitality of the *wai khruu* in the face of sweeping cultural and political changes must be acknowledged even as I allow that I am not sure why it endures. Asking why a practice should be maintained is necessary in the face of salvage scholarship, which has a continuing presence in many disciplines, including ethnomusicology. Whereas ethnomusicologists and folklorists have witnessed the demise of many traditional practices and are sometimes in the position of trying to bolster such arts against the inevitable, I have spent over a decade following an esoteric practice that is in no apparent danger of vanishing.

The *wai khruu* survives despite existing in a country that defines itself through tourism in many ways. The *wai khruu* has not been refigured as a folkloristic spectacle for tourist consumption, though many other Thai arts and crafts have been. It has not been reconstituted as "ethnographic" by Thais themselves (except in a few specific contexts, described in Chapter 6), though I have made the *wai khruu* into an ethnographic object in these pages. On the other hand, many of the same musicians and dancers who turn to the *wai khruu* at least once a year are part of the voracious network of hotels and restaurants that produce orientalist fantasy for both domestic and international tourists, so I cannot claim a distant, pristine coherence for the *wai khruu*. The belief system it represents stands offstage in the restaurants, in the wings, driving the performers' sounds and the movements but not their reception. The ritual is inevitably linked to the phantasmatic orientalism of the Tourist Authority of Thailand and its gorgeous posters of dancers, food, and flowers—the Thailand that is consumable by visitors. This too is part of the changing system of patronage for traditional music and dance, and even though I have never seen the *wai khruu* "performed" in a restaurant for tourists, its practitioners circulate between radically different environments that are nonetheless linked. In a matter of a days, I have seen my teacher Nikorn play in *wai khruu* rituals, teach university students, and play at one of the largest restaurants in the world, where the staff, in traditional Thai garb, hurtles through the aisles on roller skates, serving thousands of gastronomes as quickly as they can.

Among other things, the *wai khruu* is a theory of history. In its enactment of genealogy, it continually reconstitutes a performative construction of history and memory, but this does not mean that this history is agreed upon. Always multiple in the telling, there are as many versions of *wai khruu* histories as there are teachers who perform it, and the nonsingular character of memory and lineage creates real tensions; control over memory is directly related to the authenticity of knowledge, after all, so the stakes are high. Anthropologists Richard Handler and Eric Gable (1997, 84–89) write that the history of colonial America is constructed differently at Colonial Williamsburg by black and white "interpreters" (guides) and that they use each other "as distant and convenient foils" (88). Such contending constructions of historical "reality" are not parallel but rather are constructed dialogically, through engagement with each other. The authoritative histories enacted in *wai khruu* genealogies are no different; readings and counterreadings keep its texts alive. That multiple histories are axiomatic to the *wai khruu* is, I think, central to its vitality; its contentious, uncontrollable qualities place it beyond the reach of standardization or codification. The implications for Thai performers' understandings of "history" are therefore profound. "Facts" seem to slip away in the telling, and performers seem predisposed to tell the researcher to go ask someone else. Performers know that it's a matter of "histories," and they also know that the authority to claim certain histories is a complicated business, based on criteria far more demanding than "facts."

If the *wai khruu* seems always already to be part of the performance of the state, I should say that this study is decidedly local in its focus and intentions. I did virtually all of my research in Bangkok and its surrounding areas, and this book highlights the *wai khruu* as a "great tradition" of the nation's capital. The musicians engaged in its practice in Bangkok self-consciously carry on their activities in the shadow of the palace, even today. Performers all over Thailand practice the *wai khruu*, however, and I am sure that the ritual "speaks" in significantly different ways to performers in outlying regions. Creating educational institutions for central Thai court music and dance in Chiang Mai, for instance—six hundred miles from Bangkok, in the cool mountains of northern Thailand—is part of the larger project of pulling the rebellious north under the cultural control of central Thailand. Thus, when the Department of Fine Arts sends its performers there once a year to perform the *wai khruu*, much is being said. When those same performers fly to Wat Thai in Los Angeles to perform the ritual for young Thai American dancers, complex allegiances are foregrounded—not so much about Thai-ness versus American-ness, but about the authority of Department of Fine Arts performers over those from Chulalongkorn University, who have long been rotated out to Los Angeles to teach for brief periods. On the other hand, *mawlam* (sung poetry) performers in the northeast and *nang talung* (shadow puppet) performers in the far south also practice the *wai khruu*, and its realization in those contexts ties its practitioners into local lineages and local histories in ways I can only guess at (see Grow 1991a, 1991b for an example). This study is decidedly not an encompassing look at "the" *wai khruu*, because the ritual is always rooted in the particular concerns of the individuals who come together in its moment. In Chapter 1, I pointed out the widespread presence of *wai khruu*-like rituals in Southeast Asia and theorized this as a regional emphasis on metaperformance as central to ritual efficacy, but here I must insist on the importance of local readings that work against any flattening, supraregional theory of performance and ritual. If anything, the *wai khruu* is a complex of behaviors and beliefs that are always local and always about more than the ritual itself.

Writing Change

Finally, I must theorize my own focus on this esoteric practice during a period when Thailand was going through dramatic changes, including its new status as a Newly Industrialized Country (NIC), prodemocracy demonstrations in May 1992 that left bullet holes in restaurant walls, and the economic crisis of 1997 that transformed Bangkok into a ghost town of unfinished skyscrapers.

My time in Thailand fundamentally changed my own beliefs. I didn't plan on that. I went to Bangkok without any particular belief system at all and was hard pressed to answer Thai friends when they asked me what religion I followed. That remains true, but I do know that the Old Father is real. Having encountered him so many times and in so many places, I can't not believe, as my mask maker acquaintance said to me. Since then, I have told my own students over and over again that they need to choose their thesis and dissertation topics carefully—I tell them they must find a place or a topic that so seizes them, they cannot imagine not writing it up, or cannot imagine not feeling compelled to do so. I tell them that fieldwork doesn't matter unless you give yourself over to it in whatever way you can. The fields of anthropology, ethnomusicology, and cultural studies (to name a few) have so thoroughly problematized ethnographic authority that one necessarily addresses the construction of cultural reality through the lens of particular subjectivities, and the fact is, my subjectivity changed in the course of my research.

But shouldn't it? Ethnographic inquiry in the late 1990s demands that one address subjectivity, and I think an important implication is built into that methodological imperative. Addressing subjectivity necessitates writing reflexively about it, and this in turn calls for a change in awareness much less addressed in current critical writing—that the writer/witness/participant/one-who-experiences must allow their own subjectivity to shift in the process of having the experience and then in writing about it. I am inspired here by my colleague Hershini Bhana's radical reimagining of literary criticism (1999): Bhana's writing is "haunted by ghosts" who are at once the characters in the diasporic literary texts she examines as well as ancestral presences who walk through Bhana's meditations. Their presence raises the question of whether they *can* be controlled by the literary critic, and Bhana essentially concedes that she is haunted by them *("the chair is not empty")* and that this acknowledgment is "my attempt to disrupt claims of positivism that maintain disciplinary objects of study clearly demarcated from the expert/observer and that perpetuate mutually exclusive categories of theory and practice, the fictive and the Real, the affective 'partial' scholar and the disinterested 'accurate' scholar." In shifting her language and recognizing that ghosts occupy her text, Bhana enacts the double move in subjectivity that I ask for here: hers and theirs, writer's and reader's, and this instantly goes to the heart of how writing creates or works against alterity.[1] I cannot tell you at what point, precisely, I felt that the Old Father was touching me— at what point I felt his blessing as something tangible. I can say that there is no retreat from the moment when subjectivity shifts, no going back, though I hope a certain bifocal uneasiness enlivens this text. I have had the privilege of coming into contact with a being from another time and place, and this allowance must be part of the account, part and parcel of the critical gesture that transforms this text into a *wai khruu* of its own.

This closing chapter is thus about change in several different senses.

Even as I dwell on the question of how/why/whether the *wai khruu* doesn't change, I must also address the place of change in disciplinary focuses and in the authorial voice. Over the years that I have written and rewritten this book, ethnomusicologists have been swept up in (and have sometimes tried to resist) paradigm shifts moving through the humanities and social sciences, and I suspect that this text enacts those changes in ways that I haven't fully been able to control. The "new" ethnomusicology, presented in multivocal texts such as *Shadows in the Field* (Barz and Cooley 1997), will surely open up unforeseen ways of writing about belief and performance, and about subjectivity in/as/through performance. Several writers in that groundbreaking work (Kisliuk, Rice, Titon, Barz) suggest that ethnomusicologists have access to special ways of knowing by participating in musical performance; I would extend Michelle Kisliuk's conclusions in particular, where she considers the ways that the researcher and the people the researcher comes to know are each affected in ways beyond the researcher's or the subjects' control (1997, 43). If experience is accessible only through a certain loss of control, then the moment of threshold-crossing, when experience folds into belief, is even more difficult to write.

But writing about the challenge of writing experience/writing belief is risky—my experience in and of itself isn't the point here, it is only the entryway. This unexpectedly vulnerable observer (see also Behar 1996) doesn't want to take over the text or to have too loud a last word. I don't want to overrun the intersubjective moment that I am reaching for here. I am trying to say that the *wai khruu* and the Old Father are many things and that both are deeply pedagogical in the sense that they teach belief even as they enact and embody belief about belief, knowledge about knowledge. Through this doubled-up comprehension, this intensified framework of performance and experience, we can begin to understand.

Appendixes

Appendix A

Glossary of Terms Used

N.B.: All definitions are my own, though citations for specific related materials can be found in the text.

aacaan (Sanskrit, **achariya**) A teacher or professor at a college or university, often holding a degree beyond the college level. Used as both a title and as a pronoun. See also *khruu* for comparison.

amnaat Power, influence, authority. Used for power of all kinds, including spiritual, political, etc. See also *anuphaap*.

anuphaap Power, might. See also *amnaat*.

anusaun Commemorative books compiled in honor of a deceased person, usually distributed at the cremation.

aphinihaan A kind of spiritual, supernatural power. "The power of greatness" *(amnaat haeng baaramii)*, according to Manit 2528/1985. See also *itthirit*.

arahant Perfected monks who, through meditation, are free of human desires and often have magical powers (e.g., to fly, make rain, travel vast distances in seconds, etc.).

asom (Sanskrit, **asrama**) Hermitage, or a hermit's home in the forest. Can also imply a school, because a hermit's disciples may also live there.

Association for Assistance to Friends and Performers (Samaakhom Songkhrau Sahaai Silapin) Private organization based at Wat Phra Phireen, Bangkok, that helps sponsor the funerals of impoverished performers. Also sponsors the largest annual *wai khruu* ritual in Bangkok, usually held in mid-September. Formed in 1969.

bai mai mongkhon "Auspicious leaf," given to disciples by the officiant after the *khraup* or "covering" ritual. A leaf from the bale tree is rolled around a few blades of *phraek* grass and tied with string; the disciple usually puts it behind his or her ear for the rest of the event.

bai srii (also **bai srii paak chaam**) A ritual object necessary to most Hindu-Brahmin rituals. Made out of banana leaves, rice, flowers, and hard-boiled eggs:

259

the banana leaves are rolled and folded into an elaborate cone shape which is then filled with rice; the egg is inserted on top, and the flowers (usually jasmine buds) decorate it. Represents Mount Meru, the cosmic mountain at the center of the universe. See Heinze 1982 for more.

baht Monetary unit in Thailand, worth about four cents (U.S.) in 1988–1989.

baaramii The aura of virtuous power and greatness that surrounds great leaders. Implies a strong moral character and the ability to inspire others.

bhikku A fully ordained Theravada Buddhist monk.

boek roong Boek = "to widen, expand, open"; *roong* = "stage." A short section of the preperformance rituals in *nang yai* and *nang talung*, usually featuring the hermit and a fight between two monkeys.

Brahmin The priestly caste of Hinduism; in Southeast Asia, ritual specialists who emigrated from India and oversaw Hindu-Brahmin rituals surrounding kings (see *devaraja*). Related to the Hindu concept of *Brahman*, the supreme reality and ultimate principle underlying the world. Its associated ritual complex includes the word *om* and written power symbols called *yantra*, both of which were absorbed into Southeast Asian ritual practice.

buuchaa (Sanskrit, **puja**) "To worship," usually with flowers, incense, a candle, and a *wai*.

cap müü "To grasp the hands." This is part of the initiation ritual for passing on pieces or advancing to higher levels of the *naa phaat* repertoire. The student sits at an instrument and the teacher stands behind him or her and literally holds the student's hands in his, striking (or bowing) the notes of the first phrase of the piece.

chan "Level." In music, this refers to different metric levels or densities (similar to the Javanese musical concept of *irama*). The three most standard levels are third level, second level, and single level (*saam chan, saung chan,* and *chan dieo*): the most expansive is the third level (with a closed *ching* stroke every eight beats), while the densest is the single level (with a closed *ching* stroke every two beats). The *thao* form progresses from the third to the second to the single levels. Most older pieces are in the second level, and composers then create new pieces by expanding and contracting this second-level version into third- and single-level versions. Nearly all *naa phaat* pieces are in the second level. Twentieth-century experiments have included extremely expansive levels (the fourth and sixth), but pieces of this scope are still anomalous.

choen "To invite." Used in daily speech to invite someone to come in, sit down, or begin eating. In the language of ritual, deities are "invited" into a ritual event by reciting texts, lighting incense, and performing music or dance.

devaraja "God-king." Special royal ritual practices affirming the divine nature of the king surrounded the Hindu-Buddhist rulers of Southeast Asia, beginning around the eighth century A.D. Certain kinds of music and dance-drama were part of the rich symbolism surrounding kings and were considered such strong symbols of royal authority and legitimacy that performers were often claimed as war booty.

Dharma (Thai, **tham**) The teachings of the Buddha. See also the "Triple Gem."

dontrii "Music."

duriyaang An elegant word for "instrumental music."

Hanuman A magical monkey in the *Ramakien* who is *Phra* Ram's faithful follower.

hoomroong Prelude or overture. There are many *hoomroong* in the *seephaa mahoorii* repertoire, and three in the *naa phaat* repertoire (the Evening, Morning, and Daytime Overtures) that define its hierarchical levels (see Chapter 4 for details). *Hoom* = "to consecrate, purify"; *roong* = "building, structure."

hua khoon Masks (literally "heads") worn in *khoon* dance-drama. Most completely cover the head (those for demons, gods, and monkeys); some are worn on top of the head (those for the hermit and some animals). Performers treat masks with great respect, believing that characters' spirits reside in their masks, and are thus careful to *wai* them before and after wearing them in performance. When stored, the masks of demons should be kept apart from those of deities, refined heroes, and monkeys, since these two groups represent opposing forces in the *Ramakien*. Mask makers invite the spirit of a mask's character into it with a ritual called "opening the eyes" *(boek khaneet)*, in which the mask's eyeholes are opened.

hun krabauk Hand-puppet theater, accompanied by the *piiphaat* ensemble and the *naa phaat* repertoire. Now rarely performed.

Isuan, **Phra** One of the many names of Shiva (one of the three great deities of Hinduism, Brahma and Vishnu being the other two).

itthirit Magical, supernatural, amoral power (manifested as the ability to fly, change shape, perform feats of strength, etc.).

kae bon A vow-releasing ritual performance: *kae* = "to undo, unwrap"; *bon* = "to make a vow." When Thais have a particular problem or request, they present it to a particular deity (usually by standing in its shrine or before its statue and praying while lighting incense). If the request is granted, the person will then sponsor a *kae bon*, i.e., a performance of dance-drama (or shadow theater), in the deity's honor.

karma (Thai, **kam**) The cumulative effect of a being's deeds, both good and bad, in past and present lives. One's present form and condition is the sum total of all one's past lives. See also *merit*.

kattanyuu-kottawethii The two components of gratitude: *kattanyuu* is the feeling of gratitude that arises from the realization that parents or teachers have raised, protected, and taught you; *kottawethii* are the acts of paying them back for their generosity with respect behavior (*wai*-ing, helping them, etc.).

khaathaa A verbal spell or charm, uttered aloud when magically turning something into something else, or when consecrating something. Usually in the poetic metrical pattern of *chan*. (*Khruu* Akhom Saiyakhom's name comes from the term *khaathaa aakhom*, "a magical spell or charm uttered aloud.")

khaen Free-reed blown instrument from northeast Thailand and Laos; can be played as a solo instrument or to accompany the genre of sung narrative poetry called *maulam*.

khamphi (Sanskrit, **khamphir**) A text containing esoteric material, often of a religious or mystical nature.

Khaum A script derived from Khmer, now used in Thailand for sacred or mystical texts. Most Buddhist texts were traditionally written out in *Khaum*, which was taught to monks as part of a Buddhist education; such texts are now usually in contemporary Thai script, but some older men still know how to read and write *Khaum*.

khoon The masked dance-drama of the courts, accompanied by the *piiphaat* ensemble and the *naa phaat* repertoire. Formerly all-male, now women often perform its female and refined male roles.

khon khao song "Persons entered," that is, spirit mediums or others whose bodies are entered by spirits.

khonthap (Sanskrit, **gandharva**) Divine beings who entertain the deities with instrumental music and song. Some musicians believe that *khonthap* are the reincarnation of human musicians, others that human musicians are the reincarnation of *khonthap* that lost or did not make enough merit in their lifetime.

khraup "To cover" or "to transmit." The *khraup* ritual, which follows the *wai khruu* ritual, enacts the transmission of knowledge and power, in which the officiant literally "covers" participants' heads with a mask or a musical instrument.

khruu (Sanskrit, **guru**) "Teacher." Used in contemporary Thailand for elementary school teachers. Its older, traditional meaning, however, implies an expert of specialized knowledge, and most teachers of the performing arts are still referred to as *khruu* by their disciples. See also *luuk sit, aacaan*.

khrüang sangwoei The food offerings presented in Thai Hindu-Brahmin rituals (e.g., the *wai khruu, buang suang*, etc.). *Khrüang* = "object, goods"; *sangwoei* = "to make offerings."

kraap "To prostrate oneself in obeisance" by pressing the hands and forehead to the floor.

Krom Mahoorasop "The Department of Entertainment," which existed during the reigns of Rama V and VI (approximately 1868–1925); it was disbanded by Rama VII. The contemporary Department of Fine Arts was formed around many of the performers previously in the Department of Entertainment.

Krom Silapakaun "The Department of Fine Arts," founded in 1934; a government institution overseeing all cultural activities, including museums, archaeological sites, and the performing and visual arts.

Lak, Phra *Phra* Ram's (Rama's) younger brother, called Laksmana in the Indian *Ramayana*.

lakhon A general word for dance-drama, now used for any kind of drama or theatrical performance. Some major genres include *lakhon chaatrii* (see below), *lakhon nai* (the all-female dance-drama of the inner court), *lakhon nauk* (all-male dance-drama of the lesser courts); contemporary genres include *lakhon phuut* ("spoken," Western-style drama), *lakhon thorathat* (television drama), and *lakhon witthayu* (radio drama).

lakhon chaatrii A southern tradition of dance-drama that emerged from the confluence of *manora*, court-style *lakhon*, and *lakhon Phet* (a tradition of dance-drama from the city of Phetburi). See Grow (1991a, 1991b).

likee A genre of dance-drama found all over Thailand. It was a nonaristocratic genre patronized by the working classes and is now often seen on television. See Surapone (1980).

Luang A royally conferred noble title. Also used as a title of respect for older monks or elders.

luuk sit (Sanskrit, **shishya**) "Disciple": *luuk* = "child, offspring"; *sit* = "disciple, pupil, student."

Mahaachaat Literally "the great life," i.e., the story of Prince Wetsundaun, the penultimate life of the Gautama Buddha. Usually read aloud once a year by monks in a festive event that can take several nights; the sections of the story were traditionally marked by interludes in which a *piiphaat* ensemble played pieces from the *naa phaat* repertoire.

mahoorii A kind of classical ensemble, made up of the percussive instruments in the *piiphaat* ensemble (but with the *khlui* substituted for the *pii*) plus various stringed instruments.

manooraa A genre of southern Thai (and Malaysian) dance-drama whose core dramatic material is the story of Prince Suthaun and a magical bird-woman. It is now performed only by men and has close historical ties with *lakhon chaatrii*.

merit (bun) One of the central concepts of Buddhism and Hinduism. It is an abstract substance accumulated by all living beings when they perform good or virtuous deeds. Humans can make merit by giving gifts to monks, by sponsoring the ordination of a monk, by teaching, etc. The amount of merit one accumulates in a lifetime determines the conditions of one's next reincarnation.

Momrachawong A title (abbreviated as M.R.) for the great- or great-great-grandchildren of a king; considered aristocratic but nonroyal.

moong Suspended gongs, usually bossed, that mark strong beats of the musical structure in classical Thai pieces.

muunii A kind of hermit or *rüsii*; in India, *muunii* usually wear white and observe silence.

naa phaat, phleeng A repertoire of two hundred to three hundred pieces used for dance-drama and various rituals, including the *wai khruu*. Performed by the *piiphaat* ensemble. Considered the oldest Thai repertoire, many of these pieces and their names are also found in Cambodia and Laos, where they also center around court traditions and the worship of the *devaraja*. See Chapter 4.

nam mon Sacralized water used in many Hindu-Buddhist rituals, including the *wai khruu*. *Mon* comes from the Sanskrit word *mantra*: the basin of water is sacralized when a ritual expert (whether a monk or layperson) lights a candle and utters a *mantra* or *khaathaa* over the water, then extinguishes the candle in the water. The water is scattered over ritual participants as a blessing, to bring people out of trance, or for curing. It is mixed with powder to form a paste used in anointing rituals (such as the *khraup* ritual).

namo Related to the Indian syllable *om:* it is uttered at the beginning of Buddhist prayers. It is always recited three times in Pali as follows: *Namo tassa bhagavato arahato samma sambuddhassa,* and can be translated as "Reverence to the Lord who is worthy and fully awakened."

nang talung The shadow puppet theater of southern Thailand, performed with small articulated puppets similar to those found in Malaysia and Java.

nang yai "Great shadow theater," performed with large unarticulated puppets. *Nang yai* may be the precursor of *khoon:* many of the dance movements (performed by the men holding the puppets) are extremely similar. Dialogue was delivered by a narrator, and the musical accompaniment (of pieces from the *naa phaat* repertoire) was played by a *piiphaat* ensemble. Primarily found in central and upper southern Thailand, *nang yai* is now dying out.

Narai, Phra An incarnation of Vishnu.

natthasin A generic term for classical dance.

oongkaan (1) Sacred word of Brahmin ritual (cf. Sanskrit *om*), referring to the three major Hindu deities; see also *Namo.* In Thailand, refers to a category of recited propitiatory texts (such as those recited in the *wai khruu*) that invoke the presence of Hindu-Brahmin deities. (2) A word from Thai royal language meaning a king's decree.

phaanung A length of cloth wound around the waist and pulled up between the legs as a pair of loose trousers, extending below the knees. Worn traditionally by both men and women.

Phau Kae "The Old Father" or *Phra* Pharotmuni (Bharatamuni), the *rüsii* who was given the arts of music and dance by the deities and who then taught them to mankind. His gold-faced mask dominates altars in performers' homes and rehearsal areas and is worn by an officiant during the *wai khruu* ritual, when it is felt that he enters both the officiant and the ritual event.

phithii "Ritual, ceremony."

phleeng A generic term for a musical piece or work.

Phra An ungendered title for deities and other sacred beings.

phraek grass Used in the *wai khruu* ritual: several stems of this grass are rolled up in a leaf which is then bound with string; everyone who completes the ritual of "covering" is given one by the officiant. *Phraek* grass grows and spreads quickly and is thus a symbol of knowledge in the *wai khruu* ritual. See *bai mai mongkhon.*

phuak "Group," sometimes used to mean the group of followers surrounding a teacher or any powerful person (e.g., politicians, businessmen, leading intellectuals, etc.).

piiphaat The musical ensemble that accompanies ritual and dance-drama with the *naa phaat* repertoire, which can be performed only by a *piiphaat* ensemble.

The minimum set of instruments includes the *ranaat eek, khaung wong yai, taphoon, klaung that, pii nai,* and *ching chap;* this small ensemble is called the *piiphaat khrüang haa,* or "five-instrument *piiphaat*" (the *ching chap* are assumed and thus not counted). This basic ensemble can be enlarged by adding the *ranaat thum* and the *khaung wong lek* and is then called the *piiphaat khrüang khuu,* or "*piiphaat* ensemble of paired instruments." The largest version of the ensemble, called the *piiphaat khrüang yai,* or "large *piiphaat* ensemble," is created by adding two metal-keyed *ranaats,* called the *ranaat eek lek* and the *ranaat thum lek.* The various ensembles can be played with either hard, unpadded mallets (in which case the ensemble is called *piiphaat mai khaeng*) or soft, padded ones (*piiphaat mai nuam*), but the *naa phaat* repertoire is performed only with hard mallets.

Precepts, Buddhist **(sin)** The Precepts are enumerated codes of conduct that define correct behavior for laypersons and monks. The *Five Precepts (Sin Ha)* should be observed by all laypersons and proscribe (1) killing, (2) stealing, (3) wrongful sexual behavior, (4) lying, and (5) consuming alcohol. The *Eight Precepts (Sin Paet)* are observed by devout (usually older) persons on Buddhist holy days and by ascetics and devotees who are not monks (or cannot become monks, as in the case of women). The Eight include the Five Precepts plus three more proscribing (6) the consumption of food after noon, (7) singing, dancing, making music, or adorning oneself, and (8) sleeping on an elevated bed; also, the Eight Precepts outline total chastity rather than simply abstaining from wrongful sexual behavior as in the Five Precepts. Observers of the Eight Precepts usually dress in white to avoid the adornment of everyday clothes. Finally, monks observe 227 precepts.

Ram, **Phra** The hero of the *Ramakien,* known as Rama in the Indian *Ramayana. Phra* Ram is a reincarnation of *Phra* Narai, or Vishnu. Rama is the given name of all the kings of the Chakri Dynasty in Thailand (1782–present); the present king, King Rama IX or King Bhumibol Adulyadej, has ruled since 1946.

Ramakien (Sanskrit, **Ramayana**) The epic story of *Phra* Ram, who is tricked out of his right to the throne of Ayodhya and driven into exile in the forest, accompanied by his brother *Phra* Lak and his wife *Nang* Siidaa. When *Nang* Siidaa is abducted by the demon king Totsakan, *Phra* Ram and his army of monkeys (including Hanuman) lay siege to the demon kingdom of Langka and recover *Nang* Siidaa after fourteen years of war. The *Ramakien* is the basic dramatic material for the mainland Southeast Asian court performance arts of dance-drama and the great shadow puppet theater; unlike Java, where the Indian epic of the *Mahabharata* exists alongside the *Ramayana,* the *Ramakien* dominates the court arts of Thailand, Laos, and Cambodia, and outlines the basic metaphors of divine kingship in mainland Southeast Asia.

rap maup "To receive the right," i.e., to receive the right (1) to lead the *wai khruu* and *khraup* rituals or (2) to be a teacher of music or dance. The right to perform the *wai khruu* ritual can be received only by performers who have been initiated into the highest levels of the *naa phaat* repertoire (whether music or dance).

Ratanakosin Name of the present era (since 1782), in which Bangkok has been the Thai capital and the Chakri Dynasty has ruled.

rot nam, phithii The "ritual of pouring water," performed to express respect for a senior person. The person being honored sits with his or her hands in a *wai*, and the participants come up and pour scented water over the hands from a conch shell or small basin. Also done as part of the Thai wedding ritual, and in northern Thailand on the Thai New Year's Day in April.

rüsii *(ruesi, rsi, rishi)* An ascetic or hermit who retreats to the solitude of the forest to meditate and acquire spiritual power. *Rüsii* have access to specialized esoteric knowledge, and the heroes of traditional stories often seek them out for instruction. The One Hundred and Eight *Rüsii* received special knowledge (e.g., agriculture, medicine, etc.) from the deities and disseminated it to humans. *Rüsii* are therefore the paradigm for knowledge as well as teachers; the *rüsii* of music and dance is especially revered by performers, as discussed in detail in Chapter 3.

saaiyasaat The magical arts, derived from Brahmanism and dealing especially with spells and *khaathaa*.

saksit (Sanskrit, **shakti** + **sitthi**) "Sacred" or "holy."

saalaa A large open-air pavilion.

samniang "The sound of speech," "pronunciation," "accent." In music, *samniang* are modal and motivic "dialects" that evoke the musics of particular ethnic groups, e.g., Lao, Burmese, Chinese, European, Indian, etc. Pieces that employ these *samniang* are called "language pieces," or *phleeng phaasaa*.

seephaa mahoorii The repertoire of musical pieces used in entertainment contexts (as opposed to the ritual *naa phaat* repertoire). In the nineteenth century, the *mahoorii* ensemble began to accompany the performance of sung/chanted poetry, a tradition known as *seephaa* in which the singer would accompany him- or herself with woodblocks. Most *seephaa mahoorii* pieces consist of alternating stanzas between the instrumental ensemble and a solo singer, though purely instrumental works exist as well. See Chapter 4 for more.

shastra (Sanskrit, **sastra**) An authoritative, often sacred, treatise or scripture.

Siidaa, **Nang** The wife of *Phra* Ram in the *Ramakien*, who is abducted by the demon king Totsakan.

sit (Sanskrit, **shishya**) "Disciple." See *luuk sit*.

soet The dance headdress worn in *manooraa*, used in the *khraup* or "covering" ritual (along with the masks of the Old Father and *Phra* Phiraap) to confer power and blessings on the participants.

suat mon (**mon**, from Sanskrit **mantra**) To chant Pali prayers aloud. Usually performed by monks.

süng Strummed string instrument from northeast Thailand and Laos.

tamraa "Textbook," "reference book," or "manual."

tham khwan The "soul-tying" ritual: *tham* = "to do, make"; *khwan* = "soul." Most Thais regard this as a Hindu-Brahmin ritual. Performed in many different contexts: after a child's birth, after an accident or illness, and the night before a young man is ordained as a Buddhist monk. The ritual experts who perform the ritual are called *mau khwan* and are usually laymen who have previously been ordained as a monk. The ritual is supposed to reunite the person's soul with his or her body and to ward off evil. See Chapter 3 for more.

thaang "Way" or "path." Among musicians, used to mean "style" (i.e., of a particular instrument) or "school" (i.e., the style of a particular school or teacher).

thawaai "To offer" something to someone of higher or divine status.

theep (Sanskrit, **deva**) A divine being, similar to the Western idea of angels. Although not immortal, *theep* live for hundreds of thousands of years and never experience old age, pain, or illness. They are high in the karmic chain of rebirth, and it is possible for humans who have acquired much merit to be reborn as a *theep*. See *theewadaa*.

theepduriyaang *Theep* = "divine being"; *duriyaang* = "music." The deities of music; see Appendix C.

theewadaa (Pali, Sanskrit, **devata**) A divine being; another name for *theep*. (In Pali and Sanskrit, *devata* is the plural form of *deva*.)

Totsakan King of the demons in the *Ramakien*. Called Ravana in the Indian *Ramayana*.

Triple Gem Called the *Ratanatraai* in Thai. Refers to the Buddha, the Dharma, and the Sangha (the institution of the Thai Buddhist monkhood).

Vedas The earliest known Indian Hindu scriptures. There are four Vedas: the Rig Veda and Sama Veda, collections of hymns; the Yajur Veda, a collection of sacrificial formulas; and the Atharva Veda, a collection of charms and magic formulas. All were given to humans by *rüsii*, and all were meant to be sounded aloud. They are still regarded as the sound of eternal truth.

wai To raise the hands palm-to-palm in an expression of respect to elders, monks, deities, etc.

wai cao A ritual in which offerings are made to the spirits and souls of the ancestors on Chinese New Year's Day.

wai khruu A ritual performed to remember the virtue and kindness of teachers. When celebrated at elementary schools, colleges, and universities, students take flowers, incense, candles, *phraek* grass, and eggplant flowers, and come together to chant in praise of their teachers' virtue. The *wai khruu* was traditionally performed on the first day of study at school, when a monetary offering was usually made to the teacher. The *wai khruu* ritual is especially observed by practitioners of traditional knowledge, including traditional medicine and the arts. The *khraup* or "covering" ritual, which completes the transmission of knowledge from teacher to disciple, usually follows the *wai khruu*. Some similar rituals include *wai cao* and *wai phii*.

wai phii A ritual in which offerings are made to the souls of the ancestors on a wedding day.

"Wai Phra thoet" Words uttered by older respected persons when they receive a *wai*.

yan (Sanskrit, **yantra**) A symbol of power (drawn or written on cloth, paper, or the human body), usually activated by a *khaathaa*, or spoken formula.

List of the *Naa Phaat* Repertoire
Used in the *Wai Khruu* Ritual

This list was compiled for me by *Aacaan* Manat Khaoplüüm and *Aacaan* Sangat Phukhaothaung of the Baan Somdet Teachers College. The list seen below combines two separate lists, one that *Aacaan* Manat informally jotted down in my notebook and a second one that the two men compiled together on their own. Interestingly, the two lists were nearly identical and in virtually the same order, approximating their order of performance in a *wai khruu* ritual. Clearly, *Aacaan* Manat mentally groups and categorizes these works in a systematic and consistent fashion. The explanations for the pieces' use are from his second list; my own comments, taken from my fieldnotes and written sources, are in brackets. Total: 71 pieces.

Saathukaan [*saathu* = "to *wai*"] Performed to worship the Triple Gem [i.e., Buddha, the Dharma, and the Sangha].

Saathukaan Klaung [*klaung* = "drum"] Invites the many sacred things. Invites the great teachers.

Tra Choen [*choen* = "to invite"] Used to invite Phra Isuan and the many *theep* and *theewadaa*.

Tra Nimit [*nimit* = "friend"] Used in *khoon* and *lakhon* stories when a character changes form or shape.

Tra Baungkan [*krabaung* = "baton/club" (carried by demons)] In the *wai khruu*, used to invite the demon teachers. In *khoon* and *lakhon* performances, it is played when a character changes form or shape.

Tra Theewa Prasit [*theewa* = "deity, angel"; *prasit* = "success"] Invites the *theewadaa* and the many sacred things as they process and bestow blessings.

Tra Parakhonthap [*Parakhonthap* = deity of *piiphaat*; *khonthap* = divine beings who entertain the deities with music and song] Invites the teacher of the *taphoon* drum or the teacher of metrical patterns (*naa thap*), i.e., Phra Parakhonthap.

Tra Kring [*kring* = "bell"] [No explanation given.]

Tra Phra Phikhaneet [*Phra* Phikhaneet = Lord Ganesha] Invites *Phra* Phikhaneet, the god of all kinds of knowledge.

Tra Naun [*naun* = "to sleep"] In *khoon* and *lakhon*, used for sleeping.

Tra Banthom Phraai [*banthom* = "to sleep" (elegant); *pharai* = "forest, jungle"] In *khoon* and *lakhon*, used for sleeping or for sleeping in the forest and mountains. *Tra Naun* and *Tra Banthom Phraai* are used only for characters of high status.

Tra Narai Banthomsin [Narai = Narayana, a manifestation of Vishnu; *banthom* = "to sleep"; *sin* = "river" (Indus)] Invites *Phra* Narai.

Tra Rüsii Kalaaikot Invites the *rüsii* Kalaaikot.

Tra Phra Phrohm [*Phrohm* = Brahma] Invites *Phra* Phrohm.

Samoe Man [*man* = "demon, devil, evil spirit"; *Mara* = "devil"] Invites the god of the demons.

Samoe Theen [*theen* = "senior monk, ordained holy man"] Invites the hermit teacher to enter the ritual and to scatter water as the officiant dons the head of *Phra* Pharotrüsii.

Samoe Phii [*phii* = "spirit, ghost"] Invites the many spirit teachers.

Samoe Khao Thii [*khao* = "to enter"; *thii* = "place"] Invites the many teachers to enter and seat themselves in their prepared places.

Samoe Khaam Samut [*khaam* = "to cross"; *samut* = "bridge"] In the *wai khruu* ritual, invites the *phra* [refined heroes], i.e., the teachers of *phra* roles, who come as a group. In *khoon* and *lakhon*, used for following the road to go fight with Totsakan [i.e., Ravana, the king of the demons]. (Usually *Phra* Ram crossing the great bridge to fight with Totsakan.)

Samoe Saam Laa [*saam* = "three"; *laa* = "to depart, good-bye"] Invites the many great gods (*theepacao*). Invites *Phra* Pancasingkhaun, *Phra* Parakhonthap, or *Phra* Wisanuukaam. In the *wai khruu* for artisans, used to invite *Phra* Wisanuukaam.

Samoe Phraahm [*phraahm* = "Brahmin"] Performed to indicate [literally, "mean"] that the Brahmin who will lead the *wai khruu* ritual has entered. Similar to *Phleeng Phraahm Khao* or *Phleeng Damnoen Phraahm*.

Prooi Khao Tauk [*prooi* = "to strew, scatter"; *khao tauk* = "popped/puffed rice"] Performed while popped rice and flowers are being strewn or offered. Indicates that the *wai khruu* ritual is over.

Nang Kin–Sen Lao [*nang* = "to sit"; *kin* = "to eat"; *sen* = "to offer food to deities"; *lao* = "alcoholic beverage"] Usually performed one after the other. *Nang Kin* invites the many teachers to sit and eat the food offerings; *Sen Lao* invites them to drink the offerings of water and liquor.

Khom Wian [*khom* = "lantern"; *wian* = "to circle, circumambulate"] Invites the [illegible] *theep* or the refined heroines as a group.

Tra Yaa Paak Khauk [*yaa* = "grass"; *paak* = "mouth"; *khauk* = "stable". *Yaa paak khauk* is an idiomatic expression meaning easy, commonplace; "like grass by the barn door," i.e., so familiar as to go unnoticed (Haas 1964, 84).] [No explanation given.]

Tra Man Lamaum [*man* = "demon, devil, evil spirit"; *lamaum* = "gentle, tender"] [No explanation given.]

Tra Plaai Phra Lak [*plaai* = "end"; *Phra* Lak = Lord Laksmana] [No explanation given.]

Tra Caum Srii [*caum* = "highest, supreme"; *srii* = "magnificence, splendor"] [No explanation given.]

Tra Choeng Krachaeng [*choeng* = "lower end, foot"; *krachaeng* = "rope/rein put around an elephant's neck"] [No explanation given.]

Tra Prathan Phaun [*prathan* = "to give, offer, bestow" (royal); *phaun* = "blessing"] Played as a request to the many deities and teachers to confer their blessings on the participants in the ritual.

Tra Sannibaat [*sannibaat* = "assembly, gathering"] Invites all the sacred teachers to come together. Invites all the deities to come together as a group or gathering.

Choet Klaung [*klaung* = "drum"] In *khoon* and *lakhon*, used for traveling a long distance or afar, or traveling in a noisy, boisterous way.

Choet Ching [*ching* = "small hand cymbal"] A *naa phaat* piece from *khoon* and *lakhon*, used for traveling a long way over a long time, either quietly, noisily, or [illegible].

Choet Nauk [*nauk* = "outside"] Used in *khoon* and *lakhon* for chase or pursuit between humans and animals or between animals. Can also be used for fight scenes. Used to show off technical playing skill.

Ot [*ot* = "to cry, lament, complain in a pathetic manner"] A *naa phaat* piece from *khoon* and *lakhon*, used for crying and emotional hurt. If *Ot Em* is used, it signifies crying for happiness.

Rua Laa Dieo [*laa* = "depart, good-bye"; *dieo* = "single"] In the *wai khruu* ritual, performed at the end of various *naa phaat* pieces so that everyone will know that that piece is finished or that a set of pieces is finished.

Rua Saam Laa [*saam* = "three"; *laa* = "depart, good-bye"] In the *wai khruu* ritual, used to invite the teachers of magical power (*itthirit*) or demons of magical power. In *khoon* and *lakhon*, used for magical power.

Phleeng Chaa–Phleeng Reo [*phleeng* = "musical piece"; *chaa* = "slow"; *reo* = "fast"] Invites the teachers of *khoon* and *lakhon* and of refined heroes and heroines. Used to accompany the "Offering of the Hands" (*Thawaai Müü*). The piece *Laa* is usually played at its conclusion.

Phleeng Chaa [*phleeng* = "musical piece"; *chaa* = "slow"] In *khoon* and *lakhon*, it is a *naa phaat* piece used for traveling shorter distances in a leisurely fashion.

Phleeng Reo [*phleeng* = "musical piece"; *reo* = "fast"] Used for hurried, fast travel or escape.

Phleeng Ching [*phleeng* = "musical piece"; *ching* = "small hand cymbal"] Used for traveling shorter distances in a quiet manner.

Klom [*klom* = "to be round"] Invites the teacher-deity *Phra* Narai or *Phra* Pancasingkhaun.

Kraao Nai [*kraao* = "to be noisy, make a din, commotion"; *nai* = "inside"] Invites the teachers who are demons. In *khoon* and *lakhon*, used when the demon troops (of the left) are being inspected before going off to battle.

Kraao Nauk [*kraao* = "to be noisy, make a din, commotion"; *nauk* = "outside"] Invites the human or monkey teachers (of the right). In *khoon* and *lakhon*, used when the human or monkey troops are being inspected before going off to battle.

Hau [*hau* = "to fly magically"] Invites the deities to travel and fly through the air. In *khoon* and *lakhon*, used for flying to or from a place.

Kraao Ram [*kraao* = "to be noisy, make a din, commotion"; *ram* = "to dance"] Means happiness. In the *wai khruu* ritual, it is usually used at the end of dancing the strewing of popped rice.

Pathom [*pathom* = "first, foremost." Also the name of an ancient royal ritual in which an enemy's head was cut off and the king's feet bathed with his blood (Manit 2528/1985, 548).] Is a gathering of strength (?), or used for traveling.

Lo [*lo* = "to row, rock, swing"] Invites the teachers who live in the water or who will approach by water.

Phraahm Khao [*phraahm* = "Brahmin"; *khao* = "to enter"] Invites the hermit teachers and the many *theep* and *theewadaa* to enter the ritual. The officiant usually calls for this piece at the beginning of the ritual when he dons the "head" of *Phra* Pharotrüsii and dances into the *wai khruu* ritual.

Phraahm Auk [*phraahm* = "Brahmin"; *auk* = "to go out"] [No explanation given.]

Damnoen Phraahm [*damnoen* = "to proceed, walk, go" (royal); *phraahm* = "Brahmin"] Invites the Brahmins to enter the ritual in order to perform the *wai khruu* ritual.

Ong Phra Phiraap [*ong* = classifier for sacred or royal beings; *Phra* Phiraap = the demonic deity of masked dance-drama] Invites the teacher Phiraap. The piece *Pathom* is usually performed at its conclusion—*Pathom* can be compared to traveling.

Long Song [*long* = "to descend"; *song* = "to bathe" (royal, sacred)] For bathing the teachers with water.

Samoe For traveling a short distance.

Laa [*laa* = "to take one's leave, say good-bye"] Announces that the piece or the dance is now over.

Khuk Phaat [*khuk* = "to threaten, loom menacingly"; *phaat* = "instruments that herald, announce"] Invites the hermit teachers who have magical power *(itthirit)*, such as *Phra* Khaneet [Ganesha], *theep*, or *theewadaa*. In *khoon* and *lakhon*, used for magical power and showing off magical power.

Ruk Lon [*ruk* = "to advance, invade"; *lon* = "to fill to overflowing"] A gathering of strength [?], or invites the teachers of refined heroes, monkeys, and humans. Is usually performed before *Samoe Khaam Samut*.

Naang Doen [*naang* = "woman, lady"; *doen* = "to walk, proceed"] Invites the female teachers, that is, the dance teachers for refined heroine roles.

Plaai Khao Man [*plaai* = "end"; *khao* = "to enter"; *man* = "curtain, drape"] Used for traveling a short distance.

Khao Man [*khao* = "to enter"; *man* = "curtain, drape"] Used for traveling.

Chup/Ton Chup [*chup* = "to dip"; *ton* = "beginning"] Traveling a short distance.

Chamnaan [*chamnaan* = "to be skillful, expert, experienced in"] Invites the female teachers of *khoon*. In performance, can be used for bodily transformations.

Pluuk Ton Mai [*pluuk* = "to plant"; *ton mai* = "tree"] The name of a *naa phaat* piece used in [illegible] rituals: plowing, sowing, and planting trees.

Baatsakuunii [*baat* = "foot"; *sakuunii* = "female bird"] Is a kind of *Samoe*, called *Samoe Tiin Nok* [The Bird's Foot Samoe]. Invites the teachers of refined heroes and heroines, *Phra* Ram, and *Phra* Lak—the teachers of high status.

Hoomroong [*hoomroong* = "prelude, overture"] Invites the many sacred things to descend into the ritual.

Sooi Son [*sooi* = "ornamental string, necklace"; *son* = "to thread"] The name of a piece used in performing the dance "The Offering of the Hands." Also the name of one kind of *phleeng rüang* [suites of connected pieces].

Ram Dap [*ram* = "to dance"; *dap* = "sword] Performed before the presentation of the food offerings, while the offerings are being sliced with knives.

Choet Thawaai Khrüang [*thawaai* = "to present, offer"; *khrüang* = "objects"] Performed when the older disciples take up the food offerings and present them in dance.

Wian Thian [*wian* = "to circle, circumambulate"; *thian* = "candle"] Causes auspiciousness. When the ritual is over, this causes good luck. In music, this is also the name of a kind of *phleeng rüang* [suites of connected pieces].

Saam Tra [*saam* = "three"] A recited text *(phaat)* in the great shadow theater *(nang yai):* three texts are recited, worshiping *Phra* Pharotmuni, *Phra* Isuan, and *Phra* Narai.

Mahaachai [*mahaa* = "great"; *chai* = "victory"] Used for bestowing blessings and the many kinds of auspiciousness, for instance, during the ritual of "covering" *(khraup)*, or while monks chant prayers of blessing. This piece is used for the many kinds of auspiciousness.

Appendix C

The Deities of Thai Court Performance

Phra Isuan

Phra Isuan (Shiva) is usually grouped with *Phra* Narai and *Phra* Phrohm (Brahma) as one of the highest deities of the Thai Hindu-Brahmin cosmology, but most performers regard *Phra* Isuan with special reverence and often place his mask in a dominant place on *wai khruu* altars. His mask usually has a white face and wears the tall headdress called a *chaadaa*.

Phra Narai

Phra Narai (Vishnu), who vanquished the demon Nonthuk and started the conflict described in the *Ramakien;* the two were reborn as *Phra* Ram and the demon Totsakan.

Phra Narotmuunii

See *Phra* Parakhonthap.

Phra Pancasingkhaun

One of the main deities of music, *Phra* Pancasingkhaun's mask usually has a white face and wears a *mongkut* headdress with five spires (*panca* = "five"; *singkhaun* (or *sikhara*) = "peak, mountain top"). *Phra* Pancasingkhaun is a *khonthap* (Sanskrit, *gandharva*), a lesser deity serving the higher gods; he plays the *phin* (harp) and *kracappii* (long-necked lute) to entertain the deities. Before he was reborn as a *khonthap*, he was a particularly devout cowherd; when he died while still a young man, the deities arranged for him to be reborn in the heavens. When one high deity wishes to approach another (e.g., when Indra wanted to speak with the Buddha), he or she often sends *Phra* Pancasingkhaun ahead, to play a piece of music and ask permission for the visit.

    Phra Pancasingkhaun is generally worshipped as the deity of stringed instruments and singing. He is often contrasted with *Phra* Parakhonthap, who is the deity of all *piiphaat* instruments; in elaborate *wai khruu* rituals, an officiant may even "cover" participants with one deity's mask or the other, depending on that musician's instrumental specialty.

Phra Parakhonthap

One of the main deities of music, *Phra* Parakhonthap's mask usually has a green face and wears the tall headdress of a *rüsii*, painted to resemble tigerskin. Musicians regard him as the deity of *piiphaat* instruments, and the *taphoon* is his symbol—in fact, this drum can be used as his stand-in if a mask of him is unavailable. Some musicians say that *Phra* Parakhonthap is the deity of rhythm, whereas *Phra* Pancasingkhaun is the deity of melody.

Phra Parakhonthap and *Phra* Pancasingkhaun are both *khonthap* (Sanskrit, *gandharva*), divine beings who live in their own level of heaven but are free to visit both humans and deities alike. Some musicians say that *Phra* Parakhonthap's real name is *Phra* Narotmuunii, who is the highest of the *khonthap* as well as their teacher. As his name implies, *Phra* Narotmuunii was a *rüsii*,[1] and many *oongkaan* texts refer to him as "the old teacher" *(phra khruu kao)*. *Phra* Narotmuunii is said to have invented the *phin* (harp).

Phra Pharotrüsii (Phau Kae)

Phra Pharotrüsii is the Thai version of Bharatamuni, the sage who witnessed Shiva's cosmic dance, recorded it in a sacred treatise, and then disseminated the deity's dance positions to humankind. He is the most widely worshiped deity of performance, revered by both dancers and musicians. He is kind and benevolent, and performers regard him with respect as well as affection, frequently asking for his help and protection in all parts of their lives.

Whereas only some performers will own masks of *Phra* Parakhonthap and *Phra* Pancasingkhaun, masks of *Phra* Pharotrüsii (also known as *Phra* Rüsii, or simply *Phau Kae*, the "Old Father"), are more common. Most performers either keep a mask or a small replica of his mask on their personal altar at home or wear an amulet of his image on a chain around their neck. His mask is usually gold-skinned and depicts the face of an old man wearing the tigerskin headdress of a *rüsii*. This mask holds the central place of honor on *wai khruu* altars (usually just below the presiding Buddha image), and the officiant usually wears a mask of the Old Father during parts of the *wai khruu* and *khraup* rituals. In the *khraup* or "covering" ritual, the officiant "covers" each participant's head with three masks in succession—the Old Father, *Phra* Phiraap, and the *soet* headdress—because each imparts a different kind of power and knowledge.

Phra Phikhaneet

Phra Phikhaneet (Ganesha) has the head of an elephant and the potbellied body of a man. His mask is of a red elephant's head with one broken tusk, wearing a short *soet* headdress. *Phra* Phikhaneet was the son of *Phra* Isuan and his wife *Phra* Uma.

He is regarded by performers as the deity of knowledge and all the arts, and he is often supplicated when obstacles must be overcome. He served as the scribe for the deities and is therefore regarded as the deity of books and written knowledge.

Since the reign of Rama VI (1910–1925), *Phra* Phikhaneet has been regarded more and more specifically as the deity of the arts, especially since the 1940s, when the Department of Fine Arts adopted him as their patron deity and emblem (Ciratsa 2531/1988, 121–26, 166–67).

Phra Phiraap

Phra Phiraap is the demonic deity of masked dance-drama *(khoon)*. His mask shows the snarling face of a demon with fangs and purple skin. In the usual version, he wears no headdress and is bald or has hair of short tight curls, but some masks also depict him with gold skin, wearing a tall *mongkut* headdress.

In the *Ramakien*, *Phra* Phiraap is a demon in a minor episode no longer performed. His task is to guard a grove of fruit trees at the foot of Mount Assakan; when *Phra* Ram passes by in his travels, *Phra* Phiraap challenges him, they fight, and the demon is killed. Although his role and character in the *Ramakien* give no indication of his importance in the cosmology of performance, *Phra* Phiraap is evidently the Thai version of Bhairava, a fierce manifestation of Shiva. He is worshiped by all performers but especially by dancers and particularly by *khoon* performers. In the *khraup* or "covering" ritual for dance (and often, but not necessarily, for music), the officiant "covers" each participant's head with three masks in succession—the Old Father, *Phra* Phiraap, and the *soet* headdress—because each imparts a different kind of power and knowledge. *Phra* Phiraap is both feared and respected by performers; his wrath can result in accidents, illness, or death. His powerful and dangerous character is emblematic of the potential force of dance-drama, especially masked dance-drama.

Phra Phrohm

Along with *Phra* Isuan and *Phra* Narai, *Phra* Phrohm (Brahma) is one of the highest deities in the Thai Hindu-Brahmin cosmology. Generally regarded as the creator of the universe, he is usually depicted with four faces and four arms. He is known for his willingness to grant favors and is thus a popular deity in Thailand. The famous Erawan Shrine in Bangkok is focused on an image of *Phra* Phrohm known for its efficacy.

Phra Wisanuukaam

Phra Wisanuukaam (or Wisawakam) is another name for Vishnu and is the patron deity of all craftspersons, especially those in the arts: mask and instrument makers often have a special altar for his mask in their workshops. His mask has a green face and wears the shorter headdress called a *soet*.

Appendix D

Thai Instruments Mentioned in the Text

bandau A double-headed drum, small and light enough to be held in one hand by its wooden handle. The clapper is a cord with a small ball or knob at the end, tied to the handle. When the drum is swung or twisted back and forth, the ball strikes the drumheads, alternating between them. The *bandau* is used only in royal Brahminic rituals and originally came from India; the god Shiva is sometimes depicted holding a *bandau* in one hand, representing the rhythm of creation.

ching chap A pair of small cymbals, indispensable to most Thai classical music because they define the basic metric structure of strong/weak beats and create the framework for the metric density of any piece. Shaped like small knobbed discs about 2–3 inches in diameter, the *ching chap* are made of thick metal (either bronze or brass) and are attached to each other by a cord of string. The player holds one cymbal cupped in the left hand and strikes it with the other cymbal: the open ringing stroke is called *ching* and the closed stroke (when the two cymbals are struck rim to rim) is *chap*. The *ching chap* should have a clear, bright, penetrating sound with a long succession of overtones.

khaung wong yai/khaung wong lek A set of knobbed brass or bronze gongs set in a circular, horizontal frame of rattan. The player sits in the middle of the circle and holds a beater in each hand. The gongs are tied to the frame with leather cords with the knob upwards. The *khaung wong yai* (literally "big gong circle") plays the basic or skeletal melody around which other instruments improvise. It has sixteen gongs, with the lower ones to the player's left and proceeding upward to the right. The *khaung wong lek* (literally "small gong circle") was created later (probably during the first half of the nineteenth century), has eighteen gongs, and is an octave higher than the *khaung wong yai;* it is never played unless the *khaung wong yai* is also present.

khim A struck zither, modeled after the Chinese *yang chin.* It has a range of approximately an octave and a half and is played with two flexible bamboo beaters with felt-padded ends. Fairly easy to learn, the *khim* is often taught to children but can be played quite skillfully by accomplished musicians.

khlui A vertical bamboo flute. There are three sizes/registers that range in length from about 14–24 inches. The mouthpiece is a plug of wood that closes one end of the instrument except for a small rectangular hole. There are seven finger holes, one thumb hole on the back, and an additional hole that must be covered with a small piece of rice paper or tape. *Khlui* are now made from plastic for use in elementary school instruction but are traditionally made from bamboo and then smoked to dry the wood and to create a beautiful mottled outer surface.

klaung that A pair of barrel-like drums, played only in the *piiphaat* ensemble. Each drum is made of hardwood and has two heads made of cow or water buffalo hide held on by a number of brass tacks. A metal ring is attached to the body at the point of greatest diameter: when played, two poles (about a yard long) are passed through the drum rings, spread apart, and propped against the floor so that the drums are side by side and slightly tilted toward the player. The player has two heavy beaters about 18 inches long with padded ends. Each drumhead has a black circle painted in its center and is tuned with a patch of rice-and-ash paste applied to the circle. The two drums are tuned approximately a fifth apart but are not usually tuned to any definite pitch; the lower drum is referred to as the "female" and the higher as the "male."

kracappii Now rarely played, the *kracappii* is a long-necked, four-stringed, fretted lute. The body is oval and the long tapering neck curves at the end, giving the instrument a graceful appearance. The strings are struck with an ivory or bone plectrum. The *kracappii* originally accompanied solo singing and was later added to the *mahoorii* ensemble.

krap Two wood blocks that are struck together to coincide with the *chap* (closed) stroke of the *ching chap*. Usually made from heavy, dense wood, the four sides of the *krap* are polished and sanded and have rounded edges. When struck together, the *krap* should make a sharp snapping sound.

mahoorathuk A bronze drum, commonly known in English as a Dongson drum. Found all over Southeast Asia and in southern China, this kind of drum has ritual and military associations and is rarely used today except in some temples.

moong A single-knobbed gong, 12–18 inches in diameter, sometimes used to mark strong beats. The knob is almost always in the center of an inscribed star. The knob is struck with a padded beater, and the gong is usually suspended from a small wooden frame.

ranaat eek A xylophone with a set of twenty-one or twenty-two hardwood keys suspended over a boat-shaped wooden body. The keys are strung together with a single long cord and tuned with a mixture of lead shavings and wax stuck to their underside. The body can be plain or elaborately carved and inlaid. The beaters can be either padded or hard to create the different timbres appropriate for different genres. The *ranaat eek* is generally the ensemble leader, setting tempos, deciding on how many repeats to take, etc.

ranaat thum Paired with the *ranaat eek*, the *ranaat thum* is approximately an octave lower and has seventeen or eighteen keys of bamboo. Its musical line is often quite similar to that of the *khaung wong yai* but can be whimsical or joking. The *ranaat thum* is played only if a *ranaat eek* is present.

ranaat eek lek/ranaat thum lek A *ranaat eek* and *ranaat thum* with metal keys, usually iron (*lek*, "iron"), that lie flat on padded supports (unlike the suspended wooden keys of the *ranaat eek*). These two instruments are played only if the *ranaat eek* and *ranaat thum* are also present. The *ranaat eek lek* and *ranaat thum lek* appeared in the midnineteenth century.

phin Heavenly beings (e.g., *khonthap* and *theep*) are often described as playing the *phin*, usually translated as "harp." There are at least two kinds and possibly three. The *phin pia* and *phin nam tao* are both one-stringed, attached to a long stick or bow-like body, with a half-gourd resonator; the resonator is cupped against the bare chest, and the player plucks the string while singing. The *phin nam tao* is associated with Brahmins, while the *phin pia* is a northern Thai instrument. Morton (1970, 45–46) has an illustration of a six- or more-stringed harp shown on a fifteenth- or sixteenth-century tapestry found in northern Thailand, but many-stringed harps are not found today.

pii nai An oboe-like woodwind with a quadruple reed and a hardwood body about 16 inches long. The amount of air pressure needed to produce sound is kept constant by circular breathing, and the instrument's timbre is both piercing and very loud. The *pii nai* is played only in the *piiphaat* ensemble.

sang A conch shell blown at the beginning of royal rituals. Strongly associated with royalty, Brahmanism, and Narai (Vishnu), the lip of the shell is said to show the imprints of the deity's fingers. It is usually played along with *trae* (see below).

sau duang A two-stringed bowed instrument probably modeled on the Chinese *erhu*. The horsehair bow is inserted between the two strings, which are tuned a fifth apart. The body is a small wooden cylinder with a single head of snakeskin.

sau saam saai Literally "the three-stringed *sau*." A three-stringed bowed fiddle with no frets, the *sau saam saai* usually accompanies singing. Its body is made from half a coconut shell covered with goat- or calfskin. A small headweight, usually of silver or enamel with decorative gems, is attached to the head and creates a more sonorous timbre. Unlike the *sau duang* and *sau uu*, the bow of the *sau saam saai* is not threaded between the strings but held freely. Considered one of the most difficult instruments to learn, the *sau saam saai* is admired for its ability to blend with the human voice.

sau uu A two-stringed bowed instrument similar to the *sau duang*, but an octave lower and with a coconut-shell body, often elaborately carved and polished. The face is covered with goat- or calfskin. The *sau uu* has a deeper, mellower timbre than the *sau duang*, and its musical line is often joking or bantering in nature.

taphoon A double-headed drum, usually permanently attached to a wooden stand so that it sits in a horizontal position. The body is entirely covered with leather thongs, and each head has a black circle painted on its center where a tuning paste of rice and ashes is applied. The *taphoon* is a symbol of Parakhonthap, the deity of *piiphaat* instruments and is played only in the *piiphaat* ensemble. Because it is a symbol of Parakhonthap, it is ritually proscribed for women; it is the only instrument so proscribed.

trae A generic word for metal wind instruments played in royal ritual contexts. The *trae ngaun* is short and curved, and the *trae farang* is long and trombonelike; both are valveless. The *sang* is usually played along with them.

Appendix E

CD Contents

N.B.: Both recordings are my own, made on a Sony Professional Recorder.

The Evening Overture (Hoomroong Yen)

Played on the solo *khaung wong yai* by my teacher, Nikorn Chanthasorn.

This is the version of the *Overture* that I learned to play, as discussed in Chapter 4. Nikorn agreed to let me record him playing it for use as a teaching tool. We recorded it in the main practice room at Srinakharinwirot University–Prasanmit (where Nikorn is a professor) on October 17, 1989.

The Evening Overture (*25:57 total*):

Track 1. Saathukaan
 2. Tra Hoomroong
 3. Rua Saam Laa
 4. Khao Man
 5. Laa–Samoe
 6. Pathom
 7. Rua Laa Dieo
 8. Choet
 9. Klom
 10. Chamnaan
 11. Kraao Nai
 12. Khao Man–Laa

Excerpt from a *wai khruu* ritual

Led by the officiant *Khruu* Somyot Pobiamlot.

I made this field recording on August 17, 1989, at a small *wai khruu* ritual held at a private home. The host was a radio announcer who sponsored several troupes of nightclub comics. The participants were, therefore, mostly comics but included several well-known popular singers.

The officiant, *Khruu* Somyot, is a dance teacher unaffiliated with any major institution; he supports himself by running a small restaurant attached to a school in his neighborhood. He teaches *khoon* and *lakhon* at home on the weekends and in the evening and has a small following of loyal students. He is fairly active as an officiant and has two adult disciples to whom he has passed on the right to perform the *wai khruu* and to dance as *Phra* Phiraap.

The following transcription is approximate and intended as a listening aid. I have translated *Khruu* Somyot's general comments, but not the ritual texts as recited. The *piiphaat* ensemble was mostly made up of musicians from the Navy *Piiphaat* Ensemble *(Wong Piiphaat Bok Thahaan Rua).*

Tape Transcript *(25:47 total)*

***Track 13. Khruu* Somyot:** Now we will invite the *theewa* [deities], the *theep* [angels], and the rulers of our Siam. Let's recite together.

Everyone: [three times]
Namo tassa
bhagavato
arahato
samma sambuddhassa

***Khruu* Somyot:** Iman. [Everyone repeats the phrases after him.] *Phra* Siam theewanan. Ithi rithi. Mahaan taparan. Baramaan suthan. Eehi eehi. Ahang wan thaami. Thuk piyampi.

Iman. *Phra* Siam theewanan. Ithi rithi. Mahaan taparaan. Baramaan suthan. Eehi eehi. Ahang wan thaami. Tra piyampi.

Iman. *Phra* Siam theewanan. Ithi rithi. Mahaan taparan. Baramaan suthan. Eehi eehi. Ahang wan thaami.

"*Saa*—[stops and corrects himself]. "Tra Baungkan" and "Pathom Dusit"!

***Track 14.* [*Tra Baungkan* and *Rua*, then *Pathom Dusit* and *Rua*]**

***Khruu* Somyot:** Now we will invite *Phra* Phikaneet, the deity of success. Those who will study music and [two other subjects] must worship him, and truly worship him, or you cannot meet with success. It is therefore necessary to invite him, all of us together in this *wai khruu* today. Let's say the *Namo* together.

Everyone: [three times]
Namo tassa
bhagavato
arahato
samma sambuddhassa

***Khruu* Somyot:** Om! [Everyone repeats the phrases after him.] Khanee wanama. Mahaa phokha. Mahaa laaphra. Mahaa prasithi. Phawan thuume. Khau eehi cong maa. Thuk piyampi.

Om! Khanee wanama. Mahaa phokha. Mahaa laaphra. Mahaa prasithi. Phawan thuume. Khau eehi cong maa. Tra piyampi.

Om! Khanee wanama. Mahaa phokha. Mahaa laphra. Mahaa prasithi. Phawan thuume. Khau eehi cong maa.

"Rua Saam Laa" and then "Khao Man"!

Track 15. [*Rua Saam Laa* and then *Khao Man*]

Participants: [To each other] Light the incense! Light the incense! [Sound of a cigarette lighter.]

***Khruu* Somyot:** Now we will worship the high deities—*Phra* Isuan, *Phra* Phrohm, and *Phra* Narai, as well as all the many deities who come together here today—the "*pathiyai*" teachers, or the teachers of singing, dancing, and music. Let's say the *Namo* together.

Everyone: [three times]
Namo tassa
bhagavato
arahato
samma sambuddhassa

***Khruu* Somyot:** Iman! [Everyone repeats the phrases after him.] Akhiphahu uphaan. Ahang wan tha. Acaariyang. Sapasaaiyang. Mina santi. Sitthi kaara. Bara bachaa. Imassaming. Tawantomee. Thuk piyampi.

Iman! Akhiphahu uphaan. Ahang wan tha. Acaariyang. Sapasaaiyang. Mina santi. Sitthi kaara. Bara bachaa. Imassaming. Tawantome. Tra piyampi.

Iman! Akhiphahu uphaan. Ahang wan tha. Acaariyang. Sapasaaiyang. Mina santi. Sitthi kara. Bara bachaa. Imassaming. Tawantome.

"Saathukaan Klaung"!

Track 16. [*Saathukaan Klaung* and *Rua*]

***Khruu* Somyot:** Srii, srii! [Everyone repeats the phrases after him.] Wan nii pen wan dii. Khau hai caroen srii suk sawaat. Tangcai pathiphat. Namatsakan phrakinnasri. Yo ko khun nua klao. Phrannot niw dutsadii. Khun phra bok kee srii. Thuk kham cha lae phao nai. An nüng. Khaa ca wai. *Phra* Isuan. *Phra* Phrohm. *Phra* Narai. Wai theewadaa thang laai. Wai bidaa lae mandaa. Wai khun khruu lae aacaan. Phikhanee sang saun maa. Khau khun khruu cong raksaa. Dekha yu yen pen suk.

Namo! An waa nan massakaan. Khaaphacao khau kraap kraan. Theep chai thaang saam phra ong. *Phra* Wisukaam phuu rüang nii. Thaneeprasit sapsaan. Khruu ang len sing saarakhaan nai taairap. Iik thaang thaan theewadaa. *Phra* Pancasingkhaun. Phra kaun thoe phiw phin. Diit taang sanau sanaan. *Phra* Parakhonthap. *Phra* khruu thao. Khun khruu thaang nan lao. Thii sup saa tau kaan maa. Con thüng thuk wan nii. Khaaphacao khau anchalii. Anchoen *Phra* Rüsii 108 ton. Theewadaa nai sathaan müang bon. Cong maa chuay uayphon mongkhon. Lae saathi haeng sakolokaai. Thaa cat sia sung samnia cakanraai. Phuk phai thaang laai. Mii naa santi.

"*Hoomroong* sii naa an thananoi"!

Track 17. *Hoomroong:*
Saathukaan,
Tra Hoomroong,
Rua Saam Laa,

Khao Man–Pathom,
Laa–Samoe,
Rua Laa Dieo,
Choet–Klom,
Chamnaan,
Kraao Nai,
Ton Khao Man–Laa,
Rua Laa Dieo]

Khruu Somyot: Now we will invite the Hermit, whom we artists respect very much. He helps us at every opportunity. If you worship him, you won't be disappointed. Let's recite together.

(End of excerpt)

Appendix F

Guide to Commercial Recordings

While not numerous, some commercial recordings of Thai court music are available. This appendix provides information on the ones I find most useful in terms of recording quality, choice of repertoire, and liner notes, though some are more easily found than others. Each album uses a different system when romanizing Thai, so titles and names may be spelled in different ways.

Thai Classical Music
Performed by the Prasit Thawon Ensemble. Liner notes by Somsak Ketukaenchan and Donald Mitchell. Nimbus Records (NI 5412), 1994. Compact disc, 67 minutes, 30 seconds.

This outstanding recording features leading ritual musicians from Bangkok, all students of Prasit Thawon (whose biography appears in Chapter 6); several were mentioned in this book, including Nikorn Chanthasorn, Bunchuay Soowat, and Manat Khaoplüüm. The CD contains four long tracks: "Homrong Sornthong" (by *Luang* Pradit Phairau), "Sumran Dontri Klong" (arranged by Prasit Thawon), "Sarama" (normally used to accompany Thai boxing or sword fighting), and "Cherd Chin" (attributed to Sin Silapabanleng, father of *Luang* Pradit Phairau). Several of the pieces build up to extraordinary climaxes.

Siamese Classical Music
Performed by the ensemble Fong Nam, featuring Bruce Gaston and Bunyong Ketkhong. Marco Polo/HNH International Ltd. Compact discs available separately.

Volume 1: The Piphat Ensemble Before 1400 A.D. Liner notes by Bruce Gaston. Marco Polo/HNH International Ltd. (8.223197), 1991. Compact disc, 52 minutes, 25 seconds.

Volume 2: (There is a *Volume 2* in this series, but I have never seen it. The Marco Polo/HNH International Ltd. catalog lists it but provides no details about its contents.)

Volume 3: The String Ensemble. Liner notes by Bruce Gaston and Prasarn Wong-wirojruk. Marco Polo/HNH International Ltd. (8.223199), 1992. Compact disc, 58 minutes, 32 seconds.

Volume 4: The Piphat Sepha. Liner notes by Prasarn Wongwirojruk and Bruce Gaston. Marco Polo/HNH International Ltd. (8.223200), 1992. Compact disc, 63 minutes, 2 seconds.

These albums feature the excellent ensemble Fong Nam ("bubbles") led by American expatriate Bruce Gaston and his teacher Bunyong Ketkhong. The musicianship is outstanding, though the liner notes and the arrangements are idiosyncratic. Volume 1 is a curious attempt at historical reconstruction and should be taken with a grain of salt; the pared-down ensemble called "ancient piphat ensemble" may or may not be historically accurate, and the schematic "evolution of the piphat orchestra" provided in the liner notes has useful line drawings but is an uncritical compilation of musicians' oral histories, Montri Tramote's writings, and (presumably) iconographic evidence.

Each album contains four to six tracks, featuring everything from unusual, rarely heard pieces to the great works from the ritual repertoire. Volume 1 contains an arrangement of "Sathukarn, Tra Yapakkok, Tra Jomsri" for "ancient piphat" and a solo oboe version of "Cherd Nawk." Volume 3 contains several pieces from the ritual repertoire realized as solo works (e.g., "Sarathi" for solo two-stringed fiddle and "Kaek Mon" for zither), excerpts of the music used in marionette theater *(hun krabauk),* and one of *Luang* Pradit Phairau's more famous compositions, "Kaek Kao" (The Persian, in the *thao* form). Volume 4 features the *seephaa* chanting style—a form of narrative song—and works composed or arranged to feature it, including the long, powerful ritual work, "Grao Nai" (performed here as a xylophone solo).

Royal Court Music of Thailand
Liner notes by M.R. Chakrarot Chitrabongse. Smithsonian/Folkways (SF CD 40413), 1994. Compact disc, 54 minutes, 9 seconds.

Smithsonian/Folkways produced this unusual album in collaboration with the External Relations Division of the Thailand Office of the National Cultural Commission as part of the Thailand Program of the 1994 Smithsonian Festival of American Folklife. Like most Smithsonian/Folkways albums, its liner notes are very good. All four tracks feature works composed by Thai royalty: "Sounds of the Surf Overture" *(Pleng Homrong Kleun Kratob Fang),* by King Rama VII; "The Floating Moon" *(Pleng Bulan Loy Luen),* by King Rama II; "A Starlit Night" *(Pleng Ratri Pradab Dao Thao),* by King Rama VII; and "Heart of the Sea" *(Pleng Ok Thalay Thao),* with lyrics by Crown Princess Maha Chakri Sirindhorn (daughter of the present king, Rama IX). While not first-rank (with the exception of Natthaphong Soowat on lead xylophone), the musicians are all from the College of Dramatic Arts in the Department of Fine Arts and are thus very good.

Thailand: Ceremonial and Court Music from Central Thailand
Liner notes ("Field Notes") by James S. Upton. Multicultural Media
(MCM 3014), 1997. Compact disc, 52 minutes.

The recordings featured here were made possible by assistance from the Graduate
School and Music Department of Mahidol University, Salaya, where James Upton
taught for a year. All the recordings were made during actual events (not in a stu-
dio), so the sound quality is variable while the performances have the spontaneity
and excitement of live events. The album is especially valuable because it showcases
a variety of professional ensembles from central Thailand, from state- to temple-
sponsored, and the resulting picture of late-twentieth-century musical activity
is unique. The fourteen tracks feature the ubiquitous Department of Fine Arts
musicians as well as the Bangkok Metropolitan Ensemble, the Bangkok Police
Ensemble, the Ruam Phomburi Ensemble from Ratchaburi (featuring students of
a famous teacher), and a resident funeral ensemble from a temple in Suphanburi.
The ensemble types range from *mahoorii* to *piiphaat* to *piiphaat Mon* (funeral music). The liner notes are handsomely produced (with maps and photographs) but are
somewhat uninformed. The *piiphaat* ensemble is inaccurately called *"Phat"* throughout, and *Luang* Pradit Phairau is (I think) referred to as "Pairach." There are no
explanations for each track, though quite a few ritual works (e.g., *Saathukaan*) are
included.

The Traditional Music of Siam / Dontrii Syaam Pracam Chaat [1]
Five albums (seven CDs). Editor, Sujit Wongthes. Translator, Michael
Wright. Project Coordinator, Sugree Charoensook. Produced by the
Committee of the College of Music Project, Mahidol University, 1994.
Distributed by the Public Relations Office, Mahidol University, Pin Klao,
Bangkok 10700, tel. 433-0140-77.

This beautiful boxed set of compact discs is the best available but is also the most
difficult to find as it is not distributed outside Thailand. The featured musicians
are from the Department of Fine Arts and the Bangkok Municipal Thai Traditional Ensemble and were rehearsed by Silapi Tramote and directed by Manat
Khaoplüüm. The liner notes for each album are copious as well as bilingual (Thai
and English), even if sometimes written with a Thai reader in mind. One album,
Tham Boon, contains three compact discs and covers the entire repertoire for this
important ritual, including all three ritual overtures *(hoomroong)*—Evening, Morning, and Daytime. *Naang Hong/Sip Saung Phaasaa/Phleeng Thai Naanaa Chaat*
(61 minutes, 55 seconds) contains pieces representing the musics of other nations and cultures (a long-standing Thai tradition); the *Naang Hong* suite and *Sip
Saung Phaasaa* (The Twelve Languages) were formerly played at funerals. *Bai-Sri
Su-Khwan (Tham Khwan)* (43 minutes, 30 seconds) contains the *piiphaat* music that
accompanies the *tham khwan* ritual, a spirit-calling ceremony held for marriages,
births, housewarmings, and ordinations. *100 Pii Phra Pok Klao/King Rama VII's*

Centennial (64 minutes, 54 seconds) features five works written by Rama VII. Finally, *Wai Khru/The Worship of Teachers* (62 minutes, 48 seconds) is the definitive recording of its kind. It contains eighteen pieces, including "Sathukan," "Homrong Yen," and "Ong Phra Phirap." This album is, simply put, the sound of my fieldwork.

Notes

....

Preface

1. My second book, now in progress (provisionally titled *Speak It Louder: Asian Americans Making Music*), will be very different.

Chapter One

1. Sometime between that moment and 1994, this musician—Bunchuay Soowat, whose writings are discussed in several chapters below, was given the right to lead the *wai khruu* ritual by Montri Tramote, so these matters were on his mind for good reason.
2. This word has distinct moral overtones, implying a greatness of wisdom, compassion, and loving kindness as well as action.
3. The ritual authority of the court Brahmins was central to the *devaraja* practices of the Thai and Khmer empires. The Brahmins came to mainland Southeast Asia during the early centuries of this millennium, and wielded considerable power in Cambodia by the ninth century or even before. Their ritual activities were a mixture of Hinduism and Vajrayana Buddhism (Wales 1931, 59–60). Brahmins were imported to Thailand from Cambodia along with the "appurtenances of Khmer royalty" (ibid.) and were central to Thai court ritual by the fourteenth century if not before. Their descendants have intermarried with Thais, but the contemporary Court Brahmins still have noticeably Indian facial features and continue to conduct the royal ceremonies.
4. The *Five Precepts (Sin Ha)* proscribe (1) killing, (2) stealing, (3) wrongful sexual behavior, (4) lying, and (5) consuming alcohol. The *Eight Precepts (Sin Paet)* include the Five Precepts plus three more proscribing (6) the consumption of food after noon, (7) singing, dancing, making music, or adorning oneself, and (8) sleeping on an elevated bed; also, the Eight Precepts require total chastity rather than simply abstaining from wrongful sexual behavior. For more information, see the "Precepts" entry in the Glossary.
5. *Momrachawong* Caruunsawat Suksawat.

6. Conch shells are a symbol of Vishnu and are used in many Hindu-Brahmin rituals in Thailand, usually for pouring holy water. They are associated with the Buddha in Indian, Tibetan, and Javanese texts.

7. Officiants always bring their own mask of the hermit to the ceremony, a mask that is kept on their altar at home in a central place of honor.

8. In the *wai khruu* ceremony, each musical piece and each *khaathaa*, or magical utterance, is felt to "invite" certain deities into the ritual.

9. *Ong* is especially used as a classifier or counter for royalty and Buddha images.

Chapter Two

1. Spirits and deities, like monks, do not eat after noon.

2. Two kinds of dance-drama; see Glossary for more.

3. *Momrachawong* is an aristocratic title for male great-grandchildren of kings.

4. I don't know why these spirit mediums attended. I assumed that they were particularly devout performers until a friend pointed them out and told me they were *khon khao song*, "people who are entered." Spirit mediums usually perform their own *wai khruu* rituals in honor of their tutelary spirits, whom they usually address as their *khruu*. I can only guess that these mediums attended the ritual at Wat Phra Phireen because of its reputation for intense spirit activity. (See Muecke 1992 for more on spirit mediums and their *khruu* in northern Thailand.)

5. This ritual was at the Bangkok Bank in December 1988. Rachani is well known among performers for her ability to be entered by the Old Father; she was invited to perform in the Bangkok Bank ceremony so that this would happen, and it did.

6. Four campuses are in Bangkok, and the other four are in Bang Saen, Phitsanulok, Mahaserakham, and Songkhla. Originally called The College of Education, it was granted the title of a university in 1974 and named Srinakharinwirot ("the glory of the country") by the King himself. Although less prestigious than Chulalongkorn University or Thammasat University, Srinakharinwirot is generally regarded as a good second-rank university.

7. Hiring one's own graduates is common in Thai universities. It is seen not as favoritism but as a way of maintaining particular educational approaches and methodologies. The department thus hired two of these young professors as soon as they graduated, and then sent them abroad for graduate study (one now has a Ph.D. in ethnomusicology from York University in Great Britain and the other an M.A. in ethnomusicology from the University of the Philippines).

8. Other courses include a survey of Thai music, Thai music analysis, Thai music composition, an introduction to pedagogy, the history of Thai and "Oriental" music, classical Thai singing, music literature in classical drama, music literature in *khoon*, Thai folk music, Thai classical ensemble, religious music in Thai ceremonies, research methods (culminating in the senior thesis), and so on. Courses are also offered in Western music theory and history.

9. This has become the norm for all university music departments. At Chula-

longkorn University, for instance, the music major juniors even give a concert in which they perform the repertoire that qualifies them to advance to the next level.

10. Ordination as a Buddhist monk is a prerequisite for the fifth and highest level of the sacred music and dance repertoire as well as for leading the *wai khruu* ceremony. Only men can be ordained, though this was not true in the past. Women called nuns, or *mae chii*, who renounce the world, shave their heads, wear only white, and who usually live at Buddhist temples are not recognized by the Sangha as human vehicles for making merit, as are monks (see Van Esterik 1982; Keyes 1984).

11. Making merit is described more fully in Chapter 3.

12. Few people know that Chin passed on the right to lead the *wai khruu* ceremony to Prateep Lountratana-ari, one of the music professors at Prasanmit. As an undergraduate, Prateep was the president of the Thai Music Club and then became one of the three founding faculty members of the new Music Education Department. While still a student, he studied with Chin and was very close to her and the Silapabanleng family. Sometime in the last few years of her life, he asked for, and received from her, the right to lead the ritual. As he explained it, they were both planning for the future—for the time when *Khruu* Chüa would be too old to lead the ceremony. Prateep has never actually led the ritual. He was in his early forties in 1989, still too young to act as an officiant—most men are over fifty when they first lead the ceremony. Few people are even aware that Prateep has inherited the right: he is an extraordinarily modest man and says he isn't sure he will ever feel truly qualified to lead the ritual. Instead, he is a driving force in the department's preparations for the annual ceremony and usually assists *Khruu* Chüa during the ritual itself. He was one of the most devout lay Buddhists I knew in Bangkok, and my impression was that he believed in the efficacious power and importance of the *wai khruu* ritual more—or perhaps more openly—than some of the other music professors.

13. I videotaped this organizational meeting, the preparation of the altar and the ritual area in the auditorium, and of course the ritual event itself.

14. The music department owns a complete Mon *piiphaat* ensemble, used only at funerals. This kind of ensemble originated with the Mon people of lower Burma, and entered Thailand in the early twentieth century with a wave of Mon immigrants. See Wong (1998) for more.

15. The teachers' pictures included *Phraya* Sanau Duriyang, *Caangwaang* Thua, *Khruu* Ongkan Klipchüün, and two photographs of King Rama V (Chulalongkorn).

16. This may be related to South Asian Hindu practices. In his close examination of a *puja* (worship) for the deity Ganesha, Paul B. Courtright notes that sacred speech *(mantra)* and sacred *durva* grass are used as conduits to transfer *prana* ("vital breath," life force) from the human devotee into the image of the deity:

> The *durva* grass acts as a conduit through which passes the animating power of the *prana*, activated by the *mantra*, from the patron to the image, from giver to receiver. *Durva* is thought to be especially favored by Ganesa and some

claim it has medicinal properties in addition to its religious ones. It resembles sacred *kusa* grass which is used in Vedic sacrifice. According to one version of the myth of the churning of the ocean, when Garuda rescued the *amrta* from the thieving hands of the demons, he flew up with the vat in his claws and some of it spilled out, falling on some *durva* grass below. Hence *durva* became the receptacle of the immortality-bestowing ambrosia, the spilled leftovers of divine creative power. By virtue of this contact with the original and uncompromised substance of the universe, *durva* has acquired important capacities for transmitting the power of *prana*. (1985, 44–45)

17. Natthaphong Soowat is Bunchuay Soowat's brother. The two frequently perform together in *wai khruu* rituals, often with Natthaphong on lead and Bunchuay on supporting xylophone. Musicians at the Fine Arts Department told me that the brothers received the right to lead the *wai khruu* ritual together from Montri Tramote.

18. This sentence is recited three times at the beginning of many Buddhist rituals and can be translated as: "Reverence to the Lord who is worthy and fully awakened." The Pali spelling is *Namo tassa bhagavato arahato samma sambuddhassa* (Terwiel 1979,186).

19. The institution of Thai monkhood is called *sangha*. Together, the Buddha, the Dharma, and the Sangha are known as the Triple Gem.

20. For reasons addressed in Chapter 5, the actual ritual texts read in the ritual are forbidden to anyone but officiants. To include an actual text in this study would be unimaginable without the specific permission of an officiant, and such permission is rare.

21. Nikorn had, of course, considered this when inviting these musicians to perform in the Prasanmit ritual; he knew that all eight men (including himself) could perform the piece. *Khuk Phaat* is sometimes played alone to summon *Phra Phiraap* if some of the musicians aren't qualified to play *Phra Phiraap Tem Ong*, but this is less auspicious, and I saw it happen only once.

22. The *wai khruu* ceremony itself took almost exactly two hours to perform at Prasanmit, and eighty-three minutes of that time were filled with live performed music (and dance).

23. This kind of *yan* is from a category of such signs called *yan napathamam*, which literally means "the first/foremost letter N." The letter N is an abbreviation of the words *Namo Buddhaya*, "Hail to the Buddha," and is thus used frequently in mystical drawings and diagrams (Terwiel 1979, 141). Other officiants simply draw an *unalom* on participants' foreheads, that is, three dots in a triangular formation with a wavy vertical line extended above them. The *unalom* is another symbol of the Buddha, specifically the tuft of hair between his eyebrows that marked him as the Gautama Buddha. It is also related to the cosmic syllable *om* (88).

24. The officiant keeps this money and usually donates it to a temple, making merit in the process. One officiant told me he used the money to buy robes for monks from outside Bangkok whose temples were less affluent than those in the capital.

Chapter Three

1. The Thai words for "student" include *nakrian, naksüksaa,* and *nisit. Luuk sit* is rarely used in university contexts.
2. Other Asian-Pacific traditions similarly stress long-term ties between teachers and students in the arts. In Japan, the school or guild system called *iemoto seido* is an elaborate hierarchy of emotional and financial commitments; Joyce Malm writes that the word *sensei,* or teacher, implies "a spiritual and emotional bond between master and disciple as well as the intellectual, professional, or occupational contract to learn or teach. This bond usually lasts for the lifetime of the individuals involved. Reverence for one's *sensei,* along with one's place in the pyramidal structure of *iemoto seido,* may be passed on to succeeding generations" (1985, 160). Similarly, historical-genealogical epics in Hawaii were taught in special schools called *halau* whose teacher-priests imposed strict secrecy while the chants were being learned (Kaeppler 1980, 145--47).
3. *Luang* Pradit Phairau and *Caangwaang* Thua both invested their daughters as *wai khruu* celebrants (as discussed in Chapter 7), and Montri Tramote passed on the right to his son Silapi (as discussed in more detail in Chapter 6).
4. That is, the Triple Gem of Buddhism, three phrases that are the most fundamental expression of Buddhist belief, uttered three times at the beginning of any ritual event.
5. A similar set of verses often appears at the beginning of classical Thai poetry.
6. I have kept these final lines in Pali (rather than translate them into English) because the effect of switching from Thai into Pali words of power is central to the performative effect of reciting the prayer. This word is an entreaty for success and power *(khwaam saksit).*
7. These four words are from Pali and literally mean "age," "caste" (or, in Sanskrit, "letter, word, syllable"), "happiness," and "strength." They are recited in a number of formulaic texts asking for blessings.
8. *Mahaa* means "great." *Mahaasukho* invokes the great happiness, *mahaalaphoo* invokes the great luck or fortune, and *mahauchaiyoo* is a call expressing celebration, happiness, and the completion of an auspicious act.
9. If a contemporary teacher is being paid for private lessons, it is a sign that the student in question is an amateur or (more and more frequently) a middle-class child whose parents want the child to study music, much as Western parents send their children to study violin or piano. When such parents have their children take music lessons (whether on Thai or Western instruments), it is an attempt to make those children more sophisticated and refined. The decision whether to go with Thai or Western music indicates different attitudes—linking sophistication and refinement either with modernity or with traditional Thai culture.
10. The practice of living at a teacher's home has not completely disappeared; see, for example, the section on Sakol Kaewpenkhat in Chapter 6. Outside Bangkok, it may still be more common than I realize.
11. A male undergraduate told me that women would look extremely unattractive if they played the *pii,* because it involves puffing out the cheeks. As I explained

in a previous note, this perception, shared by Thai women and men, produces a de facto proscription against women playing the *pii*.

12. The sophomore class is initiated into the second or third level, and juniors into the fourth. For more detail, see Chapter 4.

13. There are exceptions. I knew one young woman who was a strong gong circle player, and when her music department went on tour, she was the only female instrumentalist in the *piiphaat* ensemble that accompanied their masked dance-drama performance.

14. This ceremony is called *phithii taak naam*, literally "the ritual of dipping water," and is described in detail in Chapter 2, when Professor Kamthaun Snitwong was so honored in the *wai khruu* ritual at Srinakharinwirot University–Prasanmit. The person being honored sits in a chair (or somehow elevated above everyone else), and people come up (in order of status and importance) to pour a small amount of water over his or her hands from a small silver bowl or a conch shell. The ritual is usually held to celebrate and honor someone following an important event, but it is also part of the Thai wedding ceremony and is performed in northern Thailand on Songkran, the Thai New Year's Day in April. Except at weddings, the people who ladle the water are usually expressing respect and gratitude to the person being honored, e.g., a parent, teacher, employer, etc. The ritual is not at all solemn: it is usually marked by much smiling, personal comments, and jokes between those pouring the water and those receiving it.

15. These respect behaviors are called *kattaweethii* or *kattaweethitaa*.

16. Whether rural or urban, schools are still often named after their adjacent temple.

17. In traditional rural Thailand, literacy was "indissolubly linked" with the ethical and religious training young men received at the local temple (Tambiah 1968, 121).

18. Obviously, only sons can do this. Being ordained as a monk, even for a short time, is the greatest way a child can make merit and express gratitude. Charles Keyes notes: "It is commonly said that one is ordained as a novice in order to make merit for one's mother, who cannot herself be ordained" (1983, 280).

19. Keyes relates a story (1983, 275–78) from a northern Thai text in which a son was ordained as a monk and transferred his considerable merit first to his mother (saving her from hell) and then to his dead father, who had already been reborn as a ghost because of his misdeeds. The monk received morning alms from laypersons and then transferred their merit to his parents by pouring a libation. His father was immediately reborn as a divine being *(theewadaa)*.

20. Allen Maxwell notes that in old Brunei, the root *sambah* was used in both verbs and nouns. He says,

> The Malay root *sambah*, which in its core meaning indicates "paying respect," illustrates certain relationships between persons, roles, and offices. . . . In the *sembah* the hands are closed as though in prayer with the finger-tips touching; they are then raised, not above the chin if the Chief is of less than royal blood but as high as the forehead if he is a reigning Sultan. The *sembah* proper is the way the hands are held. . . . The meaning of "obeisance" also varies. *Sembah*

is used also of vassalage to a King or State. . . . Lastly, as it is customary for a *sembah* to accompany any words addressed to a Sultan, the word is used of such speech itself. (1990, 3)

21. In her monograph on Khmer classical dance, Chan Moly Sam notes that the *sampeah* is the first movement taught to dance students. She writes:

> In dance, this gesture is stylized by joining both palms together with the fingers arched into dramatic curvatures. . . . This reverential salutation or *sampeah* is also known as *anjali* or *pranam*. This gesture occurs frequently and is seen an average of two times in each dance piece. . . . The *sampeah* is executed in three steps:
>
> 1. *Sampeah* on the chest is to a high personage such as [a] king.
> 2. *Sampeah* at the forehead is to the divinity, *krou* [teacher], or a sacred object.
> 3. *Sampeah* back at the chest is the salute to the audience or a person of an equal status.
>
> It should be noted that the above three steps are treated coherently one after the other as one movement without a break. In dance drama, *sampeah* at the chest and at the forehead signifies "worshipping, adoration, praying, an invitation to a great divinity, a greeting to a higher personage, and an agreement." When *sampeah* is placed at a distance from the temple[s], it is to a respected person such as [a] parent. (1987, 98–99)

22. With the exception of monks, who never return a *wai*—even from the King.
23. It is also the polite form, used (for instance) by an inferior speaking to a superior.
24. *Phra* Withunthamaphaun (known as *Phra* Win), who has lived at Wat Bowonniwet for almost forty years.
25. These are the spellings in Pali, as they were given to me.
26. Another, more basic metaphor, identified by Michael Reddy as "the conduit metaphor" (cited in Lakoff and Johnson 1980, 10–11), is behind the idea of the journey. This complex metaphor is summarized as:

> Ideas (or meanings) are objects.
> Linguistic expressions are containers.
> Communication is sending.

This metaphor structures our language about language, as demonstrated in expressions such as "It's difficult to put my ideas into words," "His words carry little meaning," and "It's hard to get that idea across to him." Reddy estimates that some 70 percent of our English expressions about language use this metaphor. Not surprisingly, we use the conduit metaphor in both our language about language and our language about knowledge.

27. Although the following examples can be used when talking or writing about knowledge of any kind, it happens that I found all of them in introductions to books (in Thai) about music. Most such introductions are meditations on the importance of Thai music to Thai society, and the value of musical knowledge

and understanding is nearly always addressed. Formulaic phrases of thanks and respect to the writer's teachers are always included. In fact, one such introduction (Panyaa Rungrüang 2517/1974) is titled *"Wai Khruu."*

I must also stress that, while the journey is the most common and dominant metaphor guiding Thai epistemology, it is not the only one. Knowledge is also talked about as "riches" and as something that has "value." It is also described as "deep" and "broad" and "high," or (conversely) as something shallow ("skin deep") and narrow. One writer (Mattani 1975b) warns her readers to beware of "knowledge like a duck's" *(khwaamruu yaang "pet"),* which I assume draws on the idea of floating or skimming along the surface without knowledge of the depths below.

28. Myers-Moro agrees that the "musical meanings of the word *thaang*—as 'ways' of rendering music—are consistent metaphorically with the word's other [non-musical] usages" (1993, 108). She goes on, however, to say that:

> It is by use of the word *thaang* that informants spoke most easily and naturally of the old schools. Thus it appears that—in as much as this may be verbalized—the schools are most significant or salient in the realm of musical, not social, contrasts and similarities. Musicians of the same line share a store of relatively unique or at least characteristic musical material. They also share other things: teachers, friends, experiences, and in the past, housing and household work, yet the tendency to stress shared *thaang* suggests that the social aspects of being part of a school . . . are less important than the specifically musical commonality. (108–9)

29. See Cohen (1987), which addresses "men of merit" or "saints" *(phuu mii bun* or *nak bun)* as the leaders of Thai peasant rebellions.
30. This is in direct contrast to Cohen (1987).
31. *Phra* is an honorific placed before the name of the Buddha, the names of divinities, places and things associated with Buddhism, sacred places and things, places and things associated with the King, etc.
32. It is important to note that there is no Thai word for mask. Whether made for use in performance or just for worship, all masks are called *hua* or *sirasa,* which means "head." My distinction between masks and small replicas merely indicates which are actually worn in ritual, but in Thai they are differentiated only in size, i.e., as a big head or a small head *(hua yai,* or *hua lek).* The dance masks (i.e., *hua yai)* used in *khoon* and other kinds of dance-drama such as *lakhon chaatrii* either cover the entire head of the wearer (e.g., monkey and demon masks) or are worn on top of the head (e.g., joker and *rüsii* masks), leaving the performer's real face exposed and creating a compelling double-faced effect. Referring to all of these objects as heads, whether large or small, automatically connotes respect since the paradigm of head-feet/high-low/sacred-polluted is pervasive in Thai culture.
33. Padung Cheep is on the edge of the Banglamphu district and has been at the same location, 14–20 Cakraphong Road, since 1933.
34. The cost of a mask depends on its size and materials. All of *Mom* Caruun's

sacred masks (*Phra* Siwa, *Phra* Parakhonthap, *Phra* Pancasingkhon, etc.) cost 6,000 *baht* because of the cost of gold leaf and the many tiny jewels that encrust their headdresses.

35. As far as I know, no *khoon* masks survived the Burmese sack of Ayuthaya in 1767.

36. The ritual for opening a mask's eyes and thus making it sentient is also performed for Buddha images (Tambiah 1984, 243–57). After a new Buddha image is cast, the last step before installing it in a temple for worship is to activate it by opening its eyes. This can be done by inserting jewels, painting its eyes, removing a layer of wax from over the eyes, or pretending to pierce the eyes with a needle. The ritual is performed either by the presiding Buddhist monk or by a lay ritual expert. This ritual is particularly important in northern Thailand and Cambodia, and there are Sri Lankan references to a similar ritual dating to the twelfth century A.D., as well as contemporary ethnographic accounts (by Gombrich, cited in Tambiah 1984, 255–56). It is also performed in India to consecrate the principal image in new temples. Tambiah feels that the ritual is related to the Hindu concept of *darsan*, or "auspicious sight," which is attributed to deities, saints, and renouncers; deities and holy men "give" *darsan* and worshippers "take" it.

37. These stones mark off sacred, consecrated space. Although most temples have two main assembly halls—the *wihan* and the *bot*—only the *bot* is defined by boundary stones. Eight stones define the perimeter of the building, and a ninth is buried beneath the spot where the presiding Buddha image sits. These stones are consecrated in a special ceremony, transforming the building into a space within which ordination can take place.

38. This ceremony was held on August 17, 1989, and was led by the officiant *Khruu* Somyot Pobiamlot.

39. Now called *dukun* (a more general word for a magician or specialist in non-Muslim magic), the priests of Tengger Hindu ritual were formerly called *resi pujangga*. The word *resi* is obviously from the Sanskrit *rsi*, and related to the Thai word *rüsii; pujangga* means "a man of letters." Robert Hefner (1985, 271–76) suggests a historical relationship between the Tengger *resi pujangga* and the Balinese *resi bujangga*. Though the Tengger specialist is "the preeminent officiant of a whole people's ritual tradition" and the Balinese priest is low in the priestly hierarchy, Hefner notes striking similarities in their repertoire of recited prayers and their ritual duty of transforming the demonic deities Kala and Durga back into their benevolent form as Shiva and Uma.

40. *Khruu* Nim Pho-iam.

41. See Sweeney on the Maharisi Kala Api (1972a, 43, 76–77; 1972b) and Matusky (1993) for more on preperformance ritual in the Malaysian *wayang siam*.

42. This is the Thai parallel to *sbek* in Cambodia.

43. The *wai khruu* text used at Wat Khanaun in Rachburi province is printed in its entirety in Pha-op (2520/1977, 40–49). It was transcribed and transliterated from archaic into modern Thai script by Pha-op and was taken from the traditional texts owned and used by the puppet master *Nai* La-au Thaungmisit. These texts were apparently passed down in his family.

44. Instituted in 2528/1985, this title is awarded annually by the government to about sixteen living artisans and performers.

45. Sutthiwong writes that the monkey scene is now included only when the entire performance is part of a spirit propitiation ritual called *kae bon* (2522/1979, 81).

46. Sections of the set, formal texts used in the opening sequence (e.g., the monkeys' fight, the salutation of the Hermit and Shiva, etc.) are included in Sutthiwong (2522/1978, 81–105). The verses describing the Hermit are nearly a compendium of his names and titles: he is referred to as *Phra Dabot, Than Song Phrot, Phra Yokhi, Maha Mek, Phra Muni, Phra Chidong*, and *Phra Khodom Phromcan*.

47. Endicott (1985) notes that the classification of Shiva's avatars by Malay ritual specialists reflects a sacred topography. Batara Guru is associated with the State Chamber, Toh Panjang Kuku ("Grandsire Long Claws") with the heart of the forest, Batara Kala with the dangerous boundary between land and sea (i.e., the shoreline), Raja Kala with the shore between the high- and low-water marks, and Batara Guru di Laut (Batara Guru of the Ocean) with the open sea. Toh Panjang Kuku, or Grandsire Long Claws, is a manifestation of Shiva as a tiger. Singaravelu (1970, 50) also refers to Shiva's associations with tigers: according to Indian sources, Shiva was confronted in the forest of Taragam by heretical sages who created a fierce tiger and set it upon him. Shiva seized it, stripped off its skin with one nail, and wrapped it around himself like a cloth.

48. Translated by René T. A. Lysloff.

Chapter Four

1. The Sanskrit word *vadya* means a musical instrument or instrumental piece (as contrasted to sung music). My thanks to Professor Madhav Deshpande for explaining the Sanskrit origins of this and related words.

2. He writes, "*Naa phaat* nii plae waa tham hai koet siang rüü kham phuut."

3. David Morton's monograph on Thai traditional music focuses exclusively on the *seephaa mahoorii* repertoire. He briefly mentions the *naa phaat* repertoire (referring to it as "ceremonial and theater music") in his chapter on musical form (1976, 216).

4. In Japanese Kabuki, for instance, the "offstage music," called *geza-ongaku*, fulfills much the same function (see Malm 1959; Brandon, Malm, and Shively 1978). *Gendhing lampahan* (*mlampah* = "to walk, move") in Javanese shadow theater and dance-drama are similarly iconic of action and movement (see Wong and Lysloff 1991; Lysloff 1990, 51ff.; Susilo 1988).

5. See Appendix B for a list of the ritual pieces used in the *wai khruu*, with written comments by a *piiphaat* musician describing their ritual function.

6. Uthit comments that there is also a dance for *Saathukaan*, but it is rarely performed.

7. Uthit mentions that he has seen statues of *Phra* Isuan with the Buddha seated on his head, depicting the story told to him by *Luang* Pradit Phairau.

8. *Tra* means "divine" and is probably of Khmer origin. All pieces whose names

are prefixed with *tra* are by definition from the second level of repertoire or higher.

9. Both *rua* can be heard on the accompanying CD, whose contents are listed in Appendix E.

10. Almost all kinds of dance-drama have their own overtures but most overlap considerably with the *Evening Overture* and, in fact, the *Evening Overture* is often used instead.

11. A score of the complete *Evening Overture* in Western notation was published by the Department of Fine Arts (n.d.) as *Phleeng Chut Hoomroong Yen/Evening Prelude: Chabap Ruam Khrüang (Score)*. Assembled by *piiphaat* musicians and teachers at the department, the score is an anomalous example of ritual repertoire in notation.

12. See Chapter 1, nt. 3 for more on the court Brahmins.

13. H. G. Quaritch Wales describes this ritual as it was conducted in the 1920s:

> For three days before the actual Day of Coronation [of King Prajadhipok, or Rama VII, the last absolute monarch of Thailand], the Court Brahmins performed *homa*, or sacrifices to Fire. . . . The images of the Hindu deities were placed upon three altars in a ceremonial pavilion. . . . Before the altars was placed a copper stove inscribed with the appropriate *yantra* [magical written symbols] and nine basins of water each containing a small silver coin . . . , eight of these basins being arranged around a central one. The Brahmins began their rites at 8 p.m. in accordance with the rule that Brahminical rites must be performed after dark whenever possible. The *Brah Maha Raja Gru* [the Head Brahmin] performed the usual purificatory rites . . . , [and] read the texts offering worship to the eight directions and to the Brahminic deities. . . .
>
> At the conclusion of the *homam* the fire was extinguished by some of the hallowed water being poured on it by a conch shell. This *homam* sacrifice used to be performed also in connection with the *Con Parian* [Feast of Lamps] and New Year Festivals. In the former case it was abolished by King Rama IV [r. 1851–1868], but it still survives in the New Year and Coronation Ceremonies. (1931, 72)

14. Although *hoomroong* is a noun, professional Thai musicians also tend to use it as a verb in conversation, suggesting that its older meaning still reverberates.

15. These instruments include the *trae* (a metal horn with a short, curved shape and no valves) and the *mahoorathük* (a Dongson-like bronze drum), still sometimes played to announce the King and other high-ranking nobility (Dhanit 2530/ 1987, 89–90, 64–71). See Cooler (1986) on the *mahoorathük*.

16. Unlike *ranaat eek* parts, which are easy to write out in Thai notation since the basic playing technique is octaves, the *khaung wong* part alternates freely between octaves and many other intervals (notably fourths and fifths) as well as monophonic lines. Traditional Thai notation—a solfege system, where the Thai letters for D, R, M, F, S, L, and T represent *do, re, mi*, etc.—is not well suited to representing harmony. For more on Thai notational systems, see (Myers-Moro 1990).

17. Again, the *Evening Overture*, as played by Nikorn on the solo gong circle, can be heard on the CD.

18. The same traveling piece, *Choet*, sends both deities and high-ranking humans "out" of ritual events at their conclusion.

19. I was initiated for *Tra Hoomroong* on the *khaung wong yai* by *Khruu* Bunyong Ketkhong in a *wai khruu* ritual held in Rachburi. Later, at a different *wai khruu* ritual, *Khruu* Sakol Kaewpenkhat insisted on initiating me for *Tra Hoomroong* on the xylophone as well, saying he was sure the xylophone part would come easily to me since I already knew the gong circle part.

20. The way Nikorn taught me the two pieces, and how to remember their difference, also suggests that they overlay each other conceptually. In the *Evening Overture, Tra Hoomroong* begins right after *Saathukaan* ends, with the same motive that begins *Saathukaan*. During lessons, Nikorn would at this point (without fail) say, "It's like *Saathukaan*, right? But where exactly do they separate *(yaek)?*" His consistent use of the word *separate* almost implied that they are the same piece up to that point.

21. See the CD and Appendix E for a transcript of the ritual.

22. Manat Khaoplüüm of the Department of Fine Arts and the Witthayalai Khruu Ban Somdet.

23. These three men continue to perform together in *wai khruu* rituals today.

24. *Khruu* Rongphakdi received the dance from his teacher, the great *Phraya* Natthakanurak. The four teachers who received it in turn were *Khruu* Aram Inthauranat, *Khruu* Akhom Saiyakhom, *Khruu* Yat Changthaung, and *Khruu* Yausaeng Phakdithewa.

25. In reading about other cultural systems of initiation, I came across the following passage by the anthropologist Fredrik Barth about the Baktaman people of highland Papua, New Guinea. Although it addresses a different ritual complex, the passage brought home certain important points about the Thai system:

> [N]ew information [given to] novices after initiation . . . is *not* explored in conversation to pursue its implications, not exploited to discover connections, deeper meanings, and hidden secrets. Rather, it is handled the way little boys in occupied Europe during the war handled the unexploded ammunition they found: treasured for its unknown power, potential danger, secrecy—not with any real intention to use, and not to be experimented with to discover what destruction, or noise, an explosion really makes. So, there is not only an inhibition against speaking about the revelations of Baktaman initiations, but a wariness and vagueness in *thinking* about them—it is their secrecy and exclusiveness, not their potential for enlightenment, that give them value. In this sense, the ritual symbols of the Baktaman are *not* "good to think." Their credibility and conviction arise from the fact that they are "good to act," in their proper setting. (1975, 220–21)

26. See Myers-Moro (1991).

27. Zurbuchen explains that the reader/performer "sounds a written line according to prosodic conventions that allow variation . . . within a framework of identifi-

able constraints of pitch, tone, and rhythm" (1987, 104). The method by which poetic lines are broken down into musical phrases is called *guru basa* (*guru* = "teacher"; *basa* = "language"; 106).

28. This passage can be heard on the accompanying CD; Appendix E contains a transcript.

Chapter Five

1. The word *ongkara* is found in Bali, where its derivation is given several explanations: "Some say that the individual *(wong)* can realize his or her ultimate nature as the holy syllable *(kara)*. Others interpret the word as a derivation of *wong* "person" plus *ka-rwa* "both, two together," emphasizing the unity of opposites that precedes the final realization of indivisibility" (Zurbuchen 1987, 54–55). Perhaps even more importantly, it is the "*written* form of the sound symbolizing ultimate reality" (271; emphasis mine).

2. *Oongkaan* can also mean royal command or decree.

3. *The Scripture of the Great Buddhist Magical Spells* (On 2501/1958), a small book available at many Thai bookstores, contains a number of ritual texts that invite or summon deities, including the hermits, the local place spirit, the "teacher" (to enter the speaker), and so on.

4. Reverence for written texts was inherited at least partly from Indian attitudes toward Sanskrit sources. See Deshpande (1979).

5. Sangat Phukhaothaung of the Ban Somdet Teachers College and Manat Khaoplüüm, a professional *piiphaat* musician with the National Theater troupe and a part-time instructor at the Ban Somdet Teachers College.

6. A similar publication, also published by the Department of Fine Arts, is an extremely important collection of *wai khruu* texts chosen and edited by Dhanit Yupho (2494/1951), at that time the Director of the Fine Arts Department. This booklet describes the ritual of "covering" for various dance-drama traditions (including *lakhon chaatrii*, *lakhon nauk*, and *lakhon nai*) and two "royal manuals" *(Phra Tamraa)*, i.e., the books of *oongkaan* texts used by the officiants for the royal *khoon* and *lakhon* troupes at the courts of King Rama IV and VI. These texts are quite similar to *Khruu* Akhom's described here, though the lists of offerings are detailed and elaborate.

7. *Phra* Ket (or Ketu) is *Phra* Rahu's tail.

8. This honorific is for a person of high status and saintly disposition. It means "honored father."

9. Dhanit (2494/1951, 28) notes that this magical verse is also called *Mongkut Phra Cao*, or "the Lord's Crown." *Itipisoo* is a Pali word, and seems to be a class of propitiary texts similar to *oongkaan*, though I never discovered exactly what the word means. *Piso* means "rattan shield," and *ruan tia* means "the lower house."

10. The *phin* is a strummed stringed instrument, and the *bandau* is a small double-headed drum struck with a weighted string flicked back and forth.

11. These weapons are dancers' props, symbolic of particular characters.

12. One of his disciples told me that when he died in 1994 he was eighty-seven years old.

13. *Likee* is a kind of popular street theater. *Khruu* Nim was formerly a *likee* performer, but here he uses the word *natthadontrii*, an older compound word ("dance" + "music") that the Phibul Songkhram Government instituted for the word *likee* during World War II. *Natthadontrii* was the official name for *likee* from 1942 to 1944 but did not disappear from use until 1957, when the Phibul government was overthrown. (See Surapone 1980, 90–97 for more on this period.)

14. I was unable to translate these lines.

15. This phrase is in Pali, but I was unable to discover its meaning.

16. A name for Vishnu or Narai in an earthly manifestation.

17. That is, Ganesha.

18. Manit (2528/1985, 945) merely notes that this is one of the great Brahmin kings (*thao mahaa phrohm ong nüng*).

19. The sixteenth heaven in the realm of Brahma, where there is supposed to be the greatest happiness.

20. The deity of death.

21. Uma, the wife of Shiva.

22. Saraswati, the female deity of knowledge.

23. Possibly the female deity of riches.

24. Possibly a female *rüsii*.

25. The deity of sunlight.

26. These four deities are the wives of Indra.

27. All the deities in this paragraph are female. The Thai honorific *phra* is not gender-specific, but I translate it here as "Lady" and elsewhere as "Lord."

28. This is the *rüsii* of music.

29. Karaikot (or Kalaikot) has the face of a deer and appears in the *Ramakien*.

30. These two phrases are in Pali.

31. That is, Bharatamuni.

32. Again, Bharatamuni.

33. Amarin is another name for Indra.

34. That is, Vishnu.

35. Another name for *Phra* Phiraap, the demonic deity of dance-drama.

36. Ramasun is the demonic deity of thunder (which arose from his fight with the female deity Mekkhala, mentioned below).

37. In order, they are Sunday (the sun), Monday (the moon), Tuesday, Wednesday, Thursday, Friday, and Saturday.

38. Ketu is the tail of Rahu, who causes eclipses by devouring the sun or moon. Ketu is counted as the ninth deity of the planets.

39. The female deity of the earth.

40. The Ganges.

41. The deity of fire.

42. The deity of the rain.

43. The female deity of the clouds and lightening.

44. The deity of horses, or with a horse's head.

45. A warlike deity mounted on a horse.
46. The deity of love.
47. The deity of the oceans.
48. The deity of snow.
49. This is the ruler of Catum, the first level of Heaven.
50. The king of the *naga* (magical snakes or serpents).
51. The ruler of evil spirits and ghosts; also known as Kuphen or Phasarop.
52. That is, *yak*.
53. Most Thai cities have a shrine to the guardian spirit of the city, usually represented by a pillar or *linga*. This practice is Hindu-Brahmin in origin.
54. A formal name for Bangkok.
55. That is, the various place or guardian spirits everywhere.
56. The deity of the realm of death.
57. This deity is usually considered female but here has a specifically male honorific.
58. Possibly the guardian spirit of woodworkers' chisels.
59. Another name for Bangkok.
60. Another name for Bangkok.
61. Literally *sattri*, cf. Sanskrit *kshatriya*, the warrior caste in India (prominently featured in the Hindu epics the *Mahabharata* and the *Ramayana*). The *kshatriya* were one level below the Brahmins, who had the highest status within the caste system.
62. "Insert" apparently means that the officiant is to add the names of any additional relevant cities.
63. The word *Ramayana* is used, not the Thai name *Ramakien*.
64. Another name for Totsakan or Ravana (literally "ten headed one").
65. *Khaum* is the Khmer-derived alphabet used in Thailand for esoteric scriptures and written formulas.
66. These two instruments are of Arabic origin and are usually played together. The *klaung khaek* is a drum and the *pii chawaa* is a quadruple-reed instrument (sometimes described as having a double reed though this is actually folded yet again, creating four layers of reed and thus requiring considerable lung power to play).
67. Also of Arabic origin, this is a frame drum with a single head.
68. *Nora*, also called *manooraa*, is commonly regarded as one of the oldest forms of Thai dance-drama, and is now found in the southern peninsula.
69. *Lakhon* is a general word for dance-drama.
70. *Seephaa* is a form of solo singing in which the performer accompanies him- or herself with woodblocks.
71. The twelve "languages" in Thai music are mode-specific styles of playing that imitate foreign musics, including Chinese, Khmer, Lao, Burmese, etc.
72. That is, artisans who specialize in carving out the intricately decorated leatherwork for dance headdresses, shadow puppets, etc.
73. Making elaborate objects out of folded banana leaves—trays, iconic representations of Mount Meru, containers, etc.—is a highly developed tradition in Thailand, mostly among women.
74. The *mongkut* and *chadaa* are crowns with tall spires worn by the real King in

ritual contexts and by dancers portraying kings. The *pancuret* is similar but without a spire and is primarily worn in the *Inao* stories.

75. This phrase, *khruu phak lak cam*, is a saying among musicians and was quoted by Sombat Attalakhup (2532/1989) in her thesis. It literally means, "when the teacher rests, steal his memory," and can mean learning from notation rather than by rote.

76. *Phraya* Natthakanurat (birthname Thaungdi Suwantharot) lived from 1865 to 1935 and held the position of leader of the Department of Royal *Khoon (Krom Khoon Luang)* during the reign of Rama VI. He led the *wai khruu* ceremony for dance at the court. *Phraya* Sunthaunthep Rabam (birthname Plian Sunthaunnat), a court teacher and performer who died in 1937, was "the most frequent officiant in the *wai khruu* ceremony" (presumably in and around Bangkok) during his later life according to Sombat (2532/1989, 72).

77. By "etc.," *Khruu* Nim is referring to Bangkok's full name, supposedly the longest city name in the world. Referring to Bangkok as the city of Ratanakosin also gives the text a historical weight, since Ratanakosin, Ayuthaya, Sukhothai, etc., all refer to historical periods as well as actual cities.

78. Again, he uses the word *natthadontrii* rather than *likee*.

79. I have edited this quotation to suit my own purposes, because the last sentence actually goes on and ends as follows: ". . . in a process which we must own is unique." The sacred text as a noetic palimpsest seems in fact to be true the world over, not of the Bible alone.

Chapter Six

1. This contrasts with the stricter northern Indian concept and organizational structure of the *gharana*, which is both a stylistic school and a family lineage.

2. *Prakaup* is a verb of flexible meaning, including "(1) to do, perform. (2) to add, put together, assemble, compose. (3) to consist (of), be composed (of). (4) to be a component, ingredient, constituent (of). (5) to be an accessory, an accompanying feature. . . . (6) to illustrate. (7) to support (as evidence; as a character, etc.)" (Haas 1964, 300). In the context of the officiant for the *wai khruu*, this verb could mean any or all of these things. I am especially intrigued by the suggestion that the officiant could be seen as an illustration of the ritual, or as a supporting character—this interpretation plays up its performative nature rather nicely.

3. Since then, I learned from another musician that *Khruu* Saun received the right to lead the ritual from *Phrayaa* Sanauduriyang, a court musician of the previous generation.

4. In 1996, however, I was told by one of Nikorn's colleagues that he had, in fact, received the right to lead the *wai khruu* ritual from *Khruu* Saun not long before his death. I wasn't able to substantiate this with Nikorn himself, however.

5. Bunchuay has written a number of short essays for the Chulalongkorn commemorative booklets; all emphasize standards and proper procedures for musicians. Other essays include "The Qualities of the Musicians in the *Wai Khruu*

Ritual," "The Proper Behavior of Participants in the *Wai Khruu* Ritual for Thai Music," and "Arranging the Area for the *Wai Khruu* Ritual for Thai Music." All appeared in the booklet for the *wai khruu* ritual of 2532/1989.

6. See the Glossary in Appendix A.

7. Keyes describes *baaramii* as "the virtue that comes from adherence to the teachings of the Buddha and that has long been seen as especially associated with those deemed to be righteous rulers" (1987, 209). He notes that Crown Princess Sirindhorn wrote her master's thesis on the concept and meaning of *baaramii*.

8. When I asked Montri Tramote why he hadn't yet performed the *wai khruu* ritual by a certain age, he laughed and answered, "My *baaramii* wasn't yet sufficient" *(baaramii yung mai phau)*.

9. During a long conversation about *baaramii*, one of my musician friends offered the opinion that Abraham Lincoln and Martin Luther King had had great *baaramii*, but Richard Nixon did not.

10. The concern for musical descent, and its convergence on *Luang* Pradit Phairau, will be examined in detail further on. It is strikingly similar to the concern for musical lineages in Western conservatories, as noted by Henry Kingsbury. At one point Kingsbury's teacher told him, "My teacher was Artur Schnabel, the famous pianist. Schnabel studied with Theodor Leschetitzky, Leschetitzky studied with Liszt, Liszt studied with Czerny, and of course Czerny studied with Beethoven. So you see, you come from a good pedigree here" (1988, 46).

11. Now less than two hours southwest of Bangkok by bus, Samut Songkhram was a day's journey from the capital by river and canal during *Luang* Pradit Phairau's lifetime.

12. The family had no surname until 1925, when King Rama VI gave them and other well-known teachers of music and dance family names and titles. Sorn and his father, Sin, received the family name of Silapabanleng, or "the performing arts" (Myers-Moro 1988b, 85).

13. For a description of the royal tonsure ceremony, see Gerini ([1893] 1976); Kukrit Pramoj includes a detailed description of an upper-class tonsure ritual for two young girls in his novel *Four Reigns* (1981, 97–115).

14. One of these was Prince Naris, a half-brother of Rama V, who was a gifted musician and architect.

15. The famous annual music competition was held at Khao Nguu ("the mountain of snakes"), a Buddhist temple at the foot of a mountain just outside the town of Rachburi. This competition was a major event during the reign of Rama V (1868–1910), attracting musicians from neighboring provinces and aristocrats from Bangkok, who came by boat. A large stage was erected at the foot of the mountain, but sometimes there were so many competing troupes that some would play from boats on the adjacent Mae Klaung River.

16. His actual title, *Somdet Chao Fa Krom Phraya*, indicates that he was the son of a king, in his case King Rama IV; King Rama V (Chulalongkorn) was his older half-brother.

17. David Morton gives a slightly different, more romantic, account of this fateful meeting, probably related to him by the musician's adult children in the

1950s or 1960s, after *Luang* Pradit Phairau's death: "One day Phra (Prince) Bhanurangsi, a brother of King Rama V, while out riding, heard the sound of a *ranat ek* being played. Following the sound, the Prince found the young village boy playing on the river bank. He recognized the young boy's talent and took him under his wing and saw to it that he was given the rigorous musical training of the period" (1968, 26).

18. During the late nineteenth and early twentieth centuries, the princes and aristocrats of the many palaces maintained troupes of dancers and musicians that were keenly competitive. Always on the lookout for talent, such aristocrats often asked to hear local musicians perform when they went on tour outside Bangkok and frequently recruited young performers who showed promise. One account notes that "there were not a few rural musicians who were able to further themselves as performers in the royal palaces due to this practice" ("*Khruu* Ruam Phrohmburi" 2529/1986). One palace (Bang Khau Laem, of *Somdet Cao Fa Krom Luang* Lopburi Ramesawaun) had over twenty boys in residence, all musicians, and over half were from outside Bangkok (ibid.). Such recruitment was apparently not coercive: the same account relates how Prince Boriphat (i.e., *Somdet Cao Fa* Boriphat Sukhumphan *Krom Phra* Nakhon Sawan Woraphinit, yet another half-brother of Rama V) heard the young *Khruu* Ruam play in the Khao Nguu competition as a boy and asked his grandfather whether he could take him back to his palace in Bangkok. The grandfather demurred, saying that the boy was like his own son, and the Prince "understood and didn't say anything more about it" (32).

19. Kings Rama IV and V had many children by many wives, and Bangkok was full of their royal households by the turn of the century. The proliferation of such aristocratic patrons undoubtedly helped create a golden age of Thai music and dance, as many contemporary performers view the period.

20. This Supreme Patriarch, *Somdet Phra Maha Samon Cao Krom Phraya* Vajiranana, was also the son of King Rama IV and the half-brother of Rama V. Any association with him would have been a great honor for Sorn. For more on this Supreme Patriarch, see Craig Reynolds (1979).

21. *Phraya* Prasaan lived from 1860 to 1924. A court musician from an early age, he was one of the musicians chosen by Prince Phanuphantiwong Woradet to go to England and play for Queen Victoria in 1885. He received two different titles: he was first renamed *Khun* Prasaan Duriyasap by Rama VI (while he was still Crown Prince) in 1909, and then *Phraya* Prasaan Duriyasap in 1915. An anecdote related by Phunphit Amatyakul (2529/1986, 124) suggests that he spent considerable time at Prince Phanuphantiwong Woradet's Buraphaa Palace. One day the Prince heard the palace ensemble practicing and the drum part was so beautiful that he asked who was playing. Told that it was *Phraya* Prasaan, the Prince exclaimed, "That cannot have been a person! It must have been a deity *(theewadaa)*."

22. Personal communication, Malini Sagarik.

23. That is, the uncle of Kings Rama VI and VII, who were brothers.

24. Phunphit mentions two Javanese pieces: one is called "Buten Saulk" (clearly its Javanese or Indonesian name), which he notes "is now sometimes called 'Busen

Sauk,' meaning 'to be far from worries or care'"; the other is called *Yawaa Kao*, or "old Java" (2529/1986,136). For more on these pieces, see Hughes (1992).

25. Phunphit (2528/1985, 4–6) suggests that the *angklung* may have entered Thailand sometime before this, possibly following King Rama V's (Chulalongkorn's) visits to Java in either 1896 or 1901. He notes that *Luang* Pradit Phairau's "discovery" of the *angklung* is now an important part of his perceived legacy and suggests that, though the great teacher probably wasn't the first to bring *angklung* back to Thailand, he was certainly the one who adapted it for Thai use, arranging both Thai and Javanese melodies for Thai use. He also notes that the oldest known recording of *angklung* in Thailand is from the reign of Rama VII (r. 1925–1932) and bears the name of *Luang* Pradit Phairau's troupe; he suggests that the gap between its introduction to Thailand and this (presumably) first recording shows that it took some years for the instrument to catch on in Thai musical circles.

26. This compositional technique involves taking an existing melody (usually in the second metric level) and then expanding and contracting it (into the third and first metric levels). For more on the *thao* form, see Becker (1980), Morton (1968, 22–24; 1976, 182–96), and the Glossary in Appendix A.

27. Rama VI was not (as Myers-Moro 1988b, 84 claims) the only Thai king to confer such titles and names on performers, but he certainly did it on a scale unknown before that time. Kings Rama IV and V also recognized a few performers in this way (e.g., *Khruu* Mii Khaek, renamed *Phra* Pradit Phairau), but Rama VI bestowed names and titles with such enthusiasm that some aristocrats were quite critical of him.

28. In 1913, Rama VI decreed that all Thais had to bear surnames, a practice observed only erratically before that time. Walter Vella explains the King's motivations as follows: "Administrative and social usefulness were arguments for the surname decree, but, as with so many of the King's actions, international prestige was never far from the King's mind. [His] syllogistic reasoning is clear: Western countries were progressive; Western countries had surnames; Thailand, to be progressive, must also have surnames" (1978, 130–31). District and bureaucratic officials were assigned the task of helping those under them choose surnames, and the King himself created and assigned over 3,000 names.

29. These three musicians were (1) *Khruu* Mii Khaek, or Mii Duriyangkul, during the reign of Rama IV; (2) Tat Tatanan, a musician in the Department of Entertainment and at the Ban Mau Palace during the reign of Rama V; and (3) Ewan Warasiri, later *Phraya* Warasiri, during the reign of Rama VI (Montri 2521/1978, kindly given to me by Phunphit Amatyakul). Sumonman claims that the name Pradit Phairau was created by Rama II "for Thai music teachers who had extraordinary ability in both music performance and composition; those who have received this name are therefore people who have given real life to Thai music" (2524/1981, 264).

30. Morton notes, "King Rama VI asked Son [*sic*] Silapabanleng to join the ensembles of his royal court, but although Prince Bhanu grudgingly agreed to release him, the young man loyally stayed with his original patron. Because of this, though famous, he won no royal honors until one night shortly before

Prince Bhanu died, when he was permitted to play at the Grand Palace. After his performance, the King gave him the title of *Luang* Pradit Phairo, which roughly translated means 'Maker of Beautiful Melodies.' After the death of Prince Bhanu, King Rama VI made *Luang* Pradit leader of the royal ensembles, a position which he held until after the reign of Rama VII" (1968: 26).

31. I have found no independent verification of this date, but Kumut mentions that *Luang* Pradit Phairau's daughter, Chin Silapabanleng (b. 1906), was seven years older than himself and that the Royal Uncle died when he was fourteen or fifteen.

32. Mattani (2525/1982) suggests that Rama VI centralized all royal entertainment not only for reasons of personal pleasure and enjoyment but to purposefully use them to promote national unity and the institution of the absolute monarchy.

33. These pieces are *Raatrii Pradap Daao, Khmen La'Au Ong*, and *Hoomroong Khlüün Krathop Fang*.

34. The female *mahoorii* ensemble included *Luang* Pradit Phairau's daughter Chin, as evidenced by a photograph from the period (Surachai 2524/1981, 18).

35. Until the reign of Rama VI, Thai men commonly had more than one wife, and the first wife usually had authority over later wives.

36. During the 1980s and 1990s, 150 *baht* was worth about U.S.$4–$6 but was worth considerably more in the 1930s.

37. Mattani notes, "Even after the Revolution of 1932, when Krom Mahorasop [Department of Entertainment] was transferred to Krom Silapakon [Department of Fine Arts], in the first seventeen to eighteen years of the new administration, the khon and lakhon dancers did not come to work every day. They came only for weekly rehearsals on Thursdays (Thursday is Teachers Day in [the] Thai tradition) and for performances. However, under the new administration, the khon and lakhon properties, costumes, and masks were then kept at the krom [department]. It was only after this period that the dancers became civil servants and had to comply with the rules and regulations as other government officials. Nevertheless, there is still a relaxed atmosphere and attitude among the Silapakon dancers at present, especially the senior ones and the teachers, as they regard themselves as artists. They could often be very sensitive about submitting themselves to strict administrative rules and regulations" (2525/1982,130–31). Dhanit also notes that during these first seventeen to eighteen years of the department's existence, most performers came in only for the Thursday rehearsals and performances, otherwise staying home (2526/1983, 56–57).

38. Subin now teaches in the music department at Kasetsat University and has helped perform the music initiations at the annual *wai khruu* ceremony of the *Luang* Pradit Phairau Foundation.

39. Naowarat (2532/1989, 69–70) adds that *Khruu* King was invited to *Luang* Pradit Phairau's home to perform a number of solo gong circle pieces so that David Morton, who was doing his doctoral research, could record them. *Khruu* King was a gifted gong circle player and learned these solo pieces from *Luang* Pradit Phairau: he was considered a major transmitter of the teacher's *thaang*, or style of playing.

40. Most of these jobs would have been cremations and monk's ordination ceremonies, which necessarily include *piiphaat* music.

41. *Khruu* King also noted that there was no tuition at that time for *piiphaat* ensemble students; instead, they had to be on call to perform at Department of Fine Arts functions and for the school's dance-drama performances. Prasit Thawon, another of *Luang* Pradit Phairau's disciples, was also one of these first students at the School.

42. Personal communications.

43. Acquiring this list of disciples was a long additive process that took over ten years. Few musicians are aware of all of *Luang* Pradit Phairau's conferrals. Since my dissertation work—when I knew of only seven disciples so honored—I learned of five more by showing the lineage chart in my dissertation (Wong 1991b, 332) to various musicians, e.g., to a group of musicians at the Fine Arts Department in 1994. They agreed with my configuration but provided the names of several more conferees for *Luang* Pradit Phairau, Chin Silapabanleng, and Montri Tramote. I am grateful for their help, though I still don't have biographical information for several of these disciples. Similarly, Narong Khianthongkul, a teacher at Kasetsat University and at the Luang Pradit Phairau Foundation, also provided additional names.

44. See Wong (1991b) for more extended biographical information on all of these disciples.

45. "Sit" is clearly *Luang* Pradit Phairau's nickname for Prasit; *cao* is a title placed before the first name of a child or an inferior.

46. Malini Sagarik confirmed this guess in 1998.

47. See, for instance, Prasidh's string quartet arrangement of *Luang* Pradit Phairau's *saam chan* (third-level) version of *Lao Siang Thian* (Chin 2525/1982, 540–56).

48. These eight students were her nephew Chanok Sagarik, Prasit Thawon, Prateep Lountratana-ari, Uthai Kaewla-iat, Somphop Khamprasoet, Dr. Suraphon Canthopbat, Sawit Thapthimsri, and Subin Cankaew.

49. Compared to the music contests of *Luang* Pradit Phairau's day, this contest is quite sedate: the pieces the children play are limited, and there is no improvisation—students play memorized pieces.

50. Found at www.thaikids.com.

51. That is, to the *mahoorii* and *seephaa* repertoires, or the pieces played by the ensembles that accompany singing of various kinds. The *piiphaat* repertoire of dance-drama pieces is considered both ancient and sacred and is not seen as open to expansion.

52. This is also reflected in the Thai word for "to compose," *taeng*, which literally means, "to decorate, ornament, adorn," i.e., to *add on* rather than create anew.

53. Anecdotes of this sort are reminiscent of Bach's and Mozart's ability to sit down and improvise a set of variations on any given theme.

54. The piece is called *Phleeng Asae Wun Kii*, which is felt to sound Burmese.

55. Such openings are usually taken from the first phrase of the piece. This is similar to the Javanese *buka* ("to open"), except that the *buka* is usually taken from the *final* phrase of the piece.

56. These include the rituals at Chulalongkorn University, Mahidol University, the Thai National Cultural Center, etc.

57. Most of this biographical information on Montri comes from "Samphaat Raachabandit" (2524/1981) and Phunphit (2529/1986), as well as from conversations with Silapi Tramote.

58. In 1942, the government of Prime Minister Phibul Songkhram decreed that all Thais should have surnames. Montri's father was employed as an engineer in the huge Department of Police, which was overseen by *Phra Ong Cao* Kham Rop, whose family name was Pramote (sometimes romanized as Pramoj). Along with many other employees, Montri's father asked *Phra Ong Cao* Kham Rop to give him a surname. He was given the name "Tramote"—a great honor because of its close similarity to *Phra Ong Cao* Kham Rop's. Montri then took on this surname from his father. The Pramote family continues to have great influence in Thai politics: two of *Phra Ong Cao* Kham Rop's sons, *Momrachawong* Seni Pramote and *Momrachawong* Kukrit Pramote, served as prime ministers (each during tumultuous periods of democratic reform). Kukrit is also highly regarded as a writer (of the novel *Four Reigns* as well as political newspaper columns) and as a dancer of *khoon*. The resonance of "Tramote" with "Pramote" is unmistakable to any Thai.

59. This initiation was done not by *Phraya* Prasaan Duriyasap, who had died earlier that same year, but by *Khruu* Thaungdii Chuusat, the paternal grandfather of *Caangwaang* Thua. Along with Montri, five other musicians were initiated for this piece at the same time: *Phraya* Sanau Duriyang, *Phra* Phlengphairau, *Luang* Bamrungcitcaroen, *Luang* Soisamniangson, and *Mun* Khonthapprasitson.

60. This project was sponsored by the Royal Institute, a research institute devoted to the traditional Thai arts, and was directed by Prince Damrong, the "father of Thai history." Montri dictated the supporting xylophone parts for a number of pieces.

61. In his rambling memoir, Phraya Anuman Rajdhon describes the Surawong Road area of Bangkok where he lived during the first years of the twentieth century:

> there was a small lane leading to the back of the building where a German trumpet teacher lived. His name was Fiet. As far as I know, he had two sons, one of whom, Peter Fiet, later served as the leader of a musical band at the court. He changed his name to Piti and King Rama VI gave him the surname Vadhyakorn and the title Phra Jeneduriyang. He later entered the service in the Modern Music Division of the Fine Arts Department. Khun Phra had a lot of students and is regarded as a great authority on music. He is still alive at the time of writing (1968). He must be 84 or 85 and is still living in the old house. (Sthirakoses 1996, 30)

62. In 1940, saddened and depressed by the apparent twilight of classical music, *Luang* Pradit Phairau composed a piece called "Heavy Thoughts" (*Saen Kham Nüng*, literally, "a hundred thousand thoughts"). Neither the piece's melody nor its lyrics refer directly to the cultural politics of the time, but every Thai musician knows that it is a lament for classical music—in fact, it is published

in *Luang* Pradit Phairau's collected works overlaying a photograph of Field Marshal Phibul Songkhram, the source of the cultural proscriptions. Significantly, *Luang* Pradit Phairau looked back to classical models for this eminently topical piece: although he initially wrote his own lyrics, his family convinced him that they were "too strong," and he instead used poetry from the Thai epic *Khun Chang Khun Phaen* (Chin 2525/1982, 514).

63. Some genres, such as *likee*, flourished under these restrictions; others, such as *lakhon chaatrii* (southern dance-drama) and *hun krabauk* (hand puppet drama), nearly disappeared.

64. See Mattani (1993, 190–92) for more on this period in the arts.

65. Panya claims that *Luang* Pradit Phairau also told Montri he could perform the ritual without asking permission again, and that Montri therefore led the ritual from that time on (2527/1984, 136). I haven't seen or heard this corroborated elsewhere, and it seems a bit early for Montri to have already been performing as an officiant.

66. These performance works include dance and music in the Dvaravadi, Srivijaiya, Lopburi, Chiang Saen, and Sukhothai styles, all periods of ancient Thai history.

67. That is, *Duriyangsaat Thai Phaak Wichaakaan, Kaan La Len khaung Thai, Sap Sangkhiit*, and *Kham Athibai Prawat lae Khwaam Maai khaung Phleeng Thai*.

68. Montri is clearly leading the ritual, but these two men seem to have similar or equal status: they are probably either the hosts or perhaps even officiants themselves.

69. This piece is called *Phleeng Phamaa Nimit* and was written in 1962 for the *piiphaat Mon*, an ensemble that entered Thailand from Burma in the 1930s and is now used exclusively for funerals.

70. Some of these schools included the Rachini School, the School of Dramatic Arts (the Department of Fine Arts), the Thepsirin School, the music club at Srinakharinwirot University–Prasanmit, the Teachers College of Thonburi, the Nai Rua School, the Wat Boworniwet School, Chulalongkorn University, the Sri Ayudhya School, and many others.

71. Most of the performances on David Morton's "The Traditional Music of Thailand" (Morton 1968) are by students of the Phakavali Institute.

72. The volume is also unique, as far as I know, in the Thai classical tradition. Assembling and publishing an authoritative version of a single composer's works is a Western tradition of which Chin was aware.

73. This account of the ritual and the events leading up to it are from Panya Nittayasawan (2523/1980); teachers at the Department of Fine Arts and the National Theater verified it. The four teachers invested in the ritual were Aram Inthauranat, Akhom Saiyakhom, Yat Changthaung, and Yausaeng Phakdithewa.

74. These two teachers were *Luang* Wilatwong-ngam (Ram Inthauranat), who gave Akhom the right to lead the ritual, and *Phraya* Natakanurat (Thaungdi Suwantharot), who was the leading officiant at King Rama VI's court.

75. See Chapter 7, "The Institutional Contexts of Music," in Pamela Myers-Moro (1993).

76. This is my translation of the conference title in Thai *(Watthanatham Thai Suu*

Phai Setthakit), though the official title in English was "The Cultural Campaign Against Economic Oppression." My thanks to Linda McIntosh for sharing this information with me and for her report on the conference itself, attended in the course of her research. She said that the opening presentation included a small performance showing how Western goods—clothes, music, food, etc.—bring with them cultural changes in values and morality, none for the good.

77. My thanks to Philip Bohlman for this suggestion.

Chapter Seven

1. I remember one of my first Thai language classes at the University of Michigan when my teacher, a young Thai woman in the linguistics doctoral program, explained *khrap* and *kha.* The students—all of us American—thought it was a matter of who you were speaking to, and it took considerable explanation for us to understand that the participles identify the gender of the speaker, not the person spoken to.

2. I was regarded as a *farang* (Westerner) by most Thais, but as time went on, I found that Nikorn and the other professors at Prasanmit who knew me best, and who knew that I was half Chinese American, began to ascribe my cultural *faux pas* to my *farang* background and my culturally correct behaviors to my Asian background (e.g., I knew I should help serve food because I was Asian). In short, my multiracial Asian American background led to heightened expectations of "correct" feminine behavior from the people I knew best. This elision of gender and ethnic background was frequently confusing for me because my specific sense of Asian American identity issues from an engagement with the politics of difference. Being praised for correct feminine/Asian behavior thus inverted my own values even as it scored points for me.

3. Ortner notes that she is indebted to Michelle Rosaldo's work in this area, and she summarizes Rosaldo's position as follows:

   > Rosaldo argued, *inter alia,* (1) that even though men are universally "dominant" vis-à-vis women, we should stop paying so much attention to this point; (2) that empirical work upon the lives and experiences of women should not be the primary focus of feminist research; (3) that even though the opposition between "domestic" and "public" domains (which Rosaldo herself had established as central to the analysis of gender [1974]) seems to be heuristically useful, it is actually of negative value, since it leads to an emphasis on "difference" between men and women rather than on "relations"; and (4) that ultimately gender cannot be adequately understood except in relation to other structures of social symmetry. (1996, 116–17)

   This chapter is fundamentally shaped by both Rosaldo's and Ortner's approaches.

4. Camnian Srithaiphan died sometime between 1994 and 1996; I would guess that he was born in the 1920s.

5. For instance, Heinze documents a woman medium in Bangkae routinely entered by King Chulalongkorn and the Hindu deity Brahma (1988, 259–63). both high-status beings.

6. From Prince Damrong's *Tamnan Lakhon Inao* [Legend of the *Inao* Dance-Drama].

7. In his novel *Four Reigns*, Kukrit Pramoj (1981) describes the reaction of his heroine, Mae Ploi, to the news that the newly crowned King Vajiravudh was performing in plays himself:

> "Our present Nai Luang [a title for the King] is very fond of the theatre, Mae Ploi," Khun Prem said, "all kinds of theatre—*khone, lakorn,* everything. He performs in it too, you know."
>
> Ploi gaped at her husband. She remembered during the last reign, during the festival celebrating His Late Majesty's [Rama V's] return from Europe, there had been a beautiful and unprecedented performance—unprecedented because some of the Chao Chom Maandas (Royal Consort-Mothers) had taken part in it. Ploi recalled the great excitement this had aroused and how exclusive the presentation had been, with nobody from the outside in the inside. "Now Khun Prem tells me His Majesty himself is performing!" Was this the beginning of a new tradition? . . . At the moment she could not yet take it all in, but she desisted from questioning Khun Prem any further as she did not consider it proper for her to discuss casually so lofty a subject. (2:38–39)

Later in the novel, Ploi and her husband attend a Western-style spoken drama in which the King plays the lead and his real-life fiancée is the heroine; Ploi's discomfort is so great that she cannot bring herself to watch (2:102–7).

8. That is, "*phra raachaa phithii wai khruu lae khraup khoon lakhon lae piiphaat khrang yai.*"

9. *Khunying* Phaithuun was the daughter of *Caangwaang* Thua Phatayakosol, (b. 1881 in Thonburi, Thailand, d. 1938.). As the two most highly regarded central Thai musicians during the reigns of Rama V, VI, and VII, *Caangwaang* Thua and *Luang* Pradit Phairau were rivals. *Caangwaang* Thua's parents and grandparents were musicians, and his children—notably his son and daughter, Thewaprasit Phatayakosol (1907–1973) and *Khunying* Phaithun Kittiwan (b. 1911)—followed in his footsteps. *Caangwaang* Thua's home near the bank of the Chao Phraya River in Thonburi, just across from the Grand Palace in Bangkok, was famous as a house of music. His performance style, as passed on to his students, is known as the Thonburi style. *Caangwaang* Thua directed the *piiphaat* ensemble at the Bang Khun Phrom Palace, home of Prince Boriphat, half-brother to King Rama V; the title *caangwaang* was conferred on him by Prince Boriphat. This ensemble, known for its virtuosity, made some ten recordings (on 78 r.p.m. records). *Caangwaang* Thua was considered equally good on virtually all instruments and composed a large number of musical works; at least fifteen are still played today. His descendants still live in his house, and his grandchildren direct a *piiphaat* ensemble regarded as carrying his style.

Chapter Eight

1. This point is now central to much ethnographic inquiry but remains unusual in literary criticism and other self-consciously humanistic scholarship. Bhana writes, "theorizing (by) the ghost necessitates an insertion of alternate models of identity and peoplehood" (1999), and she argues for a kind of "reading" that sounds remarkably like poststructuralist ethnographic encounter while asserting *and* interrogating the defining forces of modernity and the nation-state.

Appendix C

1. A *rüsii* named *Phra* Narotrüsii makes an appearance in the *Ramakien*: when Hanuman is traveling to Longka, he stops overnight at the *Phra* Narotrüsii's forest hermitage, and the two have a contest of magical powers (which Hanuman loses). There is no clear association between this *rüsii* and the deity of music, however, except for the name.

Appendix F

1. I would like to thank Sugree Charoensook for giving me this set of compact discs.

References

··

Note: Thailand observes the Buddhist-era calendar. Thai sources below are cited by both the Thai and Western calendar year of publication, separated by a slash (/). Following Thai practice, Thai authors are cited and alphabetized by first name, not surname.

Anderson, Benedict R. O. 1972. The idea of power in Javanese culture. In *Culture and politics in Indonesia*, edited by Claire Holt. Ithaca, N.Y.: Cornell University Press.

Anuman Rajadhon, Phya. 1968. Thai traditional salutation. In *Essays on Thai folklore* (Bangkok: Department of Fine Arts). First published as *Thai traditional salutation*, Thai Culture, n.s., vol. 14 (Bangkok: Department of Fine Arts, 1963).

Barth, Fredrik. 1975. *Ritual knowledge among the Baktaman of New Guinea*. New Haven, Conn.: Yale University Press.

Barz, Gregory F., and Timothy J. Cooley, eds. 1997. *Shadows in the field: New perspectives for fieldwork in ethnomusicology*. New York: Oxford University Press.

Bateson, Gregory. 1972. *Steps to an ecology of mind*. New York: Ballantine Books.

Bauman, Richard. 1977. *Verbal art as performance*. Prospect Heights, Ill.: Waveland Press.

Becker, Judith. 1980. A Southeast Asian musical process: Thai *thaw* and Javanese *irama*. *Ethnomusicology* 24 (3): 453–64.

——. 1988. Earth, fire, *sakti*, and the Javanese gamelan. *Ethnomusicology* 32 (3): 385–91.

——. 1993. *In the presence of the past: Gamelan stories, Tantrism, and aesthetics in central Java*. Tempe: University of Arizona, Center for Southeast Asian Studies.

Becker, Judith, and Alton Becker. 1983. A reconsideration in the form of a dialogue. *Asian Music* 24 (1): 9–16.

Behar, Ruth. 1996. *The vulnerable observer: Anthropology that breaks your heart*. Boston: Beacon Press.

Benedict, Ruth. 1934. *Patterns of culture*. New York: Houghton Mifflin.

Bhana, Hershini. 1999. The politics of methodology: Theorizing (by) the ghost. Unpublished essay.

Boisselier, Jean. 1976. *Thai painting.* Tokyo: Kodansha International.

Brandon, James R. 1967. *Theatre in Southeast Asia.* Cambridge, Mass.: Harvard University Press.

Brandon, James R., William P. Malm, and Donald H. Shively. 1978. *Studies in kabuki: Its acting, music, and historical context.* Honolulu: East-West Center, University of Hawaii Press.

Brenneis, Donald. 1994. Discourse and discipline at the National Research Council: A bureaucratic *bildungsroman. Cultural Anthropology* 9 (1): 23–36.

Brinner, Benjamin. 1995. *Knowing music, making music: Javanese* gamelan *and the theory of musical competence and interaction.* Chicago: University of Chicago Press.

Browning, Barbara. 1995. *Samba: Resistance in motion.* Bloomington: Indiana University Press.

Bruner, Edward. 1986. Experience and its expressions. In *Anthropology of experience,* edited by Victor Turner and Edward M. Bruner. Urbana: University of Illinois Press.

Brunet, Jacques. 1970. Royal music of Cambodia. UNESCO Collection of Musical Sources (Art Music from South-east Asia IX-3), 6586 002.

Bunchuay Soowat. 2531/1988. *Phuu aan Oongkaan wai khruu dontrii Thai* (Reader of the *Oongkaan* texts of Thai music). In *Nangsüü thii ralük ngaan wai khruu lae khraup dontrii thai pracam pii khaung Culaalongkorn Mahaawithiyalai, Phutthasakarat 2531.* (Commemorative book of the annual *wai khruu* and *khraup* ceremonies for Thai music at Chulalongkorn University, 1988). In Thai. Bangkok: Chulalongkorn University.

———. 2532/1989. *Khunnasombat khaung phuu banleeng nai phithii wai khruu* (Characteristics of the musicians who perform in the *wai khruu* ceremony). In *Nangsüü thii ralük ngaan wai khruu lae khraup dontrii Thai pracam pii khaung Culaalongkorn Mahaawithiyalai, Phutthasakarat 2532.* (Commemorative book of the annual *wai khruu* and *khraup* rituals for Thai music at Chulalongkorn University, 1989). In Thai. Bangkok: Chulalongkorn University.

Buntaa Khianthaungkun. 2541/1998. *Saai kaanrap maup kaanaan oongkaan nam wai khruu dontrii Thai* (Lines of transmission of the ritual texts for the *wai khruu* for Thai music). Unpublished manuscript.

Butler, Judith. 1993. *Bodies that matter.* New York: Routledge.

Cadet, J. M. 1970. *The Ramakien: The stone rubbings of the Thai epic.* Bangkok: Kodansha International.

Catlin, Amy. 1987. Apsaras and other goddesses in Khmer music, dance, and ritual. In *Apsara: The feminine in Cambodian art,* edited by Amy Catlin. Exhibition catalog. Los Angeles: The Woman's Building.

Chai-anan Samudavanija. 1991. State-identity creation, state-building and civil society, 1939–1989. In *National identity and its defenders: Thailand, 1939–1989,* edited by Craig J. Reynolds. Bangkok: Silkworm Books.

Chandler, David. 1983. Going through the motions: Ritual aspects of the reign of King Duang of Cambodia (1848–1860). In *Centers, symbols, and hierarchies*, edited by Lorraine Gesick. New Haven, Conn.: Yale University Southeast Asia Studies.

Chatsumarn Kabilsingh. 1991. *Thai women in Buddhism*. Berkeley: Parallax Press.

Chiiwit thii kieo khaung kap kaan süksaa kaan dontrii lae kaan lakhon khaung Khunying Chin Silapabanleng, phuu sup saai dontrii Thai khaung trakun Silapabanleng. 2529/1986. (Education, music, and drama in the life of *Khunying* Chin Silapabanleng, who passed on the Thai music of the Silapabanleng lineage). In *Thii ralük 80 pii: Khunying Chin Silapabanleng* (A souvenir of 80 years: *Khunying* Chin Silapabanleng). In Thai. Bangkok: *Luang* Pradit Phairau Foundation.

Chin Silapabanleng. 2531/1988. *Lamdap phithii wai khruu dontrii Thai* (Levels of the *wai khruu* ritual for Thai music). In *Thii ralük phithii wai khruu dontrii Thai lae caek raangwaan saun thaung* (A souvenir of the *wai khruu* ritual for Thai music and the distribution of the Golden Arrow Awards). Bangkok: *Luang* Pradit Phairau Foundation.

Chin Silapabanleng, ed. 2525/1982. *Saun thaung: Prachum phon ngaan phleeng khaung Luang Pradit Phairau* (The golden arrow: The collected works of *Luang* Pradit Phairau). In Thai. Bangkok: *Luang* Pradit Phairau Foundation.

Ciratsa Khachachiwa. 2531/1988. *Phra Phikhaneet: Khadi khwaam chüa lae ruup baep Phra Phikhaneet thii phop nai pratheet Thai* (*Phra* Phikhaneet: Beliefs about and images of Lord Ganesha in Thailand). In Thai. Bangkok: Department of Fine Arts.

Cohen, Paul T. 1987. From moral regeneration to confrontation: Two paths to equality in the political rhetoric of a northern Thai peasant leader. *Mankind* 17 (2): 153–67.

Cole, W. Owen. 1982. *The guru in Sikhism*. London: Darton, Longman & Todd.

Cooler, Richard M. 1986. The use of Karen bronze drums in the royal courts and Buddhist temples of Burma and Thailand: A continuing Mon tradition? In *Papers from a conference on Thai studies in honor of William J. Gedney*, edited by Robert J. Bickner, Thomas J. Hudak, and Patcharin Peyasantiwong. Ann Arbor: Center for South and Southeast Asian Studies, University of Michigan.

Courtwright, Paul B. 1985. On this holy day in my humble way: Aspects of *Puja*. In *Gods of flesh/gods of stone*, edited by Joanne Punzo Waghorne and Norman Cutler, in association with Vasudha Narayanan. Chambersburg, Penn.: Anima Publications.

Cravath, Paul. 1985. Earth in flower: An historical and descriptive study of the classical dance drama of Cambodia. Ph.D. diss., University of Hawaii.

———. 1986. Ritual origins of the classical dance drama of Cambodia. *Asian Theater Journal* 3 (2): 179–203.

Csordas, Thomas J. 1996. Imaginal performance and memory in ritual healing. In *Performance of healing*, edited by Marina Roseman and Carol Laderman. New York: Routledge.

Daniel, Yvonne. 1995. *Rumba: Dance and social change in contemporary Cuba.* Bloomington: Indiana University Press.

Daweewarn, Dawee. 1982. *Brahmanism in South-east Asia (from the earliest times to 1445 A.D.).* New Delhi: Sterling Publishers. Reprint, Atlantic Highlands, N.J.: Humanities Press.

Department of Fine Arts. 1949. *Education: The "worship of the teachers" and the staging of miscellaneous plays at the School of Dramatic Art of the Department of Fine Arts.* Bangkok: Department of Fine Arts.

———. (n.d.) *Phleeng Chut Hoomroong Yen/Evening Prelude: Chabap ruam khrüang (Score).* Bangkok: Department of Fine Arts. Bilingual commentary; Western notation.

Deshpande, Madhav. 1979. *Sociolinguistic attitudes in India: An historical reconstruction.* Ann Arbor, Mich.: Karoma Publishers.

Desjarlais, Robert R. 1996. Presence. In *Performance of healing,* edited by Marina Roseman and Carol Laderman. New York: Routledge.

Dhaninivat, H. H. Prince (Kromamun Bidyalabh Birdhyakorn). 1975. Shadowplay as a possible origin of the masked-play. In *Siamese theatre: A collection of reprints from the journals of the Siam Society,* edited by Mattani Rutnin. Bangkok: Siam Society.

———. 2531/1988. *Shadow play (The nang).* Thai Culture, n.s., vol. 3. Bangkok: Department of Fine Arts.

Dhanit Yupho. 2494/1951. *Phithii wai khruu: Tamraa khraup khoon lakhon phraum duai tamnaan lae khaam klaun wai khruu lakhon chatrii* (The *wai khruu* ceremony: A manual for the ritual of "covering" in *khoon* and *lakhon,* including the legend of and *wai khruu* verses for *lakhon chatrii*). In Thai. Bangkok: Music Division, Department of Fine Arts.

———. 1963. *Khon and lakhon.* Bangkok: Department of Fine Arts.

———. 2509/1966. *Thii maa khaung phleeng Saathukaan* (Origin of *Saathukaan*). In *Dontrii nai phrathaam winai* (Music in the rules of dharma). In Thai. Bangkok.

———. 2517/1974. *Custom and rite of paying homage to teachers of khon, lakhon and piphat.* Bangkok: Department of Fine Arts.

———. 2526/1983. *Khoon* (Masked dance-drama). 2500/1957. Bangkok: Khurusapha Suksaphan Phanit.

———. 2530/1987. *Nangsüü khrüang dontrii Thai/Thai musical instruments.* Trans. David Morton. Special bilingual edition. Bangkok: Department of Fine Arts.

———. 1990. *Custom and rite of paying homage to teachers of khon, lakhon and piphat.* 5th ed. Bangkok: Department of Fine Arts.

Dhida Saraya. 1979. *Phuu nam thaang watthanathaam kap kaan saang baan plaeng müang* (Culture heroes and the process of settlement). *Muang Boran* 6 (1): 15–23. In Thai with English translation.

Eliade, Mircea. 1988. *Symbolism, the sacred, and the arts.* Edited by Diane Apostolos-Cappadona. New York: Crossroad.

Emigh, John. 1984. Dealing with the demonic: Strategies for containment in Hindu iconography and performance. *Asian Theater Journal* 1(1): 21–39.

Endicott, K. M. 1985. *Analysis of Malay magic.* 1970. Singapore: Oxford in Asia Paperbacks.

Evans, Grant. 1998. *Politics of ritual and remembrance: Laos since 1975.* Chiang Mai: Silkworm Books.

Fabian, Johannes. 1990. *Power and performance: Ethnographic explorations through proverbial wisdom and theater in Shaba, Zaire.* Madison: University of Wisconsin Press.

Finestone, Jeffery. 1989. *Royal family of Thailand: The descendants of King Chulalongkorn.* Bangkok: Phitsanulok Publishing.

Fuller, Paul. 1983. Thai music, 1968–1981. Review essay. *Yearbook for Traditional Music:* 152–55.

Gaston, Anne-Marie. 1982. *Siva in dance, myth, and iconography.* Delhi: Oxford University Press.

Geertz, Clifford. 1963. *Agricultural involution: The processes of agricultural change in Indonesia.* Berkeley: University of California Press.

———. 1980. *Negara: The theater state in nineteenth-century Bali.* Princeton, N.J.: Princeton University Press.

———. 1986. Making experience, authoring selves. In *Anthropology of experience,* edited by Victor Turner and Edward M. Bruner. Urbana: University of Illinois Press.

George, Kenneth M. 1996. *Showing signs of violence: The cultural politics of a twentieth-century headhunting ritual.* Berkeley: University of California Press.

Gerini, G. E. 1976. *Chulakantumangala: The tonsure ceremony as performed in Siam.* 1893. Bangkok: Siam Society.

Gill, Sam. 1987. *Native American religious action: A performance approach to religion.* Columbia: University of South Carolina Press.

Griswold, A. B. 1965. *Rishis of Wat Po. Journal of the Siam Society: Felicitation volumes of Southeast Asian studies offered to H. H. Prince Dhani Nivat,* Vol. 2: 319–28.

Grow, Mary Louise. 1991a. Laughter for spirits: A vow fulfilled. Ph.D. diss. University of Wisconsin–Madison.

———. 1991b. Dancing for spirits: Lakhon chatri performers from Phetchaburi province. Paper presented at the 43rd Annual Meeting of the Association for Asian Studies, April 11–14, 1991, New Orleans.

Guskin, Alan E. 1966. Tradition and change in a Thai university. In *Cultural frontiers of the Peace Corps,* edited by Robert B. Textor. Cambridge, Mass.: Massachusetts Institute of Technology Press.

Haas, Mary. 1964. *Thai-English student's dictionary.* Stanford: Stanford University Press.

Hall, D. G. E. 1981. *History of South-east Asia.* 4th ed. New York: St. Martin's Press.

Handler, Richard, and Eric Gable. 1997. *New history in an old museum: Creating the past at colonial Williamsburg.* Durham, N.C.: Duke University Press.

Hardjowirogo. 1982. *Sejarah wayang purwa.* 1949. Jakarta: PN Balai Pustaka.

Hefner, Robert W. 1985. *Hindu Javanese: Tengger tradition and Islam*. Princeton, N.J.: Princeton University Press.

Heinze, Ruth-Inge. 1982. *Tham khwan: How to contain the essence of life; a socio-psychological comparison of a Thai custom*. Singapore: Singapore University Press.

———. 1988. *Trance and healing in Southeast Asia today*. Bangkok: White Lotus.

Hobsbawm, Eric. 1983. Introduction: Inventing traditions. In *Invention of tradition*, edited by Eric Hobsbawm and Terence Ranger, 1–14. Cambridge, England: Cambridge University Press.

Huffman, Franklin E. 1986. Khmer loanwords in Thai. In *Papers from a conference on Thai studies in honor of William J. Gedney*, edited by Robert J. Bickner, Thomas J. Hudak, and Patcharin Peyasantiwong, 199–209. Ann Arbor: Center for South and Southeast Asian Studies, University of Michigan.

Hughes, David W. 1992. Thai music in Java, Javanese music in Thailand: Two case studies. *British Journal of Ethnomusicology* 1:17–30.

Inglis, Stephen. 1985. Possession and pottery: Serving the divine in a south Indian community. In *Gods of flesh/gods of stone*, edited by Joanne Punzo Waghorne and Norman Cutler, in association with Vasudha Narayanan. Chambersburg, Penn.: Anima Publications.

Jackson, Peter A. 1995. *Dear Uncle Go: Male homosexuality in Thailand*. Bangkok: Bua Luang Books.

Jarernchai Chonpairot. 1981. Luang Pradit Phairau and his programmatic music. Unpublished manuscript.

Jit Phumisak. 2522/1979. Kralahoom. In *Phaasaa lae Niruksaat* (Language and etymology), 75–130. In Thai. Bangkok: Duang Kamol.

———. 2524/1981. *Oongkaan chaeng nam lae khau khit mai nai prawatsaat Thai lum nam Cao Phraya* (*Oongkaan* text for the water oath, and new thoughts on the Thai history of the Cao Phraya River basin). In Thai. Bangkok: Duang Kamol.

Kaeppler, Adrienne L. 1980. Polynesian music and dance. In *Musics of many cultures*, edited by Elizabeth May. Berkeley: University of California Press.

Kapchan, Deborah A. 1995. Performance. *Journal of American Folklore* 108 (430): 479–508.

Kapferer, Bruce. 1983. *Celebration of demons*. Bloomington: Indiana University Press.

———. 1986. Performance and the structuring of meaning and experience. In *Anthropology of experience*, edited by Victor Turner and Edward M. Bruner. Urbana: University of Illinois Press.

Kaungkaew Wirapracak. 2530/1987. *Kantham samut Thai lae kantriam bai laan* (Making Thai books and the preparation of palm leaves). In Thai. Bangkok: National Library and Department of Fine Arts.

Kennedy, Richard. 1994. Thailand. *Smithsonian Talk Story*, no. 5: 1, 4–6.

Keyes, Charles F. 1983. Merit-transference in the karmic theory of popular Theravada Buddhism. In *Karma: An anthropological inquiry*, edited by Charles F. Keyes and E. Valentine Daniel. Berkeley: University of California Press.

————. 1984. Mother or mistress but never a monk: Buddhist notions of female gender in rural Thailand. *American Ethnologist* 11 (2): 223–41.

————. 1987. *Thailand: Buddhist kingdom as modern nation-state.* Boulder, Colo.: Westview Press.

Khin Thitsa. 1980. *Providence and prostitution: Image and reality for women in Buddhist Thailand.* London: Change International Reports.

"*Khruu* Ruam Phrohmburi." 2529/1986. In *Anusaun ngaan phra raachaathaan phloeng sop nai Ruam Phrohmburi na meeru Wat Mahaathaat worawihaan amphoe müang cangwat Raachburi wan aathit thii 9 Phrisacikayon 2529* (Commemorative booklet of the cremation of Mr. Ruam Phrohmburi at Wat Mahathat in Rachburi on 9 November 1986). In Thai.

Khunying Chin Silapabanleng: Silapin haeng Chaat Saakhaa Silapa Kaan Sadaeng (Dontrii Thai) 2530/1987. (*Khunying* Chin Silapabanleng: National Artist of the Performing Arts [Thai Music]). In *Silapin haeng Chaat 2530.* (National Artists of 1987). Bangkok: Ministry of Education.

Kingsbury, Henry. 1988. *Music, talent, and performance: A conservatory cultural system.* Philadelphia: Temple University Press.

Kirshenblatt-Gimblett, Barbara. 1998. *Destination culture: Tourism, museums, and heritage.* Berkeley: University of California Press.

Kisliuk, Michelle. 1997. (Un)doing fieldwork: Sharing songs, sharing lives. In *Shadows in the field: New perspectives for fieldwork in ethnomusicology,* edited by Gregory F. Barz and Timothy J. Cooley, 23–44. New York: Oxford University Press.

Klausner, William J. 1987. *Reflections on Thai culture.* 3rd ed. Bangkok: Siam Society.

Kondo, Dorinne K. 1990. *Crafting selves: Power, gender, and discourses of identity in a Japanese workplace.* Chicago: University of Chicago Press.

Kornvipa Boonsue. 1989. *Buddhism and gender bias: An analysis of a jataka tale.* Working Paper Series, Thai Studies Project, Women in Development Consortium in Thailand, no. 3. Toronto: York University.

Kraisrii Nimmanhaemindaa. 1967. Lawa guardian spirits of Chiengmai. *Journal of the Siam Society* 55 (2): 185–225.

Krebs, Stephanie Laird. 1975. Nonverbal communication in khon dance-drama: Thai society onstage. Ph.D. diss., Harvard University.

Kukrit Pramoj. 1981. *Sii phaendin* (Four reigns). Trans. Tulachandra. Bangkok: Duang Kamol.

Kumut Chandruang. 1970. *My Boyhood in Siam.* 1938. London: Andre Deutsch.

La Fontaine, J. S. 1985. *Initiation.* New York: Viking Penguin.

Lakoff, G., and M. Johnson. 1980. *Metaphors we live by.* Chicago: University of Chicago Press.

Lowe, Lisa, and David Lloyd. 1997. Introduction to *Politics of culture in the shadow of culture,* edited by Lisa Lowe and David Lloyd. Durham, N.C.: Duke University Press.

Luang Pradit Phairau (Saun Silapabanleng). 2524/1981. Kaan *wai khruu* samrap duriyang Thai (*Wai khruu* for Thai music). In *Phithii wai khruu dontrii Thai* (*Wai khruu* ritual for Thai Music). In Thai. (Written sometime before the eminent teacher's death in 1954, this article has been reprinted many times.) Bangkok: Luang Pradit Phairau Foundation.

Lysa, Hong. 1998. "Of Consorts and Harlots in Thai Popular History." *Journal of Asian Studies* 57. (2): 333–53.

Lysloff, René T. A. 1990. Srikandhi dances lènggèr: A performance of music and shadow theater in Banyumas (West central Java). Ph.D. diss., University of Michigan.

Malm, Joyce Rutherford. 1985. Meaning of Iemoto Seido in the world of Nihon buyo. In *Dance as cultural heritage.* Vol. 2, edited by Betty True Jones. New York: Congress on Research in Dance.

Malm, William P. 1959. *Japanese music and musical instruments.* Rutland, Vt.: Charles Tuttle.

Manat na Chiang Mai. 2530/1987. Phithii wai *khruu* chaang silapaa hatkaam lae phithii khraup (*Wai khruu* ritual for arts and handicrafts and the "covering" ritual). In *Anusaun khrop raup wan sin phra chon Somdet Cao Fa Cuthathuut Tharadilok Krom Khun Phetchabun Inthaurachai 8. Karakhadakhom P.S. 2530.* (Commemorative book for the anniversary of the death of Prince Cuthathut Tharadilok, Prince of Phetchabun, 8 July 1987). Bangkok: Witthayalai Phau Chang.

Manit Manitcharoen. 2528/1985. *Phachananükarom Thai chabap khaung Raachaabandit Sathaan* (Thai dictionary of the Royal Academy), 9th ed. In Thai. Bangkok.

Matics, K. I. 1977. Medical arts at Wat Phra Chetuphon: Various *rishi* statues. *Journal of the Siam Society* 65 (2): 145–58.

Mattani Mojdara Rutnin. 1975a. *Siamese theatre: Collection of reprints from journals of the Siam Society.* Bangkok: Siam Society.

———. 1975b. Khau sannitthaan kieo kap khwaam pen maa khaung Phra Phiraap (Speculations on the origin of *Phra* Phiraap). *Paakkaa:* 45–69.

———. 1978. Modernization of Thai dance-drama, with special reference to the reign of King Chulalongkorn. Ph.D. diss., University of London.

———. 2525/1982. Politics of Thai classical dance-drama during the reign of King Rama VI. *Ratthasaatsaan (Journal of Political Science)* 8 (2): 126–55.

———. 1983. *Transformation of the Thai concepts of aesthetics.* Bangkok: Thai Khadi Research Institute, Thammasat University.

———. 1993. *Dance, drama, and theatre in Thailand: The process of development and modernization.* Tokyo: Centre for East Asian Cultural Studies for UNESCO, Toyo Bunko.

Matusky, Patricia Ann. 1993. *Malaysian shadow play and music: Continuity of an oral tradition.* New York: Oxford University Press.

Maxwell, Allen R. 1990. Morality in old Brunei: The language of homage and status in the *Sya'ir Awang Simaun.* Paper presented at the 42nd annual meeting of the Association for Asian Studies, Chicago.

Mayoury Ngaosyvathn. 1990. *On the edge of the pagoda: Lao women in Buddhism.* Working Paper Series, Thai Studies Project, Women in Development Consortium in Thailand, no. 5. Toronto: York University.

Metcalf, Peter. 1989. *Where are you/spirits: Style and theme in Berawan prayer.* Washington: Smithsonian Institution Press.

Miettinen, Jukka O. 1992. *Classical dance and theatre in South-east Asia.* New York: Oxford University Press.

Miller, Terry, and Jarernchai Chonpairot. 1994. History of Siamese music reconstructed from western documents, 1505–1932. *Crossroads* 8 (2): 1–192.

Miller, Terry E., and Sam-Ang Sam. 1995. Classical musics of Cambodia and Thailand: A study of distinctions. *Ethnomusicology* 39 (2): 229–43.

Mills, Mary Beth. 1995. Attack of the widow ghosts: Gender, death, and modernity in northeast Thailand. In *Bewitching women, pious men: Gender and body politics in Southeast Asia*, edited by Aihwa Ong and Michael G. Peletz, 244–73. Berkeley: University of California Press.

Mitchiner, John E. 1982. *Traditions of the seven rsis.* Delhi: Motilal Banarsidass.

Montri Tramote. 2521/1978. Raachaathinanaam nakdontrii Thai samai raachaakaan thii 6 (Names conferred on Thai musicians during the 6th reign). In Thai. Unpublished ms.

———. 2524/1981. Duriyatheep (Deities of music). In *Phithii wai khruu dontrii Thai* (*Wai khruu* ritual for Thai music). In Thai. (Bangkok: Luang Pradit Phairau Foundation). Originally published in Montri Tramote, *Dontrii Thai Parithat II* (Bangkok, 1967).

———. 2526/1983. *Hoomroong Dontrii Thai* (Thai musical overture). In Thai. Mahaserakham: Srinakharinwirot University.

———. 2527/1984. Kaanwai *khruu* lae khrâup dontrii Thai (*Wai khruu* and initiation in Thai music). In *Soom saung saeng: Chiiwit dontrii Thai khaung Montrii Tramoot* (Moonlight: Montri Tramote and the life of Thai music), edited by Scerii Wangnaithaam and Sucit Wongtheet. Bangkok: Roongphim Ruan Kaew Kaanphim.

———. 2530/1987. Thaang taang taang nai dontrii Thai (Various *thaang* in Thai music). In *Dontrii Thai Udom Süksaa Khrang thii 18.* (Thai Music in Higher Education, 18th Meeting), 42–43. In Thai. Khaun Kaen: Khaun Kaen University.

Morris, Rosalind C. 1998. Surviving pleasure at the periphery: Chiang Mai and the photographies of political trauma in Thailand, 1976–1992. *Public Culture* 10 (2): 341–70.

Morton, David. 1968. *Traditional music of Thailand: Introduction, commentary, and analyses,* with two 33 r.p.m. discs (IER 7502). Los Angeles: Institute of Ethnomusicology, University of California-Los Angeles.

———. 1975. Luang Pradit Phairo. *Selected Reports in Ethnomusicology* 2 (2): v–viii.

———. 1976. *Traditional music of Thailand.* Berkeley: University of California Press.

———. 1980. Thailand, *New Grove dictionary of music and musicians.* London: MacMillan.

Muecke, Marjorie A. 1992. Monks and mediums: Religious syncretism in northern Thailand. *Journal of the Siam Society* 80 (part 2): 97–103.

Myers-Moro, Pamela. 1988a. Thai music and musicians in contemporary Bangkok: An ethnography. Ph.D. diss., University of California–Berkeley.

———. 1988b. Names and civil service titles of Siamese musicians. *Asian Music* 19 (2): 82–92.

———. 1989. Thai music and attitudes toward the past. *Journal of American Folklore* 102: 190–94.

———. 1990. Musical notation in Thailand. *Journal of the Siam Society* 78 (1): 101–8.

———. 1991. Eclecticism and appropriation of diversity in Thai musical performance. Unpublished manuscript.

———. 1993. *Thai music and musicians in contemporary Bangkok.* Berkeley: Centers for South and Southeast Asian Studies, University of California–Berkeley.

Naowarat Phongphaibun. 2532/1989. *Khruu* King Phloipheet: Pheet phloi iik met nüng thii wup dap nai wong dontrii Thai (*Khruu* King Phloipheet: Another diamond extinguished in Thai music circles). *Silapawatthanathaam,* February, 68–73. In Thai.

Napier, A. David. 1986. *Masks, transformation, and paradox.* Berkeley: University of California Press.

Narumol Sriyanond. 2534/1991. *Satrii kap kaannam:* Prapheenii *khao maa nai witthii chiiwit khaung chumchon Thai phut nai Saharat Amerikaa* (Women leading the introduction of "tradition" into the lives of Buddhist Thais in the United States of America). In *Boek roong: Khau phitcaranaa naattakam nai sangkhom Thai/Opening the stage: Considering performance in Thai society,* edited by Paritta Chalermpow Koanantakool, 139–49. Bangkok: Sathaaban Thai Süksaa, Thammasat University.

———. 1999. Movement ethnography: Creating cultural space for the expression of identity and harmony at the Vajiradhammapadip Temple Sunday School (Centereach, Long Island). Paper presented at the 7th International Conference on Thai Studies, 4–8 July 1999, Amsterdam.

National Museum. 2514/1971. *Nithaatsakan hua khoon* (Exhibition of khon masks). March 15–May 15, 1971. In Thai. Bangkok: National Museum.

Ness, Sally Ann. 1992. *Body, movement, and culture: Kinesthetic and visual symbolism in a Philippine community.* Philadelphia: University of Pennsylvania Press.

Neuman, Daniel M. 1990. *Life of music in north India: The Organization of an artistic tradition.* 1980. Detroit: Wayne State University Press.

Nidhi Aeusriwongse. 1976. *Devaraja* cult and Khmer kingship at Angkor. In *Explorations in early Southeast Asian history: The origins of Southeast Asian statecraft,* edited by Kenneth R. Hall and John K. Whitmore, 107–48. Ann Arbor: Center for South and Southeast Asian Studies, University of Michigan.

Nim Pho-iam. 2520/1977. Lakwichaakaan chai *naa phaat* (Theory of *naa phaat*). In *Katanyuu: Wai khruu 20.* (Gratitude: *Wai khruu* '77). Bangkok: Ramkhamhaeng University.

———. 2524/1981. Laksana kit phithii taang khrüang sakkaaraa buuchaa taang khrüang phliikaam thawaai *khruu* (Characteristics of the ritual: arranging the food and sacrificial offerings for the teachers). In *Phithii wai khruu dontrii*

Thai (*Wai khruu* ritual for Thai music). In Thai. Bangkok: Luang Pradit Phairau Foundation.

———. 2530/1987a. Anusaun kaun taai, P.S. 2530: Heetphon klao wai nai saasanaa phraam khrang adiit taam khamphi phraam prawat (Memorial before dying, A.D. 1987: Concerning Brahmanism in past times, according to the scriptures of Brahman history). In Thai. Unpublished ms.

———. 2530/1987b. Anusaun kaun taai, P.S. 2530: Oongkaan noi (Memorial before dying, A.D. 1987: The lesser *Oongkaan*). In Thai. Unpublished ms.

Odzer, Cleo. 1994. *Patpong sisters: An American woman's view of the Bangkok sex world.* New York: Arcade Publishing; Bangkok: Book Siam.

Olson, Grant A. 1991a. Cries over spilled holy water: "Complex" responses to a traditional Thai religious practice. *Journal of Southeast Asian Studies* 11 (1): 75–85.

———. 1991b Thai cremation volumes: A brief history of a unique genre of literature. *Asian Folklore Studies* 51 (2): 279–94.

On Ariyawangso, compiler. 2501/1958. *Khamphii phutthaweet mahaamon: Pramuan weetmon khaathau lae yan taang taang thii saksit thuk taung taam tamraa thii thaan boruunaacaan cat tham wai thuk prakaan* (Scripture of the great Buddhist magical spells: A compilation of various sacred magical spells, formulas, and signs, exactly according to the manuals of the ancient teachers). In Thai. Bangkok: Roong Phim Liang Siang Cong Caroen.

Ong, Aihwa. 1987. *Spirits of resistance and capitalist discipline: Factory women in Malaysia.* Albany: State University of New York Press.

Ong, Walter J., S. J. 1977. *Interfaces of the word: Studies in the evolution of consciousness and culture.* Ithaca, N.Y.: Cornell University Press.

Oongkaan Kliipchüün. 2530/1987. In *Wai khruu.* Bangkok: Bangkok Bank.

Orawan Banchongsilpa. 1988. Variations in the singing of *Phleeng Pae,* a Thai classical form. M.M. thesis, University of the Philippines.

———. 2531/1988. *Phra Phiraap.* In *Nangsüü thii ralük ngaan wai khruu lae khraup dontrii Thai pracam pii khaung Culaalongkorn Mahaawithiyalai, Phutthasakarat 2531.* (Commemorative book of the annual *wai khruu* and *khraup* ceremonies for Thai music at Chulalongkorn University, 1988), 11–12. Bangkok: Chulalongkorn University.

Ortner, Sherry. 1996. *Making gender: The politics and erotics of culture.* Boston: Beacon Press.

Östor, Akos. 1980. *Play of the gods: Locality, ideology, structure, and time in the festivals of a Bengali town.* Chicago: University of Chicago Press.

Pandey, Chandra Bhanu. 1987. *Risis in ancient India.* Delhi: Sundeep Prakashan.

Panyaa Rungrüang. 2517/1974. *Prawat kaan dontrii Thai* (History of Thai music). Bangkok: Thai Watthanaa Phaanit Camkat.

Panya Nittayasawan. 2523/1980. *Sinlapin thii naa ruucak: Khruu Aram Inthauranat* (An artist worth knowing: *Khruu* Aram Inthauranat). In Thai. *Silapakon* 3 (July): 3–12.

———. 2527/1984. *Khruu* Montri Tramote. In *Soom saung saeng: Chiiwit dontrii Thai khaung Montrii Tramoot* (Moonlight: Montri Tramote's life in Thai music), edited by Seri Wangnaitham and Sucit Wongthet. Bangkok: Ruan Kaew Kan Phim.

Paritta Chalermpow Koanantakool. 1980. Popular drama in its social context: Nang talung, the shadow puppet theatre of south Thailand. Ph.D. diss., University of Cambridge.

————. 1982. Traditional and modern styles in southern Thai shadow puppet theater. Presented at the Second Thai-European Research Seminar, June 14–18, Saarbruecken, Federal Republic of Germany.

————. 1999. Community and identity of vow-fulfillment dance practitioners. Paper presented at the 7th International Conference on Thai Studies, 4–8. July 1999, Amsterdam.

Paritta Chalermpow Koanantakool, ed. 2541/1998. *Phoei raang—phraang kaai* (Revealing—masking the body). Bangkok: Faculty of Sociology and Anthropology, Thammasat University.

Parry, Jonathan. 1985. Brahmanical tradition and the technology of the intellect. In *Reason and morality*, edited by Joanna Overing. ASA Monographs 24, 200–225. London: Tavistock Publications.

Patel, Marti. 1984. Spirit cults and the position of women in northern Thailand. *Mankind* 14 (3): 308–14.

————. 1992. Trance dancing and other Mon traditions of Lampang. In *Northern miscellany: Essays from Thailand*, edited by Geoffrey Walton, 57–77. Chiang Mai: Silkworm Books.

Pemberton, John. 1994. *On the subject of "Java."* Ithaca, N.Y.: Cornell University Press.

Pha-op Posakritsanaa. 2520/1977. *Wanakaam prakaup kaan len nang yai: Wat Khanaun Cangwat Raachburi* (A work on the performance of *nang yai* at Wat Khanon, Rachburi Province). In Thai. Bangkok: Samnak Nayok Ratamontri.

Phillips, Herbert P. 1987. *Modern Thai literature, with an ethnographic interpretation.* Honolulu: University of Hawaii Press.

Phimon Saichandii. 2521/1978. Hua khoon nai phithii wai khruu (*Khoon* masks in the *wai khruu* ceremony). In *Dontrii Thai: Mathayom süksaa khrang thii 4.* (Thai music: Secondary education, 4th time). In Thai. Bangkok: Borisat Boophit kaan Phim Chamkat.

Phlaisupradit [pseud.]. 2527/1984. Sit srii kaan sut: Montri Tramote. In *Soom saung saeng: Chiiwit dontrii Thai khaung Montrii Tramoot* (Moonlight: Montri Tramote's life in Thai music), edited by Seri Wangnaithaam and Sucit Wongtheet. Bangkok: Ruan Kaew Kan Phim.

Phlu Luang. 2530/1987. *Theewalook* (World of the *devas*). In Thai. Bangkok: Muang Boran.

Phunphit Amatyakul, with Phra Cao Worawongthoe Phra Ong Cao Siriratanabutbong. 2524/1981. *Thun Kramaum Boriphat kap kaan dontrii* (Thun Kramaum Boriphat and music). In Thai. Bangkok.

Phunphit Amatyakul. 2528/1985. *Angkhalung* (Angklung). In Thai. Bangkok: Raksip.

————. 2529/1986. *Dontrii wicak: Khwaam ruu büang ton kieo kap dontrii khaung Thai phüa khwaam chun chom* (Music investigated: Elementary knowledge concerning Thai music, for appreciation). 2nd ed. Bangkok: Siam Samai.

P. Phrombhichitr. n.d. *Phutthasin saathaapatthayakaam, phaak ton* (Buddhist art and architecture, part 1). In Thai. N.p.

Pracak Praphaphitthayakaun. 2529/1986. *Theewaadaaniikarom nai wannakhadi* (Encyclopedia of *devadas* in literature). In Thai. Bangkok: Odeon Store.

Pranee Wongtheet (nee Jearaditharporn). 1973. Relationship of music and society as seen in the Thai case. M.A. thesis, Cornell University.

————. 2528/1985. Kaan lalen lae phithikaam nai sangkhom Thai (Entertainment and ritual in Thai society). In *Watthanathaam phüün baan: Khati khwan chüa* (Rural culture: Maxims and beliefs), edited by Phensrii Duk, Phathun Sinlarat, Biyanat Bunnat, and Woraphaun Thinanon. In Thai. Bangkok: Chulalongkorn University.

Prasidh Silapabanleng. 1975. Thai music at the court of Cambodia: A personal souvenir of Luang Pradit Phairoh's visit in 1930. *Selected Reports in Ethnomusicology* 2 (2): 3–5. Also in *Journal of the Siam Society* 58, no.1 (1970): 121–24.

Prasit Thawaun. 2531/1988a. Khruu phuu samuan phau (The teacher who was like my father). In *Aacaan Prasit Thaawaun: Silapin Haeng Chaat Saakhaa Silapa kaan Sadaeng (Dontrii Thai) Pracam Pii 2531*. (Professor Prasit Thawaun: National Artist of the Performing Arts (Thai Music), 1988). In Thai. Bangkok: Chulalongkorn University.

————. 2531/1988b. Wong mahaaduriyang (Great ensemble). In *Aacaan Prasit Thaawaun: Silapin Haeng Chaat Saakhaa Silapa kaan Sadaeng (Dontrii Thai) Pracam Pii 2531*. (Professor Prasit Thawaun: National Artist of the Performing Arts (Thai Music), 1988). In Thai. Bangkok: Chulalongkorn University

Praweet Thamthaadaa. 2525/1982. *Nae nam nang talung* (Introducing *nang talung*). Bangkok: Kim Nguan Kan Phim.

Prong Satsanaung. 2516/1973. *Khwaam Pen Maa khaung Samaakhom Songkhrau Sahaai Silapin* (Origin of the Association for Assistance to Friends and Performers). In *Thii ralük nai ngaan wai khruu Samuakhom Songkhrau Sahaai Silapin* (Souvenir of the *wai khruu* festival of the Association for Assistance to Friends and Performers, 6 September 2516). In Thai. Bangkok: Samaakhom Songkhrau Sahaai Silapin.

Rappaport, Roy A. 1979. Obvious aspects of ritual. In *Ecology, meaning, and religion*. Berkeley, Calif.: North Atlantic Books.

Reynolds, Craig J., trans. and ed. 1979. *Autobiography: The life of Prince-Patriarch Vajiranana*. Athens, Ohio: Ohio University Press.

————. 1991. Introduction to *National identity and its defenders: Thailand 1939–1989*, edited by Craig J. Reynolds, 1–39. Chiang Mai: Silkworm Books.

Reynolds, Frank E., and Mani B. Reynolds, trans. 1982. *Three worlds according to King Ruang: A Thai Buddhist cosmology*. Berkeley, Calif.: Asian Humanities Press.

Ricoeur, Paul. 1979. "Sacred" text and the community. In *Critical study of sacred texts*, edited by Wendy Doniger O'Flaherty. Berkeley, Calif.: Graduate Theological Union.

Rouget, Gilbert. 1985. *Music and trance: A theory of the relations between music and possession*. Chicago: University of Chicago Press.

Saksi Yaemnatdaa. 1979. "Rüsi" (Seer and hermit: The rishi). In Thai with English translation. *Muang Boran* 5 (5): 70–82.

Salmond, Anne. 1982. Theoretical landscapes: On cross-cultural conceptions of knowledge. In *Semantic anthropology*, edited by David Parkin. London: Academic Press.

———. 1985. Maori epistemologies. In *Reason and morality*, edited by Joanna Overing. ASA Monographs 24. London: Tavistock Publications.

Sam, Chan Moly. 1987. *Khmer court dance: A comprehensive study of movements, gestures, and postures as applied techniques*. Newington, Conn.: Khmer Studies Institute.

Sam, Sam-Ang. 1988. *Pin peat* ensemble: Its history, music, and context. Ph.D. diss., Wesleyan University.

Samphaat Raachabandit: Nai Montrii Tramoot (Royal Institute interview with Mr. Montri Tramote). 2524/1981. In Thai. *Waarasaan Raachabandit Sathaan* 2 (October–December): 4–11.

Sangat Phukhaothong. 2532/1989. *Kaan dontrii Thai lae thaang khao suu dontrii Thai* (Matters of Thai music, and the way to enter into Thai music). In Thai. Bangkok: Dr. Sax.

Sathian Duangcanthip. 2532/1989. King Phloipheet: *Piiphaat* aaphap (King Phloipheet: Unfortunate *piiphaat*). *Silapawatthanathaam*, February, 73–74.

Savigliano, Marta E. 1995. *Tango and the political economy of passion*. Boulder, Colo.: Westview Press.

Schechner, Richard. 1977. *Essays on performance theory, 1970–1976*. New York: Drama Book Specialists.

———. 1985. *Between theater and anthropology*. Philadelphia: University of Pennsylvania Press.

———. 1986a Magnitudes of performance. In *Anthropology of Experience*, edited by Victor Turner and Edward M. Bruner. Urbana: University of Illinois Press.

———. 1986b Victor Turner's Last Adventure. Preface to *Anthropology of Performance*, by Victor Turner. New York: Performing Arts Journal Publications.

Schechner, Richard, and Willa Appel, eds. 1990. *By means of performance: Intercultural studies of theatre and ritual*. Cambridge, England: Cambridge University Press.

Schwimmer, Erik. 1980. *Power, silence, and secrecy: The secrecy of the sacred and the power of secrecy*. Toronto Semiotic Circle Monographs, Working Papers, and Republications. Toronto: Victoria University.

Seneviratna, Anuradha. 1979. Pancaturya Nada and the Hewisi Puja. *Ethnomusicology* 23 (1): 49–56.

Seerii Wangnaithaam and Sucit Wongtheet, eds. 2527/1984. *Soom saung saeng:*

Chiiwit dontrii Thai khaung Montrii Tramoot (Moonlight: Montri Tramote's life in Thai music). In Thai. Bangkok: Ruan Kaew Kaan Phim.

Singaravelu, S. 1970. Invocations to Nataraja in the Southeast Asian shadow-plays, with special reference to the Kelantan shadow-play. *Journal of the Siam Society* 57 (2): 45–54.

Siriphong Phayomyaem. 2525/1982. *Phaap lae prawat tua lakhon Raamakien* (Images and history of the dramatic characters in the *Ramakien*). In Thai. Bangkok: O. S. Printing House.

Sirirat Praphatthong. 2530/1987. Phau Kae (Old Father). In *Wai khruu: Phanaek Dontrii Thai, Samoosaun Thanaakaan Krung Thaep, Suun Sangkhiitsin, Thanaakaan Krung Theep Camkat (Wai Khruu:* Thai Music Division of the Bangkok Bank Association, Bangkok Bank, Thursday, 10 December 2530), 36–37. In Thai. Bangkok: Bangkok Bank.

Sit buuchaa khruu (Disciple who worships the teacher). 2516/1973. Khwaam saksit khaung rian khruu (Power of the teacher's amulets). In *Thii raluuk nai ngaan wai khruu (Souvenir of the wai khruu ceremony)*, 106–19. 6 September 2516. In Thai. Bangkok: Association for Assistance to Friends and Performers.

Smithies, Michael, and Euayporn Kerdchouay. 1974. *Wai khruu* ceremony of the *nang yai. Journal of the Siam Society* 62 (1): 143–47.

Sombat Attalakhup. 2532/1989. *Wai khruu.* In Thai. Senior thesis in music, Srinakharinwirot University–Prasanmit.

Somcai Sriinuan. 2528/1985. Khwaam chüa nai kaan kae ruup nang talung (Beliefs about carving *nang talung* puppets). *Thaksin Khadi* 1: 34–38.

Sthirakoses (Phraya Anuman Rajdhon). 1996. *Looking back: Book two.* Translation Center, Faculty of Arts, Chulalongkorn University. Bangkok: Chulalongkorn University.

Stokes, Martin. 1992. *Arabesk debate: Music and musicians in modern Turkey.* Oxford: Clarendon Press, Oxford University Press.

———. 1994. Introduction: Ethnicity, identity, and music. In *Ethnicity, identity, and music: The musical construction of place*, edited by Martin Stokes. Oxford: Berg.

Stoller, Paul. 1997. *Sensuous scholarship.* Philadelphia: University of Pennsylvania Press.

Subhadradis Diskul. (n.d.) *History of the Temple of the Emerald Buddha.* Bangkok: Bureau of the Royal Household.

Subin Cankaew. 2530/1987. Khaung wong yai (Big gong circle). In *Ngaan dontrii Thai udom süksaa khrang thii 19.* (19th Annual Festival for Thai Music in Higher Education). In Thai. Bangkok: Kasetsat University.

Sulak Sivaraksa. 1991. Crisis of Thai identity. In *National identity and its defenders: Thailand, 1939–1989*, edited by Craig J. Reynolds, 41–58. Bangkok: Silkworm Books.

Sumarsam. 1995. *Gamelan: Cultural interaction and musical development in central Java.* Chicago: University of Chicago Press.

Sumonman Nimnetiphan. 2524/1981. *Eekasaan prakaup kaan saun wichaa*

Duriyaa 101. Dontrii Thai (Document for teaching Thai Music 101). In Thai. Bangkok: Srinakharinwirot University.

Surachai Khrüapradap. 2524/1981. Khwaam ruu thua pai kieo kap dontrii Thai (General knowledge of Thai music). In *Wai khruu dontrii Thai lae khwaam ruu thua pai kieo kap dontrii Thai* (*Wai khruu* for Thai music and general knowledge of Thai music). In Thai. Bangkok: *Luang* Pradit Phairau Foundation.

Surapone Virulrak. 1980. Likay: A popular theater in Thailand. Ph.D. diss., University of Hawaii.

Susilo, Hardja. 1988. Logogenesis of gendhing lampah. Manuscript.

Sutthiwong Phongphaibun. 2522/1979. *Nang talung.* Songkhla: Center for Southern Thai Culture, Srinakharinwirot University–Songkhla.

Sutton, R. Anderson. 1991. *Traditions of gamelan music in Java: Musical pluralism and regional identity.* Cambridge, England: Cambridge University Press.

Swearer, Donald K. 1974. Myth, legend, and history in the northern Thai chronicles. *Journal of the Siam Society* 62 (1): 67–88.

———. 1976a. The role of the layman *extraordinaire* in northern Thai Buddhism. *Journal of the Siam Society* 64 (1): 151–67.

———. 1976b. *Wat Haripunjaya: A study of the Royal Temple of the Buddha's Relic, Lamphun, Thailand.* Missoula, Mont.: Scholars Press.

Sweeney, Amin. 1972a. *Malay shadow puppets: The wayang Siam of Kelantan.* London: Trustees of the British Museum, Shenval Press.

———. 1972b. *The Ramayana and the Malay shadow-play.* Kuala Lumpur: National University of Malaysia Press.

Tambiah, S. J. 1968. Literacy in a Buddhist village in north-east Thailand. In *Literacy in traditional societies,* edited by Jack Goody. New York: Cambridge University Press.

———. 1970. *Buddhism and the spirit cults in north-east Thailand.* Cambridge: Cambridge University Press.

———. 1984. *Buddhist saints of the forest and the cult of amulets: A study in charisma, hagiography, sectarianism, and millennial Buddhism.* Cambridge: Cambridge University Press.

———. 1985. *Culture, thought, and social action: An anthropological perspective.* Cambridge, Mass.: Harvard University Press.

Tannenbaum, Nicola. 1995. *Who can compete against the world? Power-protection and Buddhism in Shan worldview.* Ann Arbor, Mich.: Association for Asian Studies.

Taussig, Michael. 1993. *Mimesis and alterity: A particular history of the senses.* New York: Routledge.

Tedlock, Dennis. 1983. *Spoken word and the work of interpretation.* Philadelphia: University of Pennsylvania Press.

Terwiel, B. J. 1979. *Monks and magic: An analysis of religious ceremonies in central Thailand.* 2nd rev. ed. Scandinavian Institute of Asian Studies Monograph Series, no. 24. London: Curzon Press.

Textor, Robert B. 1973. *Roster of the gods: An ethnography of the supernatural in a Thai village*. 6. vols. New Haven, Conn.: Human Relations Area Files.

Thakur, Upendra. 1987. Brahmana Panditas in Siam. In *Proceedings of the International Conference on Thai Studies*, Australian National University, Canberra, 3–6. July 1987. Vol. 1.

Thongchai Winichakul. 1994. *Siam mapped: A history of the geo-body of a nation*. Honolulu: University of Hawaii Press.

———. 1995. Changing landscape of the past: new histories in Thailand since 1973. *Journal of Southeast Asian Studies* 26 (1): 99–120.

Tokyo National Research Institute of Cultural Properties. 1987. *Masked performances in Asia*. Tenth International Symposium on the Conservation and Restoration of Cultural Property. Tokyo: Tokyo National Research Institute of Cultural Properties.

Turino, Thomas. 1993. *Moving away from silence: Music of the Peruvian Altiplano and the experience of urban migration*. Chicago: University of Chicago Press.

Turner, Victor. 1969. *Ritual process: Structure and anti-structure*. Chicago: Aldine Publishing.

———. 1974. *Dramas, fields, and metaphors*. Ithaca, N.Y.: Cornell University Press.

———. 1982. *From ritual to theatre*. New York: Performing Arts Journal Publications.

———. 1986. *Anthropology of performance*. New York: Performing Arts Journal Publications.

Turner, Victor, and Edward M. Bruner, eds. 1986. *Anthropology of Experience*. Urbana: University of Illinois Press.

Ubonrat Siriyuvasak. 1990. Commercialising the sound of the people: Pleng Luktoong and the Thai pop music industry. *Popular Music* 9 (1): 61–77.

Uthit Naksawat. 2530/1987. *Thritsadii lae kaanpatibat dontrii Thai* (Theory and practice of Thai music, Part 1). 5th ed. In Thai. Bangkok: Khana Kaammakaan Haeng Chaat Waa Duai Kaansüksaa Witthayaasaat lae Watthanaathaam Haeng Sahaaprachaachaat.

Vandergeest, Peter. 1990. Contending representations: Buddhism, Brahmanism, and polity in late nineteenth-century Thailand. Paper presented at the 42nd annual meeting of the Association for Asian Studies, Chicago, Illinois.

Van Esterik, Penny. 1982. Laywomen in Theravada Buddhism. In *Women in Southeast Asia*, edited by Penny Van Esterik. DeKalb, Ill.: Northern Illinois University, Center for Southeast Asian Studies.

———. 1989. Introduction to *Buddhism and gender bias: An analysis of a Jataka tale*, by Kornvipa Boonsue, i–vii. Working Paper Series, Thai Studies Project, Women in Development Consortium in Thailand, no.3. Toronto: York University.

———. 1996. Politics of beauty in Thailand. In *Beauty queens on the global stage: Gender, contests, and power*, edited by Colleen Ballerino Cohen, Richard Wilk, and Beverley Stoeltje, 203–16. New York: Routledge.

Van Groenendael, Victoria M. Clara. 1985. *Dalang behind the wayang: The role of the Surakarta and the Yogyakarta dalang in Indonesian-Javanese society.* Dordrecht, Holland: Foris Publications.

Vella, Walter F. 1974. Siamese nationalism in the plays of Rama VI. In *Search for identity: Modern literature and the creative arts in Asia,* edited by A. R. Davis. Sydney: Angus and Robertson.

Vella, Walter, with Dorothy B. Vella. 1978. *Chaiyo! King Vajiravudh and the development of Thai nationalism.* Honolulu: University of Hawaii Press.

Waghorne, Joanne Punzo. 1985. Introduction to *Gods of flesh/gods of stone,* edited by Joanne Punzo Waghorne and Norman Cutler, in association with Vasudha Narayanan. Chambersburg, Penn.: Anima Publications.

Wales, H. G. Quaritch. 1931. *Siamese state ceremonies: Their history and function.* London: Bernard Quaritch.

Wedel, Yuangrat (Pattanapongse). 1982. *Modern Thai radical thought: The Siamization of Marxism and its theoretical problems.* Research Series No. 4. Bangkok: Thai Khadi Research Institute, Thammasat University.

Wijeyewardene, Gehan. 1986. *Place and emotion in northern Thai ritual behavior.* Bangkok: Pandora.

Witzleben, J. Lawrence. 1995. *"Silk and bamboo" music in Shanghai: The* Jiangnan Sizhu *instrumental ensemble tradition.* Kent, Ohio: Kent State University Press.

———. 1997. Whose ethnomusicology? Western ethnomusicology and the study of Asian music. *Ethnomusicology* 41 (2): 220–42.

Wong, Deborah. 1991a. Across three generations: A solo piece for the Thai gong circle. *Balungan* 5 (1): 2–9.

———. 1991b. Empowered teacher: Ritual, performance, and epistemology in contemporary Bangkok. Ph.D. diss., University of Michigan.

———. 1998. Mon music for Thai deaths: Ethnicity and status in Thai urban funerals. *Asian Folklore Studies* 57:99–130.

———. 1999. Ethnomusicology and critical pedagogy as cultural work. *College Music Symposium* 38:80–100.

———. n.d. Ethnomusicology in Thailand: The cultural politics of redefinition and reclamation. *Ethnomusicology.* Forthcoming.

Wong, Deborah, and René T. A. Lysloff. 1991. Threshold to the sacred: The overture in Thai and Javanese ritual performance. *Ethnomusicology* 35 (3): 315–48.

Wong Dontrii Thai Krung Theep Mahaanakhon (Thai Music Ensemble of Bangkok). 2531/1988. Phleeng naa phaat nai phithii wai khruu dontrii Thai (*Naa phaat* repertoire of the *wai khruu* ceremony for music). In *Nangsüü thii ralük ngaan wai khruu lae khraup dontrii Thai pracam pii khaung Culaalongkorn Mahaawitthayalai P.S. 2531.* (Commemorative volume for the annual *wai khruu* and initiation ceremony of Chulalongkorn University, 1988.) Bangkok: Chulalongkorn University.

Wright, Barbara Ann Stein. 1980. Wayang Siam: An ethnographic study of the Malay shadow play of Kelantan. Ph.D. diss., Yale University.

Wyatt, David K. 1982. *Thailand: A short history.* New Haven, Conn.: Yale University Press.

Zurbuchen, Mary Sabina. 1987. *Language of Balinese shadow theater*. Princeton, N.J.: Princeton University Press.

———. 1989. Internal translation in Balinese poetry. In *Writing on the tongue*, edited by A. L. Becker. Michigan Papers on South and Southeast Asia. Ann Arbor: Center for South and Southeast Asian Studies, University of Michigan.

Index

Following Thai practice, Thai authors are cited and alphabetized by first name, not surname.